SELF-ENFORCING TRADE

SELF-ENFORCING TRADE

Developing Countries and WTO Dispute Settlement

CHAD P. BOWN

BROOKINGS INSTITUTION PRESS
Washington, D.C.

Library of Congress Cataloging-in-Publication data

Bown, Chad P. (Chad Philips), 1972–
    Self-enforcing trade : developing countries and WTO dispute settlement / Chad P.
Bown.
        p.   cm.
    Includes bibliographical references and index.
    Summary: "Examines challenges and costs of developing countries accessing WTO
dispute settlement process. Reviews WTO's extended litigation process, highlighting
areas countries have to master—international economics, law, and politics. Assesses
recent efforts to help countries overcome these hurdles and proposes a solution to largest
obstacle: lack of information, monitoring, and surveillance"—Provided by publisher.
    ISBN 978-0-8157-0323-5 (pbk. : alk. paper)
    1. World Trade Organization. 2. International trade. 3. Foreign trade regulation.
4. Dispute resolution (Law) 5. World Trade Organization—Developing countries.
I. Title.
    HF1385.B69 2009
    382'.92—dc22   2009033247

9 8 7 6 5 4 3 2 1

Printed on acid-free paper

Typeset in Adobe Garamond

Composition by Cynthia Stock
Silver Spring, Maryland

Printed by R. R. Donnelley
Harrisonburg, Virginia

To Rebecca, Ella, and Abigail

Contents

Tables

Acknowledgments

The intellectual seeds to this project were planted during a 2004 summer visit to the Development Research Group at the World Bank in conversations I began to have with Bernard Hoekman. Since the seeds have taken so long to fully mature, I must thank numerous sources of financial support, including the World Bank, the Brookings Institution, and the German Marshall Fund of the United States. Furthermore, I am deeply appreciative to the World Trade Organization (WTO) Secretariat and its Economic Research and Statistics Division for hosting me as its visiting scholar during my year-long sabbatical in Geneva from 2007 to 2008. Without that hospitality, I would not have been able to meet and learn from the Geneva-based extra-WTO community of practitioners and scholars whose work is central to this book. Finally, I would like to thank the Global Development Program of the Hewlett Foundation for the generous financial support that has provided me with the time and resources to research and write this book.

There are five scholars to whom I owe both a great intellectual debt and a special personal thanks. Robert Staiger provided me with the economic foundation as a graduate student over ten years ago that still carries with me today, and I am deeply appreciative of his continued time, energy, willingness, and patience that pushes me to clarify my arguments. I am also indebted to Bernard Hoekman for too many reasons to mention beyond simply planting the seeds for this project, ranging from sharing his expertise on the inner workings of the trading system to his generously allowing me to draw on much of our joint work to make the arguments in this book. Petros Mavroidis has provided me with not only energy and guidance, but a unique entry into the world of the WTO. I need to thank without implication Greg Shaffer, whose course in trade law introduced me to the WTO agreements and helped me overcome the fixed cost of communicating with trade lawyers. I am also appreciative for his introducing me, through his research and his personal efforts, to many of the people at the development-focused nongovernmental organizations (NGOs) attempting to work on the inside of the extended litigation process (ELP). Finally, I am especially indebted to Rachel McCulloch, not only for her mentoring, intellectual honesty, and generosity for allowing me to use some of our coauthored work, but also for reading and commenting on every single line in this book.

Among other academics in this interdisciplinary field, I am equally indebted to the generosity and insights of a long list of economists, legal scholars, and political scientists. Given the ELP model of chapter 5, I will first start with economists. I am appreciative of both the important intellectual contributions that have shaped how I view the WTO and the personal conversations I have had about them with economists such as Kyle Bagwell, Meredith Crowley, Henrik Horn, Doug Irwin, Robert Lawrence, Nuno Limão, Patrick Low, Patrick Messerlin, Giovanni Maggi, Håkan Nordström, Emanuel Ornelas, Andrés Rodríguez-Clare, Michele Ruta, and Kamal Saggi . I am also appreciative of the comments and suggestions by Kym Anderson, Marc Bacchetta, Mostafa Beshkar, Jean Christophe Bureau, Yvan Decreux, Kim Elliott, George Hall, Marion Jansen, Sébastien Jean, Tim Josling, Alex Keck, Rodney Ludema, Sébastien Miroudot, Jee-Hyeong Park, Roberta Piermartini, Tom Prusa, Kara Reynolds, Simon Schropp, Robert Teh, Daniel Traca, Shang-Jin Wei, and Sebastian Wilckens. I have received excellent research assistance from Aksel Erbahar and Shranutha Reddy.

I am also indebted to a number of legal specialists. Legal scholars such as Dukgeun Ahn, Steve Charnovitz, Thomas Cottier, William Davey, Jeff Dunoff, Jide Nzelibe, Joost Pauwelyn, Alan Sykes, and Joel Trachtman have patiently provided me with deeper insights into their discipline's approach to thinking about the WTO system beyond what I would have been able to attain simply by reading their scholarship. Furthermore, WTO litigators such as Scott Andersen, Arthur Appleton, Jan Bohanes, Jennifer Brant, Daniel Crosby, James Durling, Gary Horlick, Jorge Miranda, David Palmeter, Amy Porges, Edwin Verlmust, and Jasper Wauters have generously wasted many potentially billable hours explaining to me how the private sector version of step 4 of the ELP works in practice.

I owe special thanks to the intellectual generosity of a number of specialists in politics. As the book will make clear, political scientists such as Marc Busch,

Christina Davis, Cédric Dupont, Manfred Elsig, Judith Goldstein, Joanne Gowa, Helen Milner, Eric Reinhardt, and Michael Tomz have greatly influenced my work with their scholarship; however, I am also grateful to each individually for taking the time in conversation to generously share their reactions to my perspectives. A number of current or former WTO (or trade policy) "insiders" such as Patrick Allard, Geza Feketekuty, Jennifer Hillman, Alejandro Jara, Raed Safadi, and Werner Zdouc have also provided me with useful insights.

The staff at the Advisory Centre on WTO Law deserves special mention for putting up with my inquiries and musings. I am particularly grateful to Niall Meagher, Frieder Roessler, Fernando Piérola, Hunter Nottage, Thomas Sebastian, and Shandana Khan for describing to me the constraints and possibilities of the Centre in the WTO system.

Among the development-focused NGO community, I am grateful to Atul Kaushik, Gawain Kripke, and Dyebo Shabalala, as well as Nicolas Imboden and the IDEAS Centre staff for inviting me to participate in the Geneva Trade and Development Forum during my sabbatical. The International Centre for Trade and Sustainable Development (ICTSD) has been a particularly generous think tank, allowing me to test many of my ideas on diverse audiences and in venues in far-off places (Beijing, Geneva, and São Paulo). Thanks in particular to Yvonne Apea, Christophe Bellmann, Johannes Bernabe, Ricardo Meléndez-Ortiz, Sheila Sabune, Knirie Sogaard, and David Vivas-Eugui. Ann Tutwiler, Joe Guinan, and Michal Baranowski at Hewlett and the German Marshall Fund have also been extremely supportive of my work and generously opened doors for me to learn from people on the inside of the WTO system.

I also want to thank the many other individuals who patiently sat through presentations of my ideas during various seminars and conferences, including at the American Society of International Law (Bretton Woods), Brandeis, Brookings, Centre for International Governance Innovation (CIGI), Graduate Institute, Harvard Kennedy School, Johns Hopkins-SAIS (Bologna), Sciences-Po (Paris), Stanford, Yale, Wisconsin, and the World Trade Institute (Bern).

The most important support I have received is from my family. Without Rebecca, none of this book would have ever come to fruition. Abigail and Ella provided their own kind of support as well as the comic relief that makes it all worth the effort. My parents, Keith and Priscilla, and my sister Tiffany receive a lifetime of gratitude for a lifetime of encouragement.

Finally, some of the material in this book draws on collaboration with Bernard Hoekman and Rachel McCulloch that I would like to specially acknowledge. This includes Chad P. Bown and Bernard M. Hoekman, "Developing Countries and Enforcement of Trade Agreements: Why Dispute Settlement Is Not Enough," *Journal of World Trade* 42 (1) (2008): 177–203; Chad P.

Bown and Bernard M. Hoekman, "WTO Dispute Settlement and the Missing Developing Country Cases: Engaging the Private Sector," *Journal of International Economic Law* 8 (4) (2005): 861–90; and Chad P. Bown and Rachel McCulloch, "Developing Countries, Dispute Settlement, and the Advisory Centre on WTO Law," *Journal of International Trade and Economic Development* (2010 forthcoming).

.

SELF-ENFORCING TRADE

Introduction

International trade disputes between countries are an inevitable feature of economic relations in an interdependent world. Historical examples of commercial policy clashes leading to famous trade wars include the Anglo-Hanse disputes from the fourteenth to seventeenth centuries, the Anglo-French trade wars of the seventeenth to nineteenth centuries, the numerous intra-European tariff wars of the nineteenth century, as well as the Anglo-Dutch rivalry for the East India trade in the seventeenth century.[1] Prominent twentieth century episodes include the international response to the U.S. Smoot-Hawley tariffs during the Great Depression, the U.S.–European Economic Community (EEC) "chicken wars" in the 1960s, and the U.S.-Japan-EEC steel wars of the 1970s.

In contrast to earlier globalization eras, today commercial powers can turn to a multilateral institution known as the World Trade Organization (WTO) to help prevent twenty-first century trade battles from turning into trade wars. To the casual observer, the idea that the WTO might provide assistance in this arena is perhaps surprising. After all, the WTO is infamous for its more public role of attempting to facilitate multilateral trade liberalization among more than

---

1. See Conybeare (1985, 1987) for a discussion of these first three examples of trade wars escalating over import-restricting policies. On the Anglo-Dutch rivalry, Irwin (1991) provides an interpretation of the Dutch government's actions as strategic trade policy in the sense of the export subsidy policy model of Brander and Spencer (1985). Findlay and O'Rourke (2007) cover many of these trade wars, as well as a number of others taking place throughout the second millennium.

150 member countries. The latest attempt, initiated in Doha in 2001, has been subject to numerous negotiating starts and stops in Seattle, Cancún, and Hong Kong. Although the uneven progress may be typical of attempts at multilateral trade liberalization, the WTO has nevertheless come under public and official criticism for failing to deliver a timely agreement. That some failed ministerial meetings were accompanied by anti-globalization protests targeting the WTO also gave the institution a public relations black eye. Finally, because the negotiations were packaged as a "development round," whether fairly or not, the delay in arriving at an agreement has also been criticized for failing to deliver the promised benefits of globalization to developing countries.

Yet while the WTO faces public scrutiny on these other fronts, at the same time it has achieved stunning success in its other major job of managing trade disputes. Moreover, the WTO's record of success since its 1995 inception has been achieved despite an increasing number of disputes, a more diverse set of member countries to arbitrate between, an increased range of traded products and services subject to WTO rules, and more politically sensitive and sophisticated policy issues being contested. Paradoxically, the importance of the WTO dispute settlement role is underappreciated precisely because the institution has prevented dozens of obscure mini trade battles from turning into recognizable major trade wars.

Given the WTO's record of successfully mediating commercial policy disputes between member countries, several questions do arise: Has the WTO dispute settlement system actually been underutilized? Is its record of success built on a set of easy cases, indicating that it has not been sufficiently tested?[2] Could WTO dispute settlement somehow be missing an opportunity to play a larger pro-development role on behalf of poor countries in particular? Put differently, might more effective use of appropriate WTO dispute settlement actions be a useful weapon for poor countries in their arsenal of growth and development strategies? This book takes up these questions.

A Brief History of the GATT, the WTO, and Dispute Settlement

WTO dispute settlement is an arbitration process that is equal parts economics, law, and politics. The United States pushed for the current system during the Uruguay Round of trade liberalization negotiations that took place between 1986 and 1993. U.S. officials had become exasperated by the toothless and

---

2. These arguments should not be mistaken for or confused with earlier proposals to expand the legal scope of what WTO dispute settlement would cover, for example, by introducing labor and environmental standards into the agreement that would then become enforceable under WTO rules through sanctioned trade retaliation for failure to comply.

ineffective dispute settlement process of the WTO's predecessor—the General Agreement on Tariffs and Trade (GATT).

The United States, United Kingdom, Canada, and a handful of other major trading powers established the GATT in 1947. Their first intention was to avoid the mistakes of the Great Depression era, when the Smoot-Hawley tariff and international retaliatory responses developed into a trade war that virtually halted international commercial relations.[3] The GATT established itself by contributing three fundamental functions to the international trading system: providing forums in which its contracting parties could *negotiate* (additional trade liberalization commitments or disciplining rules), *illuminate* (reveal changes to national policies affecting trade or commitments), and *litigate* (challenge each other for failing to live up to obligations or commitments negotiated earlier).

Although the GATT made a major contribution to global economic integration by promoting expanded trade and international stability in the post–World War II era, by the 1980s its diplomacy-based system for resolving trade disputes had broken down. The European Community (EC) and other countries largely agreed to the new United States–backed WTO system out of political distaste for the recognized alternative at the time—increasing U.S. unilateralism under its Section 301 trade policy.[4]

Not surprisingly, many of the highest profile disputes since the 1995 inception of the WTO have been transatlantic skirmishes. To name but a few, the United States and the European Community have used the WTO as a forum for battles over bananas, hormone-treated beef, and genetically modified foods; subsidies to Boeing and Airbus and U.S. foreign sales corporations; as well as steel safeguard import restrictions. Less well-known disputes that nevertheless have important systemic implications include challenges to a U.S. policy of redistributing collected antidumping duties directly to industries under the Byrd Amendment, the United States' continued use of "zeroing" to calculate dumping margins and the size of imposed tariffs after antidumping investigations, and the European Community's changing tariff treatment for imports covered under the Information Technology Agreement.

While the United States and the European Community are allies in many other matters of geopolitical importance in international relations, the extensive trade between the two makes it inevitable that they continue to find reasons for disputes with each other. The WTO forum has provided an important and useful way to achieve harmonious economic, legal, and political solutions to most of these U.S.-EC disputes without threatening their overall trade or nontrade

---

3. For a discussion of the origins of the GATT, see Irwin, Mavroidis, and Sykes (2008).

4. For extensive discussions of the U.S. Section 301 policy, see Bhagwati and Patrick (1990); Bayard and Elliott (1994).

relations, inflicting substantial costs on other WTO members, or burdening the trading system more broadly.

Transatlantic trade is no longer the only major beneficiary to the services that WTO dispute settlement provides. Building from the U.S.-EC model, as major emerging economies such as Brazil, China, and India increasingly turn to international trade as a critical component of their development strategies, they have taken a larger ownership stake in the international trading system by relying on WTO enforcement. Brazil has taken the lead in a number of important and potentially pathbreaking South-North disputes such as challenges to U.S. and EC agricultural support policies for cotton and sugar, respectively. India has challenged how the EC implements its Generalized System of Preferences (GSP) policy, as well as a number of U.S. and EC import restrictions over textiles, apparel, and steel. Even China, a relative newcomer to the GATT/WTO system since it only acceded in 2001, recently began a long-awaited challenge to the U.S. antidumping and countervailing duty policies.[5]

However, the South-North disputes that Brazil, India, and China have initiated to enforce their access to export markets also do not tell the full WTO story. A complete examination of the WTO caseload reveals, unsurprisingly, a reciprocal pattern in disputes involving emerging economies. Just as these emerging economies have become larger exporters and thus intent on using the WTO to enforce their market access abroad, other WTO members have similarly acted to enforce their own access to the newly valuable import markets of these emerging nations. The result is a number of North-South disputes: Brazil and China have faced upwards of ten WTO challenges from developed countries, and India has faced at least eighteen.

One early message from the brief history of dispute settlement is the fundamental nature of reciprocity: the more a country challenges others by using the WTO to enforce their commitments, the more it can expect to be challenged. That reciprocity is important in disputes is not at all surprising, given that much of the WTO's success rests on the reciprocal market access opening bargains that were reached after hard-fought negotiations between countries to establish the initial agreements. The ability of the United States to keep its markets open to Brazil's exports relies, in part, on Brazil's ability to keep its market open to U.S. exports.

The importance of reciprocity is further confirmed by a third category of WTO trade disputes—the rising incidence of South-South trade frictions. Recent examples include Bangladesh challenging Indian trade restrictions on

5. Of the emerging economies commonly referred to as the BRICs (Brazil, Russia, India, China) only Russia is not a member of the WTO and thus without access to the services its dispute settlement system provides.

batteries, Argentina taking on Brazil's antidumping measures on resin imports, Indonesia fighting South Africa's import barriers on paper, and Honduras battling the Dominican Republic on cigarettes. Quite intriguing is the experience of Chile, which is a noteworthy South-South litigant in a class by itself. On the offensive side, Chile has filed disputes against five other developing Latin American trading partners (Argentina, Ecuador, Mexico, Peru, and Uruguay). On the defensive side, three neighboring developing countries (Argentina, Colombia, and Guatemala) have filed at least five different WTO complaints against Chile.

These modern commercial policy battles illustrate that WTO disputes occur between developed countries, between developed and developing countries, and between developing countries themselves. The ability of two countries to have a "useful" trade dispute—that is, a case that enforces the commitment to grant market access to exporting firms in another country—does not depend on their relative or absolute levels of economic development, but rather on whether they engage in economically meaningful, but perhaps politically contentious, international trade.[6]

A second message that comes from the dispute settlement process is the necessity of *self-enforcement* that the WTO requires. For example, consider again the WTO trade dispute involving Indian import restrictions over batteries being sold by Bangladeshi exporting firms. As in all WTO disputes, it was up to the firms and the government of Bangladesh to actively pursue their rights because the WTO does not initiate or prosecute cases itself. The WTO merely provides the neutral forum in which two disputing governments can have their skirmishes arbitrated. In this instance, India ultimately removed the import barrier, which had reduced Bangladeshi firms' exports, because the Bangladeshi government pursued the dispute and self-enforced Bangladeshi firms' access to the Indian market. Without self-enforcement and the dispute, these firms would not have been able to access the Indian market, even though they were legally entitled to it on the basis of India's earlier trade liberalization promises made through its WTO commitments.

Thus, despite or perhaps because of the WTO's success in diffusing these kinds of trade frictions, there are arguments that the WTO could be doing more. Many policymakers; economic, legal, and political scholars; and the

---

6. This is a point first confirmed empirically by Horn, Mavroidis, and Nordström (2005) and found in other studies including Bown (2005a, 2005b). Indeed, in many disputes over agricultural subsidies (for example, the *US–Upland Cotton* dispute brought by Brazil), the trade need not even be bilateral and thus between the two disputing countries—a dispute can occur over policies that affect exports to a common third market. Nevertheless, there is certainly a set of missing players in WTO dispute settlement: least developed countries, notably those in sub-Saharan Africa and much of central Asia. However, it is difficult to distinguish among possible causes of their lack of participation, as these countries are marginal participants in international trade as well as extremely poor.

increasingly influential community of nongovernmental organizations (NGOs) argue that elements of the current enforcement system make it difficult for developing countries to use, which implies that such countries are not able to enjoy the full benefits provided by the rules-based trading system. Various proposals have been made that directly aim to encourage additional developing country participation in the enforcement area of the WTO.

Is this a good idea? I argue that there is a strong pro-development case for enhancing the use of the WTO dispute settlement system by poor countries. However, I recognize the limits to what the WTO can realistically offer and identify the downside risks of improving developing country access to WTO dispute settlement. Nevertheless, developing countries face an acute need to improve their ability to self-enforce the foreign market access that WTO members have promised. Without self-enforcement there is no enforcement, and without enforcement the benefits that the rules-based WTO agreements can offer to poor countries are significantly diminished.

The purpose of this book is to make the case for strong linkages between the WTO agreements and the self-enforcing needs of developing countries. To do so, I pinpoint the systemic elements in the WTO dispute settlement process that make firms and policymakers in developing countries unable to fully self-enforce the foreign market access that has been promised to them by other WTO members. I begin with the following questions: What are the precise barriers that prevent firms, industries, and government policymakers from effectively accessing their self-enforcement needs via WTO dispute settlement? What is the right way to tackle the barriers? How has the system evolved to address them thus far? What has not yet evolved, and what needs to be done?

Outline of the Book

While the WTO currently plays the three fundamental roles that the GATT introduced into the international trading system—providing forums for its members to *negotiate, illuminate,* and *litigate*—the history of developing countries in each of the three areas of the WTO and the GATT is complex. Even though this book focuses primarily on developing countries in the third WTO function of dispute settlement, it is impossible to fully understand the self-enforcement of commitments that other countries have taken on after WTO negotiations in isolation.

Chapter 1 begins with a brief, albeit more formal, introduction to the WTO and GATT and the first of these complementary roles that the institution provides as a forum for additional liberalization negotiations. The chapter introduces the GATT/WTO *negotiating* history as well as the key institutional principles of reciprocity, national treatment, and most-favored-nation (MFN) treatment. The chapter identifies how reciprocity in particular has facilitated trade relations between countries through its influence on trade liberalization negotiations; it also foreshadows how reciprocity effectively self-enforces market access through the use of dispute settlement.

Chapter 2 provides detail on the current WTO agreements when viewed from the perspective of developing countries. It begins by presenting the evidence that the status quo agreements are largely biased against the pro-development needs of poor countries, and it also provides a discussion of the contributing causes as well as lessons to be learned. Where did these obligations and commitments—as well as the lack thereof— come from? The chapter puts the reality of the WTO commitments that face developing countries and their interests in foreign market access into context by describing the role that developing countries have played both inside and outside of GATT/WTO negotiating history.

In chapter 3, I begin our discussion of developing countries in the self-enforcing WTO dispute settlement system. Through the lens of a particular WTO trade dispute, chapter 3 identifies a number of theoretical reasons behind the need for and benefits of an effective dispute settlement system. This chapter is an essential building block for the rest of the book because it makes the case for developing country access to dispute settlement.

Do the data confirm the theory? Chapter 4 examines this by presenting the evidence to date on how developing countries have and have not used the WTO dispute settlement system. It begins by describing the countries, commercial sectors, and policies involved in the 388 formal WTO trade disputes that have taken place between 1995 and 2008. The chapter then turns to evidence from more formal empirical research analyzing the experience of developing countries in WTO trade disputes so as to identify key barriers that impede poor countries from self-enforcing commitments to foreign market access.

Given the evidence from chapter 4 on some of the key barriers affecting access to WTO self-enforcement, chapter 5 introduces a firm-level analysis of the beginning-to-end game of what I refer to as the "extended litigation process" (ELP) of WTO dispute settlement. The chapter takes the viewpoint of the exporting firms as they are the key underlying catalyst behind the need to self-enforce any foreign market access commitments that trading partners may have taken on. Drawing on insights from new scholarship analyzing the firms that successfully engage in exporting, I identify the cost to self-enforcing as an important determinant of whether firms and their government policymakers can navigate the extended litigation process.

Chapter 5 also serves as an important jumping off point for the remainder of the book—I first identify specific components to the enforcement costs that may prevent exporting firms, industries, and policymakers in developing countries from fully engaging the ELP to benefit their development needs. Then through the lens of the *targeting principle* provided by economic analysis—confronting a market failure at its source—I examine each of these hurdles individually by asking what complementary institutions have evolved to address the hurdle, how successful they have been at addressing the hurdle, and where there is still more work to be done. This approach is similar to that advocated by Dani Rodrik in his "growth diagnostics" method of determining appropriate macroeconomic policies for developing countries: look for the source of the problem and then treat it.[7] Here, the suggestion is to create the right systemic infrastructure, framework, and institutional support that allow local experts to deal with specific enforcement issues on a case-by-case basis.

One specific example of this is described in chapter 6. It has been well documented that a critical element of the ELP is, indeed, the effective WTO legal work that must take place to convince the WTO adjudicators of the merit of a country's case. For countries that may lack the internal WTO legal expertise necessary to prosecute such cases, one system has evolved that provides attorneys from external, private law firms to assist countries in need. Cost is a potential concern with such a solution, when viewed from the perspective of developing countries, because these types of law firms tend to be expensive. Chapter 6 describes one successful way of addressing this component to the problem in the WTO system: rich countries effectively subsidize litigation support to developing countries via an independent institution called the Advisory Centre on WTO Law (ACWL). The chapter highlights the important role played by the ACWL and the market failure that its existence remedies. It also identifies limits to the role that the ACWL can play, given its mandate and the other complementary needs of developing countries in the extended litigation process.

Chapter 7 turns to the emergence of civil society, NGOs, intergovernmental organizations (IGOs), think tanks, and other development-focused stakeholders and the roles that they might play in assisting developing countries in the extended litigation process. A number of advocacy groups including Oxfam, International Centre for Trade and Sustainable Development (ICTSD), and the IDEAS Centre have achieved considerable recognition and influence in the trade and development community for their work that is increasingly relevant for issues covered by WTO dispute settlement. This chapter explores how these and other lesser known NGOs such as the Environmental Working Group and Farmsubsidies.org may best contribute by providing additional nonlitigation support to developing countries in the extended litigation process. It also identifies some of the likely unintended consequences of their increased involvement—both for the developing countries themselves and also for the trading system.

7. Rodrik (2007).

Finally, given the response of the ACWL and development-focused NGOs to filling in some gaps in the ELP, chapter 8 focuses on the one remaining hole that is not likely to be filled effectively by such groups: generating and disseminating information on members' noncomplying policies that trading partners could challenge under the WTO dispute settlement system. The chapter begins by identifying the positive contributions that the WTO itself has made in its third fundamental role—the *illumination* forum for transparency—through the foundation for external monitoring that the WTO makes possible. After identifying the clear limits to the status quo, the chapter describes NGO efforts to ensure that more detailed information on potentially noncompliant policies such as subsidies (the Global Subsidies Initiative), as well as antidumping, countervailing measures, and safeguards (the Global Antidumping Database), is made publicly available.

Because such efforts are not sufficiently comprehensive to address the problem of too little information, chapter 8 proposes the establishment of a new and independent institution outside the WTO called the Institute for Assessing WTO Commitments (IAWC). The mandate of such an institution would be to provide objective information to WTO members about WTO compliance by WTO members. The chapter proposes how to establish, fund, and govern this institution to ensure its long-term success outside the WTO and the WTO's political limitations, while working within the WTO rules and with the WTO members, so that it can provide the poorest members with the information they need to use the dispute settlement system effectively. Furthermore, the chapter also describes the inevitably controversial proposal that it will be equally important to promote enforcement of developing countries' own WTO commitments.

1

The WTO and GATT: A Principled History

While the World Trade Organization in current existence provides its membership with forums for three interrelated functions—negotiation, illumination, and litigation—it is probably best known for the first of these. This chapter provides a brief overview of the negotiating forum of the General Agreement on Tariffs and Trade and its WTO successor, as well as how each has been used by the world's major trading nations since 1947.

Since the ultimate focus of this book is on developing countries and dispute settlement, it may appear strange to start with a topic that has little obvious relation to either. This chapter describes the relative success of the negotiating forum of the GATT—an agreement to which developing countries largely did not have a proactive contribution. A careful analysis of the origins of the GATT, as well as some of its later history, offers a tremendous number of lessons for developing countries and for the settlement of disputes. The underlying political and economic forces that create the incentives that shape trade relations between sovereign nations—be the countries developed or developing—remain relatively consistent over time. Thus the evidence from later chapters will substantiate that there is much to learn from the relative successes of the GATT and its negotiating history. These successes are particularly important to understand and appreciate given the extremely negative and pessimistic view that developing countries have of the current WTO bargain, which is described in chapter 2.

In the next section, I provide a brief introduction to the original GATT that was negotiated to conclusion in 1947, as well as the subsequent trade liberalization negotiations that took place over the next forty-five years. The third section presents the principles on which the GATT and the WTO are built—reciprocity, most-favored-nation treatment, and national treatment—and their practical relevance for shaping the outcomes of the negotiations. The final section describes some of the emerging evidence from more formal scholarship that finds that the GATT and the WTO (GATT/WTO), as well as these foundational principles, have an impact on government policies and subsequently on the trade flows and economic activity that such policies affect.

A Brief History of GATT Negotiations

The current WTO agreements are the legacy of commitments that countries have voluntarily negotiated with each other, on a repeat basis, in the decades since 1947. To understand the causes of the present patterns of import protection across WTO member countries as well as across products and industries within those countries, it is important to turn to the past.

The 1930s and 1940s era of the Great Depression and World War II provide important reminders of globalization's last dark episode of protectionism. The U.S. imposition of the Smoot-Hawley tariffs and the international retaliatory response in the 1930s led to the virtual halting of international commerce. Table 1-1 illustrates the pattern of the new trade barriers that were implemented by the United States and a number of other European countries during the Great Depression. What is clear is that the level of tariffs during the Depression was much higher than what most developed economies impose today.

At the conclusion of World War II, twenty-three countries, led primarily by the United States, Canada, and the United Kingdom, negotiated the General Agreement on Tariffs and Trade.[1] The goal was to create an agreement that would ensure postwar stability and avoid a repeat of the mistakes of the recent past, including the Smoot-Hawley tariffs and retaliatory responses, which had been a contributor to the devastating economic climate that culminated in the death and destruction of the Second World War. The 1947 GATT created a new basic template of rules and exceptions to regulate international trade between members (referred to as *contracting parties*) and locked in initial tariff

---

1. The twenty-three countries engaging in the Geneva negotiations that led to the signing of the GATT in 1947 were Australia, Belgium, Brazil, Burma (Myanmar), Canada, Ceylon (Sri Lanka), Chile, China, Cuba, Czechoslovakia (Czech Republic and Slovakia), France, India, Lebanon, Luxembourg, Netherlands, New Zealand, Norway, Pakistan, South Africa, Southern Rhodesia (Zimbabwe), Syria, United Kingdom, and United States. For a discussion of the negotiating history leading up to the GATT, see Irwin, Mavroidis, and Sykes (2008).

Table 1-1. *Average Tariff Levels for the United States and Major European Countries*

Country	1913	1925	1931	1952	2007[a]
Belgium	6	7	17	n.a.	5.2
France	14	9	38	19	5.2
Germany	12	15	40	16	5.2
Italy	17	16	48	24	5.2
United Kingdom	n.a.	4	17	17	5.2
United States	32	26	35	9	3.5

Source: Data for 1913, 1925, 1931, and 1952 are from Irwin (2002, table 5.1, p. 153). Data for 2007 are from WTO (2008c).

n.a. = Not available.

a. Tariff levels for each European Community member country represent the EC-wide import tariff rate.

reductions that these countries committed to establish. Even as early as 1952, the tariff cuts had reduced average tariffs substantially, as shown in table 1-1, for a number of these countries.

Over the next forty-seven years, more countries signed on to the GATT, and further trade liberalization negotiations ensued.[2] As table 1-2 documents, between 1947 and 1994, the GATT contracting parties began and concluded eight separate negotiating rounds of voluntary trade liberalization. The last of these completed rounds was the Uruguay Round, which ended the GATT era in 1994 by ushering in the World Trade Organization. By 1994, the GATT membership had simultaneously expanded from an initial 23 contracting parties to 128 participating countries. With a number of new members acceding to the WTO since its 1995 inception, more than 150 countries have signed the agreement.

The Negotiating Rounds and Negotiating Approaches

The first five rounds of GATT negotiations covering the initial 1947–61 period were typically dominated by major exporting countries, or those with a "principal supplying interest" in a particular product, getting together and negotiating reciprocal market access improvements.[3] The initial negotiators under the

2. Barton and others (2006) provide an economic, legal, and political assessment of the trade regime from the GATT through to the WTO.

3. For a discussion, see Dam (1970, chapter 5). Hoekman and Kostecki (2009, chapter 4) discuss not only the negotiating history but also the economic outcomes of different negotiating approaches of principal suppliers versus tariff formulas and exceptions. Ludema and Mayda (2009) provide an economic theory that rationalizes participation by the largest exporters in negotiations, and thus supports the principal supplier rule as a feature of the negotiations. Their theory justifies the principal supplier rule as a means to overcome the otherwise nontrivial concern of externalities that can lead to the failure of multilateral negotiations attributed to the free rider problem. Then,

Table 1-2. *GATT and WTO Negotiating Rounds of Multilateral Trade Liberalization*

Year	Name (location)	Subjects covered	Number of countries
1947	Geneva	Tariffs	23
1949	Annecy	Tariffs	13
1951	Torquay	Tariffs	38
1956	Geneva	Tariffs	26
1960–61	Dillon Round (Geneva)	Tariffs	26
1964–67	Kennedy Round (Geneva)	Tariffs and antidumping measures	62
1973–79	Tokyo Round (Geneva)	Tariffs, nontariff measures, "framework" agreements	102
1986–94	Uruguay Round (Geneva)	Tariffs, nontariff measures, rules, services, intellectual property, dispute settlement, textiles, agriculture, creation of WTO, and so on	128
2001–present	Doha Round	To be determined	To be determined

Source: WTO website, "The GATT Years: From Havana to Marrakesh" (www.wto.org/english/the wto_e/whatis_e/tif_e/fact4_e.htm).

GATT, especially those with a principal supplying interest, were developed economies. They focused their negotiation efforts on reducing import barriers in other countries that were of primary interest to their own exporters, and they used the political trade-off of expanded market access abroad for exporting industries against increased market access granted at home to foreign industries and thus the losses to industries competing against these imports.

Since the trade barriers targeted for elimination were typically those in the import markets of other developed countries, the primary result was that developed countries were asked to reduce their tariffs. Put differently, since most developing countries were neither principal suppliers nor major importing markets, little was asked of them in terms of their own trade liberalization, and little of what was of direct export interest to developing countries was liberalized by others. Such an outcome is consistent with the pattern of import tariff protection that persists today, which is explored in more depth in the next chapter, a remnant of the form of the negotiations begun in the 1940s.

---

using data on the United States, they also provide evidence for how the principal supplier rule affects the imposition of tariffs, finding that a higher concentration of exporters in a sector reduces free riding and thus results in a lower tariff.

Starting with the Kennedy Round of negotiations in 1964 through the Tokyo Round in the 1970s, countries participating in the trade negotiations used formulaic approaches to reduce further the remaining trade barriers across the board. Certain tariff-cutting formulas can be preferable to reciprocal negotiations between principal suppliers, in that they can serve to reduce average tariff levels as well as their *dispersion*. The dispersion of tariffs within a country, and even for products within an industry, is related to the difference between the average tariff and the country's highest tariffs, or the phenomenon of "tariff peaks," which is discussed in more detail in chapter 2.

Although formulas can be preferable to simple negotiations between principal suppliers if the formulas are applied rigorously, inevitably the formulaic approaches applied during the Kennedy and Tokyo Rounds did not turn out to be sufficiently "pure" in practice to fully achieve this effect. In the rounds in which formulas were applied, negotiating countries sought and were granted exemptions for "sensitive products" that they could remove from the list of goods whose import tariffs would be subject to the formula. In this manner countries typically avoided having to reduce the highest tariffs in products that the formulaic approach was trying to attack in the first place. The result is a persistent pattern of protection across countries and industries that likely looks quite similar to the reciprocity-based, bid-offer approach between principal suppliers of different products.

Important Commercial Sector Exemptions to the GATT

In addition to the general problem of certain products effectively being excluded from multilateral trade liberalization rounds because of the principal supplying interest and formula-exemption approaches to the GATT negotiations, the contracting parties deepened the severity of the problem in certain sectors by essentially taking two industries off the negotiating table—agriculture and apparel and textiles.

First, most agricultural trade was exempted from GATT disciplines beginning in the 1950s. The United States initiated the trend by requesting a GATT waiver to that effect; the emerging European Economic Community subsequently supported this decision as it undertook substantial government intervention in agricultural markets through its Common Agricultural Policy (CAP). This lack of discipline concerning trade in agricultural products would ultimately result in a complicated web of domestic policies throughout the sector— excesses in import restrictions as well as substantial domestic support (subsidies) programs, which can have the effect of choking off imports and making suppliers artificially competitive in third country (export) markets.

Second, beginning with Japan's accession to the GATT in 1955, special trading rules also were introduced to deal with potentially disruptive imports in clothing and textile products.[4] What began as the Short-Term Arrangement covering cotton textiles (1961) turned into the Long-Term Arrangement (1962–73) and subsequently the Multifibre Arrangement (MFA) (1974–94). These agreements managed global textiles and apparel trade through a complex system of quantitative restrictions and voluntary export restraints. The products covered by these agreements thus fell outside of the GATT system of rules, disciplines, and ultimately enforcement.[5]

As discussed in chapter 2, the creation of the WTO in 1995 has provided a framework to resolve these problems. Nevertheless, these particular two sectors are of fundamental interest to exporters in many developing countries. Thus the effects of the negotiating legacy of such sectors do contribute to complaints being made by developing countries about the WTO today, especially because countries continue to impose high import tariffs on these products.

The Fundamental Principles of the GATT and the WTO

The General Agreement on Tariffs and Trade established the forum for negotiations on cutting tariffs that subsequently would take place over the following decades through multilateral trade rounds. In addition, the initial negotiations resulted in an agreement that established a set of basic rules and disciplines that participating countries were to follow, as well as a forum for dispute resolution if countries deviated from them. Perhaps the most important and enduring of these basic rules embodied in the GATT 1947 are the fundamental principle of *reciprocity* and two nondiscrimination principles—*most favored-nation treatment* and *national treatment*.

Reciprocity

The GATT fundamental principle of reciprocity enters into the agreement in a number of different ways, both formally and informally.[6]

4. Japan's entry into the GATT in 1955 as a major developing country exporter of clothing and textile products, and the associated fear of disruption of economic activity due to the integration of this country into the GATT system, has a number of marked similarities with China's accession to the WTO in 2001. See the discussion in Bown and McCulloch (2007a).

5. For a more complete discussion, see Hoekman and Kostecki (2009, chapter 6).

6. Unlike the principles of nondiscrimination (most-favored-nation treatment and national treatment) described in the next two subsections, there is no article of the GATT 1947 that clearly identifies reciprocity as a foundational principle. Nevertheless, the articles in the GATT 1947 that govern how countries are to renegotiate concessions—in particular Articles XXVIII and XIX—if

First, as discussed above in the section about the process of GATT rounds of multilateral trade negotiations, these negotiations were typically undertaken on a reciprocal basis—frequently between countries with a principal supplying export interest in the other's import market. While this particular approach to negotiations was successful, it was more of a rule of thumb in the negotiations phase. There is nothing in the GATT texts that requires countries to reciprocally negotiate market access liberalization.

Second, once a contracting party had committed to opening up access to its market, reciprocity did become a formal rule for renegotiations if that country subsequently wanted to back off from its commitment. There are two broad ways that countries have backed off prior commitments, and the GATT/WTO response to both has typically been based on reciprocity.

The first instance is when a country seeks to follow GATT/WTO legal procedures when raising its import tariffs to levels higher than the "bound" commitments (or limits) it had promised to offer to the rest of the membership during an earlier negotiating round. Adversely affected trading partners are then permitted to negotiate a reciprocal market access change in another area of interest. Although it is possible that this might occur through additional trade liberalization in another sector of interest to the affected exporter, typically it is implemented through a new "market closing," which, while retaliatory, is limited by this reciprocity principle so as to rebalance the deal.

The second instance is when a country backs off commitments to opening market access in a way that is not "GATT/WTO legal," whereby adversely affected trading partners use the dispute settlement process to obtain a legal ruling that allows them to rebalance market access obligations. Case law that has emerged under the formal trade dispute settlement procedures adjudicated at the WTO has also resulted in use of the reciprocity rule for instances in which compensation needs to be allocated to adversely affected exporters after legal breaches of the GATT/WTO bargain.[7] This second point indicates that reciprocity is thus an extremely important principle when it comes to the issue of disputes and is therefore a topic that is dealt with in greater detail in subsequent chapters.

Most-Favored-Nation Treatment

The second fundamental principle of the GATT is the most-favored-nation (MFN) treatment, that is, nondiscrimination by importers across different

---

one country seeks to amend the initial bargain, do contain explicit language about reciprocity that therefore arguably feeds back to how initial negotiations are conducted. See the economic modeling framework in Bagwell and Staiger (1999, 2002) and also the discussions in Bown (2002a, 2002b).

7. See, for example, the discussion in Bown and Ruta (forthcoming) as well as a number of other chapters in Bown and Pauwelyn (forthcoming).

foreign export sources. MFN in the GATT is a rule for both negotiations and renegotiations.[8] In a negotiating round, when one GATT contracting party offers to lower its tariff to increase the market access available to foreign exporters in another GATT country, that same lower tariff and terms of market access must be then granted to all other GATT countries on a nondiscriminatory, MFN basis. This is clearly one of the most important reasons for desired membership in the agreement. Even if a country did not seek to utilize the GATT for its own tariff liberalization negotiations or as an external commitment device to facilitate internal reform (for reasons described in the next section), joining the GATT was useful because it provided some guarantee that the country's exporters would receive the "best" treatment made available to any other country in the agreement. This helps to explain why developing countries would want to join the GATT/WTO and establishes that there was some theoretical benefit to them of doing so.

Nevertheless, while MFN is an important principle in all aspects of the GATT and the WTO—during formal trade liberalization negotiations as well as renegotiations, for example, that might occur during the settlement of a dispute—this treatment becomes increasingly diluted in the presence of GATT/WTO-permitted exceptions to MFN. In particular, the GATT/WTO does permit members to sign preferential trade agreements (PTAs) between one another and thus offer lower-than-MFN tariff rates to preferred partners provided that this covers "substantially all trade." Furthermore, and as chapter 2 describes in more detail, the GATT/WTO also encourages members to offer lower-than-MFN tariff rates to developing country exporters through the Generalized System of Preferences (GSP).

National Treatment

The second fundamental principle of nondiscrimination embodied in the GATT/WTO is the rule of national treatment. The basic idea is simple—once a foreign-produced good has paid the price of entry into an import market (an import tariff), it has to be treated just like a nationally produced good.[9] The good cannot then be subject to additional taxes or regulatory barriers that would otherwise differentiate it from a domestically produced good, once the import tariff has been paid. The national treatment rule is there to prevent policymakers from eliminating the market access promised by tariff cuts through subsequent recourse to other domestic policies, such as taxes or subsidies.

8. The principle of MFN treatment is found in Article I of the GATT 1947. For a legal and economic discussion of the MFN rule, see Horn and Mavroidis (2001).

9. The principle of national treatment is found in Article III of the GATT 1947. Horn (2006) provides a recent theoretical treatment of the national treatment principle on which the GATT/WTO are modeled as an incomplete contract.

Evidence that the coverage of the national treatment principle is broad and powerful is that it is the core issue in a large number of the formal WTO disputes, many of which are examined in later chapters. In fact, in almost any dispute in which a WTO member is alleged to have differentiated unfairly between domestic and foreign-produced goods—whether it be because of a discriminatory tax code, an explicit or implicit subsidy, or a regulatory barrier motivated by concerns over environmental or consumer safety—the heart of the issue is the applicability of and the potential limits to the national treatment principle.

The Theories and Empirical Evidence that the GATT and the WTO Are Relevant

For years, even serious scholars had difficulty reconciling the apparent successes of the GATT/WTO—and what appeared to be relatively mercantilist approaches taken by negotiators under its auspices—with basic economic theory. Nevertheless, the last decade in particular has seen much research progress made in understanding the relevance of the GATT/WTO as an important and necessary component of international economic relations.

In this section I make a brief detour to highlight some of the insights provided by this increasingly sophisticated political and economic scholarship on the GATT and the WTO. In particular, I describe a substantial literature in economic theory that ascribes two potential complementary benefits to a trade agreement such as the GATT or the WTO. I refer to these as the *market access theory* and the *commitment theory*.

The market access theory is based on the well-established fact that large importing countries, whose tariff policies can affect world market prices because of the country's size, require an external motivation to agree to reduce and bind their import tariffs. The GATT and the WTO, and the principle of reciprocity in particular, provide this inducement by allowing any one country's change in trade policy—either a lowering of trade barriers under a negotiating round or a raising of trade barriers subsequently bound by the agreement—to be accompanied by an equivalent, reciprocal change in market access by trading partners.[10] The theory suggests that without the reciprocal inducement during negotiations of increased access to foreign markets, a large

---

10. More typically, the market access theory is referred to in the academic economic literature as the *terms of trade theory* and dates to the seminal work of Johnson (1953–54). A more recent treatment that now dominates the scholarly literature on international trade agreements is based on Bagwell and Staiger (1999, 2002). In particular, Bagwell and Staiger (2002, chapter 11) documented how the terms of trade theory and the market access theory are equivalent, largely addressing one issue of critics who previously found the terms of trade theory unconvincing because trade negotiators discuss import volumes (market access) rather than world prices (the terms of trade).

importing country would not unilaterally offer its own market access to foreign exporters through tariff liberalization. Furthermore, without the threat that this foreign market access will be taken away if one country deviates from the agreement by imposing new trade barriers, market access openings could not be sustained through renegotiations either.

Supporting the dominant market access theory of why the world trading system needs an institution like the GATT/WTO is increasing empirical evidence. A first study by Broda, Limão, and Weinstein uses new empirical techniques and data to provide two pieces of evidence broadly consistent with the theory.[11] They estimated disaggregated foreign export supply elasticities, which are one component in answering the important economic question of whether the importing country is "large" in its ability to affect world prices. They found that countries that are not WTO members systematically set higher tariffs on goods that are supplied inelastically. Thus WTO nonmembers—countries that have not agreed to limit their policies toward imports— tend to impose higher import tariffs on goods for which they are large and need a trade agreement inducement to get these tariffs lowered. Second, for the United States, the authors found that trade barriers are significantly higher on products not covered by the WTO agreement for which the United States has more market power.

A second recent study by Bagwell and Staiger focuses on a set of countries newly acceding to the WTO between 1995 and 2005.[12] They examined whether the motive of gaining access to markets affects these countries' tariff cut commitments and found evidence consistent with the importance of this effect. Specifically, the farther the tariff to which a country negotiates is below its original (pre-WTO) tariff level, the larger is its original, pre-WTO import volume. This result is also consistent with negotiating behavior predicted by the market access theory.

These studies seek to explain why the world needs the GATT/WTO, because the fundamental problems that these agreements are designed to tackle would not be addressed if market forces were left unfettered and government policies were not coordinated internationally. These pieces of evidence indicate that the GATT/WTO has had important real effects on countries' trade policies and the resulting trade flows.[13] The evidence is consistent with what economists predict for government behavior, especially for large, developed countries. The GATT/WTO system has created incentives for such countries to restrict their import tariff barriers compared to the tariffs they would levy in the absence of a

11. Broda, Limão, and Weinstein (2008).
12. Bagwell and Staiger (2006).
13. In chapter 2 a number of other studies are described that present related results that the GATT/WTO has affected country-level trade flows, including Subramanian and Wei (2007); Goldstein, Rivers, and Tomz (2007); Tomz, Goldstein, and Rivers (2007).

GATT/WTO-like agreement. Simply compare current policies with what these large developed economies were doing in the 1930s (see again table 1-1): unilaterally imposing mutually destructive import barriers toward one another because they could not coordinate reciprocal market access opening. This underscores one fundamental benefit that the GATT/WTO provides to the world trading system.

According to the second major theory of trade agreements, the commitment theory, even for countries that are not large (in the sense of market access described above), the GATT/WTO may help struggling governments take on efficiency-enhancing, national welfare–improving economic reforms, including trade liberalization.[14] This potential role for the GATT/WTO comes into play when a government faces entrenched political interest groups demanding special policies that make it difficult for the government to act unilaterally.[15] In this case, the GATT/WTO might also help the government convince its domestic sectors that it is serious about reform and a long-term policy of more liberal trade.

Although there has been little empirical research formally testing the practical relevance of the commitment theory, one particular element should be noted with regard to the issue of GATT/WTO enforcement. As highlighted repeatedly throughout this book, the GATT/WTO institution does virtually no enforcement on its own. Rather, the GATT/WTO is a set of self-enforcing agreements: member countries enforce trading partners' commitments embodied in the agreements by challenging each other's missteps through formal dispute settlement. Thus, as described in substantial detail in later chapters, for a country to take advantage of the potential commitment-device role that the GATT/WTO might offer to government policymakers, some other trading partner must be willing to enforce the commitments that a country takes on. If there is no external enforcement—and this is especially relevant to the case of the poorest WTO member countries whose commitments are almost never enforced through dispute settlement—the WTO essentially provides the country seeking the external commitment with nothing.

14. See the work of Tumlir (1985). More recent theoretical treatments of focus in the academic literature include the work of Maggi and Rodríguez-Clare (1998, 2007) as well as Staiger and Tabellini (1987).

15. A related problem discussed by Staiger and Tabellini (1987) is the concern over time consistency. Although a government may have an incentive to announce trade reforms, it may find it difficult to follow through with them without an external commitment device. Because firms and workers recognize that the government will eventually face this time inconsistency problem (in the absence of external enforcement via a trade agreement), they undertake too little efficiency-enhancing change—whether it be investment in or adjustment to a new and growing sector.

Conclusion

This brief introduction to the General Agreement on Tariffs and Trade and the World Trade Organization identifies a number of important lessons for the remainder of this book. First, the results from the history of the GATT and the WTO negotiations—tariff barriers in developed economies that are massively lower today when compared with those during the Great Depression era of the 1930s—is an unprecedented multilateral outcome for international economic relations. Second, the underlying principle of reciprocity that served to influence these early negotiations turns out to have been an important international force allowing governments to coordinate and simultaneously lower trade barriers. Furthermore, this reciprocal balance of trade obligations across countries is what has allowed them to keep the trade barriers low toward one another, for the most part, over the next 60 years.

Although ultimately a more detailed analysis of this latter point is of interest—how WTO members use the dispute settlement process to self-enforce the agreement and maintain this reciprocal balance in the face of relatively challenging political and economic circumstances—first, in the next chapter, the history of the GATT/WTO negotiations are retold from the perspective of developing countries.

2

Developing Countries, the WTO Agreements, and Trade Liberalization

Despite the apparent successes that the General Agreement on Tariffs and Trade and the World Trade Organization have contributed to post–World War II international economic cooperation, many critics have charged that the current bargain found in the agreements is unfriendly to developing countries. They wonder, given that developing countries are advised to engage in more trade to help them grow, exactly what does the WTO have to offer? Indeed, a newcomer looking at the WTO agreements for the first time may conclude that some elements of the World Trade Organization are hostile to the interests of developing countries. Put differently, if one were to write a multilateral trade agreement designed to disregard the interests of developing countries, many features of the current agreement would provide a template for how to start.

Where do these arguments come from and how valid are they? This chapter describes the components of the current agreement that most affect developing countries, how these components came to exist given the role of developing countries inside and outside of formal GATT and WTO negotiations, and the results of empirical research on the relevance of the WTO for their trading interests.

This chapter thus reintroduces the impact of the GATT and the WTO's negotiating forum from the perspective of developing countries. The discussion starts with the results of the negotiating process—the existing set of WTO agreements. By beginning with the end, it is easier to see two things: what developing countries have justification to complain about regarding the set of existing agreements and also what they ought to be complaining about. After describing the end, to provide some insight as to how the GATT/WTO arrived at where it is today, the next two sections explain the role that developing countries played historically with respect to the formal GATT negotiations detailed in chapter 1. This helps clarify that, while one can empathize with what developing countries are complaining about, it is not so easy to place blame for this on the WTO. The fourth section describes the evolution of the negotiation process since the inception of the WTO in 1995. The fifth section provides a brief introduction to the more formal research scholarship detailing the impact of various aspects of the WTO on developing countries' trade. In the final section I shed light on lessons learned that helps to introduce the rest of the book: concerns over developing country access to and participation in the WTO dispute settlement system.

Developing Countries' Problems with the Current WTO Agreements

A quick snapshot of the pattern of current commitments across WTO members provides conspiracy theorists with ample ammunition to support arguments that the WTO is not just indifferent toward developing countries; indeed, much of the agreement appears to have an anti-development bias.[1] There are at least four legitimate components of the WTO agreements that lead to this conclusion—three involve import-restricting policies, and one involves WTO disciplines on domestic support and subsidy policies. This section describes these four problems.

On the side of imports, GATT/WTO trade liberalization negotiations have led countries to take on commitments—or legal obligations—to limit their tariffs. In WTO legal language, there are two different types of tariff rates that are especially important to distinguish. The first is a country's *tariff binding*, defined as the country's legal commitment not to raise an applied import tax above a specified level. The second is a country's *applied tariff*, which is the actual MFN tariff rate that it imposes at the border: legally this may be at or below the country's tariff binding for the product.

Table 2-1 shows the pattern of these tariffs for three groups of WTO members in 2007—developed economies (the European Community, Japan, and the United States), emerging economies (Brazil, China, and India), and some

---

1. See, for example, the discussion in Fatoumata and Kwa (2004). Staiger (2006) provides an insightful review of some of these arguments from the perspective of economic theory.

Table 2-1. *Applied Tariffs and Bindings for Selected WTO Members, 2007*

Country or territory	Product category	Binding coverage[a]	Average bound tariff[b]	Average applied import tariff[b]	Share of duties > 3 × average[c]
European	All	100	5.4	5.2	4.2
Community	Agriculture	n.a.	15.1	15.0	8.3
	Nonagriculture	100	3.9	3.8	7.3
	Clothing	100	11.5	11.5	n.a.
Japan	All	99.6	5.1	5.1	3.6
	Agriculture	n.a.	22.7	21.8	5.8
	Nonagriculture	99.6	2.4	2.6	8.5
	Clothing	100	9.2	9.2	n.a.
United States	All	100	3.5	3.5	7.5
	Agriculture	n.a.	5.0	5.5	5.5
	Nonagriculture	100	3.3	3.2	8.5
	Clothing	100	11.4	11.7	n.a.
Brazil	All	100	31.4	12.2	0.0
	Agriculture	n.a.	35.5	10.3	0.2
	Nonagriculture	100	30.8	12.5	0.0
	Clothing	100	35.0	20.0	n.a.
China	All	100	10.0	9.9	2.4
	Agriculture	n.a.	15.8	15.8	3.2
	Nonagriculture	100	9.1	9.0	1.3
	Clothing	100	16.2	16.0	n.a.
India	All	73.8	50.2	14.5	3.7
	Agriculture	n.a.	114.2	34.4	1.2
	Nonagriculture	69.8	38.2	11.5	2.8
	Clothing	54.9	43.5	22.2	n.a.
Bangladesh	All	15.5	169.2	14.6	0.0
	Agriculture	n.a.	192.0	16.9	0.0
	Nonagriculture	2.6	34.4	14.2	0.0
	Clothing	0.0	n.a.	24.2	n.a.
Chad	All	13.5	79.9	17.9	0.0
	Agriculture	n.a.	80.0	21.9	0.0
	Nonagriculture	0.2	75.0	17.3	0.0
	Clothing	0.0	n.a.	30.0	n.a.
Colombia	All	100	42.9	12.5	0.4
	Agriculture	n.a.	91.9	16.6	3.2
	Nonagriculture	100	35.4	11.8	0.0
	Clothing	100	40.0	20.0	n.a.

Source: Author's compilations from WTO (2008c).

n.a. = Not available.

a. "Binding coverage" is defined as the share of Harmonized System (HS) six-digit subheadings containing at least one bound tariff line.

b. Simple averages are of the ad valorem (ad valorem equivalent) six-digit HS duty averages.

c. Last column is share of six-digit HS lines with applied tariffs that were more than three times the national applied tariff average.

lower-income developing countries (Bangladesh, Chad, and Colombia). The table reveals four pieces of information: the average applied tariff, the average bound tariff, the share of tariff lines the country has legally committed to the WTO for binding, and the share of the country's applied tariff lines that were more than three times the national applied tariff average. For each of the nine countries listed, the table breaks out this information for four different categories of products: all products, agriculture, nonagriculture, and clothing, which is a subset of nonagriculture imports. This simple table reveals much of the basic problem currently facing developing countries under the existing WTO bargain.

Uneven Patterns of Tariff Protection across Industries

Table 2-1 begins first with the developed economies: the European Community (EC), Japan, and the United States. Overall, these countries have legally bound almost 100 percent of their tariffs.[2] Furthermore, the binding commitments lead to import barriers that, on average, are quite low (5.4, 5.1, and 3.5 percent, respectively), as are the actual applied tariffs the countries impose at the border. Indeed, for many imported products in these countries, applied tariffs and bindings are either zero or quite close to it, so that the countries have committed effectively to free trade that is enforceable under WTO rules.

Averaging a country's tariffs can mask important information that is revealed only by a more disaggregated look at the data. First, consider what the data reveal when the tariffs are broken out by different categories of products. The tariffs these developed economies apply on imports typically thought to be of great interest to developing economy producers—for example, agricultural products and labor intensive manufacturing such as clothing—are much higher than the average. In the United States, import tariffs on agricultural products are almost twice as high as the average compared with those on nonagricultural products, while the EC average is nearly four times as high, and in Japan it is almost nine times higher (21.8 percent versus 2.6 percent). Similar patterns emerge for tariffs on clothing—the tariffs are much higher than the average for all nonagricultural products in these three markets.

It is also important not to overlook a second important fact the table reveals. The unfavorable pattern of higher-than-average protection facing export products of particular interest to developing countries is not found only in the trade policies of the northern countries, but it is sometimes even stronger for the import protection of developing countries themselves. Focusing on the applied

2. Frequently throughout this book I refer to WTO members as "countries," even though that is clearly incorrect for economies in the European Community. Nevertheless, from the perspective of the fundamental issues of concern to this book, the European Community acts as a country for the EC member states because it sets the states' common external trade policy.

tariff rates for the developing countries listed in table 2-1, one sees that aside from Brazil, each developing country also has much higher average applied import tariffs on agricultural products than it does on nonagricultural products. Clothing, also a major developing country export product, has a difficult time entering the import markets of other developing countries, given their higher than average import barriers in this sector as well.

The first problem confronting developing country exporters under the current WTO agreement is therefore the existing cross-industry pattern of import tariff protection. Specifically, almost all WTO members, both developed and developing, retain higher than average MFN applied import tariffs in products of export interest to developing countries.

Tariff Peaks and Tariff Escalation across Products within an Industry

A second concern facing exporters in developing countries is the phenomenon of import tariff escalation, which can reflect the problem of tariff peaks hinted at in chapter 1. These are particular products within an industry that have tariffs that are much larger than the size of the other tariffs within the industry.

The economic concern with such a differential between tariff rates for products *within* an industry in a given country is that it can create a disincentive for industrial development in exporting countries. For example, while important import markets may have low average applied tariffs within a sector, the remaining high tariffs that do exist may be structured so that unprocessed goods face lower import barriers than finished products. Such a pattern creates market disincentives for developing countries to process goods at home before exporting; instead they ship unprocessed goods to be processed in the importing country.

The last column of table 2-1 reveals this as a potentially important problem. While major developed economies such as the European Community, Japan, and the United States do have very low applied import tariffs both in absolute terms and especially relative to emerging and developing countries, they also have a substantial number of such tariff peaks that can lead to tariff escalation. Although some of this is simply an artifact of the statistics—that is, for a country with a very low average tariff, it is going to be easier to find more examples of products with applied tariffs more than three times that average—nevertheless tariff peaks are a significant share of tariff lines in the United States (7.5 percent), the European Community (4.2 percent), and Japan (3.6 percent).[3]

---

3. As a statistical matter, it is worth pointing out that this does not necessarily indicate relatively better performance of developing countries. Consider the case of a country with an extremely high average tariff that is effectively prohibitive at choking off imports. In this instance it is not necessary for that country to have any tariffs higher than the average (let alone three times higher than the average), as the average tariff is sufficiently high to restrict imports to zero—raising the

Finally it is worth noting that *unilateral preferences*—that is, lower applied tariff rates that many northern countries extend to exporters in developing countries, such as those provided under the Generalized System of Preferences (GSP)—typically do not take much of a bite out of these tariff peaks. Indeed, Hoekman, Ng, and Olarreaga reported that for the United States and Japan, tariff peak products had preference margins for GSP beneficiaries of only 18 and 23 percent, respectively.[4] The exception is the EC, for which the preference margin for tariff peak products was 50 percent. Thus the United States and Japan tend to grant preferences in nontariff peak products in which the applied rates were already less than 15 percent.

Lack of Binding of Developing Countries' Own Import Barriers

A third problem belongs to developing countries themselves in terms of their own import tariff policies. Thus far, the discussion has focused on how WTO commitments affect developing country exporters relative to the exporters in other countries, and thus the discussion has completely ignored half of the economic gains from trade. Equally important to the gains from exporting is what a country gains via international trade through its ability to import—through access to more varieties, higher-quality products, lower prices, technology transfer, and additional competition facing domestic firms. An important political and economic theory described in chapter 1 indicated that a country can gain from WTO membership as a commitment device that locks it into better policies than it might be able to achieve in the absence of participation in the organization. This might apply if the motive is commitment vis-à-vis otherwise strong domestic political interests or commitment to outside investors by demonstrating that the country is part of the rules-based global economy. While it sounds paternalistic, a theoretical benefit of the WTO could be that it prevents developing countries from "shooting themselves in the foot" if it induced them to adopt low tariff binding commitments.

What is clear from the data is that, for many developing countries, the WTO has not been successful in preventing them from shooting off their own feet. Consider first their tariff binding commitments and refer again to table 2-1. Some developing countries simply have not sufficiently bound their import-restricting policies—for example, Bangladesh has only placed upward tariff limit commitments on 15.5 percent of its products and Chad on only 13.5 percent.

---

tariff more will not reduce imports any further. Put differently, tariff peaks are a secondary problem that may only arise after a country has undergone import liberalization to reduce its tariffs substantially on average, which has not yet been the case for many developing countries.

4. Hoekman, Ng, and Olarreaga (2002), p. 7.

While India is a major emerging economy, it is still a country with much of its population and economy in the relatively early stages of economic development, and it has only bound 73.8 percent of its tariffs. This is the simplest component of what the WTO offers (and demands of) its member countries—and yet many developing countries do not even take advantage of this lock-in aspect to membership.

Second, even for the import tariffs that are legally bound, the bound rates are frequently extremely high. For Bangladesh, even for the few tariffs it has bound, the average binding is at 169.2 percent. For Chad, it is 79.9 percent, and for India 50.2 percent. For agricultural products in these countries, the binding commitments are even higher than the averages, at 192.0, 80.0, and 114.2 percent, respectively.

One potential counterargument might be that while few tariffs are bound and while those that are bound are bound at high levels, who cares? Tariff "bindings" refer to pure WTO legalese, and what matters to the importers and exporters out there in the global economy is only what they have to pay at the border—the *applied* import tariffs.

While this line of argument sounds okay, it is worth pointing out that for many of these countries, the applied tariff rates that exporting firms face at the border are also still relatively high. Indeed, the average applied tariff for the emerging and developing countries (with the exception of China) listed in table 2-1 is in the range of three to four times the rate applied by the European Community, Japan, and the United States. This means that consumer prices are higher and that domestic firms face reduced access to import varieties and technology in developing countries than domestic firms in developed economies face as a result of the policies that developing countries impose *on themselves.*

But second and equally important is the developing country phenomenon known as *binding overhang,* which means the existence of a large differential between the tariff binding and applied tariff rate in a country. To illustrate why a large binding overhang can be a problem, consider a situation in which the applied rate that a country imposed at the border in 2007 is relatively low. For example, take the average applied rate for Bangladesh and its agricultural products, which was only 16.9 percent in 2007—an applied rate not much higher than the European Community's (15.0 percent) and significantly lower than Japan's (21.8 percent). The major difference is the Bangladeshi binding overhang average of 175.1 percentage points versus almost zero for the EC (0.1 percentage point) and Japan (0.9 percentage point). Bangladesh thus retains the flexibility to raise its tariff to ward off imports without facing any WTO disciplines, while the European Community and Japan cannot legally do so. Foreign exporters will recognize this and thus will not invest to sell their product in the Bangladeshi market; so having a low applied tariff does not do Bangladesh much good in terms of making its import market a potential destination for foreign firms. Foreign suppliers recognize that any attempt to provide their products to Bangladeshi consumers can quickly be thwarted.

While that example is in terms of Bangladesh, it is worth noting that a large binding overhang is typical for developing countries in the WTO. With the exception of China, a large tariff binding overhang is a common phenomenon for all of the developing and emerging economies in table 2-1.[5]

Finally, while relatively high applied tariffs as well as the uncertainty created by a large binding overhang can have detrimental ("shooting one's own foot") effects on the tariff-imposing country's own economy, such restrictive trade policies also have a negative impact on economic development by hindering the export opportunities of other developing countries. Consider table 2-2, which documents the developing and emerging economy exporters that are among the top ten sources of nonoil imports for each of these countries.[6] Each of these developing economy import markets relies on developing country trading partners to supply it with imports—between three and five exporters make the top ten for each of these countries listed. This is consistent with the increasing number of South-South trade disputes described in the introduction. The barriers to trade that developing countries impose are likely to have a detrimental impact on other developing countries as well: a developing country that has high applied tariffs adversely affects developing country exports in addition to reducing its own gains from trade.

Insufficient Discipline on Domestic Support and Export Subsidies

A fourth problem is a nontariff barrier to trade that adversely affects developing country exports in agriculture. The specific concern is that, in addition to higher-than-average tariffs and other import restrictions on agricultural trade, WTO rules impose insufficient discipline on existing WTO members' policies on domestic support or government subsidies that distort incentives in agricultural markets of importance to producers in developing countries.

---

5. China's applied tariffs and its tariff bindings are quite close to each other, just as is the case for most of the developed economies in the WTO, and certainly for the three listed in table 2-1. This is mostly a result of China's WTO accession process. Unlike the case for the other developing countries listed in the table, the established WTO membership made major import market access demands of China a condition of its accession, and the result was that China negotiated tariff bindings at limits quite close to what it would end up applying.

6. This is not to suggest that developed economy exporters are also not a significant source for these countries' imports nor that their exporters would not also stand to gain from additional market access. I have simply omitted them from the table to focus attention on the developing countries that are also major exporters to these markets, since this topic is frequently overlooked.

Table 2-2. *Major Sources of Nonoil Imports, Selected WTO Members, 2004*

Importing country[a]	Developing or emerging economy exporter	Share of import market (percent)	Rank[b]
Brazil	Argentina	8.7	3
	China	7.1	4
	Chile	2.7	7
China	Malaysia	3.6	6
	Thailand	2.3	8
	Philippines	1.9	10
India	China	11.6	2
	Malaysia	3.3	8
	Indonesia	3.2	9
	Russia	1.8	10
Bangladesh	China	19.6	1
	India	11.9	2
	Indonesia	4.2	6
	Malaysia	3.8	7
	Thailand	3.3	10
Colombia	Brazil	7.8	3
	China	7.5	4
	Venezuela	5.8	5
	Mexico	5.6	6
	Ecuador	2.1	10

Source: Author's compilations from World Integrated Trade Solution (WITS), software developed by the World Bank, in close collaboration with the United Nations Conference on Trade and Development (UNCTAD).

a. Import data for Chad are not available from WITS.

b. For ranking purposes, note that this ranking counts the EC countries as one exporting entity, as well as China plus Hong Kong.

Domestic subsidies can affect developing country exporters through two channels. The first is that they can work the same way as a tariff to destroy potential market access in those countries that would be "natural" importers of developing country agricultural exports. Even if a country had low tariff bindings and applied rates in a particular product, imports may still be nonexistent if the country has sufficiently generous subsidy policies, since these increase domestic production at the expense of imports. The second is that subsidized export competition in other countries in which suppliers receive government support can destroy potential access to third country markets.[7]

Many developed countries have a legacy of substantial domestic support to the agricultural sector. Table 2-3 provides Organization for Economic Cooperation and Development (OECD) estimates of domestic support to agriculture in

7. Some developing countries will not want to discipline such subsidies. Net food importing countries benefit from agricultural subsidies in other countries, which effectively lower the price of their imports and thus improve the countries' terms of trade.

Table 2-3. *Agricultural Subsidies, by OECD and Selected Non-OECD Countries, 2007*

| Country | Producer support estimate[a] | | Total support estimate[b] (percentage of GDP) |
	Billions of U.S. dollars	Percentage of value of total gross farm receipts	
OECD			
Australia	1.7	6	0.3
Canada	7.0	18	0.7
European Union (27)	134.3	26	0.9
Iceland	0.2	61	1.2
Japan	35.2	45	1.0
Korea	25.4	60	3.0
Mexico	6.0	14	0.8
New Zealand	0.1	1	0.2
Norway	2.8	53	0.8
Switzerland	4.2	50	1.1
Turkey	13.4	21	2.8
United States	32.7	10	0.7
Total OECD	258.2	23	0.9
Non-OECD			
Brazil	4.4	6	0.8
China	35.6	8	2.3
South Africa	1.0	9	0.7

Source: OECD (2008, pp. 54–55), "Agriculture Support Estimates, 2007."

PSE = producer support estimate; TSE = total support estimate.

a. The OECD defines *PSE* as an indicator of the annual monetary value of gross transfers from consumers and taxpayers to support agricultural producers, measured at farm gate level, arising from policy measures that support agriculture, regardless of their nature, objectives, or impacts on farm production or income.

b. The OECD defines *TSE* as an indicator of the annual monetary value of all gross transfers from taxpayers and consumers arising from policy measures that support agriculture, net of the associated budgetary receipts, regardless of their objectives and impacts on farm production and income, or consumption of farm products.

2007 in a number of relatively high-income countries, as well as some of the emerging (Brazil, China) and developing (South Africa) countries for which it collects data. Notably large are the farm support policies of the EU-27 at $134.3 billion, China at $35.6 billion, Japan at $35.2 billion, the United States at $32.7 billion, South Korea at $25.4 billion, and even Turkey at $13.4 billion. Whether the subsidies are measured as a share of the value of domestic agricultural production or GDP, the levels are high. The subsidies also cover a vast array of products, and the policies are frequently implemented in a way that provides a substantial buffer between farmers and the economic incentives that would otherwise be generated by market forces.

Understanding the Sources of the Problem: Developing Countries inside and outside of GATT Negotiations

Thus far I have tried to build the following case. The current WTO agreements appear to contain some market access commitments—albeit not as much as one would hope—that are of exporting interest to developing countries. And rather than the *lack* of other desirable commitments being due to a conspiracy, when viewed from the perspective of the Great Depression era described in chapter 1, it is simply the outcome of a relatively successful set of voluntarily negotiated agreements between countries across the world. The resulting lack of sufficiently low tariff commitments and other disciplines of fundamental interest to developing country trade has been attributed to the reciprocal nature of negotiations pervasive during the GATT era that did result in substantial gains in opening up foreign market access. The developed countries were the ones at the negotiating table, so they asked for and received what was in the principal supplying interest of their major export industries. The result is, on average, low foreign tariffs in nonagricultural products, with the exception of such sectors as apparel, textiles, and footwear, which is not surprising given that those three sectors are not of significant interest to industrialized country exporters anyway.

The problems facing developing countries under the terms of the current WTO agreement appear dire. Although the major developed economy members of the WTO apply extremely low tariffs, on average, when compared with what developing countries levy or with what was done during the earlier post–World War II period, the tariffs that remain high are typically concentrated in sectors of export interest to developing countries. This is an unfortunate pattern of import protection found not only in developed economies, but in emerging and developing markets as well. Second, tariff peaks and tariff escalation may work to impede some industrial development in developing countries. Third, developing countries themselves have not taken sufficient advantage of what the WTO offers with the commitment theory under which governments can use it as an external *commitment device* to bind their trade policies to sufficiently low levels. Fourth, insufficient disciplines on domestic subsidies in sectors of interest to many developing countries can also erode the certainty of their foreign market access. These problems provide a basis for the current angst.

The next step is to determine the sources of these problems. One possibility, highlighted by the anti-globalization conspiracy theorists, is that these outcomes are the result of deliberate systematic attempts of developed countries within the WTO to write a deal that benefits only themselves while serving to marginalize developing countries. Fortunately for humanity, the existence of such a conspiracy is doubtful. The current WTO agreement is instead better interpreted as the unintended and unfortunate (although not completely unpredicted) by-product of a separate narrative partially described in chapter 1—the success of the major trading powers voluntarily negotiating with one another to open up their markets—not only toward one another but toward developing countries as well. This is not to minimize the importance of the problem, since it is indeed serious. However, allocating blame where it is not warranted is not helpful for extracting the world from this mess. This is important because there are useful lessons for all WTO members to learn from the actual GATT/WTO negotiating history, even though there may have been relatively few countries actively participating at the negotiating table throughout this history. The GATT/WTO system is not something simply to be written off or something that should be scrapped in order to start afresh.

Nevertheless, there is still one fundamental question to be tackled. Specifically, if developing countries were sitting on the sidelines during GATT negotiations, what else were they doing? As table 2-1 shows, some of the emerging markets especially do have much lower tariffs than many other developing countries. What explains this? If they too were not a formal part of GATT negotiating rounds, how did their tariffs get so low, and what are the implications for other developing countries today? To address these questions, I focus on three issues of particular interest to developing countries during the GATT era: special and differential treatment (SDT), the Generalized System of Preferences, and unilateral trade liberalization.

Special and Differential Treatment and the GATT's Part IV

Thirteen of the original twenty-three contracting parties to the 1947 GATT were developing countries. Their presence, however, did not have much effect in terms of opening up the foreign markets of interest to their potential exporting industries, and from this vantage point, one might view them as having been relatively uninfluential. While I will not attempt a full explanation of why developing countries took on a passive role in market access negotiations of interest to their potential exporters, the relevant fact is that this was the case.[8]

These thirteen developing countries were very active and quite successful at carving out special exceptions to rules and obligations that they felt were not in

8. The reasons for developing country passivity in the GATT would include the failure of the institutional framework of the International Trade Organization (ITO), which was negotiated to administer the GATT, to come into being; the dominance of the "import-substitution model" of economic development, which permeated the economic policy of developing countries during this era and led them to be skeptical of the development relevance of promoting export market access; and the rise of the United Nations Conference on Trade and Development (UNCTAD), which became the unifying voice of developing countries. More comprehensive reviews of developing country engagement in GATT negotiating rounds can be found in Hudec (1987); Srinivasan (2000).

their development interests. This was true from the start of the GATT. Although the GATT that was signed in 1947 contained nothing that explicitly linked trade to development, developing countries managed to negotiate exemptions to certain core GATT rules.[9] A number of examples illustrate how these specific exemptions limited their application and introduced the notion of special and differential treatment of developing countries. Although Article XI of the GATT sought to eliminate quantitative restrictions in favor of tariffs for GATT contracting parties, this principle was diluted to allow developing countries to impose quantitative restraints whenever they needed to safeguard the country's balance of payments (Article XII). GATT limits on import protection through tariffs or quantitative restrictions were also relaxed to allow developing countries to engage in infant industry protection (Article XVIII). The GATT contracting parties subsequently adopted other practices of SDT toward developing country participants as well. In all multilateral proceedings before the Uruguay Round, developing countries were exempted from undertaking the same sort of reciprocal market access openings expected of the developed country negotiators.

During the post–GATT 1947 era, many developing countries joined the agreement. As described earlier, membership meant that their exporters were granted MFN tariff treatment by the other contracting parties. This benefit could be enjoyed even if the countries did not commit to their own trade liberalization or to discipline their own national policies by following GATT rules. Indeed, when the GATT finally introduced the term *trade and development* into the agreement through Part IV's Article XXXVI, it repeatedly referred to the crucial role of "export earnings" in the economic development process. There is no explicit reference to the concern that import restrictions might also impede the country's economic development through insufficient access to resources, knowledge, technology, or competitive pressures.[10]

Generalized System of Preferences and the Enabling Clause

In addition to receiving through MFN treatment the benefit of trade liberalization, which was negotiated among the more active GATT contracting parties, the developing countries increasingly sought differential and more favorable

9. As is described in more detail below, a formal role for trade and development was not incorporated into the GATT text until it was amended by a 1965 protocol that added Part IV to the agreement.

10. The potential benefit of developing country import barrier reductions for other developing country exporters is hinted at in Article XXXVII: 4: "Less-developed contracting parties agree to take appropriate action in implementation of the provisions of Part IV for the benefit of the trade of other less-developed contracting parties, in so far as such action is consistent with their individual present and future development, financial and trade needs taking into account past trade developments as well as the trade interests of less-developed contracting parties as a whole."

treatment than that offered to developed country exporters. Specifically, developing countries sought and were granted preferential access to developed country markets for their manufactured exports through the offer of lower-than-MFN applied tariffs. The Tokyo Round (1973–79) of negotiations codified this into accepted practice as the Generalized System of Preferences.

Under the Tokyo Round's Enabling Clause, developing countries also enjoyed other exceptions to the basic GATT principle of MFN. They could offer lower preferential tariffs to one another without being subject to the "substantially all trade" requirement applied to developed countries engaging in a preferential trade agreement under Article XXIV of the GATT.

As I describe in more detail below, one important practical concern raised by these low preferential tariffs is their lack of enforceability in the case of violations. To the extent that WTO rules enforce tariff binding commitments, developing countries may not have much leverage under the WTO's dispute settlement provisions if a trading partner reverses itself on an offer of a lower preferential tariff. This thus creates substantial uncertainty for exporters whose trade takes place under these preferential tariffs, which, while low, are at levels that are not enforceable through the WTO dispute settlement system.

Unilateral Trade Liberalization and Preferential Trade Agreements

Eight rounds of multilateral negotiations since 1947, as well as the legacy of special and differential treatment toward developing countries, have shaped much of the cross-country and cross-industry pattern of import protection that researchers continue to observe in the data, including the average tariffs described in table 2-1. And yet, when it comes to developing countries' own import-restricting trade policies, this is not quite the full story. Missing from the discussion thus far is recognition that a number of developing countries have undertaken significant unilateral trade liberalization, at least with respect to their applied tariffs, if not necessarily their tariff bindings.

The final GATT-era element involving developing countries that is worth discussing is how some did choose to reduce applied import tariffs *unilaterally*—by which is meant outside the multilateral negotiating rounds. From table 2-1, Brazil, India, and Colombia are clear examples of such countries. For example, many of India's currently (relatively) low applied tariffs are the result of the unilateral trade liberalization that it undertook in the 1990s. This unilateral liberalization was carried out in conjunction with an International Monetary Fund (IMF) structural adjustment program developed in response to India's macroeconomic and balance of payments crisis in 1991.[11] Before it

---

11. See the discussions in Cerra and Saxena (2002); Topalova (2004); Srinivasan (2001).

implemented trade liberalization, India's average tariff was 128 percent, and some tariffs were more than 300 percent, so today's applied rates are much lower than has been the case historically. Colombia liberalized unilaterally during the late 1980s, and Brazil undertook a major unilateral liberalization in the early 1990s, which accompanied its preferential trade liberalization toward Argentina, Uruguay, and Paraguay with the formation of MERCOSUR.[12] Other developing country episodes of unilateral liberalization not presented in table 2-1 include Chile in the 1970s and Argentina and Mexico in the late 1980s.

Because these tariff liberalizations were unilateral, they were not compensated in the usual GATT reciprocal process of a multilateral trade round. One question is whether these countries should be compensated in current negotiations for binding their tariffs at these low levels. A frequent argument is that reciprocity has not worked within the GATT for developing countries because those that have liberalized have done so unilaterally and thus have gotten nothing for it from the GATT and the WTO. While it has already been noted that there is an important economic argument (removing exporter uncertainty associated with excess binding overhang) that binding these tariffs at the existing low applied rates is in these countries' own interests, are there valid counterarguments to such current demands for a payoff? I explore two related arguments that highlight the complexity of the issue.

To begin, there is at least one theoretical argument to suggest that expecting additional compensation for binding already low applied tariffs may be asking for too much in a reciprocal sense, even for small countries that cannot make themselves better off by affecting the terms of trade. Consider an instance in which the country may have already been compensated outside of the WTO structure for lowering its tariffs. For example, in exchange for its unilateral trade liberalization in the 1990s, India received financial assistance from the IMF.[13]

There are other contexts in which unilateral liberalizers may have already received some compensation, but determining the extent of that compensation can be admittedly quite complicated. Consider, for example, a country that undertakes a unilateral MFN liberalization (toward WTO members that are not PTA partners) simultaneously with a PTA liberalization. There are many instances in which a country has unilaterally liberalized its applied MFN tariffs in conjunction with preferential trade liberalization because of a regional trade

12. MERCOSUR, *Mercado Común del Sur,* or Southern Common Market, has four members: Argentina, Brazil, Paraguay, and Uruguay, with Venezuela awaiting ratification. Five other countries have associate member status: Bolivia, Chile, Colombia, Ecuador, and Peru.

13. *Unilateral* should not be confused with *voluntary*. In instances like India's experience in 1991–92, the liberalization was a condition of an IMF plan of structural adjustment and thus was in exchange for something, even if that something was not a trading partner's reciprocated trade liberalization.

agreement.[14] This may be a way to minimize potential welfare losses from the trade diversion due to the PTA. On one hand, suppose the initial payoff to the liberalization was accrued by PTA members enjoying substantially increased market access in the PTA member's market. If non-PTA members of WTO benefited little from the market access associated with the liberalization because of the simultaneous PTA, it seems to be double-counting to ask to receive WTO extra credit for binding these low MFN tariffs as well. On the other hand, if the unilateral liberalization did result in significant market access gains to non-PTA members, there may be an argument that some compensation (from the WTO membership made up of mainly non-PTA members) to the unilaterally liberalizing country is due.

Finally, regardless of the issue of potential compensation to developing countries for binding their tariffs that they may have unilaterally reduced, a significant concern does exist that these tariffs do need to be legally bound under the WTO agreement. One reason for this, which has already been addressed, is to reduce foreign exporter uncertainty and thus allow them to undertake the investment needed to develop products for the importing country market. A second reason is the legality—the WTO binding is what is the legal commitment. It is the same concern that arises when developed country importers extend tariffs that are lower than MFN bindings to developing country exporters preferentially under the GSP. Countries can only pursue trade disputes at the WTO for breaking WTO bindings. They cannot pursue disputes when a trading partner raises applied rates unexpectedly, nor can they pursue WTO trade disputes for violations of commitments to lower (unbound) tariffs under a PTA.

The Uruguay Round and the Single Undertaking

The Uruguay Round of negotiations under the GATT, begun in 1986 and completed in 1994, achieved something that had eluded all prior GATT negotiating rounds—the active participation of developing countries. Any country, including developing countries, that wished to become a member of the new World Trade Organization was required to sign onto all elements of the agreement via a "single undertaking." This required the commitment to bind tariffs

14. Estevadeordal, Freund, and Ornelas (2008), in particular, have found evidence for the case of Latin American countries that is supportive of this. For the 1990–2001 period, they found evidence that bilateral (preferential) tariff cuts led the countries to subsequently impose lower MFN tariffs in the same industry. Note that this is only one-half of the evidence, as other studies have found that preferential trade agreements can construct substantial impediments to future multilateral trade liberalization. For the case of U.S. PTAs, see Limão (2006), and for EC PTAs, see Karacaovali and Limão (2008).

in agriculture and goods trade and adhere to WTO agreements on intellectual property (IP), sanitary and phytosanitary (SPS) measures, technical barriers to trade (TBT), subsidies and countervailing measures (SCM), and so on. Unlike the GATT era, especially under the Tokyo Round, which produced a set of plurilateral agreements from which countries could pick and choose à la carte, the WTO was all or nothing.

Sylvia Ostry has referred to the Uruguay Round as the "grand bargain" between developed and developing countries.[15] For the first time, two major sectors of interest to developing country exporters—clothing and textiles through the Agreement on Textiles and Clothing and farm products through the Agreement on Agriculture—would be integrated into the GATT/WTO system and disciplines. In exchange, developed countries sought to have the WTO membership increase disciplines over trade in services through the General Agreement on Trade in Services (GATS) as well as the beginning of protection of intellectual property rights through the Agreement on Trade-Related Aspects of Intellectual Property Rights (TRIPS). Another major change of particular interest for this book was reform of the dispute settlement auspices that established the Dispute Settlement Understanding (DSU) and produced the much more comprehensive and legalistic enforcement system that is in place today.

So what happened to disappoint developing countries and cause them to become dissatisfied with this bargain ex post? At least three things.

The end of the Multifibre Arrangement (MFA) and the introduction of a more globally liberal trade regime for textile and apparel products did not result in the massive economic gains that the developing countries had expected. There are at least three contributing reasons. First, global demand for these products is downward sloping, but many developing country exporters anticipated economic gains that would accrue to them only if liberalized markets (greater export volumes) led to no change in traded prices. The export increase of many countries resulted in a fall in the prices of textile and apparel products. Second, the MFA system governing international trade in textiles and apparel products had coalesced into one that was primarily export-restraint driven, so the exporter received economic benefits via what economists refer to as *quota rents*. With the termination of quantitative restrictions when the MFA ended, gone too were the quota rents as economic welfare to the exporters. Third is China's unanticipated (in the early 1990s) and unprecedented export growth in these products. Furthermore, with China's accession to the WTO in 2001, it gained access to the same low tariffs under MFN treatment as most other textile and apparel producers in developing countries. In many instances, production

15. See Ostry (2002) and also the related discussion of Finger (2002).

shifted toward China. The combined effect of these forces is one reason why part of the anticipated benefits to the grand bargain failed to materialize for developing countries, even if it was not caused by anything that the developed countries have done or reneged on in this sector.

Second, the integration of agricultural trade into the disciplines of the GATT/WTO has not gone as smoothly as countries might have hoped. Here, there is some evidence that the inability of developing countries to take sufficient advantage of new disciplines on agriculture is due partially to developed countries reneging or not following through on commitments promised during the Uruguay Round. For example, with the violation of the terms of the WTO Agreement on Agriculture's "peace clause," a number of trade disputes over farm products have arisen because WTO members are not following through with the Uruguay Round promises. The United States was found to have provided excessive domestic support for cotton producers, and the European Community provided excessive import protection to the sugar industry. As I reveal in the data in the next chapter, the massive number of WTO disputes over agricultural trade provides evidence that overall many WTO members have found it difficult to live up to commitments to provide secure market access to foreign agricultural exporters.

Third, the commitment of developing countries to substantial protection of intellectual property has been highly controversial. Many predicted that doomsday scenarios would confront developing countries with their new commitments, which were hard to justify as having any short-run benefit: for example, northern pharmaceutical companies charging excessively high prices for life-saving drugs in AIDS-ravaged sub-Saharan Africa or biotech companies creating a dependence on imported, genetically engineered seeds. Although the worst-case scenarios have not developed, perhaps because of the political backlash that would result if IP enforcement became a higher priority via members initiating WTO disputes, certainly the public attention to this issue has created a level of suspicion on behalf of developing countries.

And yet there are also some signs with TRIPS that, for developing countries able to take on some intellectual property protection obligations, there may be an unexpected upside—a potential retaliatory tool that is particularly important in the self-enforcing arena of WTO dispute settlement. As I discuss below regarding formal trade disputes, the WTO cases over *EC–Bananas III* (Ecuador), *US–Gambling* (Antigua and Barbuda), and *US–Upland Cotton* (Brazil), each has an element in which developing countries use the threat of TRIPS nonenforcement, which is authorized under the WTO, to help their case. The idea that TRIPS might play an important enforcement role for developing countries was perhaps not fully understood by either developed or developing countries during the Uruguay Round.

The Future of WTO Negotiations and Developing Countries

In light of the unintentionally unbalanced nature of the bargain between developed and developing countries, an attempt to rebalance the overall WTO bargain began in 2001 in Doha, Qatar. There the existing membership launched its latest negotiating round and pledged to make it a development round.

Nevertheless, a template for successfully doing so has yet to emerge. Although the reciprocal negotiations framework did well to liberalize trade between developed countries over the past sixty years, a new negotiating model that I argue is based on unilateral actions (and not reciprocity) designed to rebalance the bargain between developed and developing countries has failed to gain traction.

In the context of the current Doha Round of negotiations, a number of sticking points have arisen between developed and developing countries. First, when it comes to the developing countries' past unilateral liberalization efforts, trading partners would like these countries to lock in these lower applied tariff rates by reducing their legally binding WTO tariff commitments, even though this may not lead to any additional trade liberalization through lower applied tariffs.

For their part, many developing countries have refused to do this for at least two reasons. The first is the desire to retain "policy space," the ability to increase their tariffs in unforeseen circumstances, a possibility that would be foreclosed if their tariff bindings were lowered.[16] Although there are other WTO-permitted exceptions such as safeguards, antidumping actions, and countervailing measures, which may be employed against imports (under certain conditions) with much the same effect as increasing an applied tariff, such policies are relatively costly to implement and administer bureaucratically. Second, and perhaps more important, because many of the reductions in applied tariffs were undertaken unilaterally, a number of developing countries argue that under the traditional reciprocity framework in the WTO, they are owed something in return for lowering these barriers. From their viewpoint, they are not negotiating to lock in applied rates at low levels. They are negotiating from a starting point of high tariff bindings and seek some WTO-induced incentive to cut tariff bindings.

And yet, such an approach asks that developed economies go away from what they have used in the past to facilitate and sustain politically acceptable negotiations—reciprocity—in exchange for nothing of much current value. Many developed countries are being asked to liberalize their last remaining highly protected sectors—textiles and apparel or agriculture, for example—unilaterally.

---

16. For an analysis of issues involving developing countries and policy space, see Hoekman (2005). Hoekman (2007) provides a broader discussion of developing countries in the Doha Round.

A second complicating issue facing the current state of the WTO negotiations, even building from a development-centric framework, is that developing countries themselves are diverse in terms of their interest or lack of interest in market access. They do not and should not have a common negotiating position on all key issues, given their fundamental differences in what they can successfully trade. As one extreme but important example, some developing country members of the WTO are net food-importing countries. For these countries, it is not a negotiating priority that other countries lower trade barriers for agricultural imports and increase discipline on agricultural subsidies. Not only is it something that they would not spend bargaining chips to negotiate for, all else being equal, they actually stand to lose out in terms of economic well-being if such new commitments are implemented that end up increasing the price of food products that they import.

Thus it is unrealistic to expect developing countries to collectively take on common bargaining positions in negotiations. In fact, such an expectation is wrongheaded because, for any given negotiating position on an issue, some developing countries will be in favor and others against. As the GATT negotiations from the post-1947 period have illustrated, successful and sustainable market-opening negotiations take place when they are voluntary and when they can result in a reciprocal balance of exchanges of market access.

As is clear from the discussion of the WTO's self-enforcement process beginning in the next chapter, unilateral actions may very well end up being more difficult to enforce. For if one country grants something unilaterally to a second country, the second country has nothing of value to threaten to take away should that original unilateral action be rescinded.

Economic Research on the Impact of the GATT/WTO Bargain on Trade

Recent economic research has begun to provide estimates of the impact of the GATT/WTO on international trade flows. Work by Subramanian and Wei presents a number of results that speak directly to the questions raised here of the GATT/WTO's impact on the trade of developing countries.[17] Their research uses a standard econometric gravity model to estimate the impact of GATT/WTO membership on trade across countries and industries from 1950 to 2000. They asked whether being in the GATT/WTO increases a country's

17. Subramanian and Wei (2007), as well as Goldstein, Rivers, and Tomz (2007) and Tomz, Goldstein, and Rivers (2007), are all examples of research addressing the concerns raised by the initial results in Rose (2004), who suggested that the GATT/WTO had little impact on trade across all member countries.

trade relative to an otherwise equivalent country that is not a member. The results of their regression analysis are qualitatively consistent with many of the concerns raised thus far. The first point worth noting is that, on average, developing country exports to developed economies were found to be 1.5 times higher because of GATT/WTO membership, holding a number of other things constant.[18] Therefore, although the previous discussion indicates that the current WTO bargain may be stacked against developing country interests, at least in terms of developing country exports, on average, there is a positive and significant effect of membership for developing countries.

However, there is also evidence of substantial variation across sectors as to the size of the effect of the GATT/WTO on trade—with a zero or negative impact on sectors such as agriculture and clothing (as well as footwear) and a strongly positive effect on the trade of other manufacturing sectors. One way to interpret these results is to say that, while membership in the GATT/WTO has on average had a positive effect on developing country exports, the GATT/WTO has not effectively reduced trade barriers in sectors such as agriculture, clothing, and footwear. Thus trade is not as high in these sectors as it is in other sectors and not as high for these countries as if such sectors were better covered by the GATT/WTO bargain.

Subramanian and Wei also found very little effect of GATT/WTO membership on the imports of developing countries. Thus, while the average effect on developing country exports (via trade to developed countries) has been positive, it is not surprising to find in the data that GATT/WTO membership for developing countries has not achieved a statistically significant increase in their own imports. Furthermore, there is little evidence that developing countries did much to effectively lower their applied import tariffs in response to the Uruguay Round agreement.[19]

---

18. This result, in particular, is consistent with the results of Goldstein, Rivers, and Tomz (2007), who undertook archival research from historical records to code more accurately the GATT membership variables included in the original Rose (2004) paper and also used in Subramanian and Wei (2007). However, Goldstein, Rivers, and Tomz (2007) did not address the same developing country and sectoral decomposition questions that are of particular interest to this discussion.

19. Subramanian and Wei (2007, p. 173) pointed out that "although developing countries' bound tariffs may have come down in the Uruguay Round, actual tariffs barely budged. . . . Although the percentage of tariff lines for which bindings (commitments) were taken on by developing countries increased by 50 percentage points due to the Uruguay Round, the actual tariff reductions brought about by the Round were much smaller: only 28 percent of tariff lines involved reductions in applied tariffs, and on these, the reduction was 8 percent. In other words, if tariff reductions are calculated on all tariff lines, the reduction would be about 2 percent. . . . The irony relating to [Special and Differential Treatment (SDT)] in the Uruguay Round was that it was eliminated in areas—such as TRIPS—where maintaining it may actually have been welfare-enhancing. But [SDT] was preserved in the conventional area of trade liberalization in goods where its dilution would have been welfare-enhancing."

Implications for Developing Countries and Dispute Settlement

In a nutshell, what are the implications of over sixty years of GATT and WTO negotiating history and agreements? In particular, what is the relevance of this history and the resulting WTO agreement for the argument made in the introductory chapter that giving poor countries enhanced access to the self-enforcing WTO dispute settlement system is an important component to their growth and development strategies?

First, this chapter has revealed the commercial sectors and industries in which it is expected that significant trade frictions and hence formal WTO disputes will arise. The industries most recently integrated—albeit incompletely—into the rules of the trading system are sectors such as apparel, textiles, and agriculture. If and when a developed or developing country takes on additional commitments to liberalize trade or discipline domestic subsidies, it is likely also that these areas will result in incentives to renege.

Thus these sectors require the most monitoring, enforcement, and access to WTO dispute settlement. Furthermore, at the country level, it is clear from the data on tariffs illustrated in table 2-1 that most of the additional trade liberalization that will take place in the future will be in other developing countries, as developed country tariffs for most products are already quite low. And implementing new commitments entails domestic reform and adjustment, which sometimes can result in backsliding and thus the need for other WTO members to step in and proceed with a dispute to self-enforce the agreement. The implication is that much of the dispute settlement caseload can be expected to result in formal cases being filed against developing countries.

Second, while I have painted a somewhat dire picture of the current pattern of protection across industries as being stacked against the interests of developing country exporters, I have also pointed to two important facts. First, I have explained that this outcome is not the result of a conspiracy, but of the legacy of negotiation procedures, voluntary participation, and the path that developing countries have taken to work outside of the system. But it is also important to note that WTO members—both developed countries and some developing countries as importers—have taken on substantial, enforceable commitments of interest to developing country exporters. Furthermore, as is described in the next chapter, WTO members have taken on a number of commitments that likely are not being sufficiently enforced. This thus prevents developing countries from fully realizing the benefits of the WTO. Finally, when it comes to enforcement and effective use of the WTO dispute settlement system as a development tool for poor countries, what matters for follow-through is a focus on compliance with the tariffs that are legally bound. This point ought to feed back to developing countries as a negotiation strategy—they should push harder for enforceable commitments of low binding tariffs in other countries, and they themselves should grant the concessions necessary to achieve those low foreign bindings. They should likewise focus less on preferences under GSP or other bilateral arrangements, regardless of how low the applied rates are, because ultimately those rates are not enforceable through WTO dispute settlement.

Third, I have emphasized that reciprocity matters. Reciprocity is a constant theme throughout this book, and it is important to see the many levels at which it plays a role in the international trading system. On the positive side, I have detailed how reciprocity has served as the major force in negotiations to open up previously closed markets, despite the economic forces in large developed countries that make them unwilling to do so unilaterally. Furthermore, I have shown how the lack of willingness to undertake reciprocal negotiations contributes to a failure to open the markets where developing countries need enforceable market access commitments the most.

The lessons from the reciprocity principle and the forces underlying it imply that there are limits to what the WTO can realistically achieve in terms of market access, and these limits may impose constraints especially on developing countries. For one, it is likely to be fruitless for developing countries to continue to demand something (unilaterally granted foreign market access in politically sensitive products) for nothing. Foreign market access is only as good as it is enforceable. Even in the increasingly legalized WTO system, enforceability and thus access to foreign markets is more certain when foreigners also have access to your import market. The mechanism of using something of value as a threat that can be taken away (their export market) is what keeps the whole system functioning. An increasingly interesting element of potential importance for developing countries is how this reciprocity incentive may work not only through the mechanism of imports, but also through enforcement of foreign intellectual property rights through TRIPS.

3

An Introduction to WTO Dispute Settlement

The last chapter described the set of World Trade Organization agreements resulting from rounds of multilateral negotiations over forty-seven years. The next step is to begin to explore the implications for developing countries of the WTO as a *self-enforcing* trade agreement. For the agreement to work, trading partners must find it in their own interest to remain a part of the agreement and to hold one another accountable to bargains made if one country steps away from it. Throughout most of the General Agreement on Tariffs and Trade and WTO history and for most of the commitments made, member countries do appear to have been accountable to one another, and as a result, trade frictions do not build up and boil to the surface; thus formal disputes are not necessary. But this has not been the case universally. At some points in time and over some sets of commitments, the mere existence of the agreement has not been enough—member countries have found the actual process of a formal trade dispute necessary to enforce the bargain.

This chapter introduces the WTO's formal trade dispute resolution process. Between 1995 and 2008, there have been 388 instances in which frictions between WTO members reached a point at which they required dispute settlement assistance from the institution to enforce the bargain. In introducing WTO dispute settlement, I focus on how it works and why it is important. I highlight why developing countries especially need access to WTO enforcement, what resources they need so that they can use it to enforce, the potential hurdles that may hinder their access to the process, and the implications of their failure to use it.

The next section presents basic terminology and actual legal steps of dispute resolution—that is, the "WTO speak"—associated with the formal enforcement process. While the political and economic incentives that drive the process are relatively complicated, the legal process itself is fairly straightforward and intuitive, once one understands its unique terminology.

In the second section, I introduce the actual economic, legal, and political events of one particular WTO dispute. Although this case is just one of the 388 different disputes that took place during the period 1995–2008, this particular dispute provides a revealing initiation into the WTO enforcement process. It also raises a number of fundamental questions that can only be answered by a more detailed look at the data on the full dispute settlement caseload.

The Basics of the Legal Process of WTO Dispute Settlement

Before I delve into the details of WTO enforcement actions, it is useful to become familiar with the nomenclature associated with the WTO's own unique dispute resolution process.[1] The very basics of the process followed under the WTO's Dispute Settlement Understanding (DSU) are illustrated in figure 3-1.

Suppose one WTO member country implements a new trade barrier—for example, an import restriction like a tariff or an export-promoting measure such as a subsidy—that violates WTO rules and thus reduces the market access that another WTO member country's exporters had expected to receive.[2] If the two countries do not work out the problem on their own, the exporting country's first step is to initiate a dispute at the WTO by making a formal "request for consultations." The nation of the aggrieved exporters—that is, the potential plaintiff in a dispute—is called a *complainant country,* whereas the policy-imposing defendant is called the *respondent country.*

If the countries cannot negotiate a resolution of the issue at the "consultations phase," they can request that the WTO establish a "Panel" of three independent experts to hear the two sides' evidence. Other WTO member countries with a significant interest in the dispute—perhaps because they also have

1. More detailed descriptions of the legal steps of the formal WTO dispute resolution process can be found, for example, in Mavroidis (2007, pp. 398–445); Trebilcock and Howse (1999, pp. 58–80). Seminal legal texts on the GATT legal system include Jackson (1969); Dam (1970); Hudec (1975). Jackson (1997) is an early analysis of the evolution from the GATT to the WTO.

2. In this section, the example discussed is of a trade barrier that violates WTO rules or membership obligations. The Dispute Settlement Understanding also allows for countries to pursue what are called *nonviolation complaints*—challenges to one country's action that, while not necessarily in violation of any explicit WTO rules, nevertheless eliminates market access that exporters had a reasonable expectation of receiving under the agreement.

Figure 3-1. *Basics of the WTO Dispute Settlement Process*

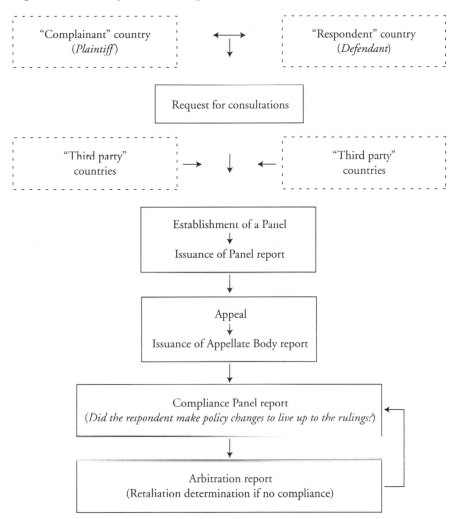

exporters that trade the same goods affected by the disputed policy—can enter into the process at this stage in the formal role that the WTO refers to as *interested third parties*. Once the Panel hears all the evidence, it issues and circulates the first legal ruling—what the WTO calls a *Panel report*—and this ends the "Panel phase" of the legal proceedings.

If either of the primary litigants (the complainant or the respondent country) is unhappy with any aspect of the rulings in the Panel report, that country can submit a request for an appeal to the WTO's Appellate Body, a sitting body of seven trade experts employed by the WTO Secretariat who act as jurists. After reviewing the case and hearing arguments from the parties, the Appellate Body then issues its ruling, which is final, thus concluding the "Appellate Body phase."

To give a rough idea of the length of time it takes for disputes to be adjudicated, in a recent study, Horn and Mavroidis report that from 1995 to 2006 WTO members' use of the consultations phase, Panel phase, and Appellate Body phase resulted in disputes that average more than two years from beginning to end.[3]

If the respondent country is found to be in violation of its WTO obligations, the WTO asks the country to bring its policies into compliance, and a reasonable period of time is established during which the country is expected to implement the change. If the complainant country is unhappy with the respondent's form of compliance, it can request that a Compliance Panel be established to rule on whether the respondent country has actually lived up to the Panel and Appellate Body legal rulings.

If the Compliance Panel rules that the respondent country has failed to change its policies and comply, the complainant can request that an Arbitration Panel be established to determine by how much the complainant is authorized to retaliate to obtain compensation for the respondent's failures.[4]

Figure 3-1 and this discussion are but a brief sketch of the formal dispute resolution process. While the legal reality is more detailed and complex, this introduction is a sufficient starting point for a deeper discussion of why dispute resolution is essential to the self-enforcing WTO agreements.

The Banana Case: An Introduction to WTO Dispute Settlement

This section introduces how the WTO dispute settlement process works and some of the reasons why it matters. Rather than describe an abstract theory of WTO dispute settlement, I begin with the *EC–Bananas III* dispute.[5] This dispute

---

3. Horn and Mavroidis (2009b, table 20) report that for the consultations phase, the length of time between the date of request for consultations until the date the Panel was established was on average 210.2 days; the length of time between the date the Panel was established until the date of the circulation of the Panel report was on average 406.4 days; and the length of time between the date of the notice of appeal until the date of the circulation of the Appellate Body report was on average 89.3 days. These three periods cumulate to 705.9 days and do not include time periods that elapse, say, between when the date at which a Panel report is circulated and the date at which one of the parties in the dispute files a notice for appeal. An alternative way to calculate time duration would be to focus only on the length of disputes for the subsample that reached the third (Appellate Body) stage of the process.

4. The dispute may not end here, because after the decision is published in the arbitration report, if the respondent claims to have complied with the rulings, the dispute must be resubmitted back to an Article 21.5 Compliance Panel.

5. In fact, there is not much theoretical research on formal WTO dispute settlement. One exception is the recent theory of Maggi and Staiger (2008) that models the dispute settlement

is a useful place to start because its history reveals many of the economic, legal, and political complexities in the WTO enforcement process. The use of this dispute provides an opportunity to question whether issues that came up in this particular case are pervasive and perhaps important in the broader WTO dispute settlement data that are examined in the next chapter.

Admittedly, this one dispute cannot perfectly capture all important or interesting elements of WTO enforcement. No single dispute can do that, and one should be wary of drawing inferences from any one particular case study, especially regarding policy reform. Indeed, there are certain elements—such as the major U.S. role as a co-complainant despite not being a physical source of grown bananas—that make the dispute unique. Nevertheless, I use this dispute to describe key features of the WTO dispute settlement process as well as how it differs from the prior GATT process. I also use it to raise eleven important questions about the implications of WTO dispute settlement, especially with regard to the interests of developing countries, a number of which can then be subject to empirical analysis.

The European Community's Banana Problem

The fundamental economic interest that boiled over into a formal trade dispute in the early 1990s involved foreign access to the European import market for bananas—the world's largest banana market with imports of roughly $2.5 billion per year.[6] While the trade dispute on which I focus erupted in the early 1990s, the issue of EC banana imports has been politically contentious on the domestic front (that is, between EC member states) dating back to the 1950s and the Treaty of Rome. Until the early 1990s, member states had different and divergent external trade policies toward bananas. At one end of the spectrum, Spain was essentially autarkic with consumption that relied on domestic production in the Canary Islands. At the other end of the spectrum, Germany had a very liberal policy toward imports of bananas, essentially free trade, so that most of its banana imports were coming from low-cost suppliers in Latin America. In the middle, politically powerful EC members like the United Kingdom and France had preferential market access programs in which they imported

---

process as completing various dimensions of an incomplete contract, which they take to be the existing WTO agreements. Horn, Maggi, and Staiger (forthcoming) provide an earlier model of the GATT/WTO as an incomplete contract. Earlier theoretical research frequently modeled trade disputes as "off the equilibrium path" behavior, and as such, these theories had little to offer regarding the determinants of trade disputes or the behavior that led to dispute settlement activity. Exceptions include Kovenock and Thursby (1992); Bown (2002a).

6. The discussion of the underlying political and economic setting and events draws from Devereaux, Lawrence, and Watkins (2006a, chapter 2); Cadot and Webber (2002); Borrell (1994).

bananas primarily from their former colonies and territories in the African, Caribbean, and Pacific (ACP) regions. Finally, other members like Belgium, Denmark, Luxembourg, Ireland, and the Netherlands were not as liberal as Germany but still imposed only a 20 percent tariff on imports of bananas that came mainly from Latin America.

The different trade policies of EC member states toward the same product managed to coexist until 1993 when, after politically rancorous internal negotiations, the members finally converged on a single, European Community–wide import regime for bananas. The new import policy, known as Regulation 404, was essentially a tariff rate quota. The quota divvied up the EC import market and established one quantitative import limit allocated to ACP producers and another to non-ACP producers (mainly Latin American exporters). Bananas coming in under the quota available to Latin American exporters would be subject to an import tariff that was not applied to imports from the ACP countries. The European Community also created a complex system of licenses to allocate the right to export under the quota.

Given the relatively large size of the total import quota allocated to ACP producers, and the relatively small size (compared with historical market shares) allocated to Latin American producers, the new EC import regime was much closer to the preexisting United Kingdom–France model than that of any other EC member. Within the EC, German consumers faced the biggest adjustment, which was higher prices. The least adjustment was faced by consumers in the United Kingdom and France and banana distributors such as the U.K. firm Fyffes and the Irish firm Geest, both of which had historically imported from ACP banana growers.

The fundamental GATT and WTO legal issues that would eventually come up in the litigation revolved around the different sizes of the market access that the European Community granted to Latin American and to ACP countries (that is, the size of the ACP share of the quota relative to that of the Latin American countries); the size of the tariff on imports from non-ACP sources; as well as the EC's allocation scheme for granting licenses to non-ACP foreign banana-distributing firms, allowing them legal access under the quota to the EC market. First, Regulation 404 led to a sharp reduction in market access for many exporting countries in Latin America. Second, the new EC system of quantitative restrictions would make internal EC banana prices much higher than the extra-EC (that is, world) price for bananas bought and sold in more open markets without quantitative limits. Thus merely acquiring the right to sell bananas at a premium price to consumers in the EC was something of value to banana traders. In addition to the EC firms, large foreign traders of bananas included the Ecuadorian firm Noboa and United States–based distributors of bananas grown in Latin America, such as Chiquita and Dole.[7] Such firms would be willing to pay a fee (what economists call *quota rents*) for access to the EC market, since there was a price premium on EC sales relative to non-EC sales.

The European Community's scheme for allocating licenses, and thus the right to collect fees from Latin American banana traders, was also quite discriminatory. First, it was not a rationing rule based on historical market share, as is typically the case under the WTO rules. Instead, the EC granted to ACP farmers some of the licenses that banana traders in Latin America would need to fill their share of the EC quota. The EC argued that allocating licenses for the non-ACP quota to ACP farmers was essentially a development assistance policy. The ACP farmers could sell the licenses and use the funds to compensate for their cost disadvantage relative to bananas grown in Latin America. But the EC also granted licenses for access to the non-ACP quota to EC firms, which they would sell to the Latin American banana sources. One likely motive for such a scheme was domestic politics: it was an attempt to create a financial transfer that would mollify those within the EC (Germany, and to a lesser extent the Netherlands, Denmark, and others) that stood to be harmed under the new, more restrictive banana import policy. Borrell estimated that the new policy cost EC consumers $2.3 billion per year and also concluded that the policy was not particularly cost-effective from a development aid perspective, as most of the transfer of quota rents under the licensing went to EC banana distributing firms and not to ACP farmers.[8]

Question 1. What are most formal disputes in the WTO about?

At the first and most fundamental level, the formal dispute that ultimately took place in this instance is typical of the vast majority taking place under the WTO and the GATT. A dispute results after one member (here the European Community) reduces the foreign market access that other members (Latin American banana-exporting countries) had expected under the terms of the bargain signed in an earlier negotiating round. Most formal WTO disputes can be boiled down to a situation in which a government initiates a case so as to enforce the foreign market access that its exporters expected to receive.

At a second level, in this instance, the form of the EC's reduced foreign market access to the Latin American exporters is typical of only a subset of formal disputes. The EC's banana regime introduced two different forms of discrimina-

7. On the U.S. side, Dole had reportedly diversified its sourcing beyond the Latin American region to be able to purchase bananas from a number of ACP countries and thus was less adversely affected by the EC policy than was Chiquita.

8. Borrell (1994, p. 16).

tion against Latin American exporters that were inconsistent with the GATT and WTO principles described in chapter 1. The first type of discrimination involved the EC's favoring its "own" industry (for example, EC banana-distributing firms) at the expense of the foreigners—a GATT/WTO violation of the principle of national treatment. The second type of discrimination involved the EC's favoring imports from one foreign source (ACP exporters) at the expense of another (Latin American exporters)—a GATT/WTO violation of most-favored-nation (MFN) treatment. When I discuss the full caseload of trade dispute activity, it will turn out that many cases involve violations of national treatment only, many cases involve violations of MFN only, and still others are like this one in that they involve violations of both.

*Question 2. Why is it important to find common economic incentives
that cross WTO litigant borders?*

Thus far the discussion has focused on a dispute based on a classic case of domestic as well as international political and economic intrigue. At first blush, this WTO dispute would appear to pit Latin American banana-exporting interests against the European Community. And yet, from the perspective of economic incentives, there are cross-border alignments of interests that are also important to recognize. Latin American exporters have allies within the EC who wanted to see the Regulation 404 policy reformed and brought more in line with WTO rules and obligations. The foremost example would be German consumers, unhappy with their reduced access to foreign bananas and the higher prices they would have to face. The EC's internal economic interests benefiting from the Regulation 404 system of import protection also had foreign allies—the banana-exporting countries of the ACP region that enjoyed preferential access to the EC market.

Cross-border alliances can be important in effectively exploiting the WTO's dispute settlement procedure to ensure that countries live up to their foreign market access commitments. As I further discuss below, cross-border alliances can also be triggered by use of the fundamental WTO principle of reciprocity, and they are particularly important when relying on the WTO process to construct retaliation threats as a means to induce respondent policy reform and compliance with WTO legal rulings.

*Question 3. Do WTO disputes typically enforce new commitments or
old commitments?*

A third interesting element to what would ultimately (in 1996) result in a WTO dispute is that it was *not* an issue of new market access commitments that the European Community promised to implement in the Uruguay Round negotiations.[9] Instead, this particular dispute arose because of a domestic political battle within the EC, in which the domestic political cost-benefit calculus was not sufficiently weighted toward liberal trading interests, and the result was a reduction in foreign market access for Latin American banana exporters.

In the data that I examine in more detail in chapter 4, there is a mix to the WTO dispute settlement caseload. Some disputes clearly arise because offending countries need help following through with new and substantial foreign market access commitments they have only just agreed to take on. In other instances, disputes arise because of market access reductions associated with old commitments—for example, a change in domestic political or economic circumstances that leads to a new demand to restrict imports and reduce foreign market access.

The GATT (pre-WTO) Banana Disputes

Before getting to the details of the eventual WTO dispute that began in 1996, it is first important to note that a number of Latin American banana-exporting countries (Colombia, Costa Rica, Guatemala, Nicaragua, and Venezuela) began legal challenges to the EC policy in June 1992 under the dispute settlement provisions of the WTO's predecessor, the GATT.[10] The legal rulings were essentially that the EC's Regulation 404 banana policy was inconsistent with its (then) GATT obligations, because it violated MFN and discriminated against bananas from Latin American sources.

Nevertheless, because of the lax dispute settlement system that was in place in the GATT era—the EC could and did veto the GATT Panel reports and thus prevented them from being adopted. It also failed to comply with the GATT legal rulings and instead chose the alternative of negotiating preferential settlements with some of the complaining countries. In particular, the European Community negotiated the Framework Agreement on Bananas, which allocated much of the share of the non-ACP countries' EC market access to Costa Rica, Colombia, Nicaragua, and Venezuela.

9. As discussed below, there were EC commitments over trade in services (under the General Agreement on Trade in Services) that did not exist before the WTO was created, which did play a fundamental role in the WTO dispute, in that arguably they allowed the U.S. government to be a primary litigant in the proceedings. Nevertheless, the discriminatory banana policies that the EC implemented in 1993 were the result of changes in domestic (intra–European Community) political and economic forces and were not the struggles of a WTO member seeking to live up to liberalization commitments made in a recent multilateral negotiating round.

10. The countries filed two separate GATT disputes that went through the dispute resolution process from 1992 to 1994: the *EEC–Bananas I* and *EEC–Bananas II* disputes. See GATT (1993, 1994).

Question 4. Why is it important for countries to join the GATT/WTO?

Left out of the negotiated Framework Agreement was Guatemala as well as a number of other major banana-exporting countries in Latin America such as Ecuador, Honduras, Panama, and Mexico.[11] The combined access of these five countries to the EC market was sharply curtailed in 1993 as an initial result of the tariff rate quota in Regulation 404, which provided a smaller overall level of market access to non-ACP exporters than they had historically received. Their market access problem was compounded by the EC's negotiated settlement with the Framework Agreement countries in which the EC subsequently granted a disproportionate share of the Regulation 404 quota for non-ACP exporters to Costa Rica, Colombia, Nicaragua, and Venezuela in exchange for the termination of their dispute activity.

Even setting aside the problem of the relatively toothless GATT dispute resolution process, a number of these countries could not do much simply because they were not even part of the GATT. Honduras did not become a GATT contracting party until April 1994, while Ecuador and Panama never signed it and did not become members of the WTO until 1996 and 1997, respectively.

In theory, the WTO (and the GATT) principle of nondiscrimination through most-favored-nation treatment is supposed to protect members against the sort of discriminatory outcome embodied in the Framework Agreement settlement. Nevertheless, the self-enforcing nature of the GATT and the WTO, as well as the reality that a number of the most adversely affected banana-exporting countries (such as Ecuador and Panama) were not parties to the GATT and thus were not entitled to MFN treatment, certainly contributed to the problem.

Question 5. What is the role of third parties in minimizing the risk of discriminatory settlements?

Why is membership in the GATT/WTO not enough? It is worth considering what would have transpired at this point in the banana case had it not been taking place during the GATT era but instead during the WTO era, in which all of these countries were WTO members. These circumstances and the set of incentives generated in this particular dispute, as well as the EC's actions, identify an important *transparency* role for third parties in dispute settlement. The fundamental concern is that, while the settlement between the EC and the Framework Agreement countries may have been a satisfactory political resolution when viewed from these countries' perspectives, it was an unsatisfactory

---

11. Guatemala had become a GATT contracting party in 1991 and Mexico in 1986. See the WTO website "GATT Members: The 128 countries That Had Signed GATT by 1994" (www.wto.org/english/theWTO_e/gattmem_e.htm).

solution either from an economic perspective or from a wider political perspective when including other countries that were affected such as Ecuador, Panama, Guatemala, Honduras, and Mexico.

A transparent process to the settlement of disputes that allows for the inclusion of third party interests could help prevent discriminatory outcomes negotiated between complainants and respondents that do not lead to a removal of policies that are illegal under the WTO (or in this case, the GATT), but instead simply restructure those policies to extend preferential treatment toward complaining countries and thus increase the adverse impact (through additional discrimination) toward noncomplaining countries that also export to the market in question.

Question 6. What are the pros and cons of making "mutually agreed solution" settlements more transparent to the public?

The process of this particular dispute raises at least one other transparency issue: the potential benefits to the WTO membership of widely publicizing the terms of any settlement, or a "mutually agreed solution," between the complainant and respondent countries. Although the legal dispute discussed thus far occurred under the GATT regime when the rules were different, many of the incentives identified in this case are common to disputes in the WTO's self-enforcing system.

It is each country's own responsibility to keep track of what is going on to continually enforce its firms' foreign market access rights. Therefore, policymakers require knowledge of the settlement terms taking place between other disputing countries. Even if a dispute is resolved in a manner that is completely consistent with the WTO rules and agreements, any dispute that leads to a policy change affecting the conditions of competition between the complainant's firms and the respondent's firms will also change the conditions of competition between at least one of those sets of firms vis-à-vis firms in third countries. Thus firms in third countries will have to adjust to the new conditions.

In many WTO disputes, the case can either fall dormant or be terminated with an announcement that the disputing countries have come to terms on a mutually agreed solution but without specifying the details of the solution. Disputing parties may prefer to keep the terms of the solution private. However, because most disputes have the potential to have an impact, either directly or indirectly, on exporting firms in third countries, an important role for the WTO is to ensure greater information dissemination concerning exactly how these disputes have been resolved.

However, transparency may have costs of its own. Requiring that the terms of settlements become transparent is likely to have other effects on the process.

For example, it is likely either to discourage the early settlement of disputes or perhaps even to discourage the use of the WTO Dispute Settlement Understanding to process enforcement claims.

The EC–Bananas III *Dispute*

After the WTO's entry into force in 1995 and shortly after Ecuador's accession in January 1996, in February five WTO members filed a request for consultations with the European Community, challenging its now modified banana regime (due to Regulation 404 and the Framework Agreement). In addition to Ecuador, the other Latin American banana producers behind the dispute were Mexico, Guatemala, and Honduras.[12] The main distinction between the WTO and the GATT disputes from the complainant perspective was the presence of the United States. Because rules over trade in services had come into the international trading system as part of the "grand bargain" via the General Agreement on Trade in Services (GATS), the United States convinced the Panel that it had a right to be a co-complainant. Specifically, U.S. firms such as Chiquita that provided distribution services by selling foreign-grown bananas to EC consumers had been adversely affected by the combination of Regulation 404 and the Framework Agreement.

The main thrust of the legal rulings in the WTO dispute was the same as the original legal rulings in the GATT disputes. The EC's banana regime was inconsistent with its obligations under the trade agreement because it discriminated against bananas exported from Latin America and against the distributors in the United States and other countries that sold bananas to EC consumers.

While the legal rulings were quite similar, the WTO dispute was fundamentally different because of the way the dispute settlement system had changed. First, because of rule changes implemented with the inception of the WTO in 1995 and the new Dispute Settlement Understanding, the European Community could no longer unilaterally block or veto the legal decisions and thus prevent them from being adopted by the WTO membership. Second, because the process could not be blocked, if and when the EC refused to bring its banana regime into compliance with the WTO ruling, the United States and other complainant countries could seek and be granted WTO authorization to retaliate as compensation.

First consider the U.S. case. The United States asked the WTO for authorization to retaliate over more than $500 million per year worth of trade to the

12. A first dispute had been initiated in September 1995 (Dispute Settlement 16, or DS16) by Guatemala, Honduras, Mexico, and the United States. However, this dispute was dropped once the February 1996 (DS27) dispute that added Ecuador as a co-complainant was initiated. Panama would join the dispute shortly upon completion of its WTO accession in 1997 (DS105).

EC that it claimed its firms had lost because of the EC's banana regime, and WTO arbiters granted the United States the right to retaliate for $191.4 million. In April 1999 the United States announced plans to carry out its $191.4 million worth of retaliation by imposing new 100 percent tariffs on coffee makers (except the Italian ones), bed linens, French-produced (Louis Vuitton) handbags, bath preparations, and a number of other products.[13] The U.S. Trade Representative presumably expected that the new 100 percent tariffs would double the prices of the targeted products and thus cause U.S. consumers to stop purchasing them—a result that would have reduced imports from the European Community by the authorized $191.4 million.

Next, consider the Ecuadorian case. Ecuador was granted the right to retaliate for $201.6 million of lost exports per year to the EC, though it did not seek to retaliate against the EC by imposing retaliatory import tariffs. As I discuss in substantial detail in chapter 5, Ecuador instead sought WTO authorization to threaten failure to protect the intellectual property of EC firms—that is, through the authorized threat not to enforce its TRIPS commitments.

Question 7. Why might respondent governments need DSU rulings and authorized retaliation threats to comply?

The idea is that the WTO dispute settlement process can help the European Community when it needs external assistance from trading partners to mobilize the domestic political forces necessary to reform the banana regime policy. Without the WTO dispute, the EC's domestic special interest constituencies were in a constellation that resulted in an inefficient policy (even from the EC's own perspective) that it could not reform on its own. If the U.S. retaliation threats could target politically powerful export interests within the EC, this could introduce new players into the EC's domestic political battle over the banana regime. While the aggrieved consumers in Germany and the Netherlands, for example, alone were not politically powerful enough to ensure a WTO-consistent banana policy, perhaps aggrieved consumers plus Louis Vuitton might be.

Rational, forward-thinking policymakers surely recognize the limits of the WTO system, which ultimately self-enforces commitments through credible, underlying threats of retaliation. If a country recognizes that it is not a sufficiently large importer of French handbags to mobilize Louis Vuitton to rebalance the domestic EC political calculus and thus get the banana policy reformed, it may hesitate to initiate the dispute settlement proceedings in the first place. It may also be more likely to drop initiated cases or to settle them on

---

13. See U.S. Trade Representative, "USTR Announces Final Product List in Bananas Dispute," Press Release 99-35 (Washington, April 9, 1999).

less advantageous terms. The potential importance of the capacity to retaliate is discussed extensively in later chapters.

The End of the WTO Dispute

In this particular case, and despite the United States being granted the right to retaliate at the end of the WTO dispute, the European Community refused to comply with the WTO ruling for a period during which the United States implemented actual retaliation against EC exports. For a period of time, this dispute was considered an abject failure—the United States was engaged in retaliation by imposing higher tariffs that choked off imports desired by its own consumers and thus reduced domestic economic well-being. And the retaliation was having no effect on the EC, which continued to maintain its banana regime, adversely affecting the exports of U.S. banana-distributing firms and Latin American banana growers.

The United States retaliated until 2001, when the United States and the EC announced a "Bananas Understanding" settlement to the *EC–Bananas III* dispute, which entailed a plan for the EC to bring its banana regime into WTO compliance. The EC agreed to modify the banana regime along three important dimensions with three different deadlines: to shift a larger share of the overall import quota toward bananas produced in Latin America by January 2002, to implement a new license allocation scheme by July 2001 in which the licenses would be granted to exporters based on their market shares from an appropriate historic reference period, and to introduce a tariff-only regime for banana imports by January 2006.[14] But despite this apparent settlement, which brought an end to U.S. retaliation, the *EC–Bananas III* dispute has been revived in recent years as the United States and Latin American countries continue to challenge how the EC is bringing its banana policy into compliance with its WTO obligations.[15]

Remaining Questions from the Banana Dispute

There are other important issues raised by this dispute that I will now discuss here.

14. See Office of the U.S. Trade Representative, "U.S. Trade Representative Announces the Lifting of Sanctions on European Products as EU Opens Market to U.S. Banana Distributors," Press Release 01-50 (Washington, July 1, 2001).

15. Many aspects of the EC's new tariff-only regime for bananas implemented in 2006 were challenged under a new dispute which led to Panel reports and even Appellate Body rulings over the "compliance phase" (Article 21.5) of the dispute settlement process, in which the WTO adjudicators are asked to assess the WTO-consistency of a country's compliance with prior rulings. In November 2008, the Appellate Body ruled that many aspects of the EC's new tariff-only regime on bananas were still inconsistent with the EC's WTO obligations.

*Question 8. Does WTO-authorized retaliation play a compliance role
and a rebalancing role?*

Although U.S. retaliation over Louis Vuitton handbags and other EC exports
may have been an attempt to induce EC compliance with WTO rulings, a second role that retaliation plays in WTO dispute settlement is very much in line
with the discussion in chapter 1 of the fundamental principle of reciprocity.
Because the WTO arbitrators limited the U.S. retaliation to a reduction of
imports from the EC by $191.4 million per year—that is, the same amount that
the arbitrators estimated that the EC's banana regime policy reduced in imports
per year from the U.S. distributors—the retaliation amounted to a *rebalancing*
of the market access bargain between the two WTO members.

While resolution of WTO disputes through retaliation, even temporarily, in
such a manner is infrequent, it does raise a difficult question for WTO
observers: how to treat this type of outcome? Was it a success or a failure? On
the one hand, the EC did not immediately comply with WTO rulings, and for
a period of time, it continued this WTO violation. Combined with the almost
two-year period in which the United States retaliated against EC exports suggests that, from a short-run perspective, this dispute highlights the failings of
the WTO system. On the other hand, from a broader perspective, the U.S.
retaliation served to settle the dispute for a period. One argument is that such
an outcome may have preserved overall U.S.-EC commercial relations by preventing the bilateral friction over bananas from spilling over to something much
larger that would have adversely affected substantially other areas of the agreement. Although the U.S. retaliation of $191.4 million per year is not trivial, this
interim outcome of retaliatory collateral damage to reciprocally rebalance the
initial bargain can be interpreted as one that produced less damage than other
likely alternatives may have.

*Question 9. How economically successful are these WTO disputes
at restoring market access?*

What has been the impact of all of this WTO dispute settlement activity on
the EC banana import market? From the perspective of the complaining countries, has this dispute resulted in an economically successful outcome of
increased EC market access that is observable in the trade data?

Figure 3-2 illustrates EC banana imports from a number of foreign exporting
countries over the 1995 to 2006 period. During the period of the WTO dispute, from 1996 through the retaliation period of 1999–2000, EC imports
from each of the foreign sources is relatively stagnant. Beginning with the 2001
U.S.-EC "Bananas Understanding" settlement, there is a noticeable increase in
the value of EC imports from a number of foreign sources. Ecuador, one of the
co-complainants in the WTO dispute, saw the value of its exports more than

Figure 3-2. *EC Banana Imports by Foreign Country Source, 1995–2006* [a]

Millions of dollars

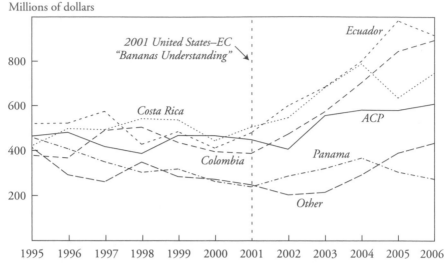

Source: Data collected by the author from Comtrade via World Integrated Trade Solution (WITS), software developed by the World Bank, in close collaboration with the United Nations Conference on Trade and Development (UNCTAD).

ACP = African, Caribbean, and Pacific and includes the major banana suppliers to the EC during this time period: Belize, Cameroon, Côte d'Ivoire, Dominica, Jamaica, and Saint Lucia.

a. The EC is defined as EC-15 consistently throughout the figure, and the data are extra-EC imports only.

double from $411 million in 2000 to $917 million in 2006. Major Latin American exporters such as Colombia ($396 million to $896 million) and Costa Rica ($444 million to $748 million) that were formal third parties in the dispute experienced similar growth for their exports between 2000 and 2006.

Furthermore, despite concerns that the restoration of less discriminatory treatment in the EC market and an increase in exports from Latin American countries would lead to *preference erosion* for ACP countries, as a group the ACP countries also had export expansion to the EC market during the 2000 to 2006 period, growing in value from $467 million to $609 million, albeit at a slower pace than that for other exporters. The largest foreign source that has faced relatively flat exports to the EC during this time period was Panama, which had exports valued at $264 million in 2000 and only $274 million in 2006.

Question 10. Why is the third party role important even when the WTO process delivers compliance?

Above I have highlighted the importance of the formal role of third parties (as well as transparency and public details on mutually agreed solutions) in potentially minimizing the likelihood that settlements between litigating parties result in discrimination against exporting firms from third countries. Nevertheless, this particular dispute and the importance of its impact on other developing countries raises the issue of the importance of third parties even when disputes end in respondent policy reform, when MFN treatment and national treatment are restored, and when the implementation is fully consistent with WTO guidelines.

In this particular dispute, the changing conditions of competition in the EC market that Latin American banana exporters faced will create the need for some ACP exporters to adjust to lost EC market access as their preference is eroded and the EC's discriminatory treatment (vis-à-vis the Latin American growers) is eliminated. Although it is not yet evident for the ACP exporters from the available EC import data through 2006 (as documented in figure 3-2), at some point ACP countries will face adjustment costs, requiring them, as well as others, to develop appropriate policies to deal with reduced exports to the EC. That this dispute has played out on a relatively transparent stage within the WTO is significant, since many of the ACP countries are participating in the WTO dispute settlement process as third parties and thus are being kept informed. It will be important to examine in the larger caseload of WTO disputes whether such a trend of third party participation is apparent overall—especially in other, lower-profile disputes.

Question 11. How pervasive (and difficult to measure) are "extra-WTO" counterretaliation threats?

As a partial response to the GATT trade dispute that resulted in the European Community signing a discriminatory settlement under the Framework Agreement on Bananas, the United States began to exert "extra-WTO" counter-retaliatory pressure against the signatory countries. First, the United States used its Section 301 trade law to investigate Costa Rica and Colombia in 1995, which could have resulted in retaliatory measures. Second, U.S. Senator (and later Republican presidential candidate) Bob Dole also backed legislation to counterretaliate against Colombia by withdrawing the United States's unilateral trade preferences granted under the 1991 Andean Trade Preference Act (ATPA) as partial compensation for its participation in the War on Drugs if Colombia did not withdraw from the Framework Agreement.[16]

In much the same way that the discussion above documented the importance of a country's capacity to retaliate through WTO-sanctioned rebalancing of the bargain, much the same can be said for extra-WTO counterretaliation threats.

16. See Daniel Mazuera, "A Trade Dispute Gone Bananas," *Wall Street Journal,* November 17, 1995, p. A19.

But whereas the capacity to make WTO-authorized retaliatory threats is something potentially measurable, it is much more difficult to capture a country's ability to make credible extra-WTO counterretaliation threats. For example, when it comes to trade preferences, it is much more difficult to measure how much of a country's exports to a trading partner arrive only because of the preference and thus are potentially subject to extra-WTO counterretaliation. Because of complex rules of origin, many "preferenced products" that a country imports may not receive the preferential tariff rate. Traders may find it too costly to meet the bureaucratic rules of origin requirements and consequently decide to simply pay the MFN tariff rate. Simply examining the value of trade under a Generalized System of Preferences (GSP) Harmonized System code category is therefore likely to overstate the true ability of the country to engage in such extra-WTO counterretaliation.

Alternatively, extra-WTO counterretaliation may take the form of threats to withdraw bilateral assistance (development or military aid). The main insight from this discussion is that, while extra-WTO threats may be very real from the perspective of developing countries in any given case, it may nevertheless be difficult to measure and thus to account for them empirically in more formal studies such as the ones to be discussed in the next chapter.

Conclusions

The *EC–Bananas III* dispute and related economic, legal, and political events surrounding the case identify a number of important issues for self-enforcement under the WTO system, especially issues that confront developing countries. The case identifies many reasons why developing countries need access to and can benefit from a transparent and accessible dispute settlement system.

Furthermore, many additional questions arise once one looks beyond this particular case. What concerns about foreign market access do developing countries tend to self-enforce through the WTO? What trading partners, sectors, and causes of lost foreign market access do developing countries target? Are many of the implicit and explicit concerns raised by *EC–Bananas III* systematically important, such as the resource costs to self-enforce foreign market access under the DSU, as the United States did in this instance, along with potential retaliation capacity and extra-WTO counterretaliation capacity? Do these concerns affect how developing countries engage the dispute settlement process and thus ultimately affect the extent to which they are able to benefit from the self-enforcing WTO system?

In the next chapter I begin the analysis on developing countries by applying some of these questions to the data. I examine the full WTO caseload of dispute settlement activity and then seek insight from more formal economic, legal, and political scholarship on self-enforcement under the WTO system.

4

Developing Countries and
WTO Trade Disputes

N ow that the events surrounding the *EC–Bananas III* dispute have portrayed how the World Trade Organization dispute settlement process can work, I turn to the full WTO caseload of data. The description of this one particular dispute in chapter 3 and the earlier discussion of the WTO agreements and historical negotiations in chapters 1 and 2 raise a number of theoretical questions that I explore in the data. After examining the raw data, I discuss the results of empirical scholarship examining how WTO members, and particularly developing countries, use self-enforcement to ensure access to foreign markets in practice.

In the next section I analyze the data on the 388 WTO disputes that were initiated between 1995 and 2008. The GATT/WTO negotiating history and the resulting agreements provide an excellent perspective from which to begin interpreting the role and importance of dispute settlement activity. First, the agreements describe what commitments WTO members have taken on and thus what is enforceable through dispute settlement—that is, what the members can be held accountable for and the possible repercussions if they refuse to comply with rulings made in the dispute settlement process. Second, the history of the negotiations—especially of the recent Uruguay Round, which introduced the North-South "grand bargain" of the Trade-Related Aspects of Intellectual Property Rights (TRIPS) Agreement and the General Agreement on Trade in Services (GATS) in exchange for market access for agriculture, textiles, and apparel—identifies areas in which frequent enforcement might be needed. Although formal trade disputes can arise over violations of commitments that countries initially made in a GATT negotiating round that took place decades ago, the recent deals are most likely to create circumstances in which it is difficult for policymakers to live up to their commitments. That obviates the need for formal WTO enforcement actions.

An examination of the WTO dispute settlement caseload from 1995 to 2008 answers many questions; however, other important issues cannot be addressed by searching for simple trends in the data. Thus, in the second section, I look deeper at the data by examining scholarly research that tests theories of WTO enforcement using more sophisticated empirical techniques. Insights from this literature are the subject of the remaining chapters of the book.

The Data on WTO Disputes

During the period from 1995 to 2008, WTO members initiated 388 formal disputes via requests for consultations.[1] To put this number into some historical perspective, WTO member countries initiated almost 50 percent more disputes during the WTO's first fourteen years than contracting parties initiated during the entire forty-eight-year era of the GATT from 1947 to 1994.[2] Reasons for this increase include more members in the WTO relative to the GATT and therefore more countries eligible to use the forum for disputing; more underlying trade and commercial interests raising disputes; more legal commitments to litigate over; and a different dispute settlement system. The result is a much more prominent role for the dispute settlement process under the WTO relative to its role under the GATT.[3]

1. The data in this section draw on two sources. First are the fundamental data on WTO dispute initiations through the end of 2008, available at the WTO website "Dispute Settlement: The Disputes—Chronological List of Disputes Cases" (www.wto.org/english/tratop_e/dispu_e/dispu_status_e.htm). The second source is the comprehensive and electronically organized data on WTO disputes through 2006 compiled and made freely available in a data collection project, funded by the World Bank and organized by Horn and Mavroidis (2008b).

2. Bown (2002a, table 1) reports 254 disputes taking place under the GATT from 1947 to 1994. Unlike the WTO system that is a result of the "single undertaking," formal trade disputes were not centralized under the prior GATT regime. Most were initiated and reported under Article XXIII of the GATT, but some came forward under various plurilateral codes that subsets of GATT contracting parties signed onto, including the Tokyo Round's subsidies or antidumping codes. The data in Bown (2002a) are compiled from WTO (1995, 1997) and Hudec (1993), the latter of which includes disputes brought forward without following the proper Article XXIII channels (for example, at ministerial meetings), though they were substantively equivalent to GATT Article XXIII disputes. See also Bown (2004a); Busch (2000); Reinhardt (2001).

3. Focusing initially on dispute initiation data is also revealing because the vast majority of WTO disputes that reach legal rulings usually result in Panel and Appellate Body reports that find some aspect of the respondent's challenged policies to be WTO-inconsistent. Using a data set of

Although the large number of WTO disputes relative to those during the GATT era suggests a more prominent role for dispute settlement within the institution, even more can be learned by breaking these data down in various ways to identify pervasive trends. The first step is to establish a consistent accounting unit for characterizing a dispute. While there are a number of possible ways to do this, depending on what one hopes to learn from the exercise, in this section I follow one strand of the literature and simply break out disputes into bilateral country pairs. For example, the *EC–Bananas III* dispute initiated by Ecuador, Guatemala, Honduras, Mexico, and the United States has been recorded in the WTO dispute initiation data as a single dispute; however, I categorize it as five bilateral disputes.[4] Because there are a number of multiple complainant disputes like this one, the basic list of 388 requests for consultations from 1995 to 2008 can be restated as 415 bilateral disputes between pairs of WTO member countries.

Figure 4-1 breaks down the WTO dispute-settlement caseload for each year over the period 1995 to 2008. As is evident from the figure, the broad time trend over the first fourteen years of the WTO is really a story of two different periods. The immediate 1995–2000 era after the conclusion of the Uruguay Round led to heavy use, with an average of forty-one disputes initiated per year, whereas the 2001–08 period has seen a decline to almost half that number, with an average of only twenty-one newly initiated cases per year. Indeed, the five-year period from 2004 to 2008 saw the fewest newly initiated disputes per year in the WTO era.

At this most aggregated level, the relative decline in the initiation of WTO disputes is likely explained by a number of contributing factors. First, the heavy usage of the WTO dispute settlement process shortly after the conclusion of the Uruguay Round is partially explained by WTO members seeking to use the "courts" to help resolve or clarify issues they were not able to resolve through the negotiating round itself. Second, given the unfamiliarity of the new dispute settlement system, in many instances countries may have thought it worthwhile to test it—even without the intention of fully utilizing the process—simply to

---

144 WTO disputes that reached a Panel ruling between 1995 and 2006, Hoekman, Horn, and Mavroidis (2009, table 9) report that 68 percent (1,398 of 2,064) of all claims on which WTO Panels issue rulings (after subtracting from submitted claims those claims that Panels did not rule on, usually for reasons of judicial economy) are won by the complainant country.

4. The *EC–Bananas III* dispute was catalogued as WTO dispute number DS27. A reason to do this relabeling is that in other instances different complainant countries do not necessarily coordinate in advance of a dispute initiation against the same respondent country over the same potentially WTO-inconsistent policy. One prominent example would be the WTO dispute revolving around the U.S. steel safeguard import restriction in 2002, in which the DSU initiation data show nine separate *US–Steel Safeguards* requests for consultations.

Figure 4-1. *WTO Dispute Initiations, 1995–2000 and 2001–08*[a]

Number of dispute initiations per year

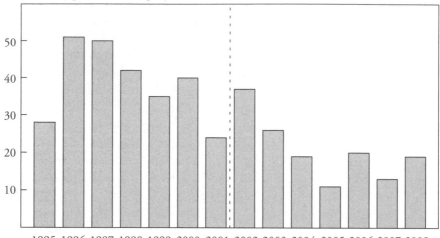

Source: Author's compilations from WTO (2009).

a. Disputes are broken down into bilateral (complainant–respondent) pairs. Because some disputes involved more than one complainant, the 388 requests for consultations initiated over the 1995–2008 period yielded 415 bilaterally paired disputes.

see what they could get out of merely triggering it. Third, the trend in initiated cases also likely reflects macroeconomic trends. Most of the period from 2001 to 2008 was associated in particular with economic growth across much of the WTO membership and a sharp acceleration in global exports—as seen in figure 4-2, especially between 2001 and 2006. When macroeconomic conditions are good, there are typically fewer calls for new import restrictions, and it is easier politically for government policymakers to fight off those that do come in. When countries are growing and exports are flowing, there is less to fight over and dispute at the WTO. This suggests that the reduction in dispute activity from 2001 to 2008 may be partially attributed to the good economic times and therefore may be reversed as times get tougher and WTO members increasingly impose new protectionist measures.

Nevertheless, macrolevel explanations are speculative and not all that useful. Examination of only aggregated data on initiated disputes and time trends hides a number of telling features of the underlying dispute settlement activity. The first subsection below explores many of these features of the data in more detail.

In the next three subsections, I focus solely on data on WTO dispute initiation: how these data differ across member countries, across sectors of commercial

Figure 4-2. *World Exports, 1995–2000 and 2001–06*

Trillions of dollars

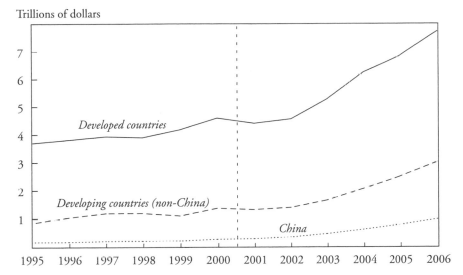

Source: Author's compilations from World Integrated Trade Solution (WITS), software developed by the World Bank, in close collaboration with the United Nations Conference on Trade and Development (UNCTAD).

activity, across types of trade barriers imposed, and over time. There is much to learn by carefully examining these data on WTO members' *initiation* of disputes—that is, the point at which they formally express displeasure when other countries do not live up to WTO commitments and obligations. After thoroughly examining the data on dispute initiation, I then turn to other aspects of the dispute resolution process. In the fourth section, I examine data on the WTO members that join dispute settlement proceedings as third parties. In the fifth section, I push deeper into the data on the actual dispute resolution process, beyond the mere initiation and participating actions of disputes, to look for patterns in the data on how the dispute resolution *process* is handled. This section in particular quickly reveals the difficulty of drawing strong insights from simple trends in the data and hence the need for the more sophisticated analysis that I review below.

What WTO Member Countries Are Involved in Disputes?

Table 4-1 documents the frequency with which various WTO members have been involved in WTO disputes as complainants and respondents during this

Table 4-1. *WTO Dispute Participation, by Complainant, Respondent, and Third Party, 1995–2008*[a]

Country	Number of times complainant	Number of times respondent	Number of times third party[b]
European Community	78	89	82
United States	91	116	73
Other industrialized countries			
Australia	7	10	47
Canada	31	15	64
Japan	13	15	90
Korea	13	13	43
New Zealand	7	0	27
Norway	3	0	27
Singapore	1	0	4
Switzerland	4	0	8
Taiwan	3	0	39
Developing countries			
Antigua and Barbuda	1	0	0
Argentina	14	16	20
Bangladesh	1	0	1
Brazil	24	14	49
Chile	10	12	22
China	3	13	62
Colombia	5	3	16
Costa Rica	4	0	9
Croatia	0	1	0
Czech Republic	1	2	0
Dominican Republic	0	3	3
Ecuador	3	3	9
Egypt	0	4	4
Guatemala	6	2	11
Honduras	6	0	12
Hong Kong	1	0	0
Hungary	5	7	2
India	18	20	51
Indonesia	4	4	4
Malaysia	1	1	2
Mexico	20	14	45
Nicaragua	1	2	6
Pakistan	3	2	9
Panama	5	1	2
Peru	2	4	8
Philippines	5	4	5
Poland	3	1	1
Romania	0	2	0
Slovakia	0	3	0

Country	Number of times complainant	Number of times respondent	Number of times third party[b]
South Africa	0	3	0
Sri Lanka	1	0	3
Thailand	13	3	37
Trinidad and Tobago	0	2	3
Turkey	2	8	18
Uruguay	1	1	5
Venezuela	1	2	15
Total	415	415	938

Source: Author's compilations from WTO (2009).

DSU = Dispute Settlement Understanding.

a. Disputes are broken down into bilateral (complainant–respondent) pairs. Because some disputes involved more than one complainant, the 388 requests for consultations initiated over the 1995–2008 period yielded 415 bilaterally paired disputes.

b. Does not include all WTO members who have only participated in DSU activities as third parties; see table 4-4 for the completion of this list. Third party data are only available up to dispute DS367, which was initiated August 31, 2007.

period.[5] The most frequent litigants are, not surprisingly, the United States and the European Community, and the two are both much more active in WTO dispute settlement than any other member. For example, the United States has initiated three times as many disputes as the third most active complainant (Canada), and it has faced nearly six times as many disputes as the third most active respondent (India). Nevertheless, a relatively long list of WTO members that initiated ten or more disputes during this era includes a group of other industrialized countries (Japan, Canada, and Korea), as well as a number of developing countries (Argentina, Brazil, Chile, India, Mexico, and Thailand).

Next I examine the time trend of data again—but now broken down by disputes initiated by different categories of complainant countries—as illustrated in figure 4-3. Immediately after establishment of the WTO, the United States and the European Community were by far the most frequent WTO litigants. Together they initiated an average of twenty new disputes per year from 1995 through 2000—as many as all other WTO members combined averaged during this era.[6] Most of the time variation of figure 4-1 is clearly revealed to reflect a

5. Throughout this chapter I sometimes wish to break apart the data associated with the U.S. and EC use of WTO dispute settlement from that of "other industrialized countries." When it is not necessary to do so, I refer to their combination as "developed countries."

6. These data do not account for the fact that the membership in the European Union (EU) expanded during this time period. For example, Poland, the Czech Republic, Slovakia, and Hungary were not members before 2004 and thus were involved in DSU activity in their own national

Figure 4-3. *Average WTO Disputes per Year, by Category of Complainant, 1995–2000 and 2001–08* [a]

Average number of WTO disputes initiated per year during period

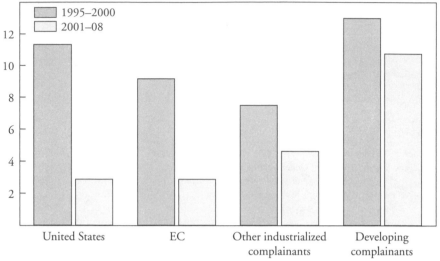

Source: Author's compilations from WTO (2009).
a. Disputes are broken down into bilateral (complainant–respondent) pairs. Because some disputes involved more than one complainant, the 388 requests for consultations initiated over the 1995–2008 period yielded 415 bilaterally paired disputes.

change in U.S. and EC complainant behavior after 2000—when the United States and the EC combined to average fewer than six newly initiated disputes per year from 2001 to 2008—less than one-third their yearly average during the 1995–2000 period.

There is a much less dramatic change between the two periods for other WTO members' dispute initiations. While the average rate of new dispute initiation has fallen across all countries, the average number of new disputes initiated by other industrialized countries as a group dropped only from 7.5 to 4.6, while developing country initiations fell only slightly, from 13.0 to 10.8 new disputes per year. For developing countries in particular, their use during the WTO era is much more stable over time—collectively they have been relatively steady users of WTO dispute settlement over the entire period.

---

capacities. Since their accession to the European Union, all of these countries' WTO dispute activity has been through the EC. Whereas the enlargement of the European Union itself created a larger internal market with both more exporters and importers and more potential WTO dispute settlement activity for the EC vis-à-vis nonmembers of the EU, the expansion also led to less potential WTO dispute settlement for these countries within the EC, since now their trade squabbles would be handled internally (within the EC) and not through the WTO.

Table 4-2. *WTO Disputes, by Complainant and Respondent Categories of Countries*[a]

| | Respondent | | | | | | | |
| | 1995–2000 | | | | 2001–08 | | | |
Complainant	*U.S. or EC*	*Other ind.*	*Developing*	*Total*	*U.S. or EC*	*Other ind.*	*Developing*	*Total*
U.S. or EC	48	30	45	123	15	7	24	46
Other ind.	24	7	14	45	31	3	3	37
Developing	45	2	31	78	42	4	40	86
Total	117	39	90	246	88	14	67	169

Source: Author's compilations from WTO (2009).

"Developing" = developing countries; "other ind." = other industrialized countries.

a. Disputes are broken down into bilateral (complainant–respondent) pairs. Because some disputes involved more than one complainant, the 388 requests for consultations initiated over the 1995–2008 period yielded 415 bilaterally paired disputes.

Even more can be learned from table 4-2, which allocates disputes into categories based on which complainant country challenged which respondent during each of these two WTO periods. Consider first the 1995–2000 period. While the United States and the European Community combined to initiate half (123 of 246) of all bilateral pairs of disputes during this era, in 39 percent of those instances, the two countries were simply challenging each other: the United States challenged the EC, or the EC challenged the United States. Put differently, a major share (19.5 percent) of the entire Dispute Settlement Understanding (DSU) caseload during the immediate post–Uruguay era consisted of the United States and the EC challenging each other. In comparison, only 9 percent (15 out of 169) of the caseload of initiated cases from 2001 to 2008 have been the United States or the EC challenging each other.

Whom are the developing country complainants *targeting* with their WTO disputes? Interestingly enough, table 4-2 reveals that in the early (1995–2000) and later (2001–08) periods, developing countries split their WTO disputes primarily between two categories of targets. Roughly 58 percent (45 of 78) of developing country disputes in the early era targeted either the United States or the EC, while in the later era it has fallen to 49 percent (42 of 86). The other major target of developing country complainants is developing country respondents—40 percent (31 of 78) of disputes from 1995 to 2000 targeted other poor countries, and the share increased to 47 percent (40 of 86) from 2001 to 2008. It has been relatively rare for developing country complainants to target other industrialized countries aside from the United States or the EC.

On the respondent side of the ledger, when developing countries are having their WTO commitments enforced by other members through formal DSU challenges, who is initiating the disputes? In the ninety instances during the 1995–2000 period in which a developing country was challenged, exactly 50 percent (45 out of 90) were initiated by either the United States or the EC, whereas another 34 percent (31 out of 90) were initiated by other developing countries. In the more recent era, these shares have flipped—out of the 67 disputes initiated against developing countries during the 2001–08 era, 60 percent (40 out of 67) were initiated by other developing country complainants, whereas less than 36 percent (24 out of 67) were initiated by the United States or the EC. And of those twenty-four cases that the United States or the EC initiated against developing country respondents in the latter period, it is noteworthy that more than one-third (9) were initiated against China alone—a country that only acceded to the WTO in 2001—and almost another one-quarter (5) were initiated against India. Thus the enforcement actions taken against developing countries (aside from India and China) increasingly are being undertaken by WTO members other than the United States and the EC, and with increasing frequency by other developing countries.

This highlights a point I make repeatedly throughout this book. When it comes to the issue of enforcement of WTO commitments, developing countries are not interested only in access to the markets of rich countries (for example, the United States and the European Community), but they are also interested in increasing and maintaining access to the markets of other developing countries as well.

What Commercial Sectors Are the Subject of Disputes?

Now that the reader has some sense of which WTO member countries are actively involved in enforcing WTO commitments, which sectors are they fighting over? In the context of the Uruguay Round grand bargain described in chapter 2—in which the developed countries were supposed to increase their available market access in textiles and apparel products and agriculture, in exchange for signing on to the TRIPS Agreement and the GATS—is there evidence that these are the predominant industries with the commitments subject to dispute?

In figure 4-4 I assign one sector to each of the WTO dispute initiations I have been describing thus far. The top half of the figure illustrates the sectors that are likely to be of greatest export interest, and hence of WTO complainant enforcement interest, to developing countries. The bottom of the figure illustrates the sectors most in line with export interests of developed countries.

The main sectors of relative importance to developing countries include industries like textiles and apparel, as well as agriculture, beverages, and seafood. Not surprisingly, the textiles and apparel sector is dominated by disputes initiated by developing countries—with nearly three times as many initiated by

Figure 4-4. *WTO Disputes, by Industrial Sector and Category of Complainant, 1995–2008* [a]

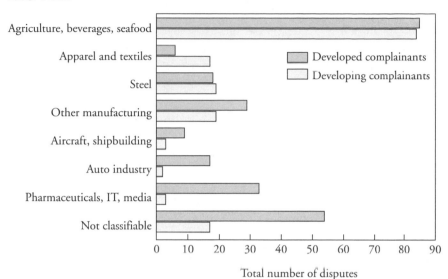

Total number of disputes

Source: Author's compilations from WTO (2009).

a. Disputes are broken down into bilateral (complainant–respondent) pairs. Because some disputes involved more than one complainant, the 388 requests for consultations initiated over the 1995–2008 period yielded 415 bilaterally paired disputes.

developing country complainants relative to those initiated by developed countries. The agriculture, beverages, and seafood industry is the most litigious industry for both developed and developing country complainants—over 50 percent of all disputes that poor countries initiated (84 out of 164) involve the enforcement of market access in agriculture, beverages, or seafood products. For developed countries, because the United States and a number of smaller economies (for example, Australia, Canada, and New Zealand) have major agricultural exporting interests, they too have been active at enforcing their WTO trading partners' foreign market access commitments, though these users account for a smaller share of the developed country overall dispute initiation caseload (85 out of 251).[7]

7. GATT/WTO trade disputes over agriculture are admittedly not a new phenomenon to the post-1995 period. Despite the agricultural sector not having nearly as many commitments over import barriers or disciplines over subsidies under the GATT regime as it has under the WTO, there is still a substantial record of GATT dispute settlement over agricultural issues. Indeed, in his analysis of formal GATT disputes covering the 1947–89 period, Hudec (1993, table 11.28, p. 327) surmised that 43 percent of GATT complaints concerned agricultural products. For an additional discussion, see Davis (2003).

The lower half of figure 4-4 focuses on industries that are relatively R&D intensive or intellectual property intensive, such as pharmaceuticals, information technology, telecommunications industries, or media. Not surprisingly, most of the disputes involving these industries have been initiated by developed countries, since the firms with foreign market access interests in these sectors are mostly headquartered there. The same basic pattern is seen in relatively capital-intensive industries that are more in the comparative advantage area of developed countries as well, sectors such as autos, aircraft, and shipbuilding. Developed economies have initiated many more disputes than developing countries in these sectors.

Finally, consider the category of "not classifiable" disputes, which are cases not readily associated with any particular industry. Most of these disputes involve one WTO member's legal challenge to another country's law or policy procedure alleged to have the potential to affect market access adversely—what lawyers refer to as *as such* claims—and not necessarily instances in which the law or policy has actually been applied to affect an industry's realized market access—referred to as *as applied* claims.[8] Examples of the former would be the challenge to the *US–1916 Act,* or the *US–Section 301 Trade Act*—instances in which Japan and the European Community challenged particular U.S. laws as being inconsistent with its WTO obligations.[9] Not surprisingly, most of such broad challenges are undertaken by developed countries. The instances in which developing countries have done so have been much more limited. One example would include broad challenges to laws with provisions that were specific to developing countries—for example, the *EC–Tariff Preferences* dispute, in which India challenged an EC scheme to allocate import tariff preferences in a potentially discriminatory manner across developing country exporters based on non-trade criteria such as the countries' willingness to combat illegal narcotics or protect labor rights or the environment. Second, there are a handful of instances in which developing countries joined as co-complainants in cases led by other developed countries—for example, *US–Offset Act (Byrd Amendment),* in which developing countries, including Brazil, Chile, India, Indonesia, Mexico, and

---

8. A handful of cases did involve "as applied" claims related to many different sectors, which it was impossible to allocate to one category alone. For this section I categorize these types of disputes into "not classifiable" (into a single industry) as well.

9. The *US-1916 Act* dispute was a challenge to the United States' Antidumping Act of 1916, an antidumping law on the U.S. books separate from the one used to regulate current U.S. antidumping procedures, that potentially allowed for a different system of (more excessive) punishment for foreign dumping and which was argued to impose a chilling effect on foreign exporters. The *US–Section 301 Trade Act* dispute was a challenge to the broad U.S. Section 301 policy described in the introduction, in which the United States conducted internal investigations of allegations of foreign market access violations that could lead to unilateral retaliation outside of the GATT/WTO dispute settlement procedures.

Thailand, joined an EC-led challenge to a U.S. law that refunded antidumping duties collected by the U.S. government to domestic U.S. firms that supported the initiation of antidumping petitions.

A final question that I investigate in this section is whether the data reveal any other obvious temporal patterns to the disputes by sector. There are a number of reasons to expect informative time variation in the data, primarily because of underlying, policy-related events specific to the market access at stake for products in each sector. Such events create differing demands for WTO enforcement of open markets over time and across sectors. Consider then figure 4-5, which illustrates WTO dispute initiations by year for four different commercial sectors of interest.

As one example, the Uruguay Round allowed for a phase-in of a number of commitments for apparel and textiles imports under the Agreement on Textiles and Clothing (ATC). This agreement phased out the previous Multifibre Arrangement (MFA) and introduced some GATT/WTO disciplines in the apparel and textiles sector for the first time. In many instances, WTO members' commitments to open up markets were relatively back end loaded and thus not expected to produce important effects on trade until 2005. From this perspective, it would not have been surprising to see a surge in WTO disputes in 2005 as trade-liberalizing countries struggled at the last minute to live up to their commitments. However, figure 4-5 shows no evidence to this effect. In fact, most disputes over textiles and apparel products took place in the 1995–2000 period, including a number of challenges to the U.S. use of the transitional safeguard for clothing and apparel available under the ATC.[10]

Agriculture is a second industry in which to expect a potential structural break in the temporal pattern of dispute settlement activity. In particular, the Uruguay Round Agreement on Agriculture contained a "peace clause" that the negotiators implemented so as to limit formal dispute settlement activity in the sector—provided certain economic conditions were met—until the clause expired at the end of 2003.[11] While one might therefore have anticipated a

10. A likely second contributor to the lack of disputes since 2005 is that important importing country markets such as those in the United States and the EC managed to live up to their import market access commitments vis-à-vis developing countries with the exception of China. The United States and the EC negotiated separate voluntary export restraints in textiles and apparel products with China that limited Chinese exports from 2005 to 2008 and thus preserved some of the market access that other developing countries were expected to lose because of the increase in Chinese export capacity. Why did U.S. and EC threats of the imposition of new import restrictions not result in a China-led trade dispute against these WTO members? One explanation is simply that the terms of China's 2001 WTO accession included a provision that permitted these members to access a China-specific safeguard import restriction, which was WTO consistent, to legally restrict imports from China in these types of products at the expiration of the ATC beginning in 2005. For a discussion, see Bown (forthcoming).

11. Steinberg and Josling (2003).

Figure 4-5. *WTO Disputes, by Industrial Sector, 1995–2008*[a]

Disputes initiated per year

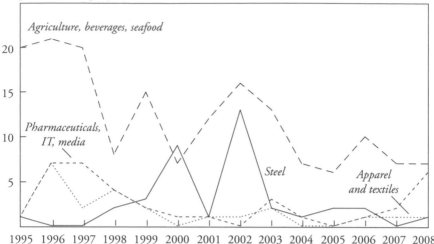

Source: Author's compilations from WTO (2009) and Horn and Mavroidis (2008b).

surge in WTO enforcement activity related to agricultural trade since the expiration of the peace clause on January 1, 2004, there is no evidence of such a surge in figure 4-5.

A surge in disputes might also have been expected in such sectors of interest to developed countries that are intensively reliant on R&D or intellectual property (IP), given that the TRIPS Agreement had a different phase-in period for developing countries, which were allocated more time to comply with obligations.[12] Nevertheless, any clustering of IP-related cases thus far appears limited to the years 1996 to 1998 in figure 4-5, or the period in which *developed* countries were supposed to have become TRIPS compliant and were thus challenging each other on various aspects of their IP-enforcement regimes. Data through 2008 show no similar clustering of WTO enforcement actions with respect to the IP commitments of developing countries.

It is therefore worth highlighting a pattern of WTO dispute settlement activity that has *not* taken place thus far, despite concerns in the immediate aftermath

12. From the date when the WTO agreements entered into force (January 1, 1995), the length of time that a country was given to ensure that its laws and practices conformed with the TRIPS Agreement varied according to whether the country was developed (one year), a developing or transition economy (five years), or least developed (eleven years, extended to twenty-one years for pharmaceutical patents). Thus one might have expected a clustering of WTO activity associated with intellectual property rights enforcement in 1996, 2000, and 2006.

of the Uruguay Round Agreement. In particular, there have not been many TRIPS disputes in which developed countries alleged that developing countries were pirating intellectual property of northern countries—especially not with respect to life-saving drugs and other related pharmaceutical products.

One final sector worth noting in figure 4-5 is steel, which had a temporal clustering of disputes. No ex ante Uruguay Round Agreement detailing guidelines of importance for this particular industry should have caused WTO enforcement actions to be concentrated over time in this industry, and yet they are. Over 50 percent (22 of 37) of WTO disputes initiated over steel products took place in just two years: 2000 and 2002.

What is the significance of this concentration of disputes over steel? The main point is that the disputes reflect underlying, nonrandom economic and policy activity during these specific years. In 2002, the United States triggered import-restricting policies over steel worldwide when it implemented steel safeguard import restrictions subsequently challenged by nine WTO members. In 2000, the United States had imposed a smaller set of safeguard import restrictions on certain steel products, as well as a number of other antidumping and countervailing measures that led to WTO challenges. The EC also imposed a number of new import barriers on steel in 2000 that led to WTO disputes.

The insight from the time clustering of activity of this particular sector is that WTO dispute settlement must be examined in the light of underlying economic as well as political conditions. In 2000 and 2002, there were many WTO disputes over steel because there were a number of newly imposed import restrictions on steel for countries to challenge. Episodes of new import restrictions under policies such as antidumping, countervailing measures, and safeguards are particularly prevalent in steel, and frequent policy changes lead to changing market access conditions and thus a reason for countries to resort to WTO enforcement.

Which Infractions That Result in Lost Foreign Market Access Are the Source of Disputes?

A third piece of data worth examining is what countries are fighting over. I categorize disputes based on the degree of "observability" of the underlying measures that are allegedly WTO inconsistent. I consider the issue of observability from the perspective of the exporting firm whose foreign market access is lost because of a potentially WTO-inconsistent measure. Consider figure 4-6, which allocates the disputes into one of five observability categories.[13]

---

13. Instead of categorizing the disputes by the specific reference to the alleged violation of a particular WTO article or agreement, I instead consider the alleged violation from the firm's perspective.

The first category at the top of the figure indicates, from the perspective of the exporting firm, the most "obvious" causes for lost foreign market access— imposed antidumping or countervailing measures. The cause of the lost foreign market access is obvious because the foreign government imposing the measure is obligated to inform the firm directly that it is doing so. Furthermore, since WTO rules on antidumping and countervailing measures require the government to collect data from the exporting firms on their sales and prices before the measures can be imposed, the firms are not only informed about the measure, but they receive information that the measure is likely to be imposed before the market access is eliminated.[14] Not surprisingly, many developing country complaints are in this category of the obvious import restriction.

Trade barriers one step away from antidumping and countervailing measures in terms of observability would include a safeguard import restriction or any explicit new trade restriction that the foreign government is required to report to WTO member governments even if it is not necessary for it to notify any particular exporting firm. This second category of "high" observability causes of lost market access also gives rise to many complaints initiated by developing countries.

As I move toward the other end of the observability spectrum of possible WTO violations, I cover measures where the government is not required by WTO rules to notify either the exporting firm or the WTO membership about policy changes. In some instances, the cause may still be apparent to the firm, even if not necessarily to its government's policymakers, because the firm identifies a differential treatment at the border. This may entail new costs or restrictions to getting access to the foreign market: for example, the importing country imposes a new quantitative restriction or higher duty, reclassifies the tariff category of a product, changes the procedure for valuing imports so as to assess higher duties, or makes it more costly for exporters to acquire the necessary licenses to engage in trade. While these "medium" observability types of disputes in figure 4-6 are more evenly balanced between developing and developed economies, it is important to note that there are a fair number of these disputes initiated by developing countries.

14. As I discuss in more detail below, there are many other reasons in addition to the observability of the measure that make antidumping measures a likely frequent target for WTO dispute settlement. First, the import restrictions are firm specific, which eliminates the need to politically organize other firms to seek government action on the exporter's behalf. Second, the use of antidumping measures has been proliferating across the WTO membership so there are many newly imposed measures to potentially challenge. Third, as more countries take on WTO commitments to bind and reduce tariffs, new antidumping measures are one of the few possible mechanisms (given the right evidentiary conditions) that allow WTO member countries to increase barriers to imports in a (potentially) WTO-consistent manner.

Figure 4-6. *WTO Disputes, by Observability of Alleged Policy Cause of Lost Market Access and Complainant Category, 1995–2008*[a]

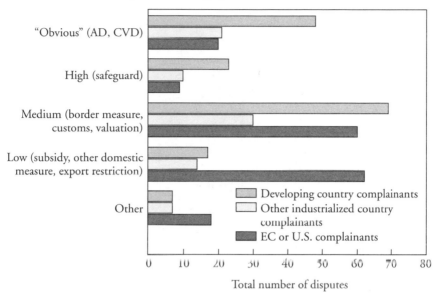

Total number of disputes

Source: Author's compilations from WTO (2009).

AD = antidumping measure; CVD = countervailing duty.

a. Disputes are broken down into bilateral (complainant–respondent) pairs. Because some disputes involved more than one complainant, the 388 requests for consultations initiated over the 1995–2008 period yielded 415 bilaterally paired disputes.

At the "low" observability end of the spectrum, however, there are fewer disputes in which the complainant is a developing country. Here, the lost foreign market access may be due to influences that do not *directly* affect the exporting firm at the border. Suppose the lost foreign market access occurs because foreign consumers chose to switch demand to another supplier, but the underlying cause of this switch was an incentive created by WTO-inconsistent means. As an example, the rival's lower price may have reflected a WTO-illegal subsidy provided by a foreign competitor's government, export restrictions on key inputs that implicitly provided such intermediates at subsidized rates to domestic producers, discriminatory domestic tax treatment, or even the failure to enforce intellectual property rights. The low observability types of disputes are dominated by the European Community and the United States as complainants and are much less frequently initiated by developing country complainants.

In figure 4-6, I classify a last set of issues as "other." These are disputes that did not directly relate to an explicit loss in foreign market access, which are frequently the "as such" claims described earlier. These disputes involve issues that

Figure 4-7. *WTO Disputes, by Observability of Alleged Policy Cause of Lost Market Access, 1995–2000 and 2001–08*[a]

Share of total disputes initiated during period

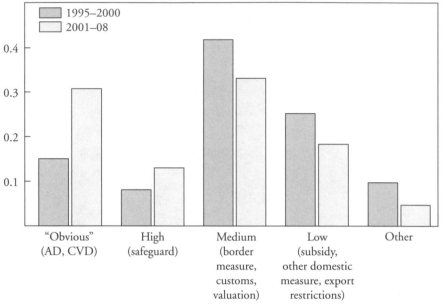

Source: Author's compilations from WTO (2009).

AD = antidumping measure; CVD = countervailing duty.

a. Disputes are broken down into bilateral (complainant–respondent) pairs. Because some disputes involved more than one complainant, the 388 requests for consultations initiated over the 1995–2008 period yielded 415 bilaterally paired disputes.

are more systemic and are less apt to involve specific industries, products, or exporters.

Figure 4-7 presents information comparing disputes over the two WTO time periods: 1995–2000 and 2001–08. An increasing share of the dispute initiation caseload concerns lost foreign market access caused by obvious and high observability measures. The share of all initiated disputes that relate to antidumping or countervailing measures alone more than doubled, from 15 percent of the caseload from 1995 to 2000 to 31 percent from 2001 to 2008. A similar increase was recorded for disputes of lost market access related to highly observable new safeguards. Combined, 43 percent (74 out of 169) of the total set of WTO disputes initiated during the 2001–08 period were over one of these three forms of administered protection—antidumping measures, countervailing measures, or safeguards. The increasingly prominent role of these particular disputes reflects how observable these measures are from the perspectives of the adversely affected firms and their governments and also the global proliferation of these measures—antidumping in particular—since the 1990s.[15]

Nevertheless, the increasing importance of these sorts of disputes is not the same thing as saying that most antidumping measures, countervailing measures, or safeguard actions against developing countries (or even developed countries) end up being challenged by formal WTO dispute settlement. In fact, as table 4-3 indicates for antidumping and countervailing measures, it is quite the opposite. For example, consider the data for the exporting industries in a WTO member such as Indonesia. Between 1995 and 2008, WTO members initiated 145 new antidumping investigations against exports from Indonesia and imposed 82 antidumping measures on Indonesian firms. Out of all this antidumping action facing its exporters, Indonesia's government initiated only two formal DSU challenges—one against a Korean and one against a South African antidumping measure on paper products. With the exception of WTO members such as the European Community and India, the pattern exhibited by Indonesia is quite typical of all WTO members. While more than 19 percent (7 percent for India) of all WTO member antidumping initiations against the European Community ultimately led to WTO challenges under the DSU, only 2 percent of the more than 2,100 antidumping initiations against the rest of the WTO membership's exporters resulted in the initiation of a formal WTO dispute.[16] Put differently, more than 90 percent of the combined new trade restrictions that WTO members imposed on exporters from other WTO members through the use of antidumping or countervailing measures during the 1995–2008 period were not challenged through the WTO self-enforcement process.

Which WTO Members Engage as Third Parties in Disputes?

Thus far the examination of the WTO dispute settlement data has focused only on the initiation of disputes and the primary litigants involved in the dispute, which is typically a complainant interested in challenging a respondent country over lost foreign market access for the complainant's exporters. In this section I turn to data on other countries that become formally involved in these disputes

15. Bown (2009a).

16. The difference between the EC and Indian responses compared with the responses of the rest of the WTO membership cannot be explained by exporters from the EC and India facing a higher ratio of imposed measures to antidumping initiations during this time period than that faced by the rest of the WTO membership. The pattern is just the opposite: the EC's share was 56.9 percent, India's share was 61.3 percent, and the rest of the WTO membership's share was 63.8 percent. Even taking out the Chinese export data from the rest of the WTO membership only decreases this share to 61.9 percent.

Table 4-3. *WTO Member Antidumping and Countervailing Measures: Initiations, Impositions, and DSU Challenges, by Targeted WTO Exporter, 1995–2008*[a]

Targeted WTO member	New AD initiations	New AD measures	Exporter uses DSU to challenge new AD	New CVM initiations	New CVMs	Exporter uses DSU to challenge new CVM
Total developed economy exporters	1,175	722	72	72	39	15
EC	283	161	55	33	22	9
Japan	144	106	2	0	0	0
United States	189	115	5	7	1	0
Korea	252	150	3	16	9	3
Taiwan[b]	92	64	2	1	0	0
Other developed countries	215	126	5	15	7	3
Total developing economy exporters	1,416	909	38	125	82	9
Argentina	30	15	3	6	4	0
Brazil	97	74	5	7	8	1
China[b]	410	295	5	23	14	5
Costa Rica	2	0	1	0	0	0
Guatemala	3	1	1	0	0	0
India	137	84	10	46	27	2
Indonesia	145	82	2	11	8	0
Malaysia	90	50	0	3	3	0
Mexico	40	27	5	0	0	0
Pakistan	10	6	0	1	1	0
Philippines	11	6	0	1	2	0
South Africa	58	38	0	6	4	0
Thailand	142	84	2	9	3	0
Turkey	44	25	2	2	1	0
Other developing countries	197	122	2	10	7	1
Total WTO member exporters	2,591	1,631	110	197	121	24

Source: Author's compilations of AD and CVM data from the Global Antidumping Database, see Bown (2009a). Author's compilations of DSU data from WTO (2009).

DSU = Dispute Settlement Understanding.

a. Data report the use of antidumping (AD) measures and countervailing measures (CVM) by WTO members against other WTO member exporters for the 1995–2008 period. Since some countries that use AD and CVM target exporters from the EC collectively, while others target exporters from EC member states in separate initiations, to make the EC data consistent, a user is characterized as having at most one AD or CVM initiation against the EC for any given product-level investigation. It is possible for a country to have more measures imposed against it than were initiated during the 1995–2008 period (for example, Brazil and CVM) because some measures imposed in 1995 resulted from initiations in 1994 or earlier.

b. Since accession to the WTO (for China, December 11, 2001, and for Taiwan, January 1, 2002), when it began to have access to formal WTO dispute settlement.

as an interested third party. Why would countries other than the primary litigants take an interest in a dispute between two WTO members? Why meddle in other countries' affairs?

In addition to those firms directly involved in the dispute, almost any change from the status quo that results from a dispute will also affect the competition that exporting firms in third countries face.[17] As one example, if the initial loss of foreign market access was due to a discriminatory (non-MFN) import restriction, one result was a policy preference vis-à-vis exporting firms from third countries. Suppose the WTO dispute results in the removal of the import restriction but does not change the policy affecting exporting firms from third countries—an illustrative dispute would be the situation facing African, Caribbean, and Pacific (ACP) exporters in *EC–Bananas III* described in chapter 3. The third country firms will need to adjust to new conditions of competition vis-à-vis the exporting firms from the complainant country that had previously been discriminated against. As a second example, if the initial loss of market access was due to a trade barrier imposed on a nondiscriminatory (MFN) basis, the exporting firms from third countries could also expect to benefit from the removal of the WTO violation pursued by the exporting firm's government in the complainant country via its WTO dispute. An illustrative dispute here would be *US–Upland Cotton* and the West African cotton exporting countries that would stand to benefit from Brazil's targeting U.S. agricultural subsidy policies.[18] Because the resolution of any dispute leads to a change in the conditions of competition in the import market of the respondent country, the main point is that firms from third countries will be interested in it so that they can plan to adjust accordingly.

Which countries take advantage of this third party access that the WTO dispute settlement system provides to keep tabs on ongoing disputes? As table 4-1 documents, the largest primary (complainant or respondent) litigants are also the countries most frequently interested in other countries' disputes as third parties. Also not surprising is that the European Community and the United States are not the most frequently active third party countries. Since they are primary litigants in such a large share of all disputes, they have less of a need to be a third party. Thus they are the second and third most active, respectively,

---

17. Bown (2009b) presents a taxonomy of ways through which changes to the conditions of competition that result from a WTO dispute can either beneficially or adversely affect firms in third countries and thus explains why these firms desire information on dispute resolution outcomes. See also Bown (2004b) for one regression-based approach to addressing the question of the extent to which the third party role increases the trade liberalization gains to third country exporters (under MFN) after a trade dispute resolution, which leads to additional foreign market access being extended from the respondent to complainant country.

18. I provide a substantial discussion of the *US–Upland Cotton* dispute in chapter 7.

behind Japan—a country that is a major exporter, though less of a litigant than the EC or the United States The next most frequent third parties are Canada and China. China's third party participation, while expected because it is also such a large exporter with interest in what policy changes are occurring in other markets, is nevertheless a surprise since it has been a WTO member only since the end of 2001.[19]

Table 4-4 presents the remaining countries that have participated in WTO disputes as formal third parties.[20] With the exception of Iceland and Israel, all of the other thirty countries are developing economies, which indicates another important way in which poor countries can track their foreign market access interests, in addition to initiating a WTO dispute.

Finally, I make two other points with respect to the basic data on interested third parties.[21] Although consideration of the third party role in addition to complainants and respondents substantially extends the list of countries that have participated in at least one dispute in some manner, it is important not to overstate the importance of merely being on this list. First, there are sixteen WTO members for whom their only dispute settlement participation experience has been in the third party role—in either the *EC–Bananas III* or the *EC–Export Subsidies on Sugar* disputes.[22] If I omit these two cases from consideration, the number of WTO members that have participated as interested third parties in one or more disputes falls from seventy-two to fifty-six. Furthermore, while seventy-two countries have participated in WTO disputes as third parties, table 4-5 identifies fifty-four additional current WTO members as never having been on the inside of any dispute—whether as a complainant, a respondent, or a third party. While some of these countries are relatively new to the WTO, which may explain their nonengagement, for most of these countries this is certainly not the explanation.

19. It is also likely that China has viewed third party involvement during this period as a learning exercise. Because of the size of its own trade, China is likely to have anticipated it would become an active primary litigant in WTO enforcement activity before too much time had passed. Indeed, whereas China was a primary litigant in only two disputes initiated between 2001 and 2005, it has subsequently been involved in fourteen disputes between 2006 and 2008.

20. The countries in table 4-4 have never served as a complainant or respondent party in any other dispute and thus are not listed in table 4-1.

21. There are also likely to be costs to third party involvement to WTO dispute settlement proceedings. For example, Busch and Reinhardt (2006a, 2006b, 2009) provide evidence that additional third party involvement in disputes can result in bottlenecks that prevent cases from settling early and thus increase the probability of a dispute reaching the stage of a Panel ruling.

22. The *EC–Export Subsidies on Sugar* dispute was initiated by Brazil, Australia, and Thailand in 2002 and involved a challenge both to EC sugar export subsidies and also to a system of providing preferential access to sugar imported from ACP countries as well as from India. For a discussion of the dispute, see Hoekman and Howse (2008).

Table 4-4. *Other WTO Members Involved as Interested Third Parties, 1995–2007*[a]

WTO member	Number of times third party[b]
Barbados	4
Belize	4
Benin	1
Bolivia	1
Cameroon	1
Chad	1
Côte d'Ivoire	4
Cuba	13
Dominica	3
El Salvador	9
Fiji	3
Ghana	1
Grenada	1
Guyana	3
Iceland	6
Israel	4
Jamaica	8
Kenya	3
Madagascar	4
Malawi	3
Mauritius	5
Nigeria	1
Paraguay	15
Saint Kitts and Nevis	3
Saint Lucia	3
Saint Vincent and the Grenadines	1
Senegal	2
Suriname	1
Swaziland	3
Tanzania	3
Vietnam	2
Zimbabwe	1
Total	117

Source: Author's compilations from WTO (2009).

a. These countries registering in formal disputes as interested third parties, unlike those countries listed in table 4-1, have never served as a complainant or respondent party in any other dispute.

b. Third party data are only available up to dispute DS367, which was initiated August 31, 2007.

How Far Do Disputes Make It through the WTO's Legal Process?

Recall again the full, legal, step-by-step dispute resolution process described in chapter 3. An important issue is identification of the determinants of how far disputes proceed through the formal legal steps of the process. What affects the likelihood of a dispute being settled by the two parties through a mutually

Table 4-5. *WTO Members with No Formal Involvement in Dispute Settlement, 1995–2008*[a]

WTO member	Membership date	WTO member	Membership date
Albania	September 8, 2000	Maldives	May 31, 1995
Angola	November 23, 1996	Mali	May 31, 1995
Armenia	February 5, 2003	Malta	January 1, 1995
Bahrain	January 1, 1995	Mauritania	May 31, 1995
Botswana	May 31, 1995	Moldova	July 26, 2001
Brunei Darussalam	January 1, 1995	Mongolia	January 29, 1997
Burkina Faso	June 3, 1995	Morocco	January 1, 1995
Burundi	July 23, 1995	Mozambique	August 26, 1995
Cambodia	October 13, 2004	Myanmar	January 1, 1995
Cape Verde	July 23, 2008	Namibia	January 1, 1995
Central African Republic	May 31, 1995	Nepal	April 23, 2004
Congo	March 27, 1997	Netherlands Antilles	January 1, 1995
Dem. Rep. of the Congo	January 1, 1997	Niger	December 13, 1996
Djibouti	May 31, 1995	Oman	November 9, 2000
Gabon	January 1, 1995	Papua New Guinea	June 9, 1996
The Gambia	October 23, 1996	Qatar	January 13, 1996
Georgia	June 14, 2000	Rwanda	May 22, 1996
Guinea	October 25, 1995	Saudi Arabia	December 11, 2005
Guinea-Bissau	May 31, 1995	Sierra Leone	July 23, 1995
Haiti	January 30, 1996	Solomon Islands	July 26, 1996
Jordan	April 11, 2000	Togo	May 31, 1995
Kuwait	January 1, 1995	Tonga	July 27, 2007
Kyrgyz	December 20, 1998	Tunisia	March 29, 1995
Lesotho	May 31, 1995	Uganda	January 1, 1995
Liechtenstein	September 1, 1995	Ukraine	May 16, 2008
Macau	January 1, 1995	United Arab Emirates	April 10, 1996
Macedonia	April 4, 2003	Zambia	January 1, 1995

Source: Author's compilations from WTO (2009).
a. Third party data are only available up to dispute DS367, which was initiated August 31, 2007.

agreeable understanding before legal rulings, as opposed to one that the complainant simply drops, or one that proceeds to Panel rulings as well as appeals and possible arbitration? Once I move beyond an examination of data on the mere initiation of disputes to measures of how the dispute settlement process is used, it is necessary to recognize that stopping the dispute resolution process is an outcome that is *jointly* determined by at least two countries. Thus it is likely to be affected by a number of factors, and not only by simple elements of the data such as the parties' income classifications.

Such a finding is evident from figure 4-8, which illustrates the share of initiated disputes between income-grouped bilateral pairs of countries that result in Panel rulings over two time periods: 1995–2000 and 2001–06. I choose to end

Figure 4-8. *WTO Disputes That Resulted in Panel Reports, 1995–2000 and 2001–06*[a]

Share of initiated disputes that result in Panel report

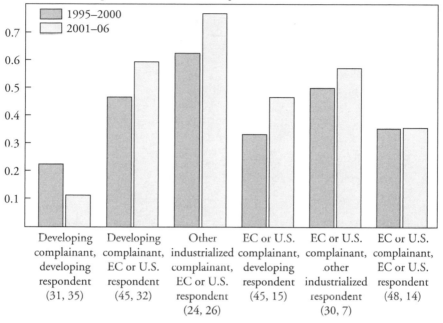

Source: Author's compilations from WTO (2009) and Horn and Mavroidis (2008b).

a. Disputes are broken down into bilateral (complainant-respondent) pairs. Because some disputes involved more than one complainant, the 356 request for consultations over 1995–2006 led to 383 bilaterally paired disputes. In parentheses are the numbers of initiated disputes between the two categories of WTO member countries during the 1995–2000, and 2001–06 periods, respectively. Three sets of bilateral pairing categories involving 31 disputes are omitted from the figure: "Developing complainant, other industrialized respondent (2, 4)"; "Other industrialized complainant, developing respondent (14, 2)"; and "Other industrialized complainant, other industrialized respondent (7, 2)."

the second period at disputes initiated by 2006 so as to allow sufficient time for cases to make it to and through the Panel process as well as for potential appeals.[23]

First, there is no obvious relationship between the levels of economic development of the parties and the outcome that a dispute reaches a Panel ruling. For example, consider first only the disputes in which the European Community or

23. I therefore end the sample with dispute initiation DS356, since DS360, which was a dispute initiated in March 2007, has already made it through the Panel process and for which an Appellate Body report was circulated in 2008. This is evidence that disputes initiated through 2006 have had sufficient time to have Panels constituted if the parties wished to pursue the matter through formal WTO dispute settlement channels.

the United States is challenged as a respondent. For these disputes, there is no simple relationship between the complainant's level of development and the outcome of the dispute reaching a Panel ruling. Cases initiated by other industrialized countries are *more* likely to result in rulings than are disputes initiated by developing countries, but disputes initiated by the United States or the EC against each other are *less* likely to result in rulings. The same can be said if I consider only the disputes in which the EC or the United States, as a complainant, is challenging another country. If the respondent is another industrialized country, the dispute is more likely to proceed to a Panel ruling than if the respondent is a developing country, but a developing country is more likely to reach a Panel ruling than if the dispute is an instance of the United States or the EC challenging the other.

There are, however, two salient features of the data in figure 4-8 regarding the share of disputes that reach the Panel ruling stage. The first is that disputes in which the two parties are both developing countries appear to be different from all of the others; disputes between developing countries are *less* likely to reach the stage of a Panel ruling. Overall, only 17 percent of the sixty-six disputes that developing countries initiated against one another during the 1995–2006 period resulted in the issuance of a Panel report compared with 48 percent (152 out of 317) of the other bilateral pairings of countries. The latter include instances in which developing countries took on other developed economies as complainants and ones in which they were faced as a respondent with a dispute initiated by developed economy complainants.[24]

The second interesting feature of the data is that the likelihood of an initiated dispute continuing to the stage in which a Panel report is issued has also increased over time—both in the aggregate and for all bilateral pairs of complainant and respondent types illustrated in figure 4-8—*except* for disputes between a developing country complainant and a developing country respondent. Not only are a smaller share of these particular dispute initiations continuing to the Panel stage, but overall this share decreased between those two time periods, from 23 percent in the 1995–2000 period to only 11 percent between 2001 and 2006.[25]

---

24. In a series of papers, Busch and Reinhardt (2001, 2003) examined the determinants of early settlement of disputes—that is, a settlement before the establishment of a Panel. They argued that disputes are more likely to result in concessions if they settle early, and at least through a sample of WTO disputes from 1995 to 2000, poor countries were less likely to secure early settlements to cases than higher-income countries were. Busch (2000) and Reinhardt (2001) presented some of the first empirical research examining GATT disputes and related questions; see also the survey in Busch and Reinhardt (2002). Alternative approaches related to the issue of whether disputes settle or result in legal rulings are presented in Butler and Hauser (2000); Guzman and Simmons (2002); Reynolds (2009).

25. For WTO disputes that make it to the Panel stage, an interesting question is whether developing countries are likely to submit fewer claims or to be less successful in them. Hoekman, Horn,

Figure 4-9. *WTO Disputes That Resulted in Panel Reports That Were Appealed, by Categories of Complainant, 1995–2000 and 2001–06*[a]

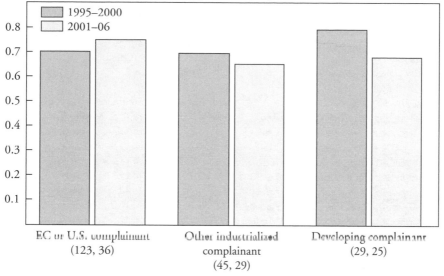

Share of Panel reports that resulted in Appellate Body report

Source: Author's compilations from WTO (2009) and Horn and Mavroidis (2008b).

a. Disputes are broken down into bilateral (complainant respondent) pairs. Because some disputes involved more than one complainant, the 356 request for consultations over 1995–2006 led to 383 bilaterally paired disputes. In parentheses are the numbers of disputes that were eligible for appeal, that is, disputes that resulted in a Panel ruling during the 1995–2000, and 2001–06 periods, respectively.

Figure 4-9 illustrates how different categories of complainant countries have used the appeals process.[26] For disputes that have made it to the stage where a WTO Panel issued a report, allowing the possibility of appeal, roughly similar shares of Panel rulings are appealed across these three groupings of complainant countries. There are a number of different reasons why the complainant and

and Mavroidis (2009) examine these and related questions using a set of 144 bilateral disputes from 1995 to 2006 between WTO members in which a Panel was formed and a report issued and in which at least one legal claim was made. Similar to the results presented in the text, there appears to be no simple relationship between country income levels and submissions or rulings. First, they find that (table 3), while developing countries filed fewer claims as complainants in disputes they initiated against the United State or the EC, relative to what other countries filed against either two, against all other targets, developing countries filed relatively more claims. Second, they find that (table 8), their overall success rate (defined as rulings on legal claims that went in their favor) is similar to other countries: they had a ruling in their favor on 57.8 percent of the claims, which was lower than the overall success rate for the United States and the EC (64.7 percent for their claims made), but it was higher than the success rate for other industrialized country complainants (56.4 percent).

26. There are too few instances of formal appeals to further break down the data into bilateral pairs of countries based on income groupings, as I have done in figure 4-5, for example.

Table 4-6. *WTO Disputes Resulting in Authorized Retaliation Threats,*
1995–2007

Dispute (complainant)	Retaliation award by the WTO arbitrators
EC–Bananas III (United States)	$191.4 million
EC–Bananas III (Ecuador)	$201.6 million
EC–Hormones (United States)	$116.8 million
EC–Hormones (Canada)	$11.3 million (Canadian)
Brazil–Aircraft (Canada)	$344.2 million
US–FSC (EC)	$4.043 billion
US–1916 Act (EC)	No specific amount
US–Offset Act (Byrd Amendment) (Brazil)	0.72 × value of U.S. subsidy payments
US–Offset Act (Byrd Amendment) (Chile)	0.72 × value of U.S. subsidy payments
US–Offset Act (Byrd Amendment) (EC)	0.72 × value of U.S. subsidy payments
US–Offset Act (Byrd Amendment) (India)	0.72 × value of U.S. subsidy payments
US–Offset Act (Byrd Amendment) (Japan)	0.72 × value of U.S. subsidy payments
US–Offset Act (Byrd Amendment) (Korea)	0.72 × value of U.S. subsidy payments
US–Offset Act (Byrd Amendment) (Canada)	0.72 × value of U.S. subsidy payments
US–Offset Act (Byrd Amendment) (Mexico)	0.72 × value of U.S. subsidy payments
Canada–Regional Aircraft (Brazil)	$247.796 million (Canadian)
US–Gambling (Antigua and Barbuda)	$21 million

Source: Bown and Ruta (2010), table 1.

respondent countries may want to utilize the appeals process. For example, certain countries may be more concerned with the systemic implications of getting the case law right and thus desire to have the Appellate Body correct Panel reports. In other cases, respondent countries may use the appeals process because it allows for an additional period of time during which WTO-inconsistent measures can remain in place.

Finally, table 4-6 shows that only seventeen of the disputes initiated between 1995 and 2007 have reached the stage at which a respondent country refused to comply with an adverse WTO ruling and the complainant country sought and was granted the right to retaliate under WTO arbitration. In even fewer of these instances did the complainant country actually carry out the authorized retaliation. A mix of developing and developed countries have sought and been granted the right to retaliate against a trading partner for the failure to comply.

I return to the data on the WTO dispute resolution process in a more formal discussion of the existing scholarship in the section below. One reason for stopping here is the difficult task of evaluating the outcomes of WTO dispute settlement proceedings. Before getting to the question of potential determinants of outcomes of WTO disputes—and whether they might vary by a country's level of economic development, the commercial sector under dispute, or the trade-restricting measure involved—a more basic issue is how to define and thus categorize and measure the outcome.

One possible measure of interest is that of compliance with legal rulings. However, data on whether the respondent country removes the offending measure in question may be difficult to obtain, especially when the WTO has little information because the dispute has been dropped or settled before the stage of a Panel ruling.[27] Furthermore, even if it were straightforward to obtain information on whether respondents remove offending measures, what if compliance with the legal ruling simply led the respondent to replace one WTO-inconsistent policy with another WTO-inconsistent policy? What if the second policy goes unchallenged at the WTO? Although this suggests using an alternative measure to evaluate the impact of rulings, such as the change in foreign market access, what benchmark should be used to evaluate the change? For example, what if the resulting policy change by the respondent restores foreign market access to the complainant, but it too is WTO inconsistent because the market access is actually taken away from third country exporters in a way that discriminates and thus violates MFN treatment?

Empirical Studies of WTO Dispute Settlement Initiation and Participation

The previous section examined the caseload of 388 WTO disputes initiated from 1995 through 2008. The inferences drawn from these data thus far are based solely on examining trends in initiated cases. I made separate comparisons of the types of countries involved, the tradable sectors that generate disputes, the trade-restricting measures at issue, and how these factors may be changing over time. While such a simplistic examination of the data is partially revealing, it nevertheless only allows one to draw limited conclusions.

In this section of the chapter, I briefly review some of the insights from the more formal empirical scholarship into WTO dispute settlement. These studies typically estimate political and economic models on large samples of WTO trade dispute data using sophisticated econometric regression frameworks. The empirical analyses search for the influence of one potentially important factor while holding constant the impact of other contributing factors.

An appropriate, and in fact the most fundamental, question of interest is whether access to the WTO dispute settlement system by developing countries to

27. Wilson (2007) presented data on compliance with WTO rulings, but this is an incomplete measure. Many disputes are terminated without a WTO ruling and thus without an official determination of whether the contested measure constituted a WTO violation and thus whether there would have been a need for the respondent country to make a policy change.

enforce their market access interests is somehow biased. Although there are many developing countries that have actively used WTO dispute settlement to enforce their foreign market access, and their (combined) use has remained much less volatile during the 1995–2008 period than that of the developed economies, nevertheless, the data also reveal some worrisome trends. The most poignant is that least developed countries, including all of those listed in table 4-5, are virtually absent from self-enforcement activity in the WTO dispute settlement system.

Can the level of a country's active engagement in WTO dispute settlement be explained by its level of economic development? To what extent does involvement also depend on other factors that were raised in the discussion of the *EC–Bananas III* dispute in chapter 3, such as the resource costs of pursuing a case when compared with the potential gains from trade associated with enforcing market access? What about the potential complainant country's capacity to induce compliance through WTO-authorized retaliation? Are developing countries particularly vulnerable to "extra-WTO" counterretaliation threats that discourage them from bringing forward disputes to enforce their foreign market access? The relative importance of any and all of these as potential explanations contributing to the observed pattern of disputes in the data can only be addressed through such formal empirical studies.

The first attempt to address empirically whether there was a bias against developing countries in their use of WTO dispute settlement was the pioneering work of Horn, Mavroidis, and Nordström.[28] Their approach was to examine whether there was an empirical link in the data between the number of cases that WTO members filed relative to the level of their international trade and the diversity of their trading partners. The basic theory is that the more a country exports, and the more trading partners to which it exports, the more frictions are likely to occur and thus the more WTO disputes the country is likely to be involved in.

Francois, Horn, and Kaunitz have expanded, refined, and extended the basic approach of Horn, Mavroidis, and Nordström to cover newly available and more detailed data for WTO disputes from 1995 to 2006, which contain the results that I reference here.[29] Their unit of analysis is a potential dispute between a complainant country i and respondent country j over exports in industry g, and their empirical question of interest is the determinants of the number of WTO disputes initiated between countries i and j in industry g between 1995 and 2006. They found convincing evidence that the composition and volume of trade matters. The larger that country i's exports are to country j

28. The Horn, Mavroidis, and Nordström (2005) approach was initially published as a working paper in 1999, and their study covered a sample of WTO dispute initiation data from 1995 to 1998. Holmes, Rollo, and Young (2003) presented a similar approach covering data from 1995 to 2002.
    29. Francois, Horn, and Kaunitz (2008); Horn, Mavroidis, and Nordström (2005).

in industry g, the more formal disputes that potential complainant i initiates against respondent j in industry g. They also found that this effect differs across the industry composition of trade and that disputes are more likely in agriculture than in other sectors. This is consistent with the pattern of results documented earlier in figure 4-4.

Result 1. The market size of disputed exports can affect the initiation of a dispute as well as the frequency of initiated disputes.

Francois, Horn, and Kaunitz provided other suggestive evidence of factors likely to affect the number of disputes a potential complainant i is likely to initiate against respondent j.[30] The first concerns the size of the two countries—as measured by their gross domestic product (GDP). Larger countries are more likely to initiate cases and have cases filed against them. The second is the possibility of extra-WTO counterretaliation via potential respondent j's bilateral aid sent to potential respondent i, as a share of country i's national income. The less dependent country i is on aid from country j, the more cases were initiated. Finally, the authors present mixed results for their proxy for each country's "legal capacity"—for which they use the "Government Efficiency Index" from the World Bank Worldwide Governance Research Indicators dataset. The higher the legal capacity of potential respondent importing country j, the fewer disputes it faced. There was no statistically significant effect of the legal capacity of potential complainant exporting country i, and in fact the coefficient estimate on this variable has the wrong sign. As the authors noted, a contributing explanation for this result is the usefulness of this particular proxy to capture the legal capacity needs of potential WTO disputing countries, an issue to which I return below.

A more general aspect of the limits of this sort of empirical study, as the authors recognized, is the implicit assumption that every i, j, g relationship faces the same basic probability of imposition of a WTO-inconsistent measure that could lead to a trade dispute. There is reason to suspect that a policy-imposing importing country j may take into consideration the likelihood of a WTO trade dispute when it decides how to structure its import protection—that is, how "WTO consistent" the importing country decides to make its protection relative to each particular exporter i.

At least two studies provide evidence in support of the theory that countries are more likely to impose new trade restrictions on partners that are less able to retaliate and self-enforce the GATT/WTO commitments that their trading counterparts have taken on.[31] First, Blonigen and Bown examined the U.S.

---

30. Francois, Horn, and Kaunitz (2008).

31. Related studies examining the influence of retaliation in antidumping behavior activity in particular includes Prusa and Skeath (2002); Feinberg and Reynolds (2006); Busch, Raciborski, and Reinhardt (2008).

antidumping process over the 1980–98 period and found that trading partners with greater capacity to retaliate against U.S. exporting firms—an important element to the WTO's self-enforcing agreement—are both less likely to be named in antidumping investigations and are less likely to have antidumping measures imposed against them after an investigation.[32] Second, in a separate study, Bown examined a set of new import restrictions that GATT contracting parties imposed over the 1974–94 period and found that countries were more likely to implement new restrictions in a GATT-inconsistent manner against trading partners with less capacity to retaliate through a change in trade policy—again, a necessary element in a self-enforcing trade agreement.[33]

Although these earlier studies do not focus on the sample of data covered by the Francois, Horn, and Kaunitz research, which examined the most recent WTO period, there is a strong presumption that the results carry over to other policy settings and time periods.[34] Governments that feel the need to implement new import protection will try to do so against trading partners through the use of policies with the lowest costs of implementing such protection. Today such costs include those associated with the prospects of a WTO trade dispute and the possibility of retaliation. The combined implication of such findings for the type of approach of Francois, Horn, and Kaunitz is that countries less able to enforce (retaliate) may be more likely to get targeted with WTO-inconsistent measures and thus might have more to fight about than do other countries.

Result 2. The imposition of WTO-inconsistent policies is unlikely to be random, as certain countries are more likely to be targeted.

Embedded in this last result is an important and underappreciated point: researchers do not have access to information about WTO-illegal policies that governments implement but that are *not* being challenged. Because of the lack of information on the nonchallenges, it is impossible to draw precise inferences regarding the determinants of challenges without making additional assumptions on the probability of countries imposing WTO-inconsistent measures.

One approach to addressing the particular hurdle of a lack of knowledge of WTO-inconsistent measures that go unchallenged is taken by Bown in a 2005 study.[35] This paper begins by noting the phenomenon documented earlier in figure 4-7: over time, an increasing share of the WTO dispute caseload is made up of challenges to WTO members' use of antidumping measures. A particular target for WTO dispute settlement has been the United States' use of

---

32. Blonigen and Bown (2003).
33. Bown (2004a).
34. Francois, Horn, and Kaunitz (2008).
35. Bown (2005a).

antidumping measures. Using the sample of data of U.S. antidumping measures imposed during the 1992–2003 period, Bown examined the determinants of which ones were challenged via GATT/WTO trade disputes.

The results are consistent with the literature described above, and they provide additional insights into the mechanisms that influence country-level decisions to initiate WTO disputes. First, Blonigen and Bown and, separately, Bown in 2004 presented evidence that retaliation capacity affects a protection-imposing country's choice of how to implement that protection—trading partners that lack the capacity to retaliate have been more likely to have GATT/WTO–inconsistent policies imposed on their exporters in the first place.[36] Similar to the evidence from those two studies, in his study from 2005 Bown found that a stronger retaliation capacity also improved the likelihood that an exporting country facing new protection will fight the matter at the GATT/WTO.[37]

Result 3. A country's underlying capacity to carry out WTO-authorized retaliation against a particular trading partner, even if not implemented in practice, can enforce compliance.

Second, the amount of trade at stake in a potential dispute matters, as Francois, Horn, and Kaunitz suggested in a setting that abstracted from country-level policy actions.[38] Bown in 2005 found a strong positive relationship between the size of the exports affected by the new U.S. import restriction and the likelihood that the antidumping measure is ultimately challenged under the WTO.[39] This last result in particular provides strong support for the theory that

---

36. Blonigen and Bown (2003); Bown (2004a).

37. Like Francois, Horn, and Kaunitz (2008), Bown (2005a) also investigated whether a foreign country's reliance on the United States for bilateral aid decreases the likelihood of filing a dispute over a U.S. antidumping measure. While the sign of the estimate is negative, as predicted by the theory, it is not statistically significant at conventional levels. That may reflect that the United States did not undertake antidumping actions during this time period against some of the poorest (and most aid-dependent) countries. Such a phenomenon may show up more robustly in the data on potential challenges to other types of trade barriers that are more likely to affect exporters from poorer countries.

38. Francois, Horn, and Kaunitz (2008).

39. Bown (2005a). In an alternative estimation framework, Bown and Crowley (2009) present a similar finding via another more precise measure. Rather than the pre-antidumping value of exports to the U.S. market, they use the value of exports to the U.S. market lost after the imposition of the new import restriction. Other research supporting this effect is Davis and Shirato (2007), which took a different empirical approach. From the perspective of a single exporting country (Japan), their paper asked which of the potential foreign market access barriers facing its exporters result in the initiation of a formal WTO dispute. They presented evidence that industries with larger levels of production and larger exports as a share of total production are likely to have their potential dispute turn into an actual WTO dispute.

the resource costs of the WTO enforcement process should be a significant determinant of which potential disputes are "realized," or initiated. A WTO dispute over an imposed U.S. antidumping measure that affects only a small dollar amount of trade and market access is more likely to be associated with small profit margins, and thus costs of the WTO enforcement process outweigh likely benefits. The various components of the extensive costs associated with fully using the WTO enforcement process are a topic to which I return in great length in the next chapter.[40]

Result 4. The resource cost of WTO dispute settlement can affect the initiation of a dispute as well as the frequency of initiated disputes.

Finally, in a second 2005 study, Bown provided additional support for these theories from a different sample of data.[41] In this research Bown used an alternative approach to examining the problem that combined elements of the frameworks from the studies described earlier.[42] Bown considered a set of actual WTO trade disputes taking place from 1995 to 2000 involving import restrictions that, as revealed by the underlying product-level trade flow data, adversely affected many exporting countries. The approach is then to examine the determinants of which of those adversely affected exporters chose to participate in the WTO dispute, whether in the complainant role or as an interested third party, as opposed to not self-enforcing their foreign market access concerns at all.

The results from this Bown approach and the sample of data are consistent with those described earlier from studies of other policy settings.[43] In particular, the market access that is at stake and the retaliation capacity of the country via its trade policy both matter. WTO members with larger product-level exports to the disputed market (measured both in value and in shares) were more likely to formally engage in the dispute, as were WTO members that had the capacity to implement trade policy retaliation against the respondent.

Further evidence that the capacity of a country's WTO-authorized retaliation matters, on the basis of the economic outcomes of the GATT/WTO dispute resolution process, is presented by Bown in two studies in 2004.[44] These

---

40. Busch, Reinhardt, and Shaffer (2008) presented a modeling approach similar to Bown (2005a), but they extended the data beyond U.S. antidumping cases to the antidumping measures imposed by a number of WTO member countries. One novel element is that their study conducted a unique survey to collect data on each WTO member's legal capacity. Their constructed measures were then used in a regression framework. Although they did not examine the case-level data such as the lost trade at stake in the potential dispute, they did present evidence that a country's lack of legal capacity reduces its ability to challenge foreign use of antidumping via a WTO dispute.

41. Bown (2005b).

42. See the studies of Bown (2005a); Francois, Horn, and Kaunitz (2008).

43. Bown (2005b).

44. Bown (2004c, 2004d).

studies focused on samples of trade disputes during the 1973–98 period and found evidence that the larger are the respondent's exports to the complainant—giving the complainant the flexibility to choose sufficiently credible trade policy retaliation targets—the more favorable is the economic outcome from the dispute. A greater capacity to retaliate increases both the likelihood that the respondent increases the foreign market access extended to the complainant and also the size of the market access (increased exports) granted to the complainant at the conclusion of the dispute.[45]

Bown's approach also provided evidence that the potential respondent country's capacity to engage in extra-WTO counterretaliation influences a country's dispute initiation and participation decision.[46] In particular, exporter dependence on the respondent for bilateral aid makes the country less likely to engage in the dispute, as is whether the countries are in a preferential trade agreement (PTA) together. After controlling for other factors, exporters that are PTA partners of the respondent are less likely to participate in the WTO legal challenge, even if they are adversely affected by the import-restricting policy.

Result 5. Potential complainants sometimes fear potential respondents' extra-WTO counterretaliation capacity.

This evidence is consistent with results from the Francois, Horn, and Kaunitz study that also found that the more dependent the exporter (potential complainant) is on bilateral aid from the importing (potential respondent) country, the fewer the number of bilateral disputes that the potential complainant initiates.[47] As these authors noted, such studies are not able to control for an exporter's reliance on a particular importer in other sectors for trade preferences that may take place unilaterally, such as the Generalized System of Preferences (GSP) and other similar types of programs.

Conclusions

The theory, data, and the emerging empirical scholarship identify a number of consistent determinants of whether and how frequently WTO members use the formal dispute settlement process to enforce their trading partners' market

45. In an interesting related piece, Evenett (2010) examines the potential retaliation capacity of twenty of the largest developing economy exporters vis-à-vis their bilateral trading partners, calculating the share of each nation's market access that is self-enforceable by the potential use of WTO-sanctioned retaliation. Within this particular subsample of major exporting developing countries, he finds that market access that is protected by retaliation capacity varies considerably across nations and that it does not appear to be related to the country's level of development.

46. Bown (2005b).

47. Francois, Horn, and Kaunitz (2008).

access commitments. First, there is fairly strong evidence, not surprisingly, that the size of the exports under potential dispute matters. Since the size of export market access is a proxy for the benefit from successful resolution of a dispute, evidence of a positive relationship indicates that the resource costs associated with using the formal WTO dispute settlement process affect which potential disputes get initiated as well as how many potential complainant countries initiate.[48] This result has important implications for the firm-level model of WTO self-enforcement that I introduce in the next chapter.

Nevertheless, there are factors other than the resource costs directly associated with using the dispute settlement process. The potential complainant's capacity to induce compliance via WTO-authorized retaliation vis-à-vis potential respondents also appears to affect the decision to use dispute settlement to self-enforce commitments. There is also evidence that potential complainant fears over subsequent extra-WTO counterretaliation (for example, respondent action on aid or preferential trade agreements) affects the WTO enforcement decision. These studies do not take into account the possibility of trade preference dependence through reliance on GSP, which may also be at play. Finally, developing countries may be more likely to have WTO-inconsistent measures imposed against them, especially if trading partners know the developing countries will not self-enforce their commitments through the use of the WTO dispute settlement process. Developing countries may thus have more to complain about in a policy sense, if not as measured by the smaller level of exports that such policies may be affecting.

Note finally the potential implications of these results for the themes I pursue in later chapters. Given the results that other factors also likely affect the self-enforcement process—for example, the WTO-authorized retaliation capacity of the potential complainant and extra-WTO counterretaliation capacity of the potential respondent—innovations that reduce the resource costs to pursuing WTO enforcement actions are not likely to result in the initiation of all potentially important disputes. Without additional actions, other impediments will continue to limit certain product-level, bilateral pairs of WTO commitments from being self-enforced. With this caveat in mind, the next chapter explores more deeply the source of the costs of participating in the WTO's self-enforcing process.

---

48. Davis and Bermeo (forthcoming) provide additional suggestive evidence that the costs of using WTO enforcement matter. They focus on a sample of developing countries and present evidence of a relationship between the number of disputes the country initiates and measures of past (historical) involvement in dispute settlement as a complainant or respondent. Such evidence suggests that one component of the cost of using WTO dispute settlement is a one-time fixed cost associated with government policymakers learning about the existence of and role for the procedure.

5

WTO Enforcement at the Firm Level: The Extended Litigation Process

The eminent legal scholar Robert Hudec has rightly suggested that dispute settlement under the current World Trade Organization system is now one of "jurist's jurisprudence" when compared with the General Agreement on Tariffs and Trade system's "diplomat's jurisprudence."[1] Nevertheless, a literal interpretation of this statement may take matters too far. Evidence shows that countries that use the WTO dispute settlement process effectively to enforce market access are forced to rely on much more than skillful lawyers. Mastery of WTO law in dispute settlement is a necessary but not sufficient condition for enforcement of market access.

Although the discussion in the last chapter focused largely on the countries involved and the economic incentives that may or may not affect government policymakers in these cases, it is critical not to miss out on the fundamental, underlying commercial interests in WTO disputes. To highlight this point, consider table 5-1.

The table presents a sample of firms from a recent *BusinessWeek* survey, "The 100 Top Brands."[2] It turns out that more than one-quarter of the 100 firms from this list can be tied to a direct enforcement interest in one or more of only

1. Robert Hudec (1970, 1999).
2. *BusinessWeek*, "The 100 Top Brands," August 1, 2005, pp. 90–94.

Table 5-1. *Developed Country Firms and WTO Trade Disputes*

Firms involved in WTO disputes[a] (global brand ranking)	WTO dispute (complainants)
Coca-Cola (1), Pepsi (23), Archer Daniels Midland, Cargill	*Mexico–Corn Syrup* (United States) *Mexico–Taxes on Soft Drinks* (United States)
Microsoft (2), Cisco (17), Siemens (45), Philips (53)	*EC–Computer Equipment* (United States)
Toyota (9), Mercedes-Benz (11), BMW (16), Honda (19), Ford (22), Audi (79), Hyundai (84), Nissan (85), Chrysler, General Motors, Daewoo, Daihatsu, Kia, Mazda, Mitsubishi, Peugeot, Suzuki, Volvo	*Indonesia–Autos* (Japan, EC, United States)
Mercedes-Benz (11), BMW (16), Honda (19), Ford (22), Volkswagen (56), Audi (79), Daimler-Chrysler, General Motors, Peugeot, Renault	*China–Auto Parts* (United States, EC, Canada)
Chiquita, Dole, Fyffes, Geest, Louis Vuitton (18)[b]	*EC–Bananas III* (United States, Mexico, Guatemala, Honduras, Ecuador)
Samsung Electronics (20), Hyundai Electronics (84), LG Semicon (97), Micron	*US–DRAMS* (Korea)
Buena Vista Pictures, Paramount Pictures, Sony Pictures (28), Twentieth Century Fox, Universal City Studios, Warner Brothers (through the Motion Picture Association of America)	*China–Intellectual Property Rights* (United States) *China–Audiovisual Services* (United States)
Nike (30), Reebok	*Argentina–Footwear* (EC, Indonesia, United States)
Pfizer (31), Novartis (43), Aventis, Bayer, Dow, Dupont, Monsanto, Syngenta	*EC–Approval and Marketing of Biotech Products* (United States, Canada, Argentina)
Harley Davidson (46),[b] Tropicana,[b] dozens of steel firms from dozens of exporting countries	*US–Steel Safeguards* (EC, Japan, Brazil, China, Korea, New Zealand, Norway, Switzerland, Taiwan)
Kodak (62), Fuji	*Japan–Film* (United States)
Thomson-Reuters (74), Bloomberg, Dow Jones, Pearson	*China–Measures Affecting Financial Information Services and Foreign Financial Information Suppliers* (United States, EC, Canada)

Firms involved in WTO disputes[a] (global brand ranking)	WTO dispute (complainants)
Boeing, Airbus	*EC–Large Civil Aircraft* (United States)
	EC–Large Civil Aircraft (2nd complaint) (United States)
	US–Large Civil Aircraft (EC)
	US–Large Civil Aircraft (2nd complaint) (EC)
Bombardier, Embraer	*Brazil–Aircraft* (Canada)
	Canada–Aircraft Credits and Guarantees (Brazil)

Source: Global brand rankings taken from *BusinessWeek,* "The 100 Top Brands," August 1, 2005, pp. 90–94.

a. Firm names linked to WTO disputes compiled by the author via official WTO dispute settlement documentation, newspaper articles, press releases, or other related government documentation.

b. Indicates firm involvement as publicly identified potential target of WTO-sanctioned retaliation instead of direct enforcement action.

fourteen WTO disputes.[3] Global firms familiar to households worldwide head-line the list of companies with commercial interests at stake in these WTO dis-putes: Coke and Pepsi; Microsoft and global computer electronics firms; the American, European, Japanese, and Korean automakers; Nike; Samsung, and Micron; pharmaceutical and biotech firms such as Pfizer, Novartis, and Bayer; Sony and Fox Hollywood film studios; the Reuters and Bloomberg financial information services firms; and Boeing and Airbus. Finally, Chiquita, Dole, and some of the other firms related to the *EC–Bananas III* dispute described in the previous chapter also find their way onto the list.

Nevertheless, these large multinational companies mostly headquartered in the North are certainly not the only firms pursuing their commercial interests of foreign market access enforcement through WTO disputes. These companies are global brands, but scores of less-recognizable firms from both developed and developing countries also have had their market access interests enforced in Geneva.

Indeed, suppose one asked the firm-level question differently. Instead of starting with a list of the world's most recognizable firms and asking if they

3. Even the global brands whose industries' trade is not highly disciplined by the WTO—for example, financial services—find the services they provide a part of dispute settlement. For exam-ple, while I do not include them in table 5-1, *BusinessWeek*'s list includes Citi, Merrill Lynch, HSBC, Morgan Stanley, JP Morgan, and Goldman Sachs, and each has found its services either discussed or used in the DSU process in a variety of different contexts, especially in cases involving subsidies and countervailing measures.

could be tied to any particular WTO disputes, one can start with a list of trade disputes and inquire as to what particular firms' interests are at stake.

In table 5-2, I do exactly this by starting with twenty WTO disputes involving a dozen different developing country complainants.[4] The right-hand column lists the names of the exporting firms with direct market access enforcement interests in each case—firms such as Rahimafrooz Batteries from Bangladesh, the Mohsin Match Factory from Pakistan, the Tubac steel company from Guatemala, and April Fine pulp and paper company from Indonesia. The firms on this list do not have the name recognition of the Cokes, Microsofts, and Toyotas of table 5-1, and indeed most of these firms would be completely unrecognizable to even the closest follower of trade policy matters. However, these firms have one important thing in common with those listed in table 5-1: they too were somehow able to engage their governments to enforce their foreign market access rights at the WTO, even if they were exporting from a country that was small or relatively poor.

This chapter describes the step-by-step and actor-by-actor process of how WTO dispute settlement works for both the well-known and the lesser-known companies involved in international trade. I use a basic descriptive model of WTO self-enforcement that I refer to as the *extended litigation process* (ELP). While any particular WTO dispute must be grounded in enforceable WTO commitments and disciplines and thus have legal merit, not surprisingly the "WTO law" at issue in any particular dispute is only the tip of the iceberg. Indeed, access to masterful knowledge of WTO law is a necessary but insufficient condition for exporters to use the WTO dispute settlement process effectively to self-enforce their access to foreign markets.

This chapter has multiple purposes. First, I describe the complexity of the WTO's extended litigation process and the many private and public actors that must participate to make it work as a means of enforcing exporters' access to foreign markets. Many find the ELP frustrating, but for predictable reasons. Economists discover that it is not only about economic incentives, lawyers discover that it is not only about the law, and political specialists discover that it is not only about domestic or international political trade-offs. The ELP is itself equal parts economics, law, and politics, and thus it can achieve a policy objective such as self-enforcing foreign market access only when these three elements work together.

---

4. A detailed discussion of all of the formal WTO disputes listed in this table and referenced throughout this book is not provided. Appendix table A-1 presents the full list of disputes, including their formal WTO names, identified in the book. The WTO's website contains detailed information on each dispute, and the WTO itself now also provides free, online one-page summaries of the Panel and Appellate Body report rulings for each dispute that has reached the stage of obtaining legal rulings. See WTO (2008b).

Table 5-2. *Developing Country Firms and WTO Trade Disputes*

WTO dispute (complainants)	Examples of exporting firms involved in WTO disputes[a]
Peru–Provisional Anti-Dumping Duties on Vegetable Oils from Argentina (Argentina)	Nidera SA, Molinos Río de la Plata SA, Aceitera General Deheza SA
US–Oil Country Tubular Goods Sunset Reviews (Argentina)	Siderca
India–Anti-Dumping Measure on Batteries from Bangladesh (Bangladesh)	Rahimafrooz Batteries (and Bangladesh Accumulator & Battery Manufacturers Association)
Argentina–Poultry Anti-Dumping Duties (Brazil)	Sadia SA, Avipal SA, Avicultura e Agropecuaria
EC–Tube or Pipe Fittings (Brazil)	Industria de Fundicao Tupy Ltda.
Mexico–Provisional Anti-Dumping Measure on Electric Transformers (Brazil)	Ansaldo Coemsa SA, Trafo Equipamentos Elétricos SA, Toshiba Do Brasil SA
US–Countervailing Duties on Certain Carbon Steel Products from Brazil (Brazil)	CSN, USIMINAS, and COSIPA
US–Definitive Anti-Dumping and Countervailing Duties on Certain Products from China (China)	Over three dozen Chinese firms from four different industries
Trinidad and Tobago–Anti-Dumping Measures on Pasta from Costa Rica (Costa Rica)	Roma Prince SA
Mexico–Steel Pipes and Tubes (Guatemala)	Tubac SA
EC–Anti-Dumping Duties on Certain Flat Rolled Iron or Non Alloy Steel Products from India (India) *US–Steel Plate* (India)	Essar Steel, Steel Authority of India Limited
EC–Bed Linen (India)	Anglo French Textiles, Madhu Industries Ltd, Omkar Exports, Prakash Cotton Mills Ltd, The Bombay Dyeing & Manufacturing Co. Ltd, Nowrosjee Wadia & Sons Ltd
South Africa–Anti-Dumping Duties on Certain Pharmaceutical Products from India (India)	M/S Randaxy Laboratories Ltd
Korea–Certain Paper (Indonesia)	Sinar Mas Group companies (Indah Kiat, Pindo Deli, and Tjiwi Kimia), April Fine
Guatemala–Cement I (Mexico) *Guatemala–Cement II* (Mexico) *Ecuador–Definitive Anti-Dumping Measure on Cement from Mexico* (Mexico)	Cemex SA

(continued)

Table 5-2 (*continued*)

WTO dispute (complainants)	Examples of exporting firms involved in WTO disputes[a]
US–Anti-Dumping Measures on Cement (Mexico)	Cemex SA
Egypt–Matches (Pakistan)	Mohsin Match Factory Ltd, Khyber Match Factory Ltd
US–Provisional Anti-Dumping Measures on Shrimp from Thailand (Thailand)	Andaman Seafood, Chanthaburi Seafoods, Chanthaburi Frozen Food, Phattana Seafood, S.C.C. Frozen Seafood, Thai I-Mei Frozen Foods, Thailand Fishery Cold Storage Public, Thai International Seafood, The Union Frozen Products, Wales & Company Universe, Y2K Frozen Food
Egypt–Steel Rebar (Turkey)	Habas, Diler, Colakoglu, ICDAS, IDC, Ekinciler

Source: Global Antidumping Database, Bown (2009a).

a. Firm names linked to WTO disputes compiled by the author via official WTO dispute settlement documentation or in national government documents.

Whereas the last chapter considered data at the macrolevel (country and industry) on how the dispute settlement process is used, this chapter reveals that at the level of the firm, the process has many additional complexities. I use the ELP model to identify how developed countries have implemented their means of self-enforcement in practice. This provides a useful benchmark for efforts to use this model to identify hurdles facing developing countries that prevent them from accessing WTO enforcement. Finally, I use this model for much of the remainder of this book to identify reform strategies to fill in existing gaps affecting developing country access to the self-enforcement process.

In the next section, I begin by applying what is known about the firms and industries that engage in international trade and are thus the commercial interests at the heart of WTO self-enforcement. I identify what will turn out to be the key issue: to engage the ELP, firms must overcome the costs associated with self-enforcing foreign market access for their products. In the second section, I describe the basic six-step extended litigation process of enforcing WTO commitments. In the third section, I take the perspective of these commercial firm interests and explain how the ELP occurs in practice, distinguishing between the incremental costs of self-enforcement that arise at each step. Admittedly this section draws primarily from the more frequent and transparent use of the process by exporting firms, industry associations, and policymakers in *developed* economies. Therefore, the fourth section draws a first set of lessons identifying the specific hurdles that confront *developing* country firms and policymakers in using the ELP.

Firms Involved in International Trade and WTO Disputes and the Fixed Costs of Exporting

Before turning to a discussion of the actual WTO dispute settlement process and examples of the firms and countries involved, it is useful to consider what is known about the firms that export. This is important because WTO dispute settlement is used only by those firms and countries that self-select into participating, such as those listed in tables 5-1 and 5-2. If the ultimate goal is to infer something about hurdles preventing other firms and countries from making it onto these lists, one needs to know more about firms that were also eligible to participate but did not. A useful first step is to compare firms that engage in trade with those that do not. Without exporting firms with commercial interests at stake pushing for the initiation of cases, their resolution, and the subsequent enforcement of foreign market access, government policymakers are not likely to pursue disputes.

Exporting Firms and Productivity

Which are the firms that export? One conclusion from recent economic research is that exporting firms are different from firms that do not export. While this may seem obvious, until recently economists did not have evidence to confirm this hypothesis. The main reason is that data were not systematically available to substantiate or refute the claim. As firm-level data have become increasingly available to researchers over the last fifteen years, economists are learning more about the ways in which firms that export are different as well as the determinants of why they have these differences.

The first interesting piece of evidence is that not all firms engage in exporting.[5] Indeed, in many countries, firms that export are much more the exception than the rule. While this may seem obvious if one is thinking about firms across industries within a country, the idea is less obvious when one begins to think about firms within the same exporting industry in a country, that is, an industry in which the country has a comparative advantage. A country's conditions may

---

5. Recent surveys include Bernard and others (2007) and also Tybout (2000). The empirical scholarship in this area that is surveyed by these articles has been accompanied by a simultaneous development in the theoretical scholarship in international trade associated with Melitz (2003)—sometimes referred to as the "new new trade theory" or the "heterogeneous firms theory." Firms are heterogeneous in these theories typically through their productivity differences.

be favorable for exporting products of a given industry because of access to land or other natural resources; because of skilled or unskilled labor abundance and physical capital; or in the case of knowledge-intensive industries, because of good institutions, financial markets, and enforcement of intellectual property rights. Firm-level data reveal that only some firms from the industry with the comparative advantage actually export. Even in the most developed economies, the majority of firms in a comparative advantage industry produce only for the domestic market and do not export.

Before turning to the natural question of causation raised by this stylized fact, economists continued to examine the data to identify other differences between exporting and nonexporting firms. First, not only do most firms not export, but the firms that do export tend to be quite distinctive in their characteristics. For example, these companies are typically quite large relative to nonexporting firms, as measured by such indicators as sales or employment. The larger scale of such firms may also explain why they are so well known to consumers (see again table 5-1). Furthermore, from society's perspective, a positive aspect of exporting firms is that typically they pay higher wages than other comparable firms.

An additional important feature consistently captured by the data is that exporting firms are more productive than nonexporters. To economists, higher productivity—producing more goods and services with fewer inputs—is important not only for reasons of basic efficiency, but also because of the tight empirical linkages between productivity and other important economic variables such as economic growth and thus living standards. As Nobel Prize–winner Paul Krugman put it, "Productivity isn't everything, but in the long run it is almost everything. A country's ability to improve its standard of living over time depends almost entirely on its ability to raise its output per worker."[6]

Yet the stylized fact that exporting firms are more productive than nonexporting firms does raise a chicken-and-egg question. Does the activity of exporting make firms productive, or are higher-productivity firms more likely to self-select into exporting?[7] The early evidence has been that high-productivity firms self-selected into exporting. Until recently, there was little evidence that becoming an exporter provided an additional boost to productivity to firms after they started exporting.[8]

6. See Krugman (1990, p. 9).
7. This question is, of course, important for many reasons including the implications for policy. On the one hand, if the mere activity of exporting generates productivity improvements, there is a case for policies that encourage exporting. On the other hand, if higher-productivity firms select into exporting but the process of exporting does not make them more productive, there is less potential benefit from policies that encourage exporting.
8. Studies that provide some evidence for learning by exporting include Van Biesebroeck (2005) for sub-Saharan African firms and De Loecker (2007) for Slovenian firms. Lileeva and Trefler

Overcoming the Cost of Exporting

For the purpose of this book, the answer to what makes an exporter is critical because it helps identify the natural question from the perspective of WTO self-enforcement: What makes an exporter able to self-enforce WTO market access? The emphasis on exporting firms and productivity is thus an important first step. Knowing that firms self-select into exporting on the basis of productivity reveals that fixed exporting costs are an important hurdle that only the most productive firms appear able to overcome.

The next question to tackle concerns the relative importance of various dimensions to the cost of exporting. The basic economic component of the overall cost of supplying a product beyond the domestic market to an export market may include such costs as the establishment of new networks, learning about new customer tastes and preferences, additional advertising and marketing to make the firm's products known in the new market, as well as shipping and other higher transport costs. The cost associated with the decision to export may also have components tied to each additional foreign market to be served. For example, a U.S. exporting firm faces a fixed cost of learning about the EC market and a separate cost of learning about the Japanese market. In addition, the cost may also be tied to each potential product that a multiproduct firm seeks to export.

When it comes to WTO enforcement activity, why is it necessary to understand the perspective provided by the underlying cost of exporting? First, the cost of exporting is likely to be affected not only by purely economic components, but by policies as well. For example, different foreign markets will have different applied import tariffs. Therefore, the firm's cost of shipping an identical product to different foreign markets may differ for foreign trade policy reasons.

Nevertheless, even many trade economists might suggest that applied import tariffs are a relatively unimportant problem and justify this by pointing to the differential in the tariff figures presented in table 1-1 (tariffs in 1931) compared with those in table 2-1 (tariffs in 2007). They would argue that yes, in 1931, when the average import tariff in the United States was 35 percent and major European markets hovered around 40 percent, overcoming that part of the cost

---

(2007) studied Canada's trade liberalization experience under the Canada–U.S. Free Trade Agreement and also found some evidence of this effect, but only for firms that were low-productivity at the beginning of this agreement. Most earlier studies fail to find evidence of additional productivity gains after entry into exporting: these studies include Bernard and Jensen (1995, 1999) for U.S. firms; Roberts and Tybout (1997) for Colombian firms; Clerides, Lach, and Tybout (1998) for Mexican and Moroccan firms; Aw, Chen, and Roberts (2001) for Taiwanese firms; Eaton, Kortum, and Kramarz (2006) for French firms; Bernard and Wagner (2001) for German firms; Trefler (2004) for Canadian firms.

to exporting might have been difficult. But certainly if today's U.S. and EC tariffs are not 35 or 40 percent but only 3.5 to 5.2 percent on average, that is a much smaller cost for a potential exporting firm to overcome. Relative to the exporting costs associated with new product development, shipping, networking, and advertising, an additional 3.5 to 5.2 percent cost disadvantage (because of tariffs) in foreign markets relative to domestic competition is tiny and in many instances can easily be overcome by cost advantages in other areas associated with underlying comparative advantage.[9] In the current global system of international commerce, aren't costs associated with trade policy almost irrelevant?

The answer is no. Even if the United States and the EC dropped all of their applied import tariffs and bindings to zero percent, there would still be costs of exporting to these markets associated with trade policies. Even if countries were to adopt zero percent MFN tariffs as their WTO commitments, exporting firms would still need to spend resources to monitor and self-enforce their access to these foreign markets in ways fundamentally different from the costs of monitoring their own domestic markets.[10]

Even with low or zero MFN tariff bindings, innovative policymakers can use other trade and domestic policies to impose additional costs on imports from a foreign firm that they do not impose on goods produced by their own firms. From the exporting firm's perspective, these costs can be different from what it has to pay to sell the same good in other foreign markets as well as its own domestic market. One prevalent example currently in use by many WTO member countries is the exporting firm–specific policy of antidumping.[11] A second

9. For example, in a recent review of economic research on the importance of transport costs in international trade, Hummels (2007, p. 136) notes, "Studies examining customs data consistently find that transportation costs pose a barrier to trade at least as large as, and frequently larger than, tariffs. . . . Transport expenditures on the median good were half as much as tariff duties for U.S. imports in 1958 (Waters 1970) and equal to tariff duties in 1965 (Finger and Yeats 1976). By 2004, aggregate expenditures on shipping for total imports were three times higher than aggregate tariff duties paid. For the median individual shipment in U.S. imports in 2004, exporters paid $9 in transportation costs for every $1 they paid in tariff duties. Moreover, the United States is actually a notable outlier in that it pays much less for transportation than other countries. In 2000, aggregate transportation expenditures for major Latin America countries were 1.5 to 2.5 times higher than for the United States."

10. Furthermore, as table 2-1 also reveals, not all tariffs are currently low, even when focusing on just the U.S. and EC import markets. There is substantial tariff dispersion ("tariff peaks"), and high tariffs remain in sectors of interest to many exporting firms in developing countries such as agriculture and clothing.

11. First, even merely initiating an antidumping investigation imposes substantial export market-specific compliance costs on the firm. The firm must collect and provide accounting and sales information to foreign investigating authorities and thus allocate company resources to a new and costly activity. Second, in many such investigations certain firms (for example, firms in the steel industry) may have a number of their different exported products investigated. Finally, any new import restriction that is imposed is a firm-specific antidumping duty and thus is a new cost to that firm for supplying a particular product to this market.

example would be product-specific costs of complying with technical, sanitary, or phytosanitary standards that foreign governments may impose, partially with the protectionist intent of limiting imports. Then, there are safeguards, special safeguards, countervailing duties, and a number of other loopholes that countries use to try to get around WTO commitments of keeping MFN tariffs low. And these are only the most prevalent policies of today. The world is likely to see new policy tools as innovative policymakers with protectionist intentions continue to look for ways around the international rules in order to impose additional costs on foreign firms. These innovations will occur because the underlying political and economic incentives for such unilateral actions are virtually impossible to eliminate, as I described in chapter 1. This creates an ongoing need not only for an agreement like the WTO, but also for constant monitoring and efficient access to the process of enforcement of that agreement.

Self-enforcement is the mechanism through which WTO market access commitments are maintained across countries in the current system. And although self-enforcement is typically portrayed theoretically as something that takes place between governments—for example, the United States keeps its markets open to EC exporters because shutting them could lead to the EC shutting its own markets and thus adversely affecting U.S. exporters—governments are not omniscient, nor do they have full control over the self-enforcement process. As I describe in detail in the next section, exporting firms have a substantial role to play. Firms that can cover the cost of engaging in the WTO's extended litigation process to protect their market access interests are the ones that can enforce the agreement.

The main point is that the cost of enforcing a WTO commitment in a given foreign market for each exported product is likely to be an important component of a firm's total cost of exporting—even, or perhaps especially, when applied tariffs or bindings are low or nonexistent. Although the importance of self-enforcement will vary across firms, industries, countries, and time, in many instances the cost is likely to be substantial. The theory on these costs is also consistent with the empirical evidence discussed in chapter 4 that exporting firms and their government policymakers are more likely to initiate formal WTO dispute settlement actions when self-enforcing larger amounts of foreign market access.[12] The existence of these costs of enforcing the commitments that other countries have taken on in the WTO system also contributes to understanding why not all firms will export, and why the firms that do export are likely to be quite different from those that do not export. The section below on

---

12. See again the discussion of the results of Bown (2005a, 2005b) and Francois, Horn, and Kaunitz (2008) in the section in chapter 4 discussing empirical studies of WTO dispute settlement initiation and participation.

the six steps of the extended litigation process highlights the particular elements of the cost of exporting associated with the WTO enforcement process.

The Exporting Firms Involved in WTO Enforcement in Light of the Theory

In light of the importance attributable to the cost of enforcing foreign market access detailed below, it is perhaps not surprising that WTO trade disputes typically boil down to conflicting commercial interests that have large, exporting firms on at least one side. Table 5-1 presents many brand-name firms, predominantly from developed countries, whose commercial interests are at stake in WTO disputes. The global brands that dominate the list are likely the largest and most productive exporting companies in their industries. Because of their presence on this dispute settlement list, these firms not only have overcome the fixed cost of exporting but also the costs of attempting to enforce their export market access interest at the WTO.

Nevertheless, as table 5-2 again indicates, these global brands are not the only firms using the WTO to enforce foreign market access. Many lesser-known exporting firms also manage to overcome the costs not only of exporting goods and services but also of engaging their governments in the enforcement of foreign market access rights to ensure their ability to export. This suggests that the costs associated with WTO enforcement are not uniform, but they are likely to vary substantially across contexts and especially across the products, firms, industries, countries, and policies involved.

While the list of firm names from table 5-2 is deliberately constructed by focusing on exporters adversely affected by a particular type of foreign policy—antidumping or countervailing duties—it is worth highlighting other relevant insights from the table. First, the countries that imposed these potentially WTO-inconsistent trade restrictions include both developed (the United States and the EC) and developing (Argentina, Egypt, India, Peru, Mexico, South Africa, and Trinidad and Tobago) WTO members.[13] This again confirms one of the fundamental points in chapter 4: exporting firms from developing countries want foreign market access enforced in both developed and developing country markets.

Furthermore, some of the exporting firms listed in table 5-2 are from very small developing countries (for example, Costa Rica and Guatemala), confirming

13. Identifying adversely affected foreign firms in antidumping cases is more straightforward than in other instances because imposed antidumping measures (such as duties or price undertakings) are typically firm-specific and based on the foreign government's calculation of a firm-specific dumping margin. This information is typically available from national government sources, and much of it is compiled in the "Global Antidumping Database"; see Bown (2009a).

that the large developing countries such as Brazil, China, and India are not the only countries interested in enforcing their foreign market access. Some of these firms are even from least developed economies (Bangladesh and Pakistan), though there are fewer examples of countries at this same economic level that stand up for their firms' foreign market access rights. Finally, the dozens of listed firms are from a wide array of industries, including foodstuffs (agriculture and seafood), pharmaceuticals, steel, textiles, and other manufacturing sectors.

To summarize, a firm's ability to enter into exporting is partly determined by whether it is a high-productivity firm and can thus overcome the fixed cost of exporting. Nevertheless, even if the firm can overcome the costs associated with establishing foreign networks and successfully marketing particular products to foreign consumers, in many instances, the additional cost of WTO enforcement must be overcome if it seeks to continue exporting. Political and economic forces in foreign countries continually seek to cut off competition from abroad, even in the face of trade agreements and even if it means violating WTO rules.

The next section describes the costs associated with using the WTO self-enforcement process. Then I analyze how firms, industries, and their governments have adopted strategies to address these costs to thus improve their ability to self-enforce their foreign market access rights. The remainder of this book explores the nature of these costs as well as ways to most efficiently target them to address the WTO self-enforcing needs of firms in developing countries.

The Six Steps of the WTO's Extended Litigation Process

Before discussing the WTO's self-enforcement process, I need to establish the setting. Suppose an exporting firm in a WTO member country has WTO-protected rights in a foreign market. The foreign government has bound its import tariff at a level that is sufficiently low for the exporting firm to have profitable export sales in this foreign market. And then, suddenly, the foreign government implements a new policy that is both WTO illegal (if litigated at the WTO and ruled upon) and that substantially reduces the exporting firm's foreign market access.[14]

Next, I use the approach introduced by Bown and Hoekman to identify the six fundamental steps of the WTO's extended litigation process and to describe the cost of WTO enforcement that arises at each step along the way.[15] As will be

14. To be clear, exporting firms and their government policymakers can also use the dispute resolution process to address another member's failure to sufficiently implement a market-opening commitment. I discuss in more detail below the additional difficulties that these sorts of disputes present when compared with disputes over policy backsliding (reneging on a market-opening commitment that was once implemented).

15. Bown and Hoekman (2005).

Figure 5-1. *The WTO's Extended Litigation Process*

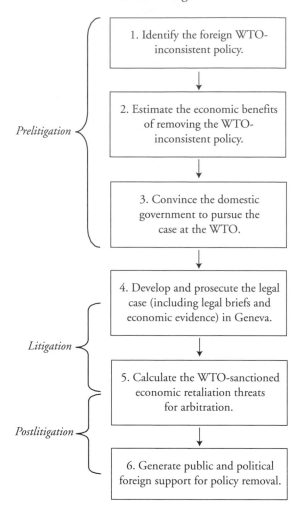

Source: Bown and Hoekman (2005), adapted from figure 1.

clear, the ELP involves much more than just the litigation of issues surrounding WTO law. The extended litigation process is illustrated in figure 5-1.

Step 1. Identify the foreign WTO-inconsistent policy.

I begin step 1 of the process with an individual I call Michele Brown. Michele works for an exporting firm in a WTO member country, and she is the firm's point person on the WTO and foreign market access. Specifically, Michele is in charge of recognizing that a foreign government has undertaken some WTO-illegal action that takes away the market access rights that the firm expected, and as a result the company has suffered lost sales (exports) and profits in that foreign market.

After Michele recognizes this, she must convince her firm that the underlying cause of lost foreign market access really is a violation of WTO rules and not some other cause that was legal under WTO commitments. For the cause of lost market access to be challengeable under the WTO dispute settlement process, it cannot be a factor that legitimately reduces foreign demand for the firm's product. For example, it cannot be a change in foreign consumer tastes or income or the introduction of a legitimately lower-priced or higher-quality foreign rival product. It also cannot be a factor that legitimately and adversely affects Michele's firm's own supply, such as the rising cost of inputs, a labor strike, bad management decisions, or a natural disaster.

The cost of the first step to an exporting country associated with WTO enforcement is therefore the firm's cost of employing Michele Brown—a woman with technical expertise in understanding the firm's legal rights and also the economic determinants of what affects her firm's exports.

Step 2. Estimate the economic benefits of removing the WTO-inconsistent policy.

In step 2 of the process, Michele needs concrete estimates of the potential economic benefit if the firm were to pursue a WTO enforcement action. What are the lost sales and profits to the firm associated with the lost foreign market access? How worthwhile is this to the company vis-à-vis its other priorities—for example, expanding into new markets, developing new products—for which it would need access to those same economic resources? Simply acquiring the information to make this case is also costly, as Michele requires resources to collect and organize these data to make a convincing argument.

Furthermore, since the main imperative of any profit-maximizing firm is to allocate resources efficiently in pursuit of its short- and long-term objectives of selling goods and services, Michele must not only have the capability of recognizing the violation of the foreign market access (knowledge of the law), how big a problem it is (knowledge of the economics), but she also must have sufficient clout within the firm to shift resources toward doing something about it.

The second cost associated with WTO enforcement, therefore, is the resources that are necessary for Michele Brown to make the convincing legal and economic case within her firm that the issue is something worth pursuing outside of the firm.

Step 3. Convince the domestic government to pursue the case at the WTO.

Once Michele has convinced her company that it is worth spending resources to attempt to engage the enforcement process to preserve foreign market access, the next step moves beyond her firm. In step 3, Michele's company must work to convince its government's policymakers to bring up the issue with its trading partner's government counterparts. Although this may happen through informal or formal government-level talks and negotiations, the important criterion is the threat point under the WTO if the negotiations break down. If the issue cannot be resolved between the two countries' governments bilaterally, Michele's government can bring it to the WTO and initiate a formal dispute settlement proceeding, which is step 4. However, Michele's government must decide to bring the issue to the WTO, as only governments, not private industries or individuals, have legal standing to pursue and respond to disputes.

Before considering the next stage, in which the government pursues the case at the WTO, I identify the costs to Michele's firm in convincing its government to take up its case with the foreign government. Step 3 of the ELP can prove very costly.

First, many government policy decisions are driven not only by special interests but also by what is in the overall interest of the country. Therefore, it is likely that Michele's firm will have to provide convincing information on the expected national payoff. For example, what are the aggregate benefits to the country of such a dispute versus the national costs? The firm must translate its expected market access gain (increased firm-level export sales and profits) that would result from the dispute into other measures of economic well-being that matter to publicly accountable government policymakers: specifically, what employment will be created and wages paid. Furthermore, for the expected payoff information provided to the government to be accurate and comprehensive, the expected size of the increased foreign market access needs to take into account the probability that the foreign country will actually reform and comply with future WTO rulings. Providing an accurate probability on foreign reform requires knowledge and expertise that go well beyond economics and law, where Michele's Brown expertise thus far lies. Her firm is now also reliant on technical expertise on the political state of affairs in the potential respondent country, an additional expertise that is, of course, costly to acquire.

Second, depending on the type of WTO violation that the foreign country has implemented, Michele and her firm may also need the political backing of the full industry to convince the government to push the case forward. For example, if the foreign policy was a trade restriction that affected all firms in the industry equally in Michele's country, it may be necessary to organize many firms to engage the government collectively to act on their mutual behalf.[16] And

16. This particular hurdle is less relevant when the WTO violation that is the cause of the lost foreign market access is an exporting firm–specific policy such as an antidumping duty. However, in this instance, a different cost may arise. If Michele's firm was hit with an illegal foreign

yet, because coordination efforts impose a cost on each firm, and the potential benefit from government action would be received by all of them, there is a collective action problem.[17] The high cost to Michele of organizing a large, diffuse industry that would lead to a low payoff to an individual firm (albeit perhaps a high payoff to the collective industry) is a classic example of what economists call the "free rider" problem. In such an instance, the government decision to engage the WTO to self-enforce the interests of many of its exporting firms is an example of that government providing its firms with a public good.

Finally, even if Michele's firm and others in her industry can overcome these costs and make a compelling case to their government, there may remain a divergence between private, firm-level interests and the interests of Michele's government. Because the government is the ultimate gatekeeper to initiating talks with the foreign government, its priorities and resource constraints will affect whether an enforcement action at the WTO is pursued. Thus, even if the case is compelling and indicative of a potentially worthwhile dispute from the industry's perspective, the government may decide against pursuing it at step 3 of the process.

What are these potential other priorities and resource constraints? There are at least two worth mentioning.

First, the government may have multiple exporting industries clamoring to use WTO enforcement services in support of their individual interests at any given point in time. As all governments are resource constrained in terms of the expertise they can allocate to WTO litigation in step 4, they must prioritize. Ultimately governments will choose to pursue the most valuable cases, leaving some with a positive expected payoff (albeit with a smaller relative payoff) on the table.

Second, a government may have other priorities because of the fear of foreign government retribution in some area outside of this particular enforcement action. The foreign government may have the ability to make extra-WTO counterretaliation threats (such as unilateral withdrawal of tariff preferences or development assistance) that, although not likely to affect Michele's firm or industry directly, may have substantial ramifications for overall economic activity in

---

antidumping duty while other firms in the industry were not, these other firms may lobby the government against Michele's proposed case to persuade it from pursuing a dispute over this issue at the WTO. Thus there is also the possibility that what may be in the interest of Michele's particular firm and even the country (in terms of net welfare) may not be in the overall interest of all of the other firms in her firm's industry.

17. See Olson (1965). Relative to the small gains that each firm receives, it may be costly for them to coordinate and organize themselves to speak with a single voice behind the potential enforcement action. Thus, because each firm waits for another to pay the costs, knowing that it cannot be excluded from the benefit, in the end, the industry is insufficiently politically organized.

Michele's country. The domestic government may also be concerned that the foreign government might be motivated to file its own counterchallenge under the WTO—the "living in glass houses" analogy—especially if the domestic government applies the same sort of policies that it would be challenging in the foreign country. This issue is not necessarily of concern to Michele's company if it is not one of the firms benefiting from those policies at home.[18]

Step 4. Develop and prosecute the legal case in Geneva.

If the first three hurdles of the process are cleared, step 4 involves the actual WTO litigation and the prosecution of the case in Geneva. The work undertaken at this stage is typically a mix of lawyers and economists, with representatives of both the government and industry working together to argue the briefs and provide the economic and other evidence in support of their case. Michele's company may choose to hire a private law firm, even if the actual arguing in Geneva is ultimately undertaken by government lawyers and officials. It will turn out that the cost to pursuing the actual litigation in Geneva can vary substantially depending on the complexity of the particular legal area at stake, the necessary supporting evidence, and a number of other factors.

Step 5. Calculate the WTO-sanctioned economic retaliation threats.

Even if Michele's firm and government lawyers win the important legal arguments in the actual Dispute Settlement Understanding (DSU) proceedings and the legal outcome of step 4 is positive, the enforcement process is far from over. Step 5 of the ELP refers to the beginning of the "postlitigation phase" of WTO enforcement. Policy reform by the respondent as required by its compliance with WTO rulings is not automatic in this system, and in many instances, the complainant country in the dispute must take explicit steps to achieve it. These steps include the threat and possible implementation of retaliation.

A set of WTO arbiters establish limits on the amount of retaliation that the complainant country is allowed to threaten and implement. The limits are typically attempts to equilibrate the future loss of market access (associated with the retaliation) with an estimate of the size of the lost market access at issue in the underlying dispute.[19] In cases in which the violation has been a WTO-illegal

18. Governments may also hesitate to initiate WTO disputes over issues that are simultaneously the source of sensitive political negotiation between members during an ongoing multilateral round.

19. The retaliation limits presented by WTO arbiters in formal disputes taking place between 1995 and 2007 are again listed in table 4-6. For a complete discussion of the economics underlying the way the WTO arbiters have arrived at these limits in practice, see Bown and Ruta (2010). The collection of research in Bown and Pauwelyn (2010) presents other legal and political elements of the retaliation threats and retaliation episodes in the first ten WTO disputes (involving seventeen complainant countries) to reach this stage of the legal process.

subsidy, arbiters have calculated the retaliation limit to be equal to the size of the subsidy benefit that the domestic firms have received as opposed to the lost trade that foreign exporting firms suffered. While the limit imposed on overall retaliation is one important element that may affect the complainant's ability to get the respondent to comply, an equally important element is how the complainant country chooses to implement its retaliation threat. In this area, the WTO process has so far imposed few constraints.

In step 5, Michele's government must therefore identify "targets" for retaliation threats intended to increase the likelihood of compliance by the offending country. WTO authorization not only to make threats but also to follow through with retaliation serves to notify the respondent government of the (soon-to-be) explicit costs that are associated with its continued failure to reform.

Products on these retaliation lists typically have a number of important political and economic characteristics, and identifying the "right" products may require again a costly acquisition of information. For example, because foreign compliance is the complainant country's ultimate goal in the case, a retaliation list may be constructed to target goods that are politically sensitive (to help catalyze reformers in the offending country) while minimizing the damage to the complainant country's own domestic economy (and thus minimizing domestic political backlash). At step 5 of the ELP, Michele's government requires costly expertise in economics and politics in addition to law to develop a retaliation list that will target just the right products.

Step 6. Generate public and political foreign support for policy removal.
The retaliation list drawn up in step 5 may suffice to mobilize political pressure for reform in the offending country. In such instances, step 5 alone may result in compliance and the end of the enforcement process for this particular dispute.

But in instances in which the retaliation list is not sufficient to induce compliance, there may be a need for one last step. Although effective retaliation lists drawn up in step 5 and the international obligation of the WTO ruling achieved in step 4 can help make the environment fertile for reform in the respondent country, some disputes require more. In particular, step 6 involves engaging other political forces to generate a public outcry within the offending country to create the momentum for policy reform to achieve WTO compliance.

For example, in democracies it may be necessary to use public relations and sophisticated media campaigns within the offending country to alert the voting public and politicians about both the internal and external adverse effects of their own policies. It may be effective to inform the public about the detrimental impact of the original policy on people in other countries. Furthermore, failure to remove the policy may also harm innocent bystanders at home through the effects of WTO-authorized retaliation on the country's own exporting industries and those who work for them. However, it is costly and complicated to fund such publicity initiatives.

To summarize, the six-step WTO extended litigation process is lengthy and complex. For exporting firms, the resources they may have spent to lobby for a negotiated improvement in foreign market access may have led to low foreign tariffs, but these low tariffs and the implied foreign market access are not guaranteed. The probability of the continuation of foreign market access implied by low tariffs depends on the subsequent willingness to spend ongoing and additional resources to monitor and enforce member compliance with WTO commitments.

The costs of the ELP include specialized inputs by firms and government policymakers, as well as experts in economic incentives, law, and foreign politics. Some of these costs are clearly borne by the exporting firm and others are clearly borne by the government. For a third set of costs it is not clear on whom the cost burden should fall, which thus raises an additional cost of coordination and uncertainty. Nevertheless, the first-order effect of failure to pay the costs of WTO enforcement falls squarely on the exporting firm, through the lost sales and lost profits associated with lost foreign market access.

How Costly Is It for Firms, Industries, and Countries to Use the WTO Enforcement Process?

The last section described the six-step extended litigation process and identified the cumulative costs of self-enforcing foreign market access under the WTO. Here I describe the process and these costs in the context of actual WTO disputes. The following discussion reveals that there is substantial variation across firms, industries, governments, and WTO-inconsistent policies as to these costs. There is no one-size-fits-all approach to learn from the firms, industries, and governments that do manage to overcome the costs of engaging the ELP. This substantial variation helps to identify the relative sizes and the binding nature of these costs.

The Cost of Monitoring and Information Collection

Steps 1 and 2 of the ELP are purely informational. In the example, the first step was that Michele Brown, who worked for the exporting firm, recognized that the firm's foreign market access had been reduced because of a WTO-illegal policy and not something else. The second step was Michele's acquisition of economic and political information to supplement her legal knowledge. Combining these data, she was able to determine that it was in the firm's profit-maximizing interest to spend the resources to do something about the problem. The cost to a firm seeking to acquire the necessary information for these first two steps can vary because of a number of factors.

Factor 1. What was the form of the WTO violation?

The first factor affecting the cost of acquiring knowledge of a WTO violation is the nature of the foreign policy that has caused the loss of market access. In some instances, the cost of acquiring knowledge can be extremely low because the firm is actually notified that it is being hit with an explicit new trade restriction. A prominent example is when an exporting firm is targeted with a new but potentially WTO-illegal antidumping duty.[20] Because of the WTO's Agreement on Antidumping and thus rules having nothing to do with dispute settlement, the foreign government had to notify the exporting firm that it was being investigated so that the firm could participate in the process by submitting potentially exculpatory data on its sales, prices, or costs.

Consider again the list of global brand-name firms found table 5-1. Firms like Archer Daniels Midland and Cargill, which were the U.S. commercial interests behind the *Mexico–Corn Syrup* dispute, did not find it costly to acquire the basic information that they had a potential WTO enforcement action to pursue. The reason is that they were notified as part of the Mexican antidumping investigation process, and so they knew that the new antidumping duty was the source of their lost sales, profits, and access to the Mexican market. The same is true for firms in table 5-1 such as Samsung Electronics, Hyundai Electronics, and LG Semicon, which were the Korean commercial interests behind the *US–DRAMS* dispute over new U.S. antidumping import restrictions imposed on their semiconductor exports.

A policy like antidumping whereby the foreign policymakers are required to notify the exporting firms of the source of their lost market access is at one end of the spectrum. One step away from antidumping measures are other measures such as a global safeguard import restriction and other explicit new trade restrictions about which the foreign government is required to alert WTO member governments, even if it is not necessary to notify any particular exporting firm. Consider, for example, the 2002 U.S. steel safeguard import restriction that resulted in *US–Steel Safeguards,* a dispute initiated by nine other WTO member governments. The U.S. government did not notify individually the dozens of steel-producing firms that lost market share because their exports to the U.S. market were adversely affected by the steel safeguard import restriction. But because the WTO's Agreement on Safeguards requires that the United States

---

20. But a second component in establishing a potential case is that the antidumping measure must be inconsistent with WTO rules. The WTO does allow for the imposition of antidumping duties under certain conditions, but virtually every antidumping measure that has been challenged at the DSU by a WTO member has been ruled to violate some aspect of the legal agreement.

conduct a public investigation and notify WTO members of the investigation and the imposition of any new import restrictions, it was not very costly for the exporting firms, whose commercial interests where affected by the WTO dispute, to identify the source of their lost market access and to mobilize to do something about it.

Now consider the other end of the spectrum of WTO violations, consisting of actions for which WTO rules do not require the importing country government to notify either the exporting firm or the WTO membership about policy changes. Suppose the lost foreign market access occurs because foreign consumers chose to switch their demand toward another supplier that is able to offer consumers a competing product at a lower price; but the underlying cause of this switch was an incentive created by WTO-inconsistent means. In many instances, for an exporting firm, the acquisition of information concerning the cause of the lost market access would involve a substantial expenditure of resources. One example already discussed in chapter 3 is the Regulation 404 policy, which was at the heart of the *EC–Bananas III* dispute. Although that particular policy implementation was likely well publicized because of the EC's relative transparency and the lobbying involved, when the EC implemented the original policy, WTO rules would not have required the EC to notify banana-exporting firms such as Chiquita and Dole that it was doing so.

More difficult for the exporting firm to observe is a competitor that is able to offer the lower price only because of a WTO-illegal subsidy provided by the foreign competitor's government. Because the rules on reporting subsidies to the WTO are much less stringent than is the case for new import restrictions, Michele Brown is likely to find that in such a case it is much costlier to identify the underlying source of the lost market access. Examples from table 5-1 would be the costs facing firms like Boeing and Airbus or Embraer and Bombardier in the various disputes over whether the U.S., EC, Brazilian, and Canadian governments provided WTO-illegal subsidies to their civil aircraft manufacturers. A second set of examples (not listed in table 5-1) would be the Brazilian exporters of sugar and cotton whose sales and foreign market access have been curtailed by the WTO-illegal subsidies challenged in the *EC–Export Subsidies on Sugar* and *US–Upland Cotton* disputes. Because the rules and requirements for reporting such subsidies to the WTO are not as stringent as those for reporting new antidumping measures or safeguard import restrictions, the adversely affected exporting firms face higher costs for private monitoring or information acquisition to identify the underlying source of the lost market access.

Table 5-1 also identifies examples of a competitor able to offer lower prices because of WTO violations that are even less transparent to the exporting firms than foreign subsidies are. Perhaps the lower price is due to alternative suppliers effectively stealing intellectual property through lax government enforcement of copyright and patent laws. These alternative suppliers (for example, DVD pirates) are what has been alleged in the *China–Intellectual Property Rights* dispute, which the United States brought on behalf of the commercial interests of the major Hollywood film studios and the Motion Picture Association of America (MPAA).

Alternatively, the lower price may be due to regulatory hurdles imposed on foreign exporters that are not imposed on domestic competitors; such standards or technical barriers are commonly justified as consumer protection measures, but in fact they are nothing more than disguised protectionism. Such are the allegations by the financial services firms of Thomson-Reuters, Bloomberg, Dow-Jones, and Pearson, which the United States, the EC, and Canada raised in the *China–Measures Affecting Financial Information Services and Foreign Financial Information Suppliers* dispute. Another example of lost market access due to a protectionist regulatory hurdle is alleged in *China–Audiovisual Services,* the second dispute that the United States filed with MPAA backing over the distribution of Hollywood movies within China.

An important difference between these latter kinds of disputes and those at the other end of the spectrum is the monitoring cost to the exporting firm. The identity and underlying characteristics of the firms that are able to bring forward WTO disputes over subsidies, intellectual property, and regulatory barriers is potentially quite revealing. Since merely acquiring information that an underlying WTO violation is part of the cause of the firm's lost foreign market access is by itself quite costly, one might expect that these disputes would involve some of the largest and most profitable firms of all of those involved in the WTO enforcement caseload.

Factor 2. Who provides the monitoring and information to the firms?

A second factor affecting the cost to exporting firms of acquiring information about potential WTO violations is the extent to which information is provided either by the private sector or by the public sector. In countries and industries in which WTO enforcement has a longer history, market forces as well as government involvement have already led to a range of burden-sharing alternatives for monitoring.

In many instances, the private sector may offer some monitoring information on potential foreign market access violations to exporting firms that are willing to pay for it. Table 5-3 lists a number of private law firms with significant experience representing corporate client interests in WTO litigation.[21] Although

---

21. Table 5-3 samples some of the major law firms involved in WTO litigation work. Other firms with significant WTO work that are not included in this table include Winston & Strawn (many members of its current trade group were formerly at Willkie Farr & Gallagher) in Washington and Budin & Partners in Geneva. In Brussels, other firms include FratiniVergano and O'Connor and Company.

Table 5-3. *Private Law Firms Providing Counsel in WTO Cases*

Law firm Trade law practice group headquarters	Examples of WTO disputes (client[a])

King & Spalding
Washington
	Guatemala–Cement I (Mexico)
	Guatemala–Cement II (Mexico)
	Korea–Dairy (Korea)
	Thailand–H-Beams (Thailand)
	US–Anti-Dumping Measures on Cement (United States)
	Mexico–Anti-Dumping Measures on Rice (United States)
	US–Countervailing Duty Investigation on DRAMS
	    (United States)
	EC–Countervailing Measures on DRAM Chips
	    (United States)
	Japan–DRAMs (Korea) (United States)

Sidley Austin
Brussels, Geneva, Washington
	EC–Trademarks and Geographical Indications (United
	    States)
	Mexico–Telecoms (United States)
	US–Upland Cotton (Brazil)
	EC–Approval and Marketing of Biotech Products
	    (United States)
	EC–Large Civil Aircraft (EC)
	EC–Large Civil Aircraft (*2nd complaint*) (EC)
	US–Large Civil Aircraft (EC)
	US–Large Civil Aircraft (*2nd complaint*) (EC)
	Brazil–Retreaded Tyres (Brazil)
	EC–Salmon (*Norway*) (Norway)

Steptoe & Johnson Brussels, Washington	*Japan–Alcoholic Beverages II* (EC) *Korea–Alcoholic Beverages* (EC) *Chile–Alcoholic Beverages* (EC) *US–Steel Safeguards* (EC) *US–Softwood Lumber IV* (Canada) *Canada–Wheat Exports and Grain Imports* (Canada) *US–Zeroing (EC)* (EC) *China–Value-Added Tax on Integrated Circuits* (China)
Van Bael & Bellis Brussels, Geneva	*Turkey–Restrictions on Imports of Textile and Clothing Products* (Hong Kong) *Argentina–Ceramic Tiles* (EC) *Egypt–Steel Rebar* (Egypt) *EC–Tube or Pipe Fittings* (Brazil)
Vermulst Verhaeghe & Graafsma Brussels	*Canada–Autos* (Brazil) *EC–Bed Linen* (India) *Korea–Various Measures on Beef* (Korea) *EC–Selected Customs Matters* (EC)

Law firm *Trade law practice group headquarters*	*Examples of WTO disputes (client*[a]*)*
White & Case Geneva, Washington	*US–Upland Cotton* (Benin, Chad) *US–Oil Country Tubular Goods Sunset Reviews* (Argentina) *US–Anti-Dumping Measures on Cement* (Mexico) *US–Anti-Dumping Measures on Oil Country Tubular Goods* (Mexico) *Japan–DRAMs (Korea)* (Japan) *Colombia–Ports of Entry* (Colombia)
WilmerHale Brussels, Washington	*EC–Hormones* (United States) *Korea–Alcoholic Beverages* (Korea) *Chile–Alcoholic Beverages* (Chile) *US–FSC* (United States) *EC–Tariff Preferences* (Andean Community) *EC–Export Subsidies on Sugar* (EC) *Canada–Wheat Exports and Grain Imports* (Canada) *EC–Large Civil Aircraft* (United States) *EC–Large Civil Aircraft (2nd complaint)* (United States) *US–Large Civil Aircraft* (United States) *US–Large Civil Aircraft (2nd complaint)* (United States)

Sources: Cases are self-reported on law firm websites, as of December 9, 2008: King & Spalding, "World Trade Organization (WTO) Dispute Settlement" (www.kslaw.com); Sidley Austin, "Our Practice. WTO Disputes" (www.sidley.com); Steptoe & Johnson, "WTO Dispute Settlement" (www.steptoe.com); Van Bael & Bellis, "WTO Dispute Settlement" (www.vanbaelbellis.com); Vermulst Verhaeghe & Graafsma and White & Case: information obtained through private correspondence with each firm's lawyers; WilmerHale, "Using International Dispute Settlement Mechanisms to Open Markets" (www.wilmerhale.com).

a. Client could be either the government or a private industry interest within that country.

many of these firms do represent large United States– or EC-based multinational corporation clients in WTO enforcement cases, a number of the law firms have also represented foreign interests—including the interests of a number of developing country industries and governments.

Many of the law firms have developed their WTO enforcement work in Geneva as an offshoot from their trade remedy litigation work in Washington or Brussels. How might this work? If a Japanese, Korean, or Brazilian steel company's lawyers are unable to prevent the U.S. or EC antidumping investigators from imposing new trade restrictions against their client during the domestic antidumping investigation, the same law firm may be called to work on behalf of the client exporting firm (as well as the Japanese, Korean, or

Brazilian government) to challenge the imposed measure at the WTO in Geneva. Furthermore, exporting firms that are repeat players, with frequent involvement in trade remedy or WTO litigation, may have long-term relationships with these law firms. Indeed, in some instances the legal advice is likely to affect the firm's business model, as firms adjust their price and sales strategies and their accounting practices in anticipation of avoiding the hassles caused by repeated foreign trade remedy investigations. Such a strategy may eliminate the need for WTO enforcement actions except as a last resort.

Nevertheless, table 5-3 does not provide information on the extent to which private law firms are ambulance chasing on their own to generate new clients, as opposed to providing these services because they have been contacted and contracted to do so by their corporate clients. If sales and profits, which could be enforced by the WTO, are large enough, private law firms would emerge to provide the monitoring services that generate information on WTO violations without being requested to look into it by the exporting firms themselves. The private lawyers would look for violations and bring them to the exporting firms in exchange for an agreement in which the firms hire them to further monitor and help develop a legal plan to engage their government to pursue the dispute formally through the government-to-government WTO process. It is not clear to what extent private law firms are currently spending their own resources in such ambulance chasing and monitoring activities to obtain future business in actual WTO litigation on behalf of commercial clients or their governments.

How much of the cost of acquiring this information any individual exporting firm will have to cover also depends on whether it is part of an industry or trade association. Industries that are relatively concentrated—either geographically or in terms of market structure—may organize for trade policy or other reasons. If firms are organized into an industry association, they can use it to monitor common foreign market access interests and thus share costs.[22]

One example from table 5-1 is again the Motion Picture Association of America, an organization of major Hollywood film studios established in 1922, thus predating even the GATT and thus originally conceived with no WTO enforcement interests in mind. Nevertheless, the MPAA is interested in enforcing its backers' WTO-protected market access and intellectual property rights in markets like China, as shown by the *China–Intellectual Property Rights* and *China–Audiovisual Services* disputes. Agricultural trade groups are also frequently politically organized, and thus they too could share the costs of monitoring foreign market access of joint interest to members. For example, the

22. The industry association may be the legacy of a network formed to lobby on issues that may initially have had nothing to do with international trade, or the association may have been part of an earlier lobbying effort to negotiate (in the context of a multilateral negotiating round) foreign market access opening.

Corn Refiners Association, established in 1913, is an industry association backed by Cargill, Archer Daniels Midland, and a number of other firms that have a commercial interest in the *Mexico–Corn Syrup* and *Mexico–Taxes on Soft Drinks* disputes that the United States filed against Mexican policies affecting high fructose corn syrup (HFCS).

In other instances, however, the monitoring and information collection function has moved beyond private firms and industry associations and has even begun to emerge at the national level of government policy. Even in the United States—a country with many law firms and industry groups monitoring and generating foreign market access information—the federal government provides two notable examples. The U.S. Department of Agriculture provides substantial information on foreign market access conditions of interest to exporters, including historical data as well as forecasts and other foreign policy-related information. A second and more targeted example for issues of potential WTO enforcement is the U.S. Department of Commerce's International Trade Administration (ITA), which has a staff dedicated to monitoring foreign market access commitments in the Market Access and Compliance (MAC) offices in the Trade and Compliance Center (TCC).[23]

Other developed economies have established similar government programs to collect and report information concerning foreign market access barriers affecting their firms' exporting interest. The European Commissioner for Trade or the Directorate General for Trade (DG Trade) has a "Market Access Database" in which EC exporting firms can register and share information on foreign market access complaints. Japan's Ministry of Economy, Trade, and Industry (METI) also collects information on such complaints and makes them public.[24]

The effectiveness of such institutional infrastructure for monitoring and information dissemination at the *national* level remains to be seen. It is one

23. As we discuss below, the U.S. government has a relatively long history of engaging commercial exporting interests to generate information on foreign market access problems—dating back at least to its Section 301 programs. The U.S. Trade Representative submits to Congress the annual *National Trade Estimate Report on Foreign Trade Barriers*, which describes foreign market access barriers facing U.S. exporters. For more information on the U.S. Department of Agriculture programs, see its website "Marketing and Trade: Exporting Goods" (www.usda.gov [December 23, 2008]). For the ITA programs, according to its government website (http://tcc.export.gov/) the TCC "is the U.S. Government's focal point for monitoring foreign compliance with trade agreements to see that U.S. firms and workers get the maximum benefits from these agreements." See also the MAC website (http://trade.gov/mac/index.asp). Of course, the monitoring is not limited to WTO commitments, as this information is presumably also of interest for those trading under NAFTA commitments as well as under other of the United States' preferential arrangements.

24. For the EC, see DG Trade's "Market Access Database: Your Guide to Cracking World Markets" (http://madb.europa.eu/mkaccdb2/indexPubli.htm [December 23, 2008]); see also the discussion in Shaffer (2003, chapter 4). For Japan, see METI's annual report, "Report on the WTO Inconsistency of Trade Policies by Major Trading Partners" (www.meti.go.jp/english/report/index_report.html [December 23, 2008]); see also the discussion in Davis and Shirato (2007).

thing to establish a government facility that allows firms to report information on a potential foreign market access violation; it is a separate matter to organize and package such information and disseminate it to interested parties that have the power and authority to act on the potential violations. Given that such programs have yet to be independently examined or assessed in light of the resources spent to operate them, it is too early to comment on institutional performance. Nevertheless, establishment of such government programs at the national level does clearly indicate that even developed countries recognize the need to share the cost burden associated with monitoring and information dissemination concerning their exporters' interests. While firms and industries with the resources to acquire such information privately may have less need for government involvement, for others there is a case for intervention. Thus policymakers are establishing new institutions to reduce the cost to exporting firms of this process of monitoring, information generation, and dissemination and to benefit politically from being perceived as doing so.

The Cost of Industry Organization and Engaging Government Policymakers

Once an exporting firm with a WTO enforcement issue at stake has the required legal, economic, and political information, the next step of the ELP is for the firm to convince its government to engage on its behalf with foreign government officials.

Part of the cost at this stage will depend on whether it is necessary for firms to spend resources to organize into political groups. As discussed in the last section, firms may have organized themselves into a larger industry group long before contacting their government to get their issue put on the WTO enforcement agenda. Firms may be organized for many reasons unrelated to trade, but the fact that they are organized into industry and trade groups may also facilitate sharing the burden of collecting information to monitor foreign market access conditions of common interest.

Nevertheless, if firms in the industry have not organized before this stage, it may be necessary for one or more firms to begin this process in step 3 of the ELP to increase the odds that government policymakers will become convinced to pursue an enforcement action. Both the importance and the cost of organizing depends on underlying circumstances. Enforcement actions related to loss of foreign market access due to antidumping measures may have a low cost where there is little need for the aggrieved firm to organize the industry because it is the only firm whose market access rights have been violated. At the other high cost extreme may be dozens of small aggrieved firms that need to act together to convince their government of the political and economic importance of taking action, say, because the cause of lost market access was a WTO-illegal foreign safeguard or subsidy.

Beyond the issue of political organization, how specifically do firms and industries get their governments to engage in WTO enforcement? Although there are certainly informal as well as formal mechanisms both within and across countries, I begin the discussion with a description of the process in countries with a relatively institutionalized framework that industries can access to draw the attention of policymakers to matters of WTO enforcement.

In the United States, industries can use the Section 301 provision to access the government by formally requesting the U.S. Trade Representative (USTR) to look into their concerns over lost foreign market access. The EC has a similar mechanism through its Article 133 Process and the Trade Barriers Regulation (TBR), whereby domestic industries can petition the government to raise the issue of potential foreign market access violations.[25] Although initiating a Section 301 claim or Article 133 or TBR procedure is not even a necessary condition for firms to get the United States or the EC to pursue a formal WTO dispute, the existence of such legal gateways does create an explicit mechanism through which exporters can apply pressure on policymakers to hear and potentially act on their concerns.

How large are the costs to firms of convincing government officials to engage the WTO enforcement process on their behalf? In addition to generating the firm-specific estimates on lost foreign market access and the potential gain to having the government act to restore the lost foreign market access, there is the cost of widening such analysis beyond the firm to the industry. The cost of collecting such information and generating support for the action depends on how organized the industry already is. An additional cost at this stage is the expected cost of obtaining political access to policymakers. Although the amount certainly differs across countries, industries, times, and political systems, there will be costs to the firm associated with formal and informal lobbying to get the issue on the agenda of government policymakers with decisionmaking power.[26]

<hr>

25. For more detailed discussions, see Shaffer (2003) and Bayard and Elliott (1994). The existence of these procedures provides exporting industries with the outside option of getting on the public record that they filed a procedure and were met with an unresponsive government—documentation of inaction that could be important for potential electoral reasons. See also Davis (2009) which, in addition, examines the Japanese process.

26. To create political goodwill to get the USTR to take up the issue at stake in the ultimate *EC–Bananas III* dispute, Carl Lindner, the CEO of Chiquita Bananas, which was the major U.S. commercial interest behind the case, reportedly organized his firm and executives to donate upwards of $1 million combined to the Democratic and Republican Parties' National Committees during the 1993–94 election cycle, including $525,000 to the Democrats after not having given any funding to them in 1992. See Devereaux, Lawrence, and Watkins (2006a, p. 110).

The Costs of the Actual WTO Enforcement Litigation

Suppose the firm and industry clear hurdles 1 through 3 of the ELP so that the domestic government is willing to engage the WTO enforcement issue on their behalf. If the government cannot resolve the concern with its foreign government counterpart through simple dialogue and negotiation, the domestic government can then initiate the fourth step of the WTO enforcement process, which begins the actual litigation phase using the WTO's Dispute Settlement Understanding.

The pure cost of time and resources to pursuing the formal litigation of a WTO dispute in Geneva can be quite high, given the cost of the technical expertise that is necessary at this stage. The cost of prosecuting a dispute depends on factors including the nature of the underlying violation, the relevance and extent of existing case law on the matter at issue, and how extensively the complainant and respondent parties in the dispute would like to make their case. There is likely to be high variation in this cost across disputes. For disputes in which the market access violation is relatively obvious and the existing WTO case law is relatively clear, the pure litigation costs of prosecuting a case may be limited to hundreds of thousands of dollars.

However, for cases covering virgin territory and in which the existing case law is relatively unclear, the legal parties may choose to expend substantially more resources to make their case, especially if the market access at stake is large. The lawyers may decide that a strategy with more numerous claims of wrongdoing and allegations of WTO inconsistencies is more likely to generate a positive legal ruling; this is a high-cost legal tactic with substantial billable hours for the lawyers involved. The lawyers may also choose to solicit and collect extensive evidence in support of their claims. Disputes such as *US–Upland Cotton* have involved technical economic studies generated by high-cost economic consultants with professional expertise that assess the market impact of agricultural subsidy policies, and disputes such as *EC–Approval and Marketing of Biotech Products* include complex scientific studies providing risk assessment evidence seeking to challenge or substantiate the impact of genetically modified organisms.

The main point is that it is largely the parties themselves that decide how many resources to devote to the dispute. In some cases, the resource expenditures have been substantial. For example, Shaffer puts the private sector litigation fees billed by the law firms to the commercial clients (Kodak and Fuji) in the *Japan–Film* dispute at more than $12 million.[27] There are other disputes with comparable amounts of legal input and evidence—for example, the United

27. Shaffer (2003, p. 38).

States and the EC in the Boeing-Airbus disputes, as well as the *EC–Approval and Marketing of Biotech Products* litigation—in which the litigation costs alone are also likely in that range.[28] Nevertheless, given the massive amounts of foreign market access that are at stake in these disputes, the parties are choosing to spend such resources. Such expenditures are, by themselves, not symptomatic of a problem in the WTO system.

Who bears the burden of the actual litigation costs? Frequently the process of WTO litigation involves government lawyers working hand in hand with the private sector lawyers representing the firms and industry associations with the commercial interests behind the dispute. Indeed, as Shaffer describes for the case of developed economies like the United States and the EC, the WTO enforcement process has evolved to a "public-private partnership" between these groups.[29] In many instances, a substantial share of the cost will therefore be borne not by the government (and hence taxpayers) but instead by the underlying industry whose commercial interest is at stake in the litigation.

Finally, it is also worth noting that firms with larger commercial interests and substantial other legal issues to contend with vis-à-vis their governments are more likely to hire private law firms. Many firms want to have their own lawyers for purposes beyond assisting government lawyers in preparing and litigating the case. Firms want their private attorneys to examine evidence and financial material before it is seen by their own (government) attorneys in WTO litigation, if only to make sure that government lawyers do not overstep their mandate and begin looking at the firm's non-WTO-related commercial interests. For example, having the United States government be the firm's only legal representation in a WTO dispute could have been troubling for major companies like Archer Daniels Midland, Micron, Microsoft, and Boeing (see again table 5-1), since each firm also recently faced U.S government lawyers as a defendant in a large antitrust-related dispute in United States courts brought by the Department of Justice, in some instances at virtually the same time as their WTO enforcement litigation.[30]

---

28. Shaffer (2009, p. 184) puts the potential litigation figure for each company in the Boeing–Airbus disputes at potentially $20 million if the WTO disputes do not settle.

29. Shaffer (2003). Shaffer, Ratton Sanchez, and Rosenberg (2008) detail how Brazil (a developing country) has adapted the public-private partnership model in support of its WTO enforcement actions.

30. As examples, see the following press releases by the U.S. Department of Justice: "Archer Daniels Midland Co. to Plead Guilty and Pay $100 Million for Role in Two International Price-Fixing Conspiracies," October 15, 1996; "Justice Department Files Antitrust Suit against Microsoft for Unlawfully Monopolizing Computer Software Markets," May 18, 1998; "Micron Executive Agrees to Plead Guilty to Obstructing a Price-Fixing Investigation Involving Computer Memory Chips," December 17, 2003; and "Boeing to Pay United States Record $615 Million to Resolve Fraud Allegations," June 30, 2006.

The Costs to Obtaining Compliance

The two final steps of the ELP are the postlitigation phase, which entails the costs associated with obtaining compliance with the legal ruling and hence policy reform in the offending country. Because there have been relatively few instances (roughly ten) to date in which formal disputes have reached the WTO-authorized formal "retaliation threat" phase, one cannot infer too much from the actual retaliation threats that have been carried out. Nevertheless, it is instructive to examine at least two high profile examples to understand the basics of how retaliation can work in practice.

The *EC–Bananas III* dispute was the first to result in WTO-authorized and implemented retaliation. After successfully challenging the EC's discriminatory import restrictions on Latin American–grown bananas that U.S. firms like Chiquita and Dole distributed internationally, the United States was granted WTO authorization to retaliate when the EC refused to reform its banana import policy sufficiently to meet WTO rulings. The WTO arbiters limited U.S. retaliation to reducing imports from the EC by $191 million per year, a figure based on the arbiters' estimate of the amount of trade that U.S. firms lost because of the WTO-illegal EC banana policy. Although the level of retaliation was constrained by the WTO ruling, the United States had flexibility in choosing particular EC exported products for retaliation. The United States focused its retaliatory tariffs on exports of Louis Vuitton handbags from France and other luxury goods from other European countries.

There are a number of political and economic arguments for targeting luxury goods. On the consumer (U.S.) side, there is less risk of a consumer backlash resulting from a tariff-induced higher price of luxury handbags, as few U.S. consumers purchased these particular products. On the exporter (EC) side, the U.S. strategy of targeting high-profile firms like Louis Vuitton may better focus the attention of EC policymakers and increase the likelihood of reform of the WTO-illegal banana policy. An economic argument for targeting luxury products is that their exporters have limited outside options if they are shut out of the U.S. market. Thus Louis Vuitton is likely to suffer a substantial reduction in profits if it is forced to sell the handbags in an alternative market with fewer wealthy consumers. The theory suggests this could be an important catalyst in getting Louis Vuitton and other affected exporters to work within the EC to reform, or even ask for the dismantling of, the banana policy.

A second example, *US–Steel Safeguards,* illustrates the potential importance and effectiveness of the underlying capacity to make retaliation threats in a dispute long before it even reaches that stage of the ELP.[31] The case involved the

---

31. Devereaux, Lawrence, and Watkins (2006a) provide an excellent account of the evolution of political and economic events in the global steel market leading up to the imposition of the 2002 U.S. steel safeguard.

EC taking the lead in a dispute that challenged new U.S. import restrictions imposed in March 2002 on a variety of steel products. By November 2003, the EC had won its legal arguments at the WTO, and it had already drawn up and made public its retaliation list of U.S exports that it would target if the United States refused to comply with the WTO ruling.[32]

The EC took advantage of the political sensitivity created by the upcoming 2004 U.S. presidential election season by concentrating its retaliation threats on products exported from U.S. swing states that were the site of highly anticipated political battles. The most publicized of the threatened sanctions would target citrus exports from Florida, the site of the previous election's (2000) Bush-Gore recount controversy in which Bush achieved a razor thin margin of victory. The Bush administration avoided the risk of alienating interests in a state critical to the upcoming election by terminating the steel import restrictions in December 2003. This particular dispute identifies a clear example of designing a retaliatory response to take advantage of political circumstances.

Although most disputes do not reach the stage of formalizing the WTO-authorized retaliation threats, let alone having countries implement them in practice, to suggest that retaliation threats are irrelevant fails to recognize the importance of economic incentives inherent in the self-enforcing WTO agreement. While it may bubble to the surface only infrequently, an undercurrent of potential retaliation is inherent in every dispute. While the threat is not necessarily explicit, policymakers always have this possibility in the back of their minds because this is the final "threat point" to which governments can resort while still remaining within the rules of the WTO system.

The implication is that Michele Brown's firm faces additional costs to use step 5 of the ELP effectively. First, her legal representatives require additional resources to pay for the technical economic and political expertise needed to generate the most useful targets for retaliation threats: political and economic interests that can be mobilized within the offending country to generate the policy reform necessary for compliance. Such expertise is likely costly and difficult to obtain; the "best" retaliation target is continually changing in the face of different respondent countries, industries, economic circumstances, and political timing.

Finally, it is worth noting that many countries have a mandatory process that allows for public hearings and feedback in the creation of the retaliation list of

32. The EC's retaliation list and threats became public long before the formal dispute reached the DSU stage when it would seek (and be granted) formal authorization to retaliate. In fact, the dispute concluded before actually reaching the arbitration phase (see figure 3-1) because the dispute ended after the WTO circulated the Appellate Body report. Indeed an early draft of the potential retaliation list was made public by the EC not long after the U.S. steel safeguard was imposed in March 2002; see Commission of the European Communities, "Proposal for a Council Regulation Establishing Additional Customs Duties on Imports of Certain Products Originating in the United States of America," COM (2002) 202 final—2002/0095 (ACC), (Brussels, April 19, 2002).

targets. If proposed retaliation is in the form of tariffs, domestic consumers of targeted goods (as well as foreign exporters) stand to lose from the retaliation, and they are likely to lobby to prevent it from taking place. This suggests that the firm and industry behind the dispute may need to spend additional counter-lobbying resources at this step of the process—one example would be actions to counter the lobbying efforts of Louis Vuitton consumers and retailers in the United States—to give well-designed retaliation threats the greatest chance to work in the respondent country.[33]

What Are the Lessons for Developing Countries?

The costs of the six steps of the ELP, and how firms, industries and governments overcome them in many developed countries, identify important lessons for developing countries regarding their WTO self-enforcement needs. While the rest of this book is dedicated to analyzing these costs in much more depth from the perspective of developing countries, I draw some basic insights here.

Developing Countries and the Costs to Monitoring and Information Collection

Steps 1 and 2 of the ELP involved the costs of monitoring WTO commitments, recognizing possible instances of WTO violations, and compiling economic, legal, and political information to persuade government officials that enforcement action should be taken. There are reasons to believe that the costs associated with these two stages are especially high and difficult for many exporting firms in developing countries to overcome.

First, to suggest that such costs are not important and that it is something else that impedes developing countries' access to WTO enforcement is to ignore the evidence revealed in table 5-2. In many of the instances in which the monitoring of WTO commitments was not an issue, as in cases such as antidumping, where the exporting firms are notified directly of the new import restrictions, the exporting firms managed to overcome the costs of at least engaging their governments to initiate WTO enforcement actions on their behalf.

Second, even the richest economies of the United States, the EC, and Japan have established government programs and policies to encourage their exporting firms to report violations of foreign market access. That these governments are helping to create new policy infrastructures to reduce the costs and to induce

---

33. In the *US–Steel Safeguards* dispute, another U.S. export on the EC's retaliation list was Harley Davidson motorcycles. Nordström (2010) provides an interesting account of the counter-lobbying that took place within EC members by consumers of Harley Davidson imports, who stood to lose if the EC retaliation was implemented.

cost sharing suggests that the costs of monitoring and information collection are substantial for exporting firms. If costs are difficult to overcome for developed economy firms that are likely to be better organized politically and have access to more detailed, comprehensive, and up-to-date data and tools for communicating, the costs are surely even more difficult for exporters in developing countries to overcome without assistance.

These points suggest a potential role for external assistance and intervention. Chapter 8 describes in more detail alternative approaches to providing this monitoring and information dissemination function to developing countries for WTO self-enforcement.

How Firms and Industries in Developing Countries Can Politically Engage Their Governments

Step 3 of the extended litigation process requires the exporting industry in the developing country to convince its domestic government to pursue the dispute against a trading partner at the WTO. Even if armed with an arsenal of legal and economic evidence in support of its case collected during the first two steps, an exporting industry may have difficulty convincing its government to pursue the dispute because of other government priorities or insufficient resource capacity on the part of policymakers.

Many developing country governments in particular do not give high priority to WTO enforcement, and many even believe that enforcement is not in the nation's overall development interest. The way to address much of this problem is through domestic political reform at home, and thus this issue goes beyond the scope of interventions proposed by this particular analysis. Nevertheless, many least developed countries (LDCs) typically lack the basic technical capacity in their Geneva missions to even keep abreast of all WTO-related activity of importance. The need for the additional capacity that is required in an actual trade dispute to represent a domestic industry during the WTO's enforcement proceeding is a burden that many LDCs have not yet been able to overcome.

These points suggest a potential role for external assistance and intervention. In chapter 7, I discuss the role that certain qualified nongovernmental organizations (NGOs) might play in assisting developing country industries and policymakers to overcome the costs associated with this particular step of the ELP.

Developing Countries and the Litigation Costs of WTO Enforcement

With few exceptions, developing country governments are unlikely to have sophisticated teams of lawyers like those that are available in developed economy governments such as the USTR or DG Trade. And although table 5-3 illustrates that private law firms are willing to work for or against almost any client—meaning that private WTO litigation services are traded internationally—the costs of hiring private law firms can be high. It may be possible to keep the costs of hiring private legal counsel under $1 million for step 4 of the ELP; however, this still is a large sum, given that for exporting firms in developing countries it is only one component of their overall exporting costs. Litigation is only one part of the extended litigation process, and these firms may export only a small value of goods, and furthermore, these goods may have low markups and the firms may have low profit margins. This type of trade may not be able to support substantial additional costs of litigation. High costs for step 4 of the process can affect the use of WTO enforcement by a developing country in ways that have already been discussed. A developing country may be likely to use the WTO only in cases in which it can find a common (cost-sharing) interest with other exporting countries. Furthermore, it may be less likely to pursue a dispute through the legal process to completion, and thus it may feed back into the dispute settlement negotiations if both sides are fully informed of its poor outside option.

Given the high cost of private litigation in step 4 of the ELP, there may be an important case for subsidizing litigation support for developing countries on issues that actually make it to that stage of WTO self-enforcement. In chapter 6, I examine one particular means by which this cost burden on developing countries has been reduced. There, I introduce the Advisory Centre on WTO Law (ACWL) and describe the implications of the ACWL on developing country access to the extended litigation process.

Developing Countries, Retaliation Threats, and Obtaining Compliance

A number of developing countries have gone through step 5 of the ELP, the stage of seeking and being granted authorization to retaliate.[34] One major explanation for why they have rarely implemented the retaliation threats in practice is surely the rational choice that developing countries make by recognizing both the domestic benefits of access to a wide range of low-priced imports (that would be reduced in the face of a tariff retaliation) as well as the relative ineffectiveness of retaliation. If the developing country is a small consumer of imports from the respondent, it may be unable to impose political and economic costs that have a significant impact on mobilizing the trading partner's domestic reform interests. Developing countries may not consume enough Louis Vuitton handbags or citrus products from Florida to convince the EC or the United States to reform. Given the limited benefit of goods (tariff) retaliation for many developing countries, two additional possibilities present themselves.

---

34. Through the end of 2008, as table 4-6 indicates, these countries include Ecuador in *EC–Bananas III;* Brazil, Chile, India, and Mexico in *US–Offset Act (Byrd Amendment);* Brazil in *Canada–Regional Aircraft;* and Antigua and Barbuda in *US–Gambling.* Brazil has also been at the stage of requesting the right to retaliate against the U.S. in *US–Upland Cotton.*

Step 5. An alternative approach: Explore the possibility of TRIPS retaliation.

In lieu of tariff retaliation over imported goods in step 5 of the ELP, developing countries have begun to explore the possibility of using retaliation under the Trade-Related Aspects of Intellectual Property Rights (TRIPS) Agreement, that is, retaliating against another country through WTO-authorized nonenforcement of the respondent country's exporting firms' intellectual property rights. The idea was first formally proposed by Ecuador at the conclusion of the *EC–Bananas III* dispute. Unlike the United States, which sought to retaliate against the EC by imposing higher import tariffs that would eliminate sales of Louis Vuitton handbags, Ecuador threatened to stop enforcing European firms' intellectual property rights for products protected from piracy by copyright or patent. Although Ecuador raised the possibility of TRIPS retaliation, it did not follow through and actually implement retaliation in this manner.

The possibility of TRIPS retaliation has been revived in a number of more recent disputes. The WTO has authorized the tiny Caribbean island nation of Antigua and Barbuda to do so after the United States failed to comply with rulings in the *US–Gambling* dispute, and TRIPS retaliation has also been under consideration by Brazil as a response to U.S. failure to comply with WTO rulings in the *US–Upland Cotton* dispute.[35] Although it is not yet clear how countries would effectively operationalize the withholding of U.S. firms' intellectual property rights in practice, TRIPS retaliation is likely to be implemented by a developing country in a future case.

Despite this possibility of enhancing the credibility of developing country retaliation threats that may empower developing countries in WTO enforcement, any successful implementation of TRIPS retaliation will still require access to the costly technical, political, and economic expertise to identify appropriate retaliation targets. Thus there are still substantial step 5 costs to developing countries in the ELP, even if they choose to do so via TRIPS retaliation.[36]

35. For a discussion of some of the practical complications of using TRIPS retaliation, see Abbott (2010).

36. There have been a number of WTO proposals to reform the DSU's underlying remedy to allow for respondent compensation in ways separate from or in addition to retaliation through increasing tariffs on goods or failing to enforce TRIPS commitments. Bagwell, Mavroidis, and Staiger (2006, 2007) examined the possible implications of a Mexican proposal to allow complainants to auction their right to retaliate to the highest bidder. Maggi (1999) explored the possible implications of permitting multilateral retaliation. Limão and Saggi (2008) examined a scheme that would introduce financial compensation to complainants in lieu of tariff retaliation, and Lawrence (2003, chapter 5) provided an additional discussion. Nordström and Shaffer (2008) examined a separate type of reform via introduction to the WTO of a small claims procedure. Since the approach of this book is to take the WTO rules and system of dispute settlement as given, I do not comment further on any of these reform proposals here.

Step 6. Alternately, obtain compliance by political mobilization of other forces.

There are still instances in which developing countries, even with access to a modified step 5 of TRIPS retaliation, do not have sufficient economic clout to mobilize commercial (exporting and intellectual property–holding) interests to induce policy reform in the offending country that will restore the complainant's lost foreign market access. In such instances, one last possibility in step 6 of the ELP is to mobilize other forces to catalyze policymakers in the foreign country to carry out the required policy reform.

The idea is to use other sources of political pressure within the offending country that will motivate reformers. Take as an example a WTO violation in the form of a taxpayer-funded subsidy in a high-income country that adversely affects the foreign market access of firms in a poor country. Increased public awareness of the subsidy itself within the domestic economy may be sufficient to stimulate public demands for reform. Suppose the public had previously been unaware that the subsidy not only adversely impacted economic activity in poor countries but also increased the incidence of poverty. Also suppose that the public had previously been unaware that the subsidy had been granted to appease domestic special interest groups and actually had regressive income distributional implications at home.

The possibility of stirring public sentiment in a way that can result in substantive policy reform certainly varies across countries and political contexts. Nevertheless the approach of targeting broad public opinion may be useful when coupled with other elements of the WTO enforcement process. I return to this issue in substantial detail in chapter 7, when I examine this possibility in light of the attempts by NGOs such as Oxfam to trigger such mechanisms in the context of the *US–Upland Cotton* dispute. While this case has had difficulty in reaching a successful policy conclusion (that is, U.S. compliance with WTO rulings and the subsequent removal of the subsidies), an investigation of how the WTO enforcement process has been used in this particular instance generates examples of new ways to exploit networks and cross-country linkages to assist developing country enforcement of their foreign market access.

Conclusion

This chapter documents how the countries that have effectively used the WTO dispute settlement process to enforce their exporting firms' foreign market access have relied on much more than just the law. Mastery and execution of the extended litigation process to self-enforce foreign market access involves complex and costly economics, law, and politics.

This chapter serves as an important jumping-off point for the remainder of the book. So far, the discussion has established that only some exporting firms are able to overcome the cost of engaging the WTO enforcement process to maintain access to foreign markets, just as only some firms are able to overcome the cost of getting into export markets to begin with. The ELP model identifies the many components of this enforcement cost and thus the many potential hurdles that confront exporting firms in developing countries and that may prevent them from benefiting fully from what the WTO agreement has to offer.

In the remainder of this book, I use the lens of the "targeting principle" provided by economic analysis to examine each of these hurdles individually.[37] The targeting principle involves confronting each market failure or underlying hurdle directly at its source. I ask what, if any, complementary institutional innovations have evolved thus far to address each cost hurdle, how successful they have been at reducing the cost at that stage of the WTO enforcement process, and what additional interventions need to take place.

---

37. The targeting principle is typically associated with Bhagwati and Ramaswami's (1963) seminal contribution.

6

The Advisory Centre on WTO Law

The last chapter highlighted examples of teams of government lawyers at the Office of the United States Trade Representative (USTR), the European Community's Directorate General for Trade (DG Trade), and other World Trade Organization members' trade offices that litigate dispute settlement cases by working in public-private partnerships with firms and industries to enforce their access to foreign markets. In other instances, private law firms with large numbers of lawyers in their international trade practice groups sometimes take the lead litigating WTO disputes on behalf of their commercial and government clients. Interestingly enough, one of the busiest groups of lawyers involved in WTO litigation is neither a private law firm nor a group of government attorneys of a WTO member. Instead, it is the Advisory Centre on WTO Law (ACWL), which is a group of fewer than ten lawyers that has participated in more than twenty-five formal WTO disputes since 2001.

In each dispute, the ACWL has worked to enforce the market access interest of firms and industries in a poor country. Furthermore, during the first seven years of its existence, the ACWL has worked on behalf of the complainant country in more disputes than all other WTO members except for the United States and the EC. Put differently, if the ACWL were not an intergovernmental organization but instead were itself a WTO member country, it would be considered as the third most frequently active complainant litigant in the Dispute Settlement Understanding (DSU) system during this time period.

The establishment of the ACWL and its resulting assistance to developing countries provide a major contribution to the WTO enforcement process. In much the same way that the economic incentives discussed in chapter 1 create the need for some multilateral institution to do what the WTO does, many of the same economic incentive-based arguments can be used to describe the need for an organization like the ACWL—that is, if it did not exist, countries would have to invent it.[1]

Although the ACWL fills a major gap in the enforcement needs of the international trading system, its institutional design does not allow it to take care of all the problems associated with providing necessary WTO enforcement assistance to poor countries. The ACWL's commercial clients are obscure firms like Rahimafrooz Batteries from Bangladesh, the Mohsin Match Factory from Pakistan, the Tubac steel company from Guatemala, and April Fine pulp and paper company from Indonesia. However, unlike Boeing and Airbus, Chiquita, Kodak and other multinational corporations whose legal representation may be USTR, DG Trade, or some other major legal participant in the WTO enforcement system, the ACWL's commercial clients are not permitted to have unsolicited contact with their WTO lawyers. Such constraints, as well as other economic incentives generated by the creation of the ACWL, do impose limits on its ability to assist developing countries and their industries to navigate the WTO's self-enforcement process.

The first major section of this chapter begins by describing the origins of the ACWL and what it was intended to do. Within the context of the extended litigation process (ELP) model of WTO self enforcement described in chapter 5 (see figure 5-1), I conclude that the ACWL mandate appears limited in addressing the problem of the costs of step 4 that impede developing countries' access to expensive lawyers to litigate their WTO disputes. Thus, in the second major section, I examine potential implications of the ACWL using data on its WTO dispute settlement activities over the 2001–08 period. In particular, I assess various ways in which the ACWL may be affecting whether and how developing countries use the WTO to self-enforce their foreign market access. Combining the theory behind the institution with the data reveals the key role of, as well as the limits to, the ACWL and thus indicates other areas of assistance that are still missing from the ELP. Therefore, in the last section, I explore concerns raised by the data on how countries are using the ACWL as well as the implications for additional reform.

---

1. Earlier reviews of the ACWL include Van der Borght (1999); Hoekman and Mavroidis (2000); Jackson (2002); Bown and Hoekman (2005); Shaffer (2006).

Background of the ACWL

The Advisory Centre on WTO Law was established in Geneva in 2001 by a group of nations as a legal services center for developing countries. In addition to providing general legal advice on WTO matters, a fundamental purpose of the ACWL was to offer developing countries subsidized, low-cost, legal support when they acted as complainants, respondents, or third parties in WTO dispute settlement proceedings.[2] The ACWL is an intergovernmental organization (IGO) and its organizational structure consists of a general assembly (which comprises all ACWL member countries and representatives of the least developed countries), a six-person management board, and an executive director.

The ACWL can supply services to developing countries, customs territories, or economies in transition.[3] As of 2008, services provided by the Centre were available to twenty-eight developing countries that had become members and two additional developing countries in the process of accession to the ACWL. Another forty-five WTO members and countries in the process of acceding to the WTO (but which are not members of the ACWL), designated by the United Nations as least developed countries (LDCs), are also eligible for the services the ACWL offers.[4] Table 6-1 lists the members of the ACWL as well as the non-member countries that are eligible for ACWL services at reduced rate fees.

Why establish a legal assistance center for poor countries so that they can access advice on WTO legal issues? One motivation is similar to why centers are set up for individual workers regarding violations of employment law via wrongful termination or discrimination in the context of domestic legal systems. In employment law, the argument is that private lawyers may be discouraged from taking on cases when the damages that would be awarded to successful plaintiffs are small relative to the costs of litigation—for example, a potential dispute involving an injured worker who either earns low wages or suffers small damages in which awards would be limited to lost wages or reemployment. The provision of legal services to poor individuals may be beneficial to society if it encourages

2. The ACWL does more than litigation work for WTO disputes. It also helps advise countries on WTO obligations and rules (for example, if country x were to implement such and such law, would it be WTO compatible?), and it offers training programs to assist WTO capacity building in developing countries. It has an internship program that helps Geneva-based WTO missions develop their own staff competencies in matters of WTO law. See ACWL's website, "Secondment Programme for Trade Lawyers" (www.acwl.ch/e/training/secondement_e.aspx [December 10, 2008]).

3. A "customs territory" refers to a geographic territory that may not necessarily satisfy the international legal definition of a country but is nevertheless in charge of levying its own customs duties at its border. "Economies in transition" refer to the formerly centrally planned, nonmarket economies (for example, the former Soviet bloc of Eastern Europe countries) that are in the process of becoming more market oriented.

4. All information on the ACWL was taken from its website (www.acwl.ch [December 10, 2008]).

Table 6-1. *ACWL Members and Countries Eligible for Subsidized ACWL Services*

	Countries eligible for ACWL services		
Developed country members not eligible for ACWL services	*Developing country members of the ACWL*	*LDCs that are nonmembers of the ACWL but are eligible for ACWL services*[a]	
Canada	*Category A*	Afghanistan	Madagascar
Denmark	Taiwan	Angola	Malawi
Finland	Hong Kong	Bangladesh	Maldives
Ireland		Benin	Mali
Italy	*Category B*	Bhutan	Mauritania
Netherlands	Colombia	Burkina Faso	Mozambique
Norway	Egypt	Burundi	Myanmar
Sweden	India	Cambodia	Nepal
Switzerland	Indonesia	Cape Verde	Niger
United Kingdom	Mauritius	Central African Rep.	Rwanda
	Oman	Chad	Samoa
	Pakistan	Comoros	São Tomé and Príncipe
	Philippines	Dem. Rep. of Congo	Senegal
	Thailand	Djibouti	Sierra Leone
	Turkey	Equatorial Guinea	Solomon Islands
	Uruguay	Ethiopia	Sudan
	Venezuela	The Gambia	Tanzania
		Guinea	Togo
	Category C	Guinea Bissau	Uganda
	Bolivia	Haiti	Vanuatu
	Costa Rica[b]	Laos	Yemen
	Dominican Rep.	Lesotho	Zambia
	Ecuador	Liberia	
	El Salvador		
	Georgia[b]		
	Guatemala		
	Honduras		
	Jordan		
	Kenya		
	Nicaragua		
	Panama		
	Paraguay		
	Peru		
	Sri Lanka		
	Tunisia		

Source: Advisory Centre on WTO Law's website (www.acwl.ch/e/index_e.aspx [December 10, 2008]). LDCs = least developed countries.

a. Countries that are designated by the United Nations as LDCs and that are also members of the WTO or are in the process of acceding to the WTO are entitled to the services of the ACWL without becoming ACWL members.

b. Developing countries in the process of accession to the ACWL.

individuals to stand up for their rights, which then encourages employers to adhere to the law and not mistreat workers. Because attorneys have lucrative outside options, local or federal government funding typically subsidizes legal service centers to encourage work in such public interest law.

From the perspective of economic analysis, the creation of a legal assistance center for poor countries in the WTO system can also be seen as partially addressing a market failure associated with positive externalities and providing a public good. In the absence of any intervention, a "free rider" problem of too little self-enforcement can emerge over WTO violations of foreign market access that negatively affect exporters in a number countries. Because there are positive externalities associated with each individual country self-enforcing, in that the adversely affected exporters in other countries stand to also benefit from the effort of another exporting country, too few private resources are allocated to self-enforcement by each exporting country. Furthermore, the public good in this setting is the improvement of property rights—in this context, market access rights—and how they are treated and valued in the trading system. Nevertheless, despite the underlying economic rationale for the ACWL, not all developing countries that are eligible for membership have chosen to participate in the institution. Table 6-2 lists the developing countries that, while eligible for ACWL accession, have not yet begun the process of formal membership.[5]

The next two subsections describe the inputs, costs, and services that the ACWL provides as well as the prices and terms of access to those services that the ACWL offers to developing country clients.

The Supply Side: Funding and the ACWL's Legal Team of Inputs

Funding for the ACWL is through a hybrid model. Its membership, with the exception of the LDCs, contributes in a cooperative approach to the ACWL's Endowment Fund. Contributions for developing country members are made on a sliding scale based on country characteristics (share of global trade, corrected for per capita income)—$50,000 for members in category C, $100,000 for members in category B, and $300,000 for members in category A (see table 6-1).[6]

---

5. In the empirical section below, I do not examine the determinants of a country's choice to accede to the ACWL: why some countries become members and others do not, or why some members use the ACWL services and others do not. As the ACWL is a relatively new institution, the research literature is relatively scant, and to my knowledge, these and other related questions have not yet been addressed empirically.

6. These are converted from the fee schedule, which is listed in Swiss francs: CHF81,000 for members in category C, CHF162,000 for members in category B, and CHF486,000 for members in category A, using the fixed conversion rate of CHF1.62 per U.S.$1, as specified under the UN Operational Rates of Exchange applicable for the month of May 2002. As of December 2007, the Endowment Fund was valued at CHF23 million (ACWL 2007, p. 4).

Table 6-2. *Developing Countries That Are Not ACWL Members*

Category A	Category B	Category C
Korea	Antigua and Barbuda	Belize
Mexico	Argentina	Botswana
Singapore	Bahrain	Bulgaria
Brunei Darussalam	Barbados	Cameroon
Cyprus	Brazil	Congo
Israel	Chile	Côte d'Ivoire
Kuwait	Czech Republic	Cuba
Macau	Gabon	Dominica
	Hungary	Estonia
	Malaysia	Fiji
	Malta	Ghana
	Morocco	Grenada
	Nigeria	Guyana
	Poland	Jamaica
	Romania	Kyrgyz Republic
	Slovakia	Latvia
	Slovenia	Mongolia
	South Africa	Namibia
	St. Kitts and Nevis	Papua New Guinea
	St. Lucia	Senegal
	Trinidad and Tobago	St. Vincent and the Grenadines
		Suriname
		Swaziland
		Zimbabwe

Source: Advisory Centre on WTO Law's website (www.acwl.ch/e/index_e.aspx [December 10, 2008]). Compiled by the author as the difference between the list of ACWL membership and the list of ACWL eligible countries, including the category schedule, from Annex II of the Agreement Establishing the ACWL.

While the developing countries that use the ACWL services do make financial contributions to the institution, the bulk of the funding for the ACWL has been obtained from high-income members of the ACWL, which are the developed country donors listed in table 6-1 that do not qualify for the legal services the Centre provides. These countries have made substantial contributions to the Endowment Fund, and many have also made separate contributions to the ACWL's annual operating budget, collectively contributing more than $13 million between 2001 and 2007 to establish the ACWL and make it operational.[7]

7. Developed countries that each have contributed $1 million or more to the Endowment Fund include Canada, Denmark, Finland, Ireland, Italy, the Netherlands, Norway, and Sweden. The following countries also contributed $1.25 million each to the annual budget sometime during the ACWL's first five years: Ireland, the Netherlands, Norway, and the United Kingdom. See Annex I of the Agreement Establishing the ACWL (www.acwl.ch/e/about/organisational_e.aspx [December 10, 2008]).

The developed country members of the ACWL include Canada, Norway, Switzerland, and the more liberal bloc of typically northern EC member states (Denmark, Finland, Ireland, Italy, the Netherlands, Sweden, the United Kingdom). Notably absent from the list of developed country ACWL members and financial contributors are, of course, the United States, Japan, Australia, France, and Germany, as well as the EC as a whole. Despite the lack of financial support from some of the major trading nations, the contribution that a number of other developed countries have made is noteworthy and should affect the broader debate of more systemic DSU reform. The $13 million spent by developed countries constitutes a substantial subsidy to developing countries to improve their access to litigation and thus enforcement of WTO commitments.

The current ACWL funding structure has additional benefits, relative to other models, that are particularly pertinent to the issue of providing self-enforcement support to developing countries according to their own needs. First, the current endowment approach is less likely to affect the composition of disputes that the ACWL handles, which is not necessarily the case when donor funding derives from nongovernmental sources that may be "issue based."[8] As an example from the United States in particular, the absence of official U.S. public sector (government) funding in a particular area can frequently give rise to nongovernmental organizations and civil society groups from the private sector filling the void. Such groups frequently receive their financial support from private foundations. The ACWL's current policy would appear to rule out private foundation funding, at least with respect to funding that could be used to cover the cost of WTO litigation, as opposed to funding for general training programs.[9] While this may limit the scope of the ACWL's potential donors to national governments, this also has potential benefits. Since many private funders are issues based, accepting their funding could have ramifications for the scope of legal assistance that the Centre implicitly felt it had to emphasize to please donors. One theoretical benefit of the current ACWL approach in which funding is not tied to issues-based organizations is that the ACWL is free to pursue the cases of greatest interest to its members and not necessarily those of interest to its funders. Because it is not funded by interest groups, it is not expected to develop an issues-oriented agenda and seek publicity by trying to influence the composition of cases that come its way.

In addition to the implications of the source of ACWL funding, it is also relevant to examine the "input mix" that generates the "output" of the ACWL's

8. I describe this concern in substantially more detail in chapter 7.

9. ACWL current policy is that "the ACWL may also accept, under strict conditions, contributions from other governmental and non-governmental sources for specific purposes that are not related to dispute settlement cases, such as training and the traineeship programme." See its website (www.acwl.ch/e/about/organisational_e.aspx [December 10, 2008]).

services. One possibility is that the ACWL is able to offer a product at low cost not because it is a subsidized, high-quality product but instead because the ACWL puts out a low-quality product derived from low-quality inputs. The data available on ACWL staff would appear to rule out such an explanation.

While I discuss below the challenges to measuring and hence evaluating the output of the services provided by the ACWL, I can describe the apparent quality of the inputs that go into the provision of ACWL services. The ACWL staff includes the executive director and deputy director and, as of December 2008, six lawyers, two administrators, and a handful of apprentice-type trainees in the ACWL's secondment program for trade lawyers. The professional staff of eight lawyers plus directors includes citizens of eight different countries: Canada, Germany, India, Ireland, New Zealand, Peru, Philippines, and Zimbabwe.

While small, the ACWL serves its clients with a staff that has measurable indicators of relevant and useful diversity and talent. For such a small group, the lawyers bring a considerable variety of WTO-relevant experience from their employment before they joined the ACWL—ranging from private practice at major law firms involved in WTO litigation, to trade ministries of various WTO member governments, to working within the WTO Secretariat itself in the area of the DSU.

As another measure of quality, the members of the ACWL legal team were educated at some of the best programs worldwide for international economic law (for example, Cambridge University, University of Chicago, Oxford University, and the World Trade Institute). Finally, they are recognized by peers as experts in the field, as evidenced by invitations to lecture on the WTO around the world and their published articles on the WTO in top-level professional journals.

The Demand Side for ACWL Services: Fees and Access

Once a developing country accedes to the ACWL and pays the membership cost to the cooperative Endowment Fund, it is entitled to use the ACWL's legal services at relatively modest fees. These fees are well below the typical market rates for lawyers at the private law firms involved in WTO litigation.[10] For ACWL members, there is generally no charge for obtaining legal advice on an issue of WTO law. For example, there would be no cost for a short opinion or a brief answer to a government official's question on whether a piece of proposed domestic legislation would be consistent with the country's WTO obligations.

Fees for using the ACWL's services in the context of an actual WTO trade dispute are based on a sliding scale, depending on whether the ACWL member is in

10. The schedule of fees is set out in Annex IV of the Agreement Establishing the ACWL (www.acwl.ch/e/about/organisational_e.aspx [December 10, 2008]).

category A ($200 per hour), B ($150 per hour), or C ($100 per hour), or is classified as a least developed country ($25 per hour). Developing countries that are nonmembers of the ACWL can also access ACWL legal services at slightly higher rates than ACWL members pay, thus maintaining an incentive for membership.

In addition to creating a sliding scale of hourly billing rates depending on the developing countries' categories, the ACWL has also sought to reduce cost uncertainty associated with DSU litigation by creating an expected time budget that establishes a maximum number of billable hours that clients will be charged, which is based on each phase of the DSU proceeding. As of 2007, the ACWL's estimates of the maximum number of hours indicate that the bill for hourly legal services related to a dispute could not exceed $170,800, even for a dispute that went all the way from consultations through a Panel proceeding and ruling and then through to the Appellate Body.[11] This, of course, is significantly lower than the private attorney fees for some of the disputes described in chapter 5, which have reached into the millions of dollars.

Although access to high-quality, low-cost WTO legal advice may be available at the ACWL, there are procedural barriers that may impose other costs on the firms and industries most in need of the legal assistance that the ACWL provides. One obvious cost to firms and other private entities reflects the ACWL's mandate as an IGO, which allows only ACWL members' governments, rather than exporting firms, to initiate contact with the ACWL.[12]

Consider the implications of this limited access to the ACWL in the context of the hypothetical case I introduced in chapter 5. Michele Brown, who works for a firm in a developing country, believes her firm's, and country's, foreign market access interests have been violated. Before Michele can raise her questions of WTO enforcement with the experts at the ACWL, she first has to convince her government to initiate discussions with the ACWL. Michele cannot contact the Centre directly.

This mandate imposes a sharp limit on the contribution that the ACWL can make to the overall extended litigation process of WTO enforcement. Specifically, the ACWL cannot subsidize the cost of acquiring the economic, legal, and political information that Michele will need to convince her firm and her government that a foreign market access complaint is worth pursuing. Within the

11. Converted at the exchange rate of CHF1.62 per U.S.$1, see ACWL (2007, pp. 26–27). The ACWL breaks down its maximum charges according to the three distinct phases of the DSU process: consultations (a maximum of $29,400, or CHF47,628), Panel proceedings (a maximum of $88,800, or CHF143,856), and Appellate Body proceedings (a maximum of $52,600, or CHF85,212).

12. In particular, the ACWL states, "The ACWL's mandate is limited to giving advice to developing countries and LDCs [Least Developed Countries]. It cannot, therefore, respond to requests for advice by developed countries, non-governmental organizations, *private entities within a developing country or groupings of countries,* unless the government of a country entitled to the ACWL's services has endorsed that request." See ACWL (2007, p. 12, emphasis added).

context of the six-step ELP (figure 5-1) described in chapter 5, the ACWL can only enter after step 3 and after the firm and industry have already petitioned their government and convinced it to look into the WTO enforcement issue in more depth. Therefore, the ACWL's substantive contribution is likely to take place mainly in step 4 of the ELP, when it provides relatively low-cost legal assistance in cases that have already reached the stage of potential WTO litigation under the DSU.[13]

A final question to consider on the demand side for ACWL services is what happens if two developing countries both seek access to the subsidized, high-quality legal assistance that the ACWL provides and they are on opposing sides in a dispute? Can the ACWL represent both sides of a dispute? This is likely to be an issue, especially given the data in chapters 2 and 4, which indicate that many trade barriers that WTO enforcement seeks to remove involve developing country challenges to other developing countries.

In fact, the ACWL cannot represent both sides of any given WTO dispute. However, the ACWL has institutionalized a procedure to handle this problem. For example, if it cannot represent a developing country as a respondent in a particular dispute because it has already agreed to represent a developing country on the complainant side, the respondent can still access subsidized, high-quality legal assistance from an alternative source. The alternative source is the ACWL's roster of external legal counsel, which is a list of individuals and law firms to which the ACWL outsources clients in cases of conflict of interest. The client that is "second to show up" chooses a law firm or individual from the list and pays fees to the ACWL.[14] The ACWL then makes up the difference between those fees and the charges imposed by the private law firm or lawyer doing the work.

ACWL Involvement in WTO Disputes

The next step is a first attempt to assess empirically some elements of the theory justifying the creation of the ACWL. I have described the ACWL as an institution designed to assist developing countries in their enforcement of WTO market

---

13. This is not to suggest that the ACWL does not work with clients to help them determine whether any particular dispute is worth pursuing. The ACWL surely uses its WTO legal expertise to inform governments that certain cases are not worth pursuing, despite the information that Michele Brown has compiled. The point is that the ACWL does not enter the extended litigation process at all until it is so requested by Michele's government, and chapter 5 identified many hurdles that may create barriers to potential disputes reaching step 4 and hence the ACWL.

14. Using law firms from the external counsel list is more expensive than accessing ACWL legal services because the price is 20 percent higher than the listed hourly rate for ACWL lawyers. See the schedule of fees set out in Annex IV of the Agreement Establishing the ACWL at the ACWL's website (www.acwl.ch/e/about/organisational_e.aspx [December 10, 2008]).

access through the DSU. What can be learned by examining the data on how the ACWL has actually been used?

This section begins by examining the ACWL's WTO caseload using data on members' use of the ACWL's litigation services: which countries the ACWL has represented in DSU cases, how frequently the ACWL has represented countries, and against which respondent countries the ACWL has represented developing country complainants.

To determine whether the introduction of the ACWL has affected the WTO dispute caseload, I then turn to economic theory to identify a number of different ways in which the mere introduction of the ACWL might affect a country's access to WTO dispute settlement through the number or the composition of enforcement cases that a country pursues. In addition to the ACWL's existence simply increasing the number of disputes that developing countries bring before the DSU, theory also suggests particular channels through which the ACWL may affect the pattern of cases initiated.

First, I examine the country composition of complainants. The ACWL's existence lowers the cost to a country of pursuing a WTO dispute, which may affect the observed country-level DSU caseload pattern through at least two different margins. The ACWL could affect the DSU caseload through what economists call the *intensive margin*—lower enforcement costs could lead to more disputes brought forward by the same countries that have brought disputes forward previously. The ACWL may also affect the pattern of DSU cases through the *extensive margin*—new complainant countries using the DSU for the first time. Results based on the limited evidence on the use of the ACWL to date suggest that the ACWL may be affecting the country composition of disputes through the intensive margin, that is, more disputes by the same countries, not through the extensive margin, that is, disputes by new countries.

The underlying theory also suggests that within countries, introduction of the ACWL may result in those countries that have used the DSU previously pursuing different *types* of cases, as well as pursuing the same types of cases *differently*. For example, I examine evidence on whether the availability of ACWL assistance may be empowering these particular countries through two specific channels. For the first channel, countries that would not otherwise have been able to do so can now pursue sole-complainant disputes on behalf of their exporters. Concerning the second channel, countries now are able to pursue the actual DSU legal process more extensively in support of any given market access enforcement interest. These possibilities in the data are explored below.

Next, because the ACWL reduces the costs faced by exporting firms, industries, and countries in enforcing their foreign market access, subsidized litigation costs may also have a scale effect even within the countries that are the historical users of the DSU and seem to be pursuing more disputes. In addition to a cost-shifting effect (litigation costs are transferred from developing country exporters to developed country funders of the ACWL), the cost reduction due to the ACWL may reduce the *threshold scale* of market access at stake that is necessary to initiate a dispute. As discussed below, the empirical analysis of ACWL-backed cases compared with disputes brought forward by ACWL-eligible countries but without ACWL assistance finds some evidence in the data of such a differential pattern based on the scale of market access.

Finally, in the last three subsections I examine other aspects to the data of how the ACWL may be affecting developing country access to WTO enforcement. One section examines the data on the provision of legal opinions by the ACWL and thus potential information generation. The second focuses on the externality benefits derived from ACWL coordination of outside lawyers through its roster of external counsel. The last section concludes with a brief discussion of the outcomes of ACWL-backed disputes.

The ACWL in WTO Disputes: What Role? For Whom? How Frequently?

To justify the existence of the ACWL, it is easiest simply to describe the use of its WTO dispute settlement services. I begin by examining the ACWL workload on behalf of developing countries in WTO litigation over its first seven years of existence.[15] Table 6-3 provides a breakdown of ACWL involvement in WTO dispute settlement cases between 2001 and 2008.

The time period studied begins with the ACWL's first case in 2001 assisting Peru in *EC–Sardines* (DS231) and ends with the request in 2008 for consultations on behalf of Indonesia for *South Africa–AD Measures on Uncoated Woodfree Paper* (DS374). During this period, WTO members initiated 144 formal disputes against one another. Of these cases, the ACWL has been involved in twenty-three, or 16 percent of all disputes.[16] So the ACWL has been busy.

What services did the ACWL provide in these cases? The ACWL is most frequently involved in the DSU process standing behind one of the primary litigants, typically representing the complainant that initiated the case. Of the

15. I focus the discussion of the data for the DSU cases initiated between the establishment of the ACWL in 2001 and 2008. As of December 2008, the last listed ACWL dispute for 2008 was DS374, for which the request for consultations was May 2008. The date of that dispute thus forms the benchmark period for this comparative exercise analyzing dispute participation by the ACWL.

16. The ACWL has been involved in three other disputes (for example, DS141, DS146, and DS192) that were initiated before 2001 and thus before the ACWL came into existence. While the ACWL did not assist developing countries in the initiation of these cases, the ACWL was asked to assist a developing country at a later phase of the multiyear dispute settlement process.

Table 6-3. *ACWL Participation in WTO Trade Disputes, 2001–08*[a]

WTO dispute, year initiated	ACWL client, role in dispute
EC–Bed Linen, 1998[b]	India, potential appellant
India–Autos, 1998[b]	India, respondent
US–Cotton Yarn, 2000[b]	Pakistan, complainant
EC–Sardines, 2001	Peru, complainant
Turkey–Fresh Fruit Import Procedures, 2001	Ecuador, complainant
US–Textiles Rules of Origin, 2002	India, complainant
EC–Tariff Preferences, 2002	India, complainant; Paraguay, Colombia,[c] Ecuador,[c] Peru,[c] and Venezuela[c] as third parties
US–Softwood Lumber V, 2002	Thailand, third party
US–Upland Cotton, 2002	Chad, third party
Australia–Fresh Fruit and Vegetables, 2002	Philippines, complainant
Australia–Certain Measures Affecting the Importation of Fresh Pineapple, 2002	Philippines, complainant
EC–Export Subsidies on Sugar, 2003	Thailand, complainant
Mexico–Certain Measures Preventing the Importation of Black Beans from Nicaragua, 2003	Nicaragua, complainant
EC–Chicken Cuts, 2003	Thailand, complainant
Dominican Republic–Import and Sale of Cigarettes, 2003	Honduras, complainant; Dominican Republic,[c] respondent
India–AD Measure on Batteries from Bangladesh, 2004	Bangladesh, complainant
Korea–Certain Paper, 2004	Indonesia, complainant
US–Zeroing (Japan), 2004	Thailand, third party
Egypt–Matches, 2005	Pakistan, complainant
Mexico–Steel Pipes and Tubes, 2005	Guatemala, complainant
Turkey–Rice, 2006	Turkey,[c] respondent
US–Shrimp (Thailand), 2006	Thailand, complainant
Colombia–Customs Measures on Importation of Certain Goods from Panama, 2006	Panama, complainant
EC–Regime for the Importation of Bananas, 2007	Colombia, complainant

WTO dispute, year initiated	ACWL client, role in dispute
Colombia–Ports of Entry, 2007	Panama, complainant; Colombia,[c] respondent
South Africa–AD Measures on Uncoated Woodfree Paper, 2008	Indonesia, complainant

Sources: Advisory Centre on WTO Law, "Assistance in WTO Dispute Settlement Proceedings since July 2001" (www.acwl.ch/e/dispute/wto_e.aspx).

a. Through May 2008.

b. Dispute initiated before the establishment of the ACWL in 2001; the ACWL assisted at a later phase of the multiyear dispute settlement process, such as the appeal.

Though information was not updated on its website, the ACWL is also advising Thailand in *Thailand–Customs and Fiscal Measures on Cigarettes from the Philippines* (DS371) and *US–Anti-Dumping Measures on Polyethylene Retail Carrier Bags from Thailand* (DS383); this information is from private correspondence with the ACWL.

c. Legal assistance provided not by the ACWL but through a firm hired from ACWL's roster of external legal counsel.

twenty-three disputes from 2001 to 2008 in which the ACWL has played some role on behalf of a developing country, in nineteen instances it assisted the complainant country. In the other four instances, the ACWL weighed into a dispute by assisting a country participating as an interested third party, and in none of these twenty-three cases did it assist the respondent country directly—though in three cases a law firm from the ACWL's external counsel roster was used to provide ACWL-like assistance to developing country respondents.[17]

To put the role and the magnitude of the ACWL contribution to the DSU caseload into some perspective, during the dispute initiation period covered between 2001 and 2008, the ACWL (nineteen times) has worked legally on behalf of complainant members in more disputes than any WTO member acted as a complainant in its own disputes except for the United States (also nineteen times) and the EC (twenty-one times).[18]

17. The three respondent developing countries given ACWL-like assistance (in terms of prices) were the Dominican Republic in DS302, Colombia in DS366, and Turkey in DS344. The ACWL could not provide the legal assistance itself in the first two disputes, since it was representing the complainants. In the DS344 dispute, the ACWL could not represent Turkey because of a separate conflict of interest. (In DS146, the ACWL did assist India as a respondent country, but this dispute was initiated before the establishment of the ACWL.)

18. The ACWL has not been as busy as the WTO trade litigators in the USTR and DG Trade offices during this time period for other reasons. While the ACWL has been able to focus its DSU work almost exclusively on legal support of complainant countries, these other two WTO members have also had to defend themselves as respondents in forty-six (United States) and twenty-eight (EC) cases and have served as an interested third party in another thirty-four (United States) and forty-seven (EC) cases.

The ACWL has provided DSU litigation services directly to seventeen developing countries. Its most frequent clients have been Thailand (5 times) and India (4 times). Other repeat clients for ACWL DSU support services include Indonesia, Pakistan, Panama, and the Philippines. To the extent that repeat clients are broadly indicative of satisfaction with the quality of services provided, repeat demand for ACWL services suggests that at least some clients are pleased with the output.

Who are the targets of ACWL clients for WTO enforcement? As discussed in chapter 4, a large share of all DSU cases involve either the United States or the EC, given their dominant import markets and importance in world trade. ACWL involvement in cases against the United States and the EC is therefore not surprising; the ACWL represented complainant countries filing cases most frequently against the United States (three times) and the EC (six times). Because the United States and the EC are often the dominant import markets for developing country exports, the ACWL will frequently line up against these particular respondent countries representing developing country complainant export interests.[19]

Any allegation of ACWL bias against the EC and the United States is quickly dismissed once the next simple feature of the data is examined. As the main legal assistance center for developing countries, the ACWL has been asked by clients to help bring forward nine disputes that challenge other developing countries. To put this differently, of the total of fifty-four complaints that WTO members lodged against developing countries during this 2001–08 period, the ACWL worked on behalf of the complainant country in 17 percent of them. The ACWL has therefore worked on behalf of complainants who have filed more disputes against developing countries than all other WTO members have filed during this time period except the EC (ten times) and the United States (twelve times).[20] This reinforces one of the central points made repeatedly throughout this book—firms in developing countries are not interested solely in

19. However, when the ACWL works on behalf of a complainant taking on either the United States or the EC, the other frequently aligns with the ACWL and its client's position as an interested third party. Examples would include DS283, *EC–Export Subsidies on Sugar,* in which the United States as a third party supported the position of the ACWL client Thailand, and in DS343, *US–Shrimp (Thailand),* in which the EC as a third party also supported the ACWL client Thailand.

20. It is also worth pointing out that the ACWL's clients tend to focus on initiating disputes against different developing countries compared with those disputes initiated by the United States or the EC. Of these twenty-two disputes that the United States and the EC filed collectively against developing countries during this time period, twelve were filed against either India or China. The ACWL, however, has only been involved in one case filed against India (the case brought by Bangladesh) and none against China. This is further evidence that exporters in developing countries are interested in self-enforcing access in different foreign markets in developing countries than are exporters in the United States and the EC.

enforcing access to northern markets. Firms and industries in developing countries also want reduced trade barriers in southern markets, and this evidence from the ACWL caseload confirms that developing country governments use the WTO for this purpose.

As particular examples from table 6-3, the ACWL has worked for Guatemala and Nicaragua in separate cases against Mexico, Honduras against the Dominican Republic, Ecuador against Turkey, Pakistan against Egypt, Indonesia against South Africa, Bangladesh against India, and Panama against Colombia.

Another interesting element of this list is the symbolism attached to these last two disputes: the ACWL working for Bangladesh against India, and for Panama against Colombia. These disputes are particularly noteworthy because table 6-3 also indicates that the ACWL worked on behalf of India and Colombia on the complainant side during the same time period. If the ACWL can be trusted by government officials from Bangladesh and Panama to act as their advocate in taking on the Indian or Colombian policies in one dispute, and then also be trusted by government officials from India or Colombia as their advocate in a different dispute, the ACWL must play a very diplomatic game. The fact that the ACWL must be able to play this diplomatic game does create explicit limits as to where the ACWL can step into the ELP on behalf of developing countries. The fact that it cannot cover the entire ELP and is essentially limited to step 4 therefore creates gaps and a demand for other groups to step in, which is a concern that is discussed in substantial detail below.

Finally, most of the disputes are in sectors of export market access that are of broad interest to developing countries. As the list in table 6-3 indicates, the WTO member was interested in enforcing foreign market access in either agriculture (including foodstuffs and fisheries) or textiles and apparel in thirteen out of the twenty-one disputes in which the ACWL represented the complainant. This fits into the expectations based on the chapter 2 discussion of developing country trading interests and the WTO Agreements.

Now that I have described data on the provision of ACWL services in the WTO caseload, I turn next to the more difficult questions concerning whether and how the introduction of the ACWL might be affecting the DSU caseload relative to counterfactual scenarios in which the ACWL did not exist.

The ACWL's Effect on the DSU Caseload: More Cases by Developing Countries since 2001?

The first place to examine whether the ACWL is affecting WTO dispute settlement activity is simply in the time series of data. Is there is a sharp increase in developing country WTO dispute settlement activity since the ACWL's establishment in 2001?

Figure 6-1. *WTO Dispute Initiations, by Category of Complainant,
1995–2001 and 2002–08*[a]

Disputes initiated per year

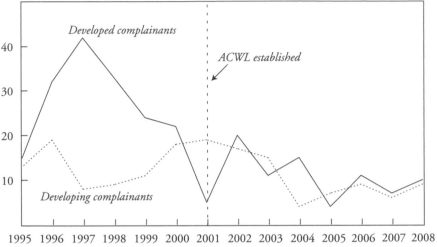

Source: Author's compilations from WTO (2009).

Figure 6-1 illustrates the initiation of WTO disputes by developed and
developing country complainants over the 1995–2008 period. In terms of the
number of disputes initiated by developing countries, there does not appear to
be an obvious break in the pattern of the data associated with the arrival of the
ACWL in 2001. Developing countries initiated, on average, almost twelve
WTO disputes per year during the sample. During the 2000–04 period, the
average was higher at seventeen disputes per year, but otherwise the rate of initiation by developing countries is relatively steady throughout the sample. Figure
6-1 does not suggest that the introduction of the ACWL has dramatically
increased the number of developing country–initiated disputes relative to the
pre-ACWL period.

As I have already discussed in substantial length in chapter 4, the major trend
in the data illustrated in figure 6-1 comes from the change in the relative frequency with which developed countries (especially the United States and the
EC) have initiated WTO disputes over time. The immediate establishment of
the WTO in 1995 at the end of the Uruguay Round led to an average of
twenty-eight developed country complainant disputes per year before 2001.
After 2001, developed countries have averaged less than half that number of initiations, or roughly eleven per year.

Thus a larger share of WTO disputes has been initiated by developing countries since the July 2001 establishment of the ACWL. On the one hand, between January 1, 1995, and June 30, 2001, developed countries initiated 172 disputes compared with 90 disputes initiated by developing countries—almost a 2:1 ratio.[21] On the other hand, between July 1, 2001, and December 31, 2008, developed countries initiated only 80 disputes to the 73 initiations by developing country complainants, an almost 1:1 ratio.

The difficulty in attempting to assess from the dispute initiation data alone the impact of the ACWL is that many other things are changing during this time period that can also be expected to affect countries' relative demands for WTO enforcement. As already observed in chapter 4 (see figure 4-2), good export performance for both developed and developing countries during this time period lowers the incidence of grievances and thus demands for WTO enforcement overall and is therefore one contributing explanation for a relative decline in the aggregate number of dispute initiations since 2001.

To summarize, the post-2001 period has seen a relative increase in developing country initiations of WTO disputes vis-à-vis the number of disputes initiated by developed countries. Although the total number of disputes initiated by developing countries per year has been relatively stable over time, this change in relative share is dominated by the fact that the number of disputes initiated by developed countries fell dramatically. Because many things were changing during this time period in addition to the establishment of the ACWL, one cannot rely on this as a definitive indicator of an empirical relationship. Thus in the next sections, I look more closely at the data to identify potential channels and margins through which the ACWL may affect the composition of WTO enforcement cases that developing countries pursue.

The ACWL's Effect on the DSU Caseload: New Countries or More Cases by the Same Countries?

An additional way to investigate the channels through which the ACWL may affect the DSU enforcement caseload is through a more detailed analysis of the countries using its services. Once again, in the context of the ELP model developed in chapter 5, the ACWL lowers the cost of enforcing a trading partner's WTO commitment to keep market access open to foreign firms.

Here I examine data on whether the ACWL may have an impact on the country-level composition of cases. The ACWL could affect the DSU caseload

---

21. Again, to be consistent with the way in which the data were broken down in chapter 4, I convert the 388 dispute initiations between 1995 and 2008 into 415 bilateral pairs of disputes, since there are some disputes with multiple complainant countries.

Table 6-4. *ACWL Clients in WTO Disputes before and after First ACWL Experience, 2001–08*[a]

Country	First time ACWL client	No. of times ACWL client	No. of times WTO disputant before first ACWL experience as			No. of times WTO disputant after first ACWL experience as		
			Com-plainant	Respon-dent	Third party	Com-plainant	Respon-dent	Third party
Bangladesh	2004	1	0	0	1	0	0	0
Chad	2007	1	0	0	0	0	0	0
Colombia	2007	2	4	2	16	0	1	0
Dominican Rep.	2003	1	0	1	3	0	1	0
Ecuador	2001	2	1	2	6	1	1	3
Guatemala	2005	1	5	2	9	0	0	2
Honduras	2003	1	4	0	10	0	0	2
India	2001	4	11	13	31	4	7	20
Indonesia	2004	2	2	4	4	1	0	0
Nicaragua	2003	1	0	2	5	0	0	1
Pakistan	2001	2	1	2	4	1	0	5
Panama	2006	2	2	1	2	2	0	0
Paraguay	2002	1	0	0	5	0	0	9
Peru	2001	2	1	2	4	0	2	4
Philippines	2002	2	2	4	4	1	0	1
Thailand	2003	5	8	1	23	4	2	14
Venezuela	2001	1	1	1	4	0	1	10

Source: Data compiled by the author from matching public records from Advisory Centre on WTO Law's website with public information on World Trade Organization's website.

a. Through May 2008 and dispute DS374.

through the intensive margin, that is, lower enforcement costs could lead to more disputes brought forward by the same countries that have brought disputes forward previously. Second, the ACWL may also affect the pattern of DSU cases through the extensive margin, that is, new complainants with no prior history of using WTO dispute settlement may use the DSU for the first time because of the lower enforcement costs that the ACWL provides.

Table 6-4 examines the relative importance of the intensive or extensive margins at the country level. For each ACWL client, the table shows the year the country first used the ACWL for DSU services, how many times it had used the DSU prior to being an ACWL client (broken down by instances as complainant, respondent, or interested third party), and how many times it has subsequently turned to DSU enforcement after it used the ACWL for the first time.

To interpret the information in table 6-4, consider what it implies for a country like Ecuador. Ecuador first used the ACWL for a WTO dispute initiated in 2001. Before this dispute, Ecuador had been involved in nine WTO cases: one prior experience as a complainant, two as a respondent, and six as a third party. Overall it has used ACWL services twice. Since its initial involvement with the ACWL in its 2001 dispute, Ecuador has only been involved in five additional WTO disputes—once as a complainant, once as a respondent, and three times as a third party.

Ecuador is quite representative of the ACWL's clients thus far. When we measure experience by involvement in initiated cases, most clients had substantial prior experience in WTO enforcement before their first use of ACWL services. Almost all of the countries using the ACWL during the 2001–08 period appear to be countries with past experience in the DSU, and they are thus using the ACWL to assist in the initiation of additional disputes (the intensive margin). Although this conclusion is based on data for only seven years and seventeen countries, there is nevertheless almost no evidence that the ACWL has served to introduce more countries (the extensive margin) to formal WTO enforcement. The only example of a country that had no prior experience in a formal WTO dispute before working with the ACWL was Chad, which used the ACWL to represent it as a third party in the *US–Upland Cotton* dispute.[22] All other ACWL clients had prior DSU litigation experience. Although there is nothing to rule out the possibility that as more time passes, word of the ACWL and its services will spread to new countries that will use the ACWL to start enforcing foreign market access commitments, there is little evidence that that has taken place thus far.

The data show that countries with prior DSU experience use the ACWL to pursue more cases. The intensive margin effect suggests that the ACWL may have lowered the cost to WTO self-enforcement, but not by enough to introduce completely new countries to formal DSU activity. The countries that use and benefit from the ACWL are able to lower the costs of the actual litigation involved in the ELP (step 4)—costs that would be higher if the country's government were to do it all itself or if it were to outsource it to a private sector law firm.

Given the ACWL mandate that limits ACWL assistance to only step 4 in the ELP, it is not surprising that the ACWL is primarily affecting the intensive margin: more disputes initiated by the same historical DSU-using countries. The ACWL cannot independently and proactively gather information at the prelitigation stage about possible violations of WTO commitments to alert developing countries that their market access might be at risk. Furthermore, the ACWL cannot even have direct (nonauthorized) contact with the exporting firms with

---

22. Even in this instance, the ACWL assisted Chad in the dispute's latter phase of an Article 21.5 Compliance Panel (ACWL 2008). As an interested third party, Chad received pro bono assistance during the earlier Panel and Appellate Body phases (see figure 5-1) of the dispute from the Geneva office of the law firm White & Case (see table 5-3).

foreign market access concerns and questions that they might like to have answered, but only with their governments. Given these institutional constraints, the ACWL is really only a mechanism to assist countries that are already relatively knowledgeable about the WTO and the ELP.[23]

The ACWL's Effect on the DSU Caseload: The Same Countries but More Empowered?

Although there is scant evidence that the ACWL has introduced WTO enforcement to new countries without previous DSU experience, the Centre may still have an effect if it empowers previous users with new resources to pursue different cases, as well as to pursue cases differently, than they otherwise would without ACWL assistance. Here I examine two particular channels through which ACWL resources may affect developing countries. The first channel is concerned with countries filing more sole-complainant disputes on behalf of their exporters. The second channel pertains to countries pursuing the DSU legal process more extensively in support of any given market access enforcement interest.

Table 6-5 presents some evidence consistent with the theory that the ACWL is empowering developing countries through these two channels to undertake DSU-related activities that they might not otherwise have the resource capacity to pursue.[24] The table lists the thirteen developing countries that used the ACWL between 2001 and 2008 to file at least one sole-complainant WTO enforcement action. While eleven out of these thirteen countries had filed at least one complaint at the WTO previously, eight out of the thirteen had never previously filed a WTO complaint on their own. Most of these countries' experience in dispute settlement was therefore in instances in which they either rode the coattails of a more powerful WTO member in a dispute—for example, following the U.S. lead in *EC–Bananas III,* or the EC lead in *US–Offset Act (Byrd Amendment)*—or in which they pooled their resources as part of a collective action—for example, *US–Shrimp.*[25]

---

23. As I describe in more detail in chapter 7, Chad's introduction to the ACWL in the *US–Upland Cotton* dispute was facilitated by relatively sophisticated nongovernmental organizations—such as the IDEAS Centre, Oxfam, and the International Centre for Trade and Sustainable Development (ICTSD)—that have offices in Geneva and work on WTO issues.

24. This evidence is merely consistent with this theory. Because all of these countries have some prior DSU experience, these data do not allow one to disentangle this theory from an alternative theory suggesting that it is not the access to new litigation support resources that matters but that these countries are more likely both to pursue sole-complainant disputes and to more completely engage the process through to an issuance of a legal ruling because of the knowledge they obtained by participating, albeit tangentially, in prior DSU activity.

25. *US–Shrimp* was a collective challenge brought by a number of Southeast Asian shrimp-exporting countries to a U.S. ban on shrimp sourced from countries that did not mandate that

Table 6-5. *Countries Using the ACWL to Initiate Sole-Complainant WTO Disputes, 2001–08*[a]

Country	No. of prior disputes as complainant	No. of prior disputes as sole complainant	No. of prior disputes as sole complainant resulting in at least a Panel report	No. of ACWL-backed disputes as sole complainant resulting in at least a Panel report
Bangladesh	0	0	0	0[b]
Colombia	4	3	0	0
Ecuador	1	0	0	1[b]
Guatemala	5	2	0	1
Honduras	4	0	0	1
India	11	8	3	2
Indonesia	2	0[c]	0	1
Nicaragua	0	0	0	0[b]
Pakistan	1	0	0	1[b]
Panama	2	0[c]	0	0
Peru	1	0	0	1
Philippines	2	1[c]	1	0
Thailand	8	2[c]	0	1[c]

Source: Data compiled by the author from matching public records from Advisory Centre on WTO Law's website with public information on World Trade Organization's website.

a. Through May 2008 and dispute DS374. "Prior" indicates before the instance of the country first using ACWL services as a complainant in DSU proceedings.

b. Indicates at least one additional sole-complainant dispute that resulted in a settlement communicated to the WTO as a "mutually agreed upon solution."

c. Sole-complainant disputes that were tied into larger disputes pursued by other WTO members: for India: *Turkey–Textiles*; for Indonesia: *Argentina–Safeguard Measures on Imports of Footwear*; for Panama: *EC–Regime for the Importation of Bananas*; for the Philippines: *US–Import Prohibition of Certain Shrimp and Shrimp Products*; for Thailand, for prior ACWL experience disputes: *EC–Duties on Imports of Rice*, *Turkey–Restrictions on Imports of Textile and Clothing Products, EC–Tariff Preferences*; for ACWL-backed disputes: *EC–Export Subsidies on Sugar* and *EC–Chicken Cuts*.

Access to the ACWL may therefore provide resources for developing countries to start pursuing a greater range of enforcement cases in which their firms alone have a foreign market concern and in which they do not have the option to share the litigation cost burden with other exporting countries facing the same trade restriction. This may be increasingly important given the ongoing proliferation of discriminatory, country-specific trade barriers imposed by

their shrimp were caught using turtle excluder devices (TEDs) that reduced the death of endangered sea turtles. *US–Offset Act (Byrd Amendment)* was a dispute in which the EC led a group of developed and developing economies challenging a change in the U.S. law that mandated that the U.S. government pass on the antidumping duties that had been collected to the firms that were behind the domestic petition for new antidumping measures. The *EC–Bananas III* dispute is discussed extensively in chapter 3.

WTO members, such as antidumping measures. For foreign market access violations like these, it may be impossible for exporters in one country to organize with exporters of another country to challenge a foreign country's action collectively because the foreign country's actions against each exporting country are unique and thus may involve different WTO violations.[26]

The second empowerment channel examines whether the ACWL's sole-complainant clients are able to pursue the DSU process more extensively within any given initiated case. Merely looking at data on initiated disputes hides important elements of the story. A dispute may get initiated to draw attention to an enforcement issue but then subsequently is dropped if there are insufficient resources to pursue it all the way through the dispute settlement process.[27] Is there evidence that, by providing its clients with deeper pockets, ACWL services encourage developing countries to use the legal process more extensively, so as to generate rulings and potentially public support to assist their enforcement actions?

The third column of table 6-5 reveals that only two (India and the Philippines) out of these thirteen ACWL sole-complainant client countries had ever been part of a prior sole-complainant DSU proceeding that pushed the legal process sufficiently so as to obtain even a Panel ruling. Compare this with the data of the last column, which indicate that, with the backing of the ACWL, seven "new" countries have pushed their sole-complainant cases to a Panel ruling for the first time. Furthermore, the data for the other four out of the eleven sole-complainant ACWL clients (without prior experience of litigating to a Panel report) are not entirely negative. Two of the countries (Bangladesh and Nicaragua) settled their disputes through "mutually agreed upon understanding" notifications to the WTO before there was a need to obtain a Panel ruling. As for the other two countries (Colombia and Panama), their ACWL-backed disputes were initiated too recently to know whether they will proceed to a legal ruling.

Although the previous section found almost no evidence that the ACWL is introducing completely new countries without prior DSU experience to WTO self-enforcement, the evidence does suggest that the ACWL is empowering

---

26. Because such measures are also applied on an exporting country–specific basis, it may also be the case that there are no other countries with exporters adversely affected with which to act collectively.

27. Disputes can also terminate early if countries in the dispute reach a settlement that resolves the issue. Nevertheless, even respondent countries may decide not to stop the legal process of a dispute (despite it being a "losing" case) for a number of reasons, including the desire to obtain impartial legal rulings and potential retaliation threats to take back to domestic political constituencies to help convince them of the need to undertake reform. (See again the issues raised in the discussion of *EC–Bananas III* in chapter 3 and also the two sections in chapter 5 on the costs of obtaining compliance and retaliation threats by developing countries to obtain compliance.) Furthermore, a developing country complainant with access to resources to fully litigate the case may be less likely to settle a dispute early when doing so would result in a bad economic outcome.

many developing countries with prior, albeit sometimes minimal, DSU experience to do more. The evidence is consistent with the theory that access to ACWL resources affects developing countries through at least two different channels. In particular, the ACWL has backed thirteen developing countries that initiated at least one sole-complainant DSU case during the 2001–08 period. Eight of these thirteen countries had never before initiated a sole-complainant dispute, and eleven of these thirteen had never pushed a sole-complainant dispute at the WTO even so far as to achieve a first-level Panel ruling. Of these eleven countries without prior sole-complainant experience, the ACWL has provided the litigation support to allow seven to pursue their own sole-complainant action to at least a Panel ruling for the first time.

The ACWL's Effect on the DSU Caseload: Is There a Scale Effect?

Even though the ACWL may have yet to introduce new countries to WTO enforcement (refer back to table 6-4), an additional mechanism through which it may affect dispute settlement is through the composition of cases initiated. Recall that the ACWL offers legal assistance to developing countries at a lower cost than they would be able to find in the marketplace. Consider that fact within the context of the ELP model that I developed in chapter 5 and the example of the exporting firm facing a cost of enforcing WTO commitments. Even though the introduction of the ACWL has not yet resulted in new countries actively enforcing their exporters' WTO market access interests, in this section I examine whether the provision of subsidized litigation affects the pattern of cases pursued within a given country through two different channels—a *cost-shifting* effect, as well as a *scale* effect.

The first possibility is that while the introduction of the ACWL subsidizes the litigation costs for poor countries, it does not lower the overall costs of the ELP enough to affect the composition of cases litigated at the WTO. If so, the cases are the same cases that would have been brought without the ACWL. Although there is no change in the composition of the overall DSU caseload (relative to a hypothetical world without the ACWL), existence of the ACWL makes it cheaper (to the developing country) to bring the same cases that it would have brought anyway. The main mechanism through which the ACWL's existence would then benefit developing countries is through a cost-shifting effect—that is, while the rate of WTO enforcement with an ACWL in existence is unchanged, the cost of enforcement to developing countries using the ACWL is lower because developed country funders of the Centre have borne a substantial share of the financial burden.

A second possibility is that introducing the ACWL lowers the costs of self-enforcement enough to change the *scale* of enforcement cases that countries can pursue at the WTO. Holding constant the potential ACWL benefit to developing countries that occurs through the cost-shifting effect, the ACWL may allow more and more commitments of foreign market access, and hence more overall trade, to be enforceable given this lower cost at the WTO. To explain how the scale effect might work, suppose that without the ACWL, the high cost of litigation makes it only cost-effective for exporters to initiate cases over WTO violations that concern lost annual exports of $15 million or more for any given product. Lowering the enforcement cost may allow countries that can only export annually less than $15 million of a given product to be able to self-enforce foreign commitments that would not be enforceable in the face of high costs. It is through this channel that *more* commitments would become enforceable. In this section I examine the data for one sign of evidence of such a scale effect.[28]

One indicator of a scale effect that is consistent with the underlying theory would be if the ACWL were picking off a distinct class of cases according to the size of the market access at stake. To examine this possibility, I focus on a subset of disputes from table 6-3: specifically the cases in which the ACWL worked for a complainant country on a challenge to a respondent's antidumping (AD) measure. I then compare features of the data from these disputes with the data from another, otherwise comparable, set of disputes. The comparable disputes are WTO enforcement cases that also involve developing country challenges to foreign AD actions that were initiated during the same time period. These are cases in which the ACWL-eligible complainant country could have enjoyed access to subsidized legal support (from the ACWL) in bringing forward the case but chose not to do so and instead brought the dispute forward independently. The list of non-ACWL-backed disputes includes disputes initiated by developing countries that did not accede to the ACWL (Argentina and Brazil), as well as ACWL members that simply chose not to use the ACWL services in this particular case (India, Taiwan, and Turkey).

Table 6-6 provides data from these two sets of ACWL-eligible developing countries that filed WTO disputes over challenges to a WTO member's use of antidumping measures. The top half of the table lists DSU challenges in which countries did not use the ACWL services; the lower half of the table lists challenges in which WTO members used the ACWL. Consider first a WTO dispute such as *EC–Anti-Dumping Duties on Certain Flat Rolled Iron or Non-Alloy Steel Products from India,* a case that India brought without ACWL assistance against the EC. In the three years before the EC import restriction, Indian

---

28. These results are necessarily preliminary because the ACWL has been in existence only since 2001, and the number of cases in which it has been involved is relatively small. It is important to note that, in principle, it is impossible to know that the introduction of the ACWL allowed an otherwise infeasible case to be brought forward. Nevertheless, one can look for certain features in the WTO dispute data that suggest that the ACWL is having an effect along this dimension.

Table 6-6. *Value of Market Access at Stake in ACWL versus Non-ACWL WTO Disputes, AD Cases Involving Developing Country Complainants, 2001–08*

WTO dispute (developing country complainant)	Average value of complainant exports in three years before AD measure[a] (U.S. dollars)	Estimated value of lost exports due to AD measure[b] (U.S. dollars)
Non-ACWL client cases		
Argentina–Poultry Anti-Dumping Duties (Brazil)	41,464,128	−25,128,358
Peru–Provisional Anti-Dumping Duties on Vegetable Oils from Argentina (Argentina)	11,000,726	−9,720,227
South Africa–Definitive Anti-Dumping Measures on Blanketing from Turkey (Turkey)	5,906,750	−5,766,517
EC–Anti-Dumping Duties on Certain Flat Rolled Iron or Non-Alloy Steel Products from India (India)	39,868,190	−8,481,772
India–Anti-Dumping Measures on Certain Products from the Separate Customs Territory of Taiwan, Penghu, Kinmen and Matsu (Taiwan)	3,072,471	−1,432,583
Brazil–Anti-Dumping Measure on Resins (Argentina)	71,215,545	69,672,704
Mean value in non-ACWL cases:	28,754,635	−20,033,693
ACWL client cases		
India–Anti-Dumping Measure on Batteries from Bangladesh (Bangladesh)	315,430	−315,430
Korea—Certain Paper (Indonesia)	42,136,886	3,853,435
Egypt–Matches (Pakistan)	2,608,283	−2,453,799
Mexico–Steel Pipes and Tubes (Guatemala)	2,693,535	−2,242,200
South Africa–Anti-Dumping Measures on Uncoated Woodfree Paper (Indonesia)	844,778	−802,930
Mean value in ACWL cases:	9,719,782	−1,933,559

Source: Author's compilations. To make samples comparable, all disputes are over recently imposed AD measures against developing countries eligible for membership in the Advisory Centre on WTO Law (ACWL). Complainant exports are of six-digit Harmonized System (HS) products subject to the AD import restriction; HS export data taken from World Integrated Trade Solution (WITS), software developed by the World Bank, in close collaboration with the United Nations Conference on Trade and Development (UNCTAD).

AD = antidumping.

a. Average annual value in the three years before the AD investigation.

b. Value of lost exports calculated as value of exports two years after the AD investigation minus the average annual exports in the three years before the AD investigation.

exporting firms averaged $39.9 million in sales to the EC per year. A mere two years after the imposition of the EC AD restriction, the Indian exporters had lost $8.5 million in sales to that market. India did not use the ACWL in this dispute, although it had used the ACWL in a number of other disputes (see again table 6-3).

Compare this with a similar WTO challenge to an antidumping measure involving steel that Guatemala brought against Mexico in *Mexico–Anti-Dumping Duties on Steel Pipes and Tubes from Guatemala,* in which Guatemala did use the ACWL services. Guatemalan exporting firms averaged only $2.7 million in sales to Mexico per year in the three years before the Mexican import restriction. Two years after the imposition of the Mexican AD restriction, $2.2 million of exports had been wiped out.

Although a comparison of these two cases is admittedly anecdotal, this pattern is typical across cases in the two categories of ACWL-assisted versus non-ACWL-assisted disputes over antidumping actions. Both the initial value of trade as well as the value of trade lost due to the new import restriction (both are proxies for the size of market access at stake) are typically much smaller in the WTO disputes involving the ACWL. In four of the six non-ACWL disputes, the pre-antidumping value of exports was greater than $10 million per year, whereas in four of the five ACWL-backed disputes, the pre-antidumping value of exports was less than $3 million per year. Comparing these two sets of otherwise similar disputes, the average size of exports for non-ACWL cases was larger ($28.7 million versus $9.7 million), and the average value of lost exports for non-ACWL cases was larger ($20.0 million versus $1.9 million).

The results from the ACWL's early cases in table 6-6 support the theory that the existence of the ACWL does more than just shift the cost of litigation from developing to developed country funders, it may be inducing a scale effect. In a set of comparable disputes over lost market access that was due to a WTO member's potentially WTO-inconsistent use of antidumping measures, on average, developing countries are using the ACWL when the market access stakes are smaller.[29] The non-ACWL cases are disputes with larger market access implications—perhaps larger profits are at stake and firms are better able to privately cover the fixed cost of enforcing foreign market access.

This finding is also consistent with the results in table 6-4. While experienced DSU-using countries are taking advantage of the lower litigation costs provided by the ACWL and pursue more cases, there is some evidence of a scale effect. Specifically, countries bringing more cases may be initiating cases that are different from non-ACWL cases in that they seek to enforce smaller dollar-value amounts of trade and thus additional market access commitments that otherwise would not be self-enforced. These are disputes that countries, without the ACWL, might not otherwise bring because it would be more difficult to cover the costs of enforcement without the subsidized assistance.

---

29. The analysis does not control for many other factors that may affect whether a country chooses to use the ACWL, and it is based on a small sample of observations. Nevertheless, it illustrates the sort of comparison that ought to be made more comprehensively when additional data are available.

A final question involves the type of cases the ACWL may be pursuing on behalf of poor countries. I argued that the current funding approach does not allow the outside influences of funders to affect the composition of cases that countries would bring forward; countries could use the ACWL to pursue cases that have development priorities, even though such cases are not necessarily important to private funders caught up in the latest fad-related, "trade and . . ." issue that is only tangentially about market access and economic development and is more likely about something else.

Although based on a small sample again, the data on the types of disputes covered by the ACWL caseload support this benefit of the current funding model. Fewer of the cases in table 6-3 are the headline-grabbing types of disputes of interest to funders, let alone academics and legal scholars. Instead, the ACWL has been asked to pursue disputes in which developing countries challenge important, albeit technical, topics such as customs misclassification of a product as a nontariff barrier to trade (manipulation of rules of origin requirements), antidumping measures (including zeroing), customs bonds, indicative prices, and ports of entry. The ACWL has also shown that it is capable of making substantive contributions to disputes that may be quite important for reasons of WTO jurisprudence. Indeed, the ACWL has played a major role in such important disputes as the first antidumping case concerning the issue of zeroing (*EC–Bed Linen*), the Generalized System of Preferences (GSP) case (*EC–Tariff Preferences*), as well as the groundbreaking agricultural domestic support cases (*EC–Export Subsidies on Sugar* and *US–Upland Cotton*).

From a development perspective, it is refreshing to observe the ACWL taking up cases over topics that, while perhaps not as intellectually stimulating as big social issues, are likely to be economically quite important for developing country market access.

Is the ACWL Introducing New Countries to the DSU through Legal Opinions That Do Not Lead to Litigation?

Thus far the analysis of ACWL activities in WTO dispute settlement has focused on how ACWL clients have used its services over issues that eventually resulted in DSU litigation. Of course, the ACWL may also affect the DSU caseload by issuing legal opinions to client countries that request them.

The ACWL issues legal opinions that fall into three different categories. The first category has little to do with potential DSU litigation and involves systemic questions about the WTO, legal aspects of various negotiating proposals undertaken during the Doha Round, and so forth. The second and third categories of ACWL opinions deal with questions that could ultimately end up as WTO enforcement cases. The second class of questions concerns whether a measure

Table 6-7. *Legal Opinions Provided by the ACWL, 2005–08*

Legal opinions provided by the ACWL	2005	2006	2007	2008
Total	82	96	110	175
Concerning				
Advice on systemic or procedural issues	47	66	48	83
Advice on country's own measures (for example, possibility that measures imposed would be challenged)	17	11	39	61
Advice on measures imposed by other countries	18	19	23	31
As requested by				
Category A countries	n.a.	n.a.	16	19
Category B countries	n.a.	n.a.	47	57
Category C countries	n.a.	n.a.	29	82
LDCs	n.a.	21	18	17
Newly initiated ACWL-backed disputes against measures by other countries	2	2	2	1

Source: Advisory Centre on WTO Law, "The ACWL Report on Operations," various years (www. acwl.ch/e/about/reports_e.aspx), and its website "Assistance in WTO Dispute Settlement Proceedings since July 2001" (www.acwl.ch/e/dispute/wto_e.aspx), through May 2008.
n.a. = Not available.

that the questioning country has imposed or is considering imposing is consistent with WTO rules and obligations—for example, does the questioning government need to worry that this trade restriction would be challenged at the WTO? The third class of questions concerns whether a trading partner's measure is consistent with the WTO—for example, would the questioning country have a potential legal case to pursue?

Table 6-7 documents the number of legal opinions requested and issued by the ACWL over the 2005–08 period, a trend that is increasing over time. The top panel of the table breaks down the legal opinions according to the issue about which the requesting countries are seeking information. It is interesting that countries appear to have as many, if not more, inquiries about the WTO-consistency of their own measures than the WTO-consistency of other countries' measures. This suggests that the ACWL also may be performing a substantive role of encouraging countries to comply with their WTO obligations so as to reduce the incidence of possible foreign market access violations that may lead to disputes.

The bottom row of table 6-7 notes simply that the vast majority of developing country inquiries about other countries' measures do not result in formal WTO enforcement cases. For example, in 2007 countries used the ACWL to make twenty-three inquiries into the WTO-inconsistency of another country's policy. However, the ACWL was asked to back the initiation of only two WTO disputes. The failure to turn inquiries into actual WTO disputes may be due to a number of factors that are impossible to discern from the data. It could be that the ACWL response is that the issue has insufficient legal merit to form the basis for a dispute. It could also be that although the ACWL suggests that the issue has legal merit, when the developing country brings it up with the potential respondent, they resolve the issue without need for a formal dispute. Another potential explanation is that although the ACWL's opinion suggests that there is scope for a dispute and the developing country is unable to resolve the issue with the potential respondent, some hurdle prevents that country from bringing the dispute forward and through step 4 of the ELP.

Finally, the middle panel of table 6-7 breaks out the requests for information from the ACWL based on the requesting country's classification category (see again table 6-1), which is largely related to its level of development. The table indicates that the poorest of the ACWL's clientele, as revealed by their requests for legal opinions, are making some attempt to participate in the WTO system, even in issues of enforcement. Thus while there may be no evidence so far that these countries are being introduced into formal WTO dispute settlement, they are at least using the ACWL to be introduced to WTO law.

ACWL Spillovers—Is It Inducing and Coordinating the Pro Bono Work of Law Firms?

Consider again the data on the ACWL-backed cases in table 6-3. One issue that I have yet to fully address is that in nine of the nineteen instances in which the ACWL represented a client as a complainant in a WTO dispute, the respondent was another developing country. In many such disputes, the respondent may also seek access to the subsidized litigation support offered by the ACWL. As discussed in earlier chapters, many cases also have the probability of significant external effects on the trade of other developing countries that might have a third party legal interest—for example, *EC–Bananas III*, *EC–Export Subsidies on Sugar*, and *US–Upland Cotton*. Although the ACWL cannot represent these other countries and thus both sides of the same dispute, as it would obviously have a legal conflict of interest, the Centre's external counsel program offers the developing country respondents and third parties in these disputes subsidized access to WTO legal support.[30]

Table 6-8 lists the 2008 roster of eleven law firms registered with the ACWL to offer their services. This roster provides names of law firms and attorneys willing to provide counsel to LDCs and other ACWL members if a conflict of

---

30. Table 6-3 indicates the four instances in which developing countries have accessed the roster of external legal counsel in these disputes taking place from 2001 to 2008.

Table 6-8. *ACWL's Roster of External Legal Counsel*

Law firm	Trade law practice group headquarters
Akin Gump Strauss Hauer & Feld	Washington
Borden Ladner Gervais	Canada (Ottawa)
FratiniVergano	Brussels
Gide Loyrette Nouel	Brussels
King & Spalding	Washington
Minter Ellison	Australia (Canberra)
O'Connor & Company	Brussels
Sidley Austin	Brussels, Geneva, Washington
Van Bael & Bellis	Brussels, Geneva
Vermulst Verhaeghe & Graafsma	Brussels
White & Case	Geneva, Washington

Source: Advisory Centre on WTO Law, "Roster of External Legal Counsel" (www.acwl.ch/e/ dispute/counsel_e.aspx [December 9, 2008]). The ACWL also lists individuals with which it has external counsel arrangements, including Edmond McGovern and Donald McRae.

interest prevents the ACWL from providing services through its own attorneys; in such a situation, the ACWL subcontracts the legal services out to the private sector. The developing country that uses lawyers from the external counsel list then pays the ACWL.

A first item to note is that many of the names on the ACWL's roster are the same firms offering their own private services to governments and industries that were documented in the last chapter (table 5-3). This suggests that developing countries are still getting assistance from high-quality teams of lawyers, even when they are not able to access the ACWL.

Perhaps equally important, the ACWL is able to use external counsel informally to facilitate a sort of pro bono work by the trade litigation practice groups at these law firms. In the context of domestic litigation, pro bono work is a major means through which legal assistance is provided to poor clients. A large law firm in particular may provide pro bono services to low-income clients, which in effect are cross-subsidized by the fees paid by its high-income clients and which perhaps are undertaken to improve the firm's reputation as a contributor to its community.[31]

The ACWL coordination of pro bono work carried out by private law firms may ultimately be a major resource to developing countries. Thanks to the long history of international trade litigation in the United States and the EC through

31. Galanter and Palay (1995, p. 46) indicate that a "high volume of pro bono work may offer an inducement for recruiting talented associates and may enable the firm to facilitate development of its lawyers' professional skills while projecting a coveted image of public service."

antidumping and countervailing measures and safeguard investigations and actions, the supply of the world's practicing attorneys in the field of international trade law is concentrated not in Geneva, the physical site of the ACWL, but in Washington and Brussels, again as indicated by the location of the law firms' trade practice groups documented in table 5-3. One important contribution of the ACWL is that it maintains a network of law firms in Washington and Brussels, which are available to represent the interests of developing countries, thus taking advantage of the high concentration of trade litigation expertise located in those cities.

Facilitating pro bono work through the ACWL instead of through the law firms directly can provide other benefits to the developing countries because of differences in the pattern of cases that would be brought forward through the ACWL as opposed to through a pure pro bono model. To maximize the public relations benefit of its efforts, an unconstrained law firm would prefer pro bono work related to high-profile cases that offer the firm the possibility of precedent value or the ability to grab headlines and significant media attention, as opposed to cases that are more rudimentary and unglamorous, involving straightforward enforcement of existing and well-understood provisions, which are major components of the ACWL-backed caseload found in table 6-3.

ACWL Performance—Is the ACWL Doing a Good Job?

The ACWL has done much to offset the lack of litigation assistance available to poor countries. The large number of cases in which it has participated indicates a demand for its services. Although the empirical analysis is based on a short time period and a small sample of observations, there is evidence that the existence of the ACWL may be shifting the composition of cases that arrive before the DSU toward enforcing smaller-scale market access cases of interest to poor countries, as well as allowing them to pursue more sole-complainant WTO disputes deeper into the extended litigation process.

Nevertheless, the value of the ACWL will ultimately be assessed not only by whether it provides developing countries with increased access to WTO enforcement, since access and participation are only one part of dispute settlement. The ultimate question is whether the ACWL is actually helping developing countries to enforce their foreign market access commitments in ways that would not be possible without the ACWL. There are important questions to consider including how does the ACWL's won-loss record on legal arguments compare with the won-loss record of other litigants, after controlling for the complexity of cases and a number of other features of the data? Although such output indicators are difficult to measure and evaluate, such output-related questions are the next important issue to address. It may be too early to address such questions empirically, given the paucity of data available to conduct such an exercise. Nonetheless, two final comments are in order.

First, there is already some evidence that the ACWL is on the right track, given its mandate and available resources. The clearest evidence is repeat requests by ACWL members for its services, which indicates some level of satisfaction with the job that it has done thus far.

Second, one needs to know not only whether developing countries are winning their WTO legal arguments at step 4 of the ELP, but also and more fundamentally whether developing countries obtain compliance in the legal proceedings they win and whether the lost market access at stake is restored. How does the ACWL's record compare in terms of obtaining an economically successful resolution of the dispute for its complainant client? Because the ACWL contributes just one part to the ELP, the answers to these questions go well beyond an isolated analysis of how the ACWL does in its part (step 4), but the answers are also influenced by many other elements of WTO self-enforcement covered throughout this book.

Concerns Raised by the Theory and Data on the ACWL

The theoretical discussion concerning the existence and institutional structure of the ACWL, as well as an early assessment of the data on its participation in WTO dispute settlement, raises a number of questions for policy. In this section, I comment on the remaining gaps in the extended litigation process of WTO self-enforcement.

No Independent Prelitigation Investigation, No New Countries, and a Disincentive for the Private Sector

The first problem relates to prelitigation investigation and access to legal services. As it stands, the ACWL can advise clients in need of assistance only after a country's government officials request it. The ACWL has neither the resources nor the mandate to go out into the field and offer information to developing country exporters that they have a legally viable case they could pursue at the WTO to enforce their market access rights. That the ACWL cannot do these things is consistent with the data on the DSU cases in which it has been active. Countries with prior knowledge and experience with the DSU are using the ACWL, but the mere existence of the ACWL has not yet induced additional countries to start enforcing their market access rights through the DSU.

Furthermore, the introduction of the ACWL into the ELP does have the potential to worsen the problem of inadequate predispute information gathering that private law firms might undertake to generate information on foreign market access violations to prospective developing country clients. Because the existence of the ACWL allows a potential client to bring disputes to ACWL lawyers at a lower cost than a private firm would be able to offer, private law firms are less likely to recoup their costs in generating such information. This suggests that the introduction of the ACWL may have had the unintended side effect of private firms generating even less information needed in steps 1 to 3 of the ELP than would otherwise be the case, since the economic incentives have changed.

Related to these problems is the question of who has access to the legal services provided by the ACWL. The current format allows only developing country governments to seek subsidized legal assistance, rather than the exporting firms or industry associations themselves. In the context of the example from chapter 5, the ACWL cannot work directly with Michele Brown, or Michele Brown's firm, or Michele Brown's firm's industry association. It can only work with Michele Brown's government once Michele Brown's firm has cleared all other hurdles of engaging the government to work on its behalf. Thus Michele Brown cannot go to the ACWL, request that it investigate whether there is a legal basis for her country to present a WTO challenge, and then report back to her government. First, she must convince her government that it is worth bringing the problem to the ACWL. Thus not only can the ACWL not research whether there is a violation of market access, but the ACWL also cannot communicate with potential exporters that might be affected by this issue until the government intermediary authorizes it.

The ACWL cannot proactively be involved in information gathering because of its mandate and because to do so is likely to impinge upon its most important role as an advocate within the legal phase (step 4) of the ELP. This is very much related to the prescient suggestion made by another eminent GATT/WTO legal scholar, John Jackson, who in a speech at the inauguration of the ACWL in 2001 stated that "the Advisory Centre will necessarily need to separate its advocacy role from its policy preferences. It has an obligation to its clients under professional ethics . . . to be a vigorous advocate, and utilize strong arguments on behalf of its clients. But it will need to consider, probably on a case-by-case basis, the degree to which its advocacy role is consistent with expressions of policy preferences or suggestions about reform of the dispute settlement system."[32]

Furthermore, and for much the same reason why it cannot engage in unsolicited information gathering, even after winning its case, the ACWL's role in the postlitigation step 5 and step 6 of the ELP is somewhat limited. The ACWL can advise a complainant country on the likely WTO-compatibility of its retaliation list of goods, services, or intellectual property commitments that it will

32. See Jackson (2002, p. 113).

threaten to pursue if the respondent refuses to comply with DSU rulings. However, the ACWL cannot lobby or mount a public relations campaign to induce policy reform in the respondent country. And as discussed in chapter 5, and to be pursued further in chapter 7, in many instances inducing policy reform in the respondent country requires engaging exporter and other diverse public interests in the respondent's economy to come to the rescue of the other economic interests at stake—specifically, the complainant's exporters and the respondent's consumer interests.

Third Parties

The data indicate that the ACWL is not used frequently by developing countries to track their market access interests in other countries' WTO disputes in the role of an interested third party. The primary potential explanation, that the disputes in which developing countries are most likely to have a third party interest already involve the ACWL representing a developing country as a respondent or complainant, is ruled out since the ACWL makes alternative legal assistance available via its roster of external counsel.

Developing countries do not appear to be increasing their participation as interested third parties, even though there is a strong economic interest in many cases to do so. As chapter 3 discussed extensively in the context of the *EC–Bananas III* case, if a dispute leads to compliance, it will almost always have an impact on a third country, whether imposing adjustment costs on other countries or creating export opportunities. It is therefore worrisome that countries have not taken up the ACWL services more vigorously as an opportunity to keep themselves informed (and to be able to weigh in on) the DSU process as interested third parties.

Since the ACWL offers legal support for LDCs as third parties in DSU proceedings free of charge, the failure of a sufficient number of developing countries to take up this service, despite the potential need for it that was identified in chapter 3, suggests that there is still a missing link.[33] This implies the existence of an additional cost, specifically the cost of acquiring information about the country's economic stake in the WTO enforcement—that is, step 1 in the ELP. Since the ACWL cannot even alert developing countries that they should be paying attention to a particular dispute as a third party whose economic interests are at stake, this is symptomatic of a more systemic problem.

---

33. Concerning free services for LDCs, see ACWL (2007, p. 28).

Developing Country Reform Demands: What Should DSU Reforms Target?

More evidence that the ACWL cannot do it all can be gleaned from developing countries' own demands for DSU reform. In particular, a number of developing countries have proposed major DSU reform that would create a fund internal to the WTO itself to cover the costs of litigation faced by developing countries in their DSU enforcement cases.[34]

Given this chapter's discussion of the ACWL and its major function of shifting the litigation cost burden of WTO enforcement from developing countries to developed countries (which are the primary ACWL funders), a developing country proposal to create a separate fund and infrastructure within the WTO to do the same thing would appear to promote creation of something that is redundant. It is also a potential waste of the developing countries' political capital to spend it negotiating for something that effectively already exists.[35] That a number of countries have made such a proposal suggests that problems in the current system continue to impede their access to dispute settlement. Even after the introduction of the ACWL, developing countries are still unhappy with the system.

Yet many developing country proposals call for more of the same kind of funding and support that already exists. I have found no evidence that more of the same assistance is needed. While the ACWL has been busy, it has not had to resort to external counsel often enough to suggest that current demand for its services is above its capacity. I would argue that a different sort of funding is needed—not an internal WTO fund. Specifically, what is needed is funding to create information on WTO violations as this would spur the appropriate level of developing country demand for ACWL services.

34. Examples include a proposal from Cuba, Egypt, India, Malaysia, and Pakistan (the "Like-Minded Group"); see "Dispute Settlement Understanding Proposals: Legal Text; Revisions in Some of the Proposals in TN/DS/W/47," WTO JOB 06/222 (Geneva: WTO, July 10, 2006); as well as one from the African Group; see "Text for the African Group Proposals on Dispute Settlement Understanding Negotiations," WTO TN/DS/W/92 (Geneva: WTO, March 5, 2008).

35. Although one can argue both that the ACWL may need more funding (to ensure that it would not run short of funds to provide this assistance) and that other areas of support aside from the actual litigation (step 4) in the ELP need funding, the funding and infrastructure for subsidizing developing country access to their actual litigation needs is already largely in place. Developing countries should be spending their negotiating capital on other more important issues; access to good, cheap litigation support for the DSU would seem already to be achieved. But as I discuss in subsequent chapters, it is not clear that the missing funding and gaps in the ELP could be effectively addressed within the WTO Secretariat either, primarily for political reasons. Thus, while I agree with the general developing country argument that more resources need to be allocated to market access enforcement, the critical question is where (in step 1 through step 6 of the ELP) and how this support should be provided.

The remainder of this book makes the case that what developing country governments need, and what assistance is currently missing from the ELP, is information on potentially enforceable WTO commitments that trading partners are violating. This information would identify potential DSU cases that developing countries could pursue, and which some might pursue with the assistance already available and affordable through the ACWL. It is not clear that the developing countries' own proposals for reform would confront any of the weaknesses of the current model, particularly the lack of information on potentially enforceable WTO commitments that are being violated.

Conclusions

Theory and early evidence on ACWL activities in WTO enforcement cases suggests that it is playing a critical role. Although the ACWL has not yet been able to spread WTO enforcement access to new countries that do not have prior experience in the DSU, evidence on how developing countries are using its services indicates it is improving enforcement in instances in which the market access at stake for exporters in poor countries is too small to make market-provided legal counsel a practical option.

Nevertheless, in creating a successful ACWL, the founders and implementers have had to limit its role in the WTO's overall extended litigation process. While the ACWL can and does act as effective legal counsel for firms and industries in poor countries that make it to step 4 of the ELP, its effectiveness is constrained by the services it cannot offer. It cannot assist in the information gathering and political organizing phases of steps 1 to 3, and the role that it can play in inducing reform in steps 5 to 6 may also be somewhat limited. Thus there is a need for others to step in, as I discuss next.

7

Development-Focused NGOs in WTO Enforcement

Introducing the role of nongovernmental organizations (NGOs) in the World Trade Organization system immediately brings to mind the fiery street protests and anti-globalization activists at the failed Seattle ministerial meetings in December 1999. Although the media coverage from Seattle was a public relations fiasco for the WTO, the spotlight transformed the institution from a virtual unknown entity into a familiar, if not necessarily welcome, presence on the world scene.[1] Moreover, the role of nongovernmental organizations—including many "civil society" groups, which focus on the needs of developing countries—has subsequently evolved so that some now attempt to make substantive contributions by engaging within the WTO system.

---

1. Evidence of this transformation includes the role that trade negotiations and the WTO have played in feature films—albeit not necessarily blockbusters—in recent years. These include the 2008 box office failure, *The Battle in Seattle*, starring Charlize Theron (a previous Oscar Award winner), Woody Harrelson (a previous Oscar Award nominee), and Ray Liotta. While not strictly about the WTO but about trade negotiations and developing countries more broadly, the 2005 HBO film *The Girl in the Café*, starring Bill Nighy and Kelly Macdonald, received sufficient critical acclaim to receive two Golden Globe nominations and three Emmy Awards. A cult film that received attention on college campuses and among anti-globalization activists was the 2003 spoof of the WTO, *The Yes Men*. Jones (2003) provides an interesting analysis of how economic insecurities associated with trade and globalization have manifested into fears and activism against the WTO. See also Irwin (2002).

The claim that development-focused NGOs might better serve the interests of their "clients" by embracing globalization instead of attacking it is admittedly far from novel.[2] The intention here is to do more. The goal of this chapter is to identify specific means by which NGOs might assist poor countries in overcoming the hurdles that impede their use of the WTO's extended litigation process (ELP) and thus facilitate their self-enforcement of the foreign market access they need for achieving development goals through expanded trade. I focus on ways NGOs with appropriate technical skills could make use of the WTO system, and WTO enforcement in particular, more effectively to help poor countries take advantage of globalization. I also note some problems that could arise as NGOs transform themselves along these lines.

Because NGOs have so far played little role in the WTO's enforcement process, I begin the first section with a brief discussion of how such groups have been active in the WTO thus far, which has been primarily through attempts to influence multilateral negotiations. Such an approach provides at least two important insights. First, it equips us with a basic understanding of the existing "supply side" of NGOs with some expertise in WTO matters. Second, examination of WTO-provided data from areas in which NGOs actively engage with the institution highlights the continuing importance of economic incentives. The list is dominated by commercial interest groups such as industry associations; only to a lesser extent is it populated by nonprofit NGOs or civil society groups. Thus, surveying the full list of WTO-active NGOs does not provide much assistance in helping narrow in on which development-focused NGOs have become (and may increasingly become) a component of the WTO self-enforcement process, especially from the perspective of providing assistance to developing countries.

Therefore, beginning in the second section the discussion turns back to the extended litigation process model of WTO enforcement in chapter 5. Given how the ELP works in WTO dispute settlement practice, I use "demand-side" considerations to identify how development-focused NGOs may assist exporting firms, industries, and policymakers in developing countries to overcome the hurdles of WTO self-enforcement. The demand is driven by developing country needs for assistance to overcome the costs of completing each of the six steps of the ELP. Therefore, unlike other scholarly assessments, this one is intentionally not a comprehensive description of NGOs and related civil society activity in the global trading system.[3] I match demand-driven needs with a discussion of

2. See, for example, the discussions of NGOs in recent books on globalization including Collier (2007, chapter 10); Bhagwati (2004, chapter 4); Friedman (2005, pp. 382–91).

3. For more comprehensive approaches to examining civil society groups and the WTO, for example, differentiating NGOs by their approaches as "conformers," "reformers," or "radicals," see Scholte, O'Brien, and Williams (1999) as well as Williams (2005). The legal scholarship by Dunoff (1998) and

the existing (albeit limited) development-focused NGO services that are supplied in this area.

Where possible, the approach of this chapter draws inferences from development-focused NGO engagement in the ELP of actual WTO disputes, which includes engagement by large and well-known advocacy groups such as Oxfam International. I also highlight the role that smaller and lesser-known NGOs such as the Geneva-based IDEAS Centre can play by helping firms in developing countries overcome the cost of politically organizing and engaging with their policymakers on the issue of WTO self-enforcement. Nevertheless, I also go beyond the historical record of NGO involvement in actual WTO disputes so as to identify useful resources and services that NGOs might adapt for developing country use in future cases. After introducing NGOs such as the United States–based Environmental Working Group and the EC-based Farmsubsidies.org, I speculate as to how the information they provide might be used on behalf of developing countries in the ELP.

An important theme of the chapter is the need for NGO personnel to acquire the competencies in areas of economics, law, and politics that are required to assist developing countries in gaining access to the benefits of the WTO through the use of the ELP (see again figure 5-1). The second section explores the possible roles that NGOs might play in the initial prelitigation phase (step 1 through step 3), while the third section describes a role for NGOs in the postlitigation phase (step 6) of promoting policy change within respondent countries to generate compliance with WTO rulings. While I find a substantial role for NGOs to play in these phases of the ELP, I also identify a remaining gap in information generation that the current set of NGOs cannot fill. I explore implications of this gap and proposals to address it in chapter 8.

In the fourth section I assess the impact that NGOs could have in the middle stage of the ELP (step 4)—by offering formal litigation support similar to that provided by the Advisory Centre on WTO Law (ACWL). Although I would not be surprised to observe NGOs playing a larger role in this part of the ELP in future WTO enforcement activity because of its high profile nature, nevertheless, I also explain why this particular use of donor resources is not likely to generate the biggest benefit in terms of providing developing countries with an enhanced ability to self-enforce their ability to trade.

Finally, the last section identifies important roles for academics, think tanks, research institutes, and other scholars in the WTO enforcement process, even though they may not overcome barriers to entry for any given developing

---

Esty (1998) provides historical context regarding ways NGOs sought engagement in the WTO in the 1990s. Charnovitz (2000) expands on this and discusses even earlier NGO participation during the GATT era. For a more recent treatment, see Van den Bossche (2008).

country in any particular dispute. I highlight the role of these other outside actors in making critical assessments and stimulating improvements to the DSU process, reviewing work that has been done and areas in which more research is needed.

NGOs in the WTO System: Attempts to Influence Multilateral Negotiations

Which NGOs are most engaged in the WTO system, and what have they been attempting to do? To provide some description of the NGO supply side, I begin with data on NGO participation in WTO-related activities, which indicate that NGOs have become increasingly interested in the business of the WTO since its 1995 inception.

Table 7-1 presents data on formal registered involvement of NGOs in two types of high profile WTO events. Table 7-1a provides data on registered attendance at WTO ministerial meetings. These meetings between government officials take place sporadically at various cities around the world; they include the 1999 ministerial meetings in Seattle and another in 2001 in Doha, Qatar, which launched the Doha Development Round of multilateral trade liberalization negotiations. Table 7-1b shows data for the now annual WTO Public Forum held at the WTO Secretariat in Geneva, an event designed to increase WTO transparency and the availability of the institution to outsiders. The purpose of the forum is to encourage public dialogue, partly in response to the increased demand for transparency that manifested itself in the Seattle protests. Each table reveals that hundreds of NGOs and thousands of individuals have registered to take part in these events.[4] These numbers signal both a greater NGO interest in following what happens in the WTO as well as attempts to influence the WTO both directly and by advising officials of countries involved in negotiations and other related activities.

Figure 7-1 presents an additional indicator of NGO involvement by documenting the number of NGO position papers that the WTO Secretariat received over the 1999–2007 period. As their name suggests, these papers articulate an NGO's policy perspective on some issue of relevance to the WTO. The WTO received an average of sixty-one NGO position papers per year over this period. However, there is substantial heterogeneity in the timing of the submissions, with spikes at the dates of ministerial meetings. This was especially true in 1999 (Seattle) and 2003 (Cancún), which saw nearly double the yearly average,

---

4. Attendance was down in Doha in 2001, partially because of the travel difficulties in the wake of 9/11 and also because of the cost and visa challenges associated with attending a meeting in this hard-to-reach city.

Table 7-1. *NGO Involvement in WTO Events*

a. Participation at Ministerial Meetings

Ministerial conference	NGOs registered	NGOs that attended	Number of individual participants
Singapore 1996	159	108	235
Geneva 1998	153	128	362
Seattle 1999	776	686	1,500 (approx.)
Doha 2001	651	370	370
Cancún 2003	961	795	1,578
Hong Kong 2005	1,065	812	1,596

b. Participation at Annual WTO Public Forum[a]

WTO public forum date	Number of individuals registered[b]
July 6–7, 2001	n.a.
April 29–May 1, 2002	n.a.
June 16–18, 2003	n.a.
May 25–27, 2004	n.a.
April 20–22, 2005	n.a.
September 25–26, 2006	1,396
October 4–5, 2007	1,741
September 24–25, 2008	1,425

Source: Data compiled by the author from the WTO's External Relations Division website, "For NGOs" (www.wto.org/english/forums_e/ngo_e/ngo_e.htm), and correspondence with the division.

n.a. = Not available.

a. Before 2006 the annual event was called the WTO Public Symposium.

b. For the 2001 symposium, 269 NGOs registered, and more than 350 individuals who registered for the 2006, 2007, and 2008 public forums indicated that they represented NGOs.

and to a lesser extent in 2001 (Doha) and 2005 (Hong Kong). The high level of submissions during the years of ministerial meetings is evidence of NGO efforts to influence WTO-spawned multilateral negotiations.

Table 7-2 presents examples of NGOs from the list of more than 200 different groups that submitted the position papers presented in figure 7-1.[5] In the next subsections, I further describe the NGOs behind these WTO position papers, before turning to a consideration of how some of the more development-focused NGOs might play a role in the self-enforcement process helping to ensure developing country access to foreign markets.

5. Appendix table A-2 presents the entire list of NGOs that have submitted at least one position paper to the WTO during this period from 1999 to 2007.

Figure 7-1. *NGO Position Papers Received by the WTO Secretariat, 1999–2007*

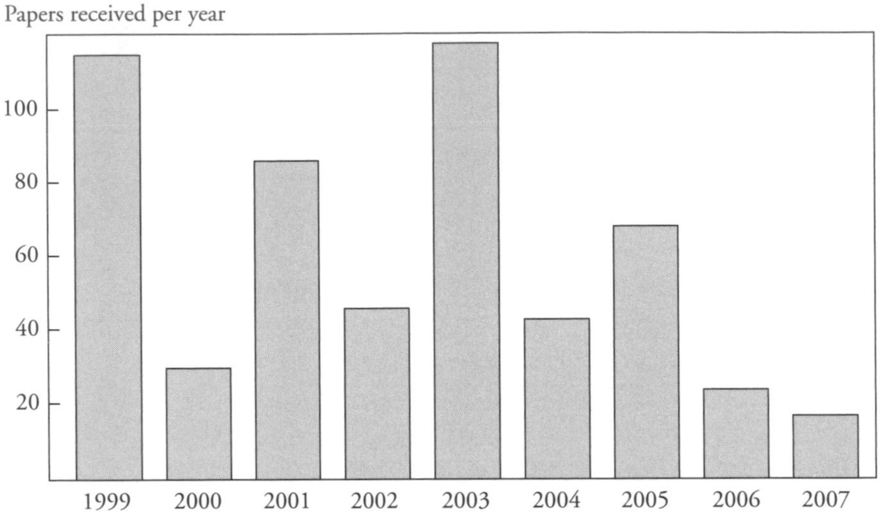

Papers received per year

Source: Data compiled by the author from the WTO's website "NGO Position Papers Received by the WTO Secretariat" (www.wto.org/english/forums_e/ngo_e/pospap_e.htm [January 5, 2009]).

Coalitions of Commercial Exporting Interests in Developed Countries

From the perspective of chapters 1 and 2, which described the process and results of the GATT/WTO negotiating history, it is not surprising that many position papers submitted by NGOs (listed in table 7-2) are from the political and lobbying arms of the commercial interests in developed countries with foreign market access interests that have been negotiated into the existing WTO agreements. For example, the business interests represented by the American Chamber of Commerce, the International Chamber of Commerce, the European Services Forum, and the Union of Industrial and Employers' Confederation (formerly UNICE, now renamed BUSINESSEUROPE) account for nearly 20 percent of the position papers received by the WTO Secretariat during the 1999–2007 period. There are also industry-specific submissions for numerous sectors, including some of the latecomers to coverage in the GATT/WTO system that I described in chapters 1 and 2. These include submissions from producer coalitions in sectors including agriculture, fisheries, chemical manufacturing, services, and pharmaceuticals.

Within the example of Michele Brown in chapter 5, many of these NGOs are simply an extension of the political organization representing Michele's self-interested firm and her industry. Although the political organization that I described in chapter 5 was limited to the other firms in her industry in her country, many of these groups extend such coalitions across either borders (two or more countries) or industries (two or more sectors).[6] These groups are clearly not marginalized players in the WTO system. The mere existence of these coalitions signals that many firms do not lack either the resources or the capacity to organize with other firms, and thus they are able to influence their own governments to self-enforce foreign market access commitments in the WTO. These are not the sort of NGOs I have in mind as providing help to the exporting industries in developing countries that need assistance in the ELP, nor are they the groups that might assist developing countries in using the ELP to maintain their foreign market interests.

Emergence of Coalitions of Commercial Exporting Interests in Developing Countries

Table 7-2 also shows three NGO position paper submissions from industry coalitions in developing countries. This includes submissions from the Brazilian National Confederation of Industry (CNI), Brazilian Business Coalition (CEB), and the All India Association of Industries (AIAI). These submissions are not nearly as numerous as those of industry coalitions in the United States, Europe, or even Canada and Japan; nevertheless, the emergence of such developing country organizations signals that some industries in developing countries recognize how the WTO system works. Industry coalitions from poor countries need to engage the WTO to obtain and then enforce access to foreign markets to promote their development in the same way that industries in the North have used the WTO to obtain and then enforce their own access to foreign markets. And while I explore below how some development-focused NGOs can work with or on behalf of these developing country industries, a more efficient approach is for these industry groups to be empowered to organize and speak for themselves in the WTO process without external assistance from foreign NGOs.

In the second section I turn to the next step for these developing country industry coalitions, which is to move beyond negotiations and engage the self-enforcement process of WTO dispute settlement and thus ensure that foreign commitments negotiated are implemented in practice.

---

6. For example, the International Federation of Pharmaceutical Manufacturers Associations (IFPMA) is largely an international extension of the U.S.-based pharmaceutical coalition PhRMA (Pharmaceutical Research and Manufacturers of America). If I were to extend the discussion of Michele Brown in chapter 5 beyond WTO enforcement to broader issues of WTO negotiations, domestic firms would sometimes organize politically beyond their own national borders or their own sectoral borders.

Table 7-2. *Examples of NGOs Submitting Position Papers to the WTO,*
1999–2007

Nongovernmental organization	Total no. submitted
Developed country commercial coalitions	
A. General	
American Chamber of Commerce	21
International Chamber of Commerce	37
European Services Forum	17
Union of Industrial and Employers' Confederation (UNICE)	31
B. Industry-specific NGO (agriculture, fisheries, chemicals, services, pharmaceuticals)	
International Food and Agricultural Trade Policy Council	8
Committee of Agricultural Organizations in the European Union (COPA)	4
Korea Fisheries Association	1
National Federation of Fisheries Cooperative Associations	1
International Council of Chemical Associations (ICCA)	9
International Financial Services London	3
World Information Technology Services Alliance	2
International Federation of Pharmaceutical Manufacturers Associations (IFPMA)	6
Developing country commercial coalitions	
Brazilian National Confederation of Industry (CNI)	1
Brazilian Business Coalition (CEB)	1
All India Association of Industries (AIAI)	1
Other "issue-based" NGOs (consumers, labor, environment, others)	
Médecins Sans Frontières (MSF)	3
Consumers Unity & Trust Society (CUTS)	7
International Confederation of Free Trade Unions (ICFTU)	6
World Federation of Trade Unions (WFTU)	3
Performing Arts Employers Associations League Europe (PEARLE)	1
International Federation of Intellectual Property Attorneys (FICPI)	7
Greenpeace	9
World Wide Fund for Nature International (WWF)	20
International Gender and Trade Network	2
World Council of Churches (WCC)	1
Bahá'í International Community	1
Development-focused NGOs	
ActionAid	5
Oxfam	7
International Centre for Trade and Sustainable Development (ICTSD)	14
International Institute for Sustainable Development (IISD)	19

Source: Data compiled by the author from the WTO's website "NGO Position Papers Received by the WTO Secretariat" (www.wto.org/english/forums_e/ngo_e/pospap_e.htm [January 5, 2009]).

Issue-Based NGOs

Other types of NGOs aside from political coalitions of exporting industries have also attempted to influence the multilateral negotiations taking place under WTO auspices. Although these groups listed in table 7-2 are also "issue based," their issues are not commercial exporting interests but instead the concerns of consumers, labor, the environment, or something else.

Consider first the interest of consumers. On the issue of intellectual property rights, and the protection for medicine in particular, countering the pharmaceutical industry collective represented by IFPMA are groups such as Médecins Sans Frontières (MSF), which advocate for consumer health interests in developing countries. The major India-based NGO Consumers Unity & Trust Society (CUTS) has also made a number of its positions known on WTO-related issues.

There are other examples of submissions from issue-based NGOs. The interests of organized labor are represented by submissions from broad union confederations. Workers from specific industries such as the theater and the performing arts or in professions such as intellectual property rights law are also represented by submissions. Environmental advocates including Greenpeace and the World Wide Fund for Nature International (WWF) have made numerous submissions. And although these are less frequent, there are submissions relating to issues such as trade and gender and religion.

At this stage, it is important to recall that many of these issue-based organizations representing consumers, labor, or even the environment need not take a general anti-globalization perspective, nor is it even necessary that they be at odds with the exporting industry coalitions listed in table 7-2. Natural political alliances based on common economic incentives are likely to form between such groups.[7] For example, groups representing workers in exporting sectors have many of the same short run interests as the exporting firms and industries themselves, and thus an alignment of interest in enforcing foreign market access makes sense. Such coalitions might be joined by foreign consumer organizations

---

7. An interesting example of such a diverse coalition is the U.S.-based groups behind a letter sent to President Obama and congressional leaders in March 2009 during the midst of the global economic crisis asking the new administration to reaffirm the "critical importance of rejecting destructive protectionism" and "[to] work vigorously for a successful conclusion of the WTO Doha Development Agenda that will open major markets for both developed and developing countries." The letter was signed by the heads of Oxfam America, Business Roundtable, United States Conference of Catholic Bishops, National Foreign Trade Council, Women Thrive Worldwide, among others. The letter has been posted to the websites of various NGOs including the National Foreign Trade Council. See its press release announcing the letter, "U.S. Business Community and NGO Leaders Unite to Urge the President and Congress to Take Action on Trade & Investment Agenda," with a link to the full letter (www.nftc.org/newsflash/newsflash.asp?Mode=View&id=236&articleid=2701&category=All).

that have an interest in access to the goods and services those exporting firms and their workers provide: imports benefit consumers through lower domestic prices as well as new varieties of differentiated products beyond those available from domestic producers.[8] And in some instances there may even be the scope for environmental interests to join such coalitions. Strengthening WTO disciplines over international trade can sometimes help reduce pollution and other environmental problems—for example, reduction of fisheries and agricultural subsidies—and thereby enhance sustainable development. This indicates the potential for case-by case coalitions between some exporting groups and environmental NGOs.[9] And while there may not be a natural coalition between MSF and the IFPMA, it is not far-fetched to imagine political coalitions between MSF and an industry group representing exporters that produce off-patent, generic pharmaceutical products.[10]

Development-Focused NGOs

When it comes to the specific concerns of developing countries, table 7-2 also identifies a number of submissions from development-focused NGOs whose "issue" is economic development or poverty alleviation in poor countries. These submissions include contributions from advocacy groups such as Oxfam and ActionAid, which are NGOs that have moved their focus beyond development assistance and humanitarian aid. Their participation reflects the recognition that the WTO system can provide benefits to developing countries if these countries can engage effectively in the system. Many other development-oriented groups have similarly shifted their advocacy role to establishing a voice within the Doha Round debate instead of simply fighting against it.

Table 7-2 also shows contributions from important think tanks with a development focus, such as the International Centre for Trade and Sustainable Development (ICTSD) and the International Institute for Sustainable Development

8. In the fourth section I describe a specific WTO dispute over an illegal EC product labeling scheme for sardines in which a U.K. consumer group formed such an alliance with Peruvian exporters.

9. For example, increased access to agricultural imports could decrease some local environmental problems in countries whose own agricultural production relies on extensive use of chemical fertilizers or energy to produce crops because of unfavorable climate, poor quality of land, and the unavailability of labor. For the general relationship between international trade and the environment, see Copeland and Taylor (2003).

10. The primary conflict between developing country consumers of pharmaceuticals (represented by Médecins Sans Frontières) and the IFPMA is not about international trade in these products. Rather, it is about the higher prices for imported products relative to domestically produced "equivalents" that may result from the intellectual property rights protection scheme found in the Trade-Related Aspects of Intellectual Property Rights (TRIPS) Agreement. The opposite result (a fall in consumer prices) typically occurs with increased access to imports.

(IISD) and academic institutions throughout the world. I return to a discussion of these groups in substantial depth below.

Beyond the position papers relating to multilateral negotiations listed in table 7-2 that this eclectic mix of NGOs have submitted directly to the WTO, a cottage industry of NGOs and intergovernmental organizations (IGOs) has arisen to advise developing country policymakers and thus affect WTO negotiation outcomes by directly influencing developing country policymakers themselves. These NGOs and IGOs have provided formal and informal advice as government officials sought to identify, solidify, and articulate their negotiating positions and priorities in the Doha Round. Examples of IGOs include the South Centre and International Lawyers and Economists Against Poverty (ILEAP). Many other groups have evolved to assist understaffed developing country policymakers with capacity building in trade policy to help them define and defend their interests in negotiations and to form coalitions with other countries sharing these interests.

A final category of groups seeking to influence the positions of developing country policymakers includes the teams of economic researchers at a variety of institutions that now provide developing (and developed) country policymakers with sophisticated analysis of various negotiating proposals in the Doha Round using tools such as computable general equilibrium (CGE) modeling projections.[11] Prominent examples of such efforts include the Global Trade Analysis Project (GTAP) at Purdue University, Centre d'Études Prospectives et d'Informations Internationales (CEPII) in Paris, the Development Research Group at the World Bank, and the United Nations Conference on Trade and Development's (UNCTAD's) Agriculture Trade Policy Simulation Model (ATPSM).[12] Such studies can help to identify the costs and benefits of various proposals and also some of the adjustments—including industry contraction and expansion and labor reallocation—that would take place within countries once the negotiations conclude and implementation begins. These studies also indicate where additional resources and policy attention (such as aid for trade) may be needed domestically to facilitate the politically contentious adjustment process at the conclusion of the round and mitigate concerns for nonimplementation, noncompliance, and backsliding.[13] Although the modeling efforts of such groups

---

11. Such models were used during earlier negotiating rounds to generate estimates on projected outcomes, so this is not a new phenomenon. However, advances in computing power have enabled more researchers to provide this service, thus generating more information of potential use to the policy community as it collectively converges on a negotiating outcome.

12. For a discussion of differences in results from different approaches, see Bouët and Krasniqi (2006). Numerous other academics are also contributing to these CGE efforts, and the literature is too extensive to allow full reference to them here.

13. Bown and McCulloch (2007b) explore the range of adjustment problems confronting the current (and future) international trading system, including issues that have impeded progress in the Doha Round.

sometimes generate conflicting results and estimates, having a variety of such studies providing a range of forecasts can also help identify the key areas of uncertainty regarding likely gains and losses. Consumption of such studies requires additional technical capacity on the part of policymakers.

The increasing number and diversity of these economic modeling groups itself signals an important technical advancement within the WTO system. The need for information has created a market in which highly skilled researchers are competing to generate products (useful information) for policymakers and negotiators. As earlier chapters describe, the extended litigation process for WTO enforcement of foreign market access also requires firms and countries to have access to technical knowledge and economic, legal, and political expertise to make sure that other countries live up to their negotiating promises. An important question is whether the improved technical capacity currently helping to inform the WTO negotiating process (such as economic-based modeling) can subsequently be adapted into the technical capacity needed to assist developing country interests in their follow-up through WTO enforcement in the future.

Donors and NGO Investment to Influence WTO Negotiations: Implications for WTO Enforcement

Hundreds of NGOs seek to influence the WTO system, including many that have a development focus. Most of their efforts seek to influence the process or outcomes of WTO negotiations as opposed to the process of WTO enforcement.[14] I conclude this section by identifying reasons why I expect issue-based groups to shift their focus toward WTO enforcement.

First and foremost are the demand-side motives. Developing countries have many needs for assistance as they seek to self-enforce. In chapter 5, I documented the scope of the problem confronting exporting industries in developing countries.[15] As trade barriers fall across the world because WTO members have taken on legal commitments to lower and bind tariffs, fewer barriers remain over which to negotiate in the context of a multilateral round. At the same time, new liberalization commitments mean a substantial increase in countries' enforcement needs to ensure that foreign market access promises are kept. Thus I expect developing country interests to divert their demand for assistance from NGO help in negotiations toward NGO help in WTO enforcement.

Second, on the supply side, many private foundations and aid agencies in developed countries have created powerful incentives for NGOs and civil society

14. As described in chapter 5, the industry associations representing particular commercial interests, which make up an important part of the extended litigation process of WTO enforcement, are the exception to this.

15. In particular, see the section on lessons for developing countries.

Table 7-3. *Some Private Foundations of Importance to Development-Focused NGOs*

Foundation	Grants paid in 2007 (U.S. dollars)
Bill and Melinda Gates Foundation—Global Development Program	308.0 million
Ford Foundation[a]	129.1 million
William and Flora Hewlett Foundation—Global Development Program	97.3 million
John D. and Catherine T. MacArthur Foundation—International Program in Global Security and Sustainability	87.2 million
Charles Stewart Mott Foundation[b]	26.3 million

Source: Data collected by the author by aggregating relevant subcategories of grant making reported in each foundation's 2007 annual report.

a. For the Ford Foundation, data were constructed as the difference between total grants and U.S. grant making for the "Asset Building and Community Development" and "Peace and Social Justice" categories.

b. Data for the Mott Foundation combined several categories: "Civil Society (Non-U.S.)," "International Finance for Sustainability," and "Reform of International Finance and Trade."

groups to play a more active role in shaping global development policy.[16] Table 7-3 illustrates annual grants made under various categories of global development programs in some of these major private foundations. The largest of these donors is the Gates Foundation; its Global Development Program gave more than $300 million in grants in 2007 alone.[17] Other major foundations that have worked substantially in the area of global development and therefore have influenced NGO activities relating to the WTO include the Ford Foundation, the William and Flora Hewlett Foundation, the John D. and Catherine T. MacArthur Foundation, and the Charles Stewart Mott Foundation.[18]

An examination of the annual reports of the development-focused NGOs mentioned in this chapter indicates that many receive significant funding from these foundations. These NGOs have already invested significant resources to learn about and engage in the WTO system—a feat that is not trivial—so as to influence negotiations. Thus these groups are likely to seek to make further use of that investment by transforming their knowledge of the WTO negotiations process to another area in which it would be useful—WTO self-enforcement.

16. Examples of northern aid agencies that provide substantial donor funding to NGOs and civil society groups in the policy arena of global development include the U.K. Department for International Development (DFID), the Dutch Ministry of Foreign Affairs, the Swiss Agency for Development and Cooperation (SDC), and the Swedish International Development Cooperation Agency (SIDA).

17. This grant-making program is completely separate from its more highly publicized Global Health Program, which granted $1.2 billion in 2007 under various initiatives to address AIDS, malaria, and other pressing public health concerns around the world.

18. The Rockefeller Foundation is another major donor; its data are not listed because the foundation's annual report does not break out grants into a global development category comparable with the others on this list.

Furthermore, the NGOs that have been advising policymakers in the negotiations arena risk losing their credibility if they do not adapt to assist developing countries as they seek to self-enforce their market access; the expected foreign market access will not materialize and the benefits to trade will not be realized.

How will NGOs and civil society groups transform themselves to become useful to the workers, firms, industries, and policymakers within developing countries that need assistance in self-enforcing foreign market access? The expertise that many NGOs currently have to offer is admittedly not well tailored to the needs of developing countries for assistance in self-enforcement. To examine a path that NGOs might take, I move the discussion beyond the current NGOs, their current priorities, and their current skills. In the remainder of this chapter, I focus on NGO transformations—frequently discussed in terms of technical capacity and skill upgrading—that are needed for them to offer substantive assistance to developing countries in the area of WTO self-enforcement. To organize these ideas, the rest of this chapter refers back to the extended litigation process model of WTO enforcement in chapter 5.

Steps 1 to 3 of the Extended Litigation Process: NGOs as Information-Generating Watchdogs and Political Organizers

In chapter 5, I introduced the six-step extended litigation process model of WTO enforcement and identified the hurdles that may prevent or discourage exporting firms in developing countries from self-enforcing their foreign market access. In exploring potential NGO roles in the provision of useful assistance, I begin with the initial problems that exporters face in merely identifying the source of lost foreign market access and organizing to do something about it. Specific hurdles include the acquisition of accurate and complete information regarding potential enforcement actions to pursue, the calculation of expected payoffs and costs to pursuing such actions, and the political organization of firms that may be needed to engage and convince government policymakers that the enforcement action is worth pursuing.

For NGOs with a substantial network of affiliates in developing countries, they may be well positioned to play an enhanced role in some aspects of the information-gathering stage of the ELP. Such NGOs are potentially useful sources of local knowledge of exporting firms, industries, and worker interests. They also may know how to initiate and then mediate policy conversations between local exporters and national government officials on how and whether to self-enforce market access commitments through WTO dispute settlement.

The WTO dispute over *US–Upland Cotton* provides an example in which NGOs helped developing countries overcome some hurdles inherent in this phase of the enforcement process. As I have described earlier, in September 2002 Brazil initiated a formal WTO dispute challenging U.S. cotton subsidy programs. Brazil claimed that U.S. payments to the sector had exceeded U.S. commitments from the Uruguay Round, violating the terms of the "peace clause," which had put a truce on potential disputes relating to agriculture. The U.S. subsidy encouraged U.S. farmers to increase domestic production and exports, subsequently driving down the world price for cotton. The reduction of the world price resulting from this U.S. policy caused injury to Brazil's cotton farmers and exporters by reducing their market access in third countries that imported cotton for consumption.[19]

Once the dispute initiated by Brazil was under way, the IDEAS Centre, a small, Geneva-based NGO, joined with Oxfam International and the Geneva-based think tank ICTSD to organize and mobilize cotton farmers in other countries to engage in the dispute.[20] They focused on engaging policymakers in such West African countries as Benin, Burkina Faso, Chad, and Mali—countries that were relatively poor and whose economies were heavily dependent on cotton exports. As producers and exporters of cotton, these countries had the same foreign market access interest at stake as the complainant Brazil and thus were natural (economic) allies in Brazil's efforts to get the U.S. to remove what was ultimately ruled to be a WTO-inconsistent policy.

NGO engagement in this particular dispute reveals the contributions that NGOs can make to the process as well as some of their limitations in helping developing countries engage the ELP.[21] Identifying the limitations then helps to pinpoint where additional technical assistance will be needed.

19. Although it is frequently neglected in the discussion of this dispute, many developing country importers of cotton actually benefit from the (WTO-inconsistent) U.S. subsidy, because the subsidy results in a lower price. Cotton is a key input for many textiles and apparel products that developing countries export. Removal of the U.S. subsidy, which would lead to an increase in the price of cotton, would thus have an adverse impact on cotton-consuming industries in these countries. As I first identified in chapter 3 (in particular, the section "Remaining Questions from the Banana Dispute"), the effects on a third country of even an economically successful resolution to a WTO dispute highlight the need for transparency in the dispute resolution process. Third party rights can provide an important monitoring role within the dispute resolution process, which in this particular dispute would mean that cotton-consuming firms in such third countries are also prepared to adjust to the increase in price of a key input.

20. For a discussion of the political and economic events involved in this dispute, including the roles of NGOs such as the IDEAS Centre, Oxfam, and the ICTSD in particular, see Devereaux, Lawrence, and Watkins (2006b, chapter 5) and also Heinisch (2006). For the West African perspective, see Zunckel (2005). The IDEAS Centre and its efforts to engage the West African countries on cotton were led by two former diplomats from Switzerland, Nicolas Imboden and Arthur Dunkel. Dunkel served as director general of the GATT from 1980 until 1993. Oxfam, which is based in the United Kingdom, has offices all over the world, including Geneva and the United States.

21. The ultimate measure of success in this particular NGO effort to engage West African countries in support of the foreign market access is as yet unknown as the dispute is not yet fully resolved. At the end of 2008, the United States had still failed to comply with all of the WTO legal rulings in the formal dispute that Brazil initiated, and Brazil was at the stage of formulating formal retaliation threats—one possibility is through withdrawal of TRIPS commitments discussed in chapter 5—if the United States continued to not comply.

First, NGOs with local knowledge about exporting firms, industries, and their workers can be useful at helping them organize politically. A critical component of the ELP in disputes involving many different causes of lost foreign market access involves the example in chapter 5 of Michele Brown organizing with other firms within her exporting industry to politically engage domestic policymakers. NGOs with resources and expertise to facilitate this process may be particularly important in a developing country that is unable to engage industry interests efficiently and fairly with its government representatives because the country's institutions have poor technical capacity. Most developing countries lack, for example, the policy gateway that is available to exporters in the United States (through Section 301) or the EC (through Trade Barriers Regulation) to make their foreign market access concerns known to government officials.

It is also noteworthy that NGOs were contributors to the fact that the *US–Upland Cotton* dispute introduced Benin and Chad into a formal role, as interested third parties, in the WTO dispute settlement process for the first time.[22] As I have already documented in chapter 6, this dispute may have important longer-run implications for these countries if their participation helps their policymakers increase the depth of the countries' engagement in the WTO system in the future.

However, it is important to identify some important limitations to the potential effectiveness of NGOs at this stage of information generation and identification of WTO violations. The IDEAS Centre and Oxfam were able to engage West African countries on the cotton issue because Brazil was already initiating a trade dispute over the issue. Had Brazil not taken the lead in the WTO dispute, it is difficult to envision that these NGOs would have had the capacity on their own to convince the West African countries to act in the same way.

Most NGOs do not yet have the economic, legal, and political technical capacity required to facilitate WTO self-enforcement. Such technical expertise is necessary, as in the cotton case, to identify and convincingly demonstrate to industries and government policymakers that the U.S. cotton subsidy program is WTO-inconsistent and that such a dispute is a market access issue of considerable economic importance—the U.S. subsidy was the reason that West African farmers lost access to the global cotton market. The current lack of NGO capacity in information generation and identification of WTO violations

---

22. Benin and Chad received legal support from the law firm White & Case (refer back to table 5-3) during the Panel and Appellate Body phases, and Chad also received legal support from the ACWL during a later Article 21.5 phase that assessed whether the U.S. policy reforms brought it into sufficient compliance with the earlier WTO rulings.

reinforces the need for others to provide these activities in the process. Thus some other group needs to step in to collect information on potential WTO violations and to provide accurate and complete economic, legal, and political information on the expected value (in terms of foreign market access) and costs to developing countries to pursue such disputes.

Step 1 contains a fundamental obstacle that limits the use of the FLP by exporting interests in developing countries. As documented in chapter 4, evidence from the WTO dispute settlement caseload indicates that developing countries do frequently initiate disputes when their exporting firms can easily recognize the source of the foreign market access violations (highly observable violations such as antidumping measures, safeguards, or other border measures) and do not typically initiate disputes over less transparent types of trade barriers. Additional evidence is provided by the case of Benin and Chad in the *US–Upland Cotton* dispute. When Brazil initiated the dispute and revealed information on the source of Benin and Chad's lost foreign market access, these two countries were willing to act on it by involving themselves in the WTO dispute as third parties. But when a potential ally like Brazil does not exist, how can such technical information be made available to countries such as Benin and Chad?

In chapter 8 I describe new initiatives to provide this information. To be of use to developing countries, NGOs that disseminate such information and politically organize firms require a sufficient level of technical capacity to consume the information intelligently, even if they cannot produce it themselves. NGOs need to develop this skill to make decisions and recommendations to developing country policymakers that are based on the economic interests of the countries themselves.

Finally, it is important to recall that development-focused groups like Oxfam and the IDEAS Centre are also not indigenous to the developing countries. As outsiders, an implication is that they must consume donor resources to acquire sufficient expertise about local political and economic conditions so that they can help exporting firms and industries organize. Although development-focused NGOs offer important services to protect developing country industries' interests in the WTO self-enforcement process, it is encouraging to recall from table 7-2 that local NGOs are also emerging in developing countries. The association groups of developing country industries—Brazilian National Confederation of Industry (CNI), Brazilian Business Coalition (CEB), and All India Association of Industries (AIAI), as well as an India-based NGO such as Consumers Unity & Trust Society (CUTS)—signal that local groups are expanding their own capacity to be sufficiently informed consumers of information regarding WTO enforcement so that they can take on these political organization functions themselves.

Step 6—NGOs, the Media, and Advocacy for Respondent Compliance and Reform

Before turning to the role NGOs might play in providing actual legal support services in the middle phase (step 4) of the ELP, I explore the ability of such groups to affect the postlitigation phase of step 6. How might NGOs facilitate policy reform in respondent countries and compliance with WTO rulings that enforce the foreign market access expected by exporting firms and industries in developing countries?

Consider step 6 of the ELP when the developing country complainant, having made its legal arguments successfully, is now trying to get the respondent to comply with the WTO rulings. The complainant has already made whatever credible retaliatory threats it can—whether it be goods retaliation, cross-retaliation by withdrawing TRIPS commitments, or possibly making no retaliatory threats at all. This section explores the role of NGOs in the public relations sphere, as they engage the media to enhance the political climate for reform in the respondent country. To provide context, recall again the discussion of the *EC–Bananas III* (chapter 3) and *US–Steel Safeguards* (chapter 5) disputes and the associated media attention that accompanied the complainant country seeking to mobilize forces for policy reform in the respondent country. To this discussion I add one more dispute, the *EC–Hormones* case, in which the United States was authorized in 1999 to retaliate after the EC failed to lift a WTO-inconsistent ban on imports of U.S. beef that was treated with hormones.

In these two disputes involving the United States as complainant, the United States retaliated against the EC after its failure to comply immediately with WTO legal rulings and to restore U.S. exporters' market access. In the *EC–Bananas III* dispute, the United States sought to mobilize forces within the EC to dismantle the discriminatory import regime against bananas grown in Latin America and distributed by U.S. companies (Chiquita and Dole). After winning the necessary WTO legal arguments in the formal dispute, the United States captured media attention in Europe by threatening and then implementing retaliatory tariffs on European exports of a number of luxury products, including Louis Vuitton handbags. A second dispute from that same year is the *EC–Hormones* dispute. After the WTO legal rulings determined that the EC had violated its commitments by banning imports of U.S. hormone-treated beef, the United States retaliated over other high profile products that were cultural exports from France, including Roquefort cheese, foie gras, and truffles.[23]

---

23. See USTR (1999). In this dispute, U.S. retaliatory action did not achieve the goal of inducing EC officials to remove the WTO-inconsistent policy. In addition to the luxury items listed in the text, the United States also retaliated over EC exports of pork and a number of other products. Much of the media longevity of this particular dispute was due to the reaction of the French activist José Bové, himself

A third example is the EC-backed dispute over *US–Steel Safeguards*, in which the United States was the respondent country. Here the United States agreed to comply with WTO rulings partially out of political concern over European threats to impose retaliatory tariffs on U.S. exports. The EC grabbed media headlines after threatening to impose higher duties on well-known products exported from swing states of critical interest to the Bush administration in the upcoming 2004 Presidential election—for example, citrus products from Florida, and high-profile products from Ohio, Pennsylvania, and Wisconsin, which included Harley Davidson motorcycles. The EC's idea in this dispute was to generate a targeted political backlash within the United States—Americans speaking out against their government's WTO-inconsistent policy—by mobilizing key U.S. export interests with political influence in the Bush administration due to their geographic importance in a timely election.

Do such headline grabbing media episodes create useful lessons for developing country complainants at the step 6 phase of obtaining compliance and policy reform? In fact, media attention may be even more important for developing countries in their complainant disputes than it is for larger developed countries. One reason is that many developing countries lack a sufficiently large volume of imports from politically powerful commercial exporting interests in the respondent country that can be used to threaten new trade barriers. With limited retaliation capacity to engage exporting interests in the respondent country on their behalf, developing countries need creative, alternative strategies to induce compliance. One potential strategy is to mobilize other groups within the respondent country that are also adversely affected by their government's WTO-inconsistent policy.[24]

There are at least two categories of adversely affected groups that developing countries might target to mobilize for reform. The first category includes potential allies that have a common interest in removing the WTO-inconsistent policy because of the economic losses that they suffer. For example, a WTO-inconsistent

---

a Roquefort farmer, who subsequently dismantled a McDonald's restaurant in southern France and was sent to prison. As an interesting side note, the Bush administration's last USTR (Susan Schwab) increased the retaliatory tariff on Roquefort cheese from 100 to 300 percent in January 2009 just before leaving office (USTR 2009), once again making WTO enforcement an issue of media attention.

24. This strategy is an alternative approach for developing countries in addition to cross-retaliation within the TRIPS Agreement to induce compliance by developed economy respondents. For example, chapter 5 (see the section "Developing Countries, Retaliation Threats, and Obtaining Compliance") describes countries such as Ecuador (*EC–Bananas III*), Antigua and Barbuda (*US–Gambling*), and Brazil (*US–Upland Cotton*) potentially retaliating by failing to enforce the intellectual property rights (patent or copyright protection, for example) of exporting firms in the EC or the United States in industries such as pharmaceuticals, films or other media, or software that are intellectual property intensive. Retaliating under the TRIPS Agreement would be an alternative way to mobilize exporting industry forces within the respondent country to obtain compliance.

policy that restricts imports, such as a quota or excessive duty, imposes losses on domestic consumers via the higher prices they have to pay. An alternative WTO-inconsistent policy that promotes exports, such as a subsidy, also imposes losses on domestic citizens via the tax burden they suffer for financing the subsidy. The second category includes individuals who do not necessarily experience economic losses, but who nevertheless suffer a loss in well-being (what economists refer to as "utility" loss) after being informed of the WTO-inconsistent policy. This might occur for voters who are newly informed about various consequences of their own government's policies: the *international consequences* because of the significant harm they are causing to the economic well-being of people in other countries, the *income distributional consequences* because such policies are domestically more regressive than was previously known, and even the *environmental consequences* because the policies are causing harm in terms of increased pollution.

The next three subsections explore how NGOs have exploited (or could exploit) elements of the strategy of information generation and public relations to help mobilize potential allies in promoting reform in respondent countries. I begin first with Oxfam's attempt to use the international consequences strategy to generate demands for political reform in the *US–Upland Cotton* dispute. Next, I explore how NGOs might tap into the category of people who themselves experience economic losses as well as the possibility that an electorate might be engaged to push for reform based on new knowledge of how their government's own policies create unanticipated income distributional or environmental consequences. In the third subsection I discuss recent economic research assessing evidence that NGO activism in this realm may have payoffs. Although some researchers have found that NGOs can have an effect, their work also reveals important limitations to such efforts and possible unintended consequences of NGOs increasing their activism in this area. I explore this concern in the last subsection.

Educating the Public on the International Consequences of WTO-Inconsistent Policies: Oxfam in the US–Upland Cotton *Dispute*

The *US–Upland Cotton* dispute provides another important but also unique example of an attempt to engage media attention around a particular WTO enforcement action. The focus of the dispute was potentially WTO-inconsistent U.S. agricultural subsidy policies that adversely affected developing countries' abilities to export their own cotton. The approach in this instance would be different from the EC's tactics in the *US–Steel Safeguards* case. Some of the countries seeking U.S compliance were small and poor: Benin, Burkina Faso, Chad, and Mali did not consume sufficient volumes of U.S. exports and thus did not have the capacity to credibly retaliate against U.S. export industries so as to convert them into potential allies within the U.S. political process to help obtain the desired policy reform.[25]

Oxfam worked effectively on behalf of the West African cotton-producing countries in *US–Upland Cotton* to engage the U.S. media from a different angle. During their "Make Trade Fair" campaign, which was working to improve the terms of commerce between coffee growers in developing countries and coffee retailers and consumers in northern markets, Oxfam also commissioned research and developed policy briefs on the cotton issue.[26] Most important, Oxfam used the experience learned from the "Make Trade Fair" campaign and its public relations savvy to tap into its U.S. media connections to influence and highlight reporting on the cotton issue. The cotton issue surfaced in an impressive list of op-eds and articles placed in major newspapers and other media outlets (the *New York Times, Wall Street Journal, Economist, Washington Post*) in 2003 and 2004—many of them citing Oxfam's work identifying with the plight of West African farmers who had suffered lost market access because of the subsidy payments to U.S. cotton farmers.[27] Oxfam's strategy was to use the media to convince the American public that its own government's policies were harming already poor farmers in West Africa. The intention was to enhance the climate for policy reform, with the U.S. public demanding cuts to U.S. agricultural subsidies.

Although Oxfam and other groups were successful at generating U.S. media attention on the cotton issue and placing it in the headlines of news outlets famous for shaping public opinion, these efforts had little short-term effect on U.S. public opinion. A telephone survey of 1,000 U.S. households carried out by the German Marshall Fund of the United States (GMFUS) between September and October 2005 asked the following question: "Are U.S. farm subsidies acceptable even though developing country farmers suffer?" Despite the recent media attention, 53 percent of the respondents answered that it was "acceptable," and another 15 percent indicated it was "acceptable to avoid domestic farm closures."[28] This evidence suggests that it may be difficult for NGOs to

---

25. A separate issue is whether the West African countries would even be permitted legally to retaliate against the United States in this dispute. The answer, based on how the dispute has evolved, is no, since these countries were not complainants in the actual dispute. (Benin and Chad did register formally as an interested third party.) Of course, their decision not to become complainants may have reflected their lack of retaliation capacity.

26. Examples of Oxfam's studies include Watkins (2002); Baden (2004).

27. See also the discussion of Heinisch (2006) and the documentation of the media efforts described there.

28. See GMFUS (2005, p. 18). GMFUS performed the same survey in different countries within the EC and found results that were not much different: in the EC, 45 percent of the respondents answered that it was "acceptable," and another 21 percent indicated it was "acceptable to avoid domestic farm closures."

influence public opinion about policies such as domestic subsidies using descriptions of their adverse international consequences.

There are other potential lessons to learn from the problems that likely plagued Oxfam's media effort to generate support for policy reform and induce compliance. The case does highlight important technical capacities that NGOs must possess to be effective in assisting developing countries in the ELP.

First, NGOs must have a very sophisticated understanding of the political process within the respondent country. To be able to contribute to the reform first requires detailed knowledge of the policymaking process in the respondent country and thus knowledge of how to implement a change in the WTO-inconsistent policy. For example, does the reforming country's institutional infrastructure and its political system allow the required policy change to be achieved by an executive decision—administratively or bureaucratically—or does it require a more concerted act of legislation?

As the experience of the *US–Upland Cotton* dispute reveals, agricultural policy reform in the United States is extremely difficult politically. Traditionally legislators negotiate U.S. farm policy once every five years as part of an overall farm bill. A key question from the *US–Upland Cotton* case is the extent of the U.S. Department of Agriculture's discretion in its administration of the cotton subsidy program. If the program can only be reformed by a legislative act of Congress, NGOs therefore need to understand the complicated legislative cycle in which farm bills are debated so that they can time the media blitz for maximum political impact. Oxfam's efforts to engage the media to paint a dire picture during the 2003–04 period may have been ineffective in promoting major reform of the U.S. subsidy policies because they were not being debated in Congress at the time. The most recent debates and reforms of U.S. farm bills occurred in 2002 and 2007. The poor timing in this case is in direct contrast to the EC's successful actions in *US–Steel Safeguards,* which took political advantage of the timing of an election to improve its chances at achieving compliance and policy reform.

Second, NGOs must have the technical capacity to recognize why respondent countries may need to rely on the WTO's dispute settlement process, and legal rulings in particular, to facilitate domestic policy reform. The media effort to publicize the cotton issue from 2003 to 2004 came well before the actual WTO dispute had fully exhausted the legal process.[29] Thus the media campaign

29. The timing of the media blitz in the fall of 2003 was surely designed to coincide with the Cancún ministerial meeting, which took place in September. This turned out to be successful in that cotton worked its way onto the negotiating agenda of the Doha Round of negotiations, but it also contributed to the failure of that particular ministerial meeting, and it is not clear that taking the West African cotton issue out of the WTO enforcement (trade dispute) forum and moving it to the negotiations forum will be more effective in achieving reduction of the U.S. subsidies, U.S. compliance with WTO obligations, and restoration of foreign market access for cotton exporters in West Africa. In addition, Brazil has continued to pursue the issue as a WTO dispute in attempts to achieve U.S. compliance.

occurred before an impartial set of arbitrators (the WTO Panel and subsequent appeals to the Appellate Body) had determined that the United States was indeed in violation of its obligations.[30] With the benefit of hindsight, legal rulings were likely to play an important role in this particular dispute. The dispute set an important precedent because a developing country (Brazil) was challenging a developed country over the issue of agricultural subsidy payments. Much of the argument covered virgin legal territory and introduced new forms of economic evidence.[31] It would also set a precedent for other U.S. agricultural support programs for other crops. If the United States ultimately does reform its cotton subsidy policies, an impartial set of WTO legal rulings and thus the mandate to live up to its international obligations can be of political value to the U.S. government, which would otherwise have to struggle to piece together sufficient domestic political coalitions in support of the reform.

Despite the failure of the media effort in this instance, the *US–Upland Cotton* case does identify a creative strategy and a template that developing countries can follow as they seek foreign compliance with WTO rulings when they arrive at step 6 of the ELP. The utility of the approach will be case specific. It must be tailored to the particular political context and climate and combined with other strategies that I identify next.

Educating the Public on the Domestic Consequences of WTO-Inconsistent Policies

Thus far I have described how, in the final stage of the ELP, complainant countries and their advocates seek to generate political support in the respondent country in two ways: via mobilization of exporting industries that are fearful of suffering retaliation or mobilization of the voting public suffering utility losses when confronted with evidence that their own government's policies were harming poor people in other countries. In this section I identify an additional target that complainants and their advocates might mobilize as an ally for reform—the domestic groups in the respondent country that also lose economically from the WTO-inconsistent policy or those that may become more politically active in the face of new knowledge of the income distributional consequences or environmental consequences of their government's own domestic policies.

---

30. The Appellate Body did not issue its report in the original dispute until March 2005. Furthermore, the process by which the WTO assesses U.S. compliance with the rulings—whereby the U.S. can argue that it has complied with rulings, and subsequent rulings determine whether this was the case—was not completed until June 2008.

31. Sapir and Trachtman (2008) discuss the technical economic evidence that played an important role in the case.

Each WTO-inconsistent policy will result in a different set of losers even within the respondent country. Thus the appropriate groups to mobilize will vary on a case-by-case basis. For disputes that involve import restrictions, a natural ally will be consumers with their consumption interests.[32] For disputes that involve subsidies, a natural ally will also be taxpayers. Mobilizing either of these groups is not easy, of course, because much the same "free rider" incentives that I discussed in the context of the example of Michele Brown in chapter 5 operate here. A WTO-inconsistent policy may harm domestic consumers and taxpayers, but it typically hurts each by only a little bit. While the aggregated costs may be large, the cost imposed on each individual is likely to be small, thus creating little incentive for any consumer or taxpayer to spend the resources to organize and engage in collective efforts to change the policy.

Though it is a challenge to engage consumers and taxpayers politically, some newer NGOs provide important information and resources that could be useful in efforts to mobilize these groups. Consider, for example, the U.S. nonprofit organization Environmental Working Group (EWG)—and in particular its Farm Subsidies Database.[33] The EWG takes advantage of information available from official U.S. government sources under the Freedom of Information Act to publish data on who in the United States is receiving agricultural support payments from the U.S. government.

The EWG's data collection exercise increases transparency and disseminates information that can be used to mobilize U.S. taxpayers and consumers to support efforts to reform agricultural subsidies.[34] For example, the Farm Subsidies Database could be used to evaluate the statement that agricultural support programs are targeted at ensuring the viability of small family farms and thus helping preserve the rural way of life in the United States. While the data reveal that some of the payments indeed do go to small farmers, the Farm Subsidies Database also documents that the subsidy payments are concentrated on a relatively small number of large (and politically active) corporate farms.

How might such information be useful in the context of WTO enforcement and the step 6 phase of generating compliance? Consider how NGOs might use

32. Researchers at the Peterson Institute for International Economics (then called the Institute for International Economics) have estimated the cost to consumers of each job saved by a particular U.S. policy that was enacted to protect import-competing industries. See Hufbauer and Elliott (1994). Such an approach might also be applied to WTO disputes to obtain compliance by revealing to the consuming public just how much the WTO-inconsistent policy is costing them.

33. The Environmental Working Group's Farm Subsidies Database can be located at (http://farm.ewg.org/farm/index.php [February 7, 2009]).

34. The EWG's data are frequently referenced in major media outlet reports on U.S. agricultural subsidy programs. For example, see Alexei Barrionuevo, "Mountains of Corn and a Sea of Farm Subsidies," *New York Times,* November 9, 2005, p. A1; Lauren Etter and Greg Hitt, "Bountiful Harvest: Farm Lobby Beats Back Assault on Subsidies," *Wall Street Journal,* March 27, 2008, p. A1; and Andrew Martin, "Awash in Milk and Headaches," *New York Times,* January 2, 2009, p. A1.

such a database as a tool to complement the other strategies in promoting reform of U.S. agricultural subsidies in the *US–Upland Cotton* dispute. In addition to Oxfam's efforts to convince the American public that the policy harmed poor cotton farmers in West Africa, NGOs could use the media to highlight the domestic consequences of U.S. cotton subsidies. Alerting the public as to the recipients of U.S. cotton subsidy payments could mobilize taxpayer demands for policy reform. For example, cotton was the third largest U.S. agricultural subsidy program for the 1995–2006 period ($21 billion total), trailing only the corn and wheat industries. Furthermore, payments to cotton farmers were not widely disbursed. The top 10 percent of cotton subsidy recipients were paid 81 percent of the total cotton subsidy payments received over the 1995–2006 period. The bulk went to corporate farms, such as Tyler Farms in Arkansas, which received $24 million in cotton subsidy payments, and Due West Farms in Mississippi, which collected close to $16 million. Information on subsidy payments to farms from this publicly accessible database could be combined with data on congressional districts, voting records, and campaign contributions.

In addition to highlighting the regressive income distribution consequences, the public might also be better informed about the adverse environmental consequences of agricultural subsidies. EWG data on subsidies could be combined with data on pollution problems to highlight the linkages between agricultural subsidies and the environmental concerns associated with runoff of chemical fertilizers. This strategy could provide additional transparency on how the WTO-inconsistent policies also reduce domestic economic efficiency and increase inequality within the respondent country, in addition to concerns over their negative consequences abroad.

Finally, it is not only groups in the United States like EWG that are seeking to provide additional transparency on agricultural subsidy policies. A similar group, Farmsubsidy.org, has launched comparable efforts to construct a publicly accessible database on European Community agricultural subsidy payments, although data collection efforts for Europe are likely to be more difficult given the additional layers of governments involved.[35] Although the efforts of EWG and Farmsubsidy.org generate potentially useful products, ultimately it is up to the developing country complainants, as well as potential development-focused NGO advocates working on their behalf within the ELP, to access this information and turn it into something that captures public attention and contributes to the policy reform.

---

35. Farmsubsidy.org's data have also recently become an important media reference for EC agricultural subsidy programs. For example, see Stephen Castle and Doreen Carvajal, "Recipients of Europe Farm Grants Disclosed," *New York Times*, May 8, 2009, p. A7.

Lessons from Research on the Effectiveness of NGO Activism

I have thus far identified past attempts and theoretical possibilities of NGOs engaging the public in respondent countries as political allies on behalf of developing country complainants. The strategy is to generate and disseminate information on the adverse, unintended, and perhaps previously unknown consequences of government policies—both internationally and domestically—and use the NGOs' considerable public relations skills to mobilize support from politically disparate interest groups (such as consumers and taxpayers).

Emerging scholarship provides the basic theory underlying NGO activism in this realm, as well as evidence as to its effectiveness. Since much of this research derives from a slightly different set of NGO activists than I have detailed thus far, it is important to describe the context. Consider the potential impact of human rights advocates on labor standards in developing countries. A good example is Jeff Ballinger, the activist who mobilized an NGO movement in the 1990s to take on Nike's sweatshops in Southeast Asia.[36] The sneaker giant was accused of using subcontractors whose plants paid below-market wages, employed child labor, and subjected workers to dangerous conditions. The NGO movement was extremely successful in generating media attention that brought the issue of labor standards of Nike's Southeast Asian sneaker plants to the attention of the U.S. public.

Elliott and Freeman model such human rights activists as "supplying" a product to developed country consumers, specifically information on the working conditions associated with the goods that consumers buy.[37] Elliot and Freeman conducted surveys to obtain data, which were then used to estimate the consumer latent demand curve for labor standards, and attempted to account for the difference in consumer responsiveness to products made under good conditions as opposed to those made under bad (sweatshop) conditions. The elasticity estimates from the survey data suggest an asymmetric consumer response to information on labor standards. Consumers are likely to make dramatic changes to behavior when provided with information about the poor conditions associated with their consumer products, whereas they make only slight modifications of behavior (willingness to pay a higher price) when provided with good information on the source of the products they purchase.

---

36. For the anti-sweatshop movement, see Winston (2002), who categorizes the activist groups as "confronters"—those who would focus on generating media attention and publicity—and "engagers"—those who would sit down with firms and policymakers to identify possible compromises and areas of reform.

37. See Elliott and Freeman (2005). Spar (2002) discussed groups involved in the publicity of Nike and sweatshops in the 1990s. More extensive coverage of labor standards, NGOs, and globalization can be found in Elliott and Freeman (2003).

Harrison and Scorse examine the related question of whether anti-sweatshop activity affected firm-level decisions at plants owned by subcontractors of brand-name firms in industries such as footwear and apparel and textiles in Southeast Asia in the 1990s.[38] They provide evidence that NGO activist campaigns against companies such as Nike, Adidas, and Reebok are positively correlated with large wage increases for unskilled workers employed by subcontractors. Furthermore, although the campaigns imposed costs on the subcontractors in terms of reduced investment, reduced profits, and increased probability of closing for smaller plants, their research finds no evidence that the higher wages resulted in a significant reduction in employment or in a relocation of plants.

The results from Elliott and Freeman and Harrison and Scorse together indicate that NGO activists can affect individual consumer choices, which in turn induce firms to change their behavior.[39] However, these results for NGO activists targeting labor conditions in factories in foreign countries producing goods sold under U.S. name brands are somewhat at odds with the 2005 GMFUS survey results reported earlier for cotton subsidies. Recall that 68 percent of the U.S. public found U.S. farm subsidies were acceptable (or acceptable with a qualification) even if they hurt poor farmers in developing countries.

There are at least three contributing explanations for these seemingly inconsistent public responses, with implications for even the most sophisticated NGOs to bear in mind. First, NGO activists in the successful cases of labor standards benefited from being able to target brand-name products whose sales and profitability rely on their reputations. Whereas Nike and Reebok are names that ring a bell with the public, even the U.S. cotton farms that are the largest recipients of federal agricultural support payments (Tyler Farms and Due West Farms) are not. Second, consumer products may be easier to target with media attention than intermediate inputs. Whereas consumers buy shoes or coffee directly (which a "Make Trade Fair"–type campaign can target), a product like cotton is an input into the production of other goods and thus is much more difficult for end-consumers to track. Third, it is likely to be easier to affect an individual's one-time consumption decision than his or her political choice, given that most members of the public are not single-issue voters whose votes in elections depend mainly on the candidates' positions on trade policy or agricultural subsidies.

Therefore, for NGOs to generate a groundswell of public opinion against child labor appears to be a much easier public relations task than to promote public support for political action against agricultural subsidies by publicizing

38. See Harrison and Scorse (forthcoming). Harrison and Scorse (2006) present confirming results from a similar study.
39. Elliott and Freeman (2005); Harrison and Scorse (forthcoming).

their adverse impact on foreign welfare, implications for domestic income distribution, or their adverse environmental impact. And in relative terms, explaining
agricultural subsidies to the public may be easier than the equally worrisome but
more complex implications of policies such as antidumping or any of the multi-
tudes of other nontariff barriers to trade that developing country complainants
may need assistance in getting respondents to remove.

For NGOs hoping to use public opinion to promote policy changes on behalf
of developing country complainants, this suggests a tough row to hoe. Oxfam's
approach in the *US–Upland Cotton* dispute as well as possible NGO efforts to
publicize the inequitable distribution of U.S. farm subsidy payments (using and
publicizing information provided by the Environmental Working Group) need
to be well conceived and complemented with other strategies. To ensure that
developing country clients have realistic expectations, NGOs should provide
caveats regarding uncertainties about the likely effectiveness of their efforts.

Additional Cautions to NGO Activism for Issues of WTO Enforcement

Increased activism by NGOs in this area is likely to have important side effects.
Moreover, some NGOs continue to maintain a Seattle-like anti-globalization
mind-set. Finally, issue-oriented NGOs, even if not hostile to the WTO, may
have no interest in using WTO enforcement to advance the interests of developing countries. Indeed there are examples of NGOs playing a substantial role
in generating WTO-inconsistent policies that lead to new disputes.

One prominent example is the activity of environmental advocates such as
the Earth Island Institute, a U.S. NGO that successfully targeted the use of the
purse seine method of fishing for tuna in the late 1980s because dolphins were
killed as "by-catch."[40] NGO activism engaged the American public to such an
extent that Congress enacted a law ultimately leading to an import ban on tuna
from countries that did not impose on their fishing boats sufficiently rigorous
standards to prevent dolphin by-catch mortality. However, the NGO activism
that influenced the U.S. government to impose the import ban also resulted in
controversial "tuna-dolphin" trade disputes in the GATT in the early 1990s.[41]

---

40. Vietor and Reinhardt (1995) provide a discussion of some of the groups involved in the publicity
surrounding the issue of tuna and dolphins in the late 1980s.

41. See the unadopted GATT Panel reports, *US–Restrictions on Imports of Tuna: Report of the Panel,*
DS21/R (Geneva, September 3, 1991), for the dispute initiated by Mexico (*US–Tuna/Dolphin I*) and
US–Restrictions on Imports of Tuna: Report of the Panel, DS29/R (Geneva, June 16, 1994), for the dispute
initiated by the EEC (*US–Tuna/Dolphin II*). The Panel reports in the dispute are associated with the
infamous "product-process" doctrine that infuriated environmentalists by ruling that countries could not
differentiate between domestic- and foreign-produced goods on the basis of the process by which each
was created, even if one process was environmentally damaging because it resulted in dolphins killed as
by-catch. For a discussion of the "product-process" doctrine, see Hudec (1998).

Although these disputes were settled before the establishment of the WTO, the issue of Mexico's tuna export access to the U.S. market was revived in a formal WTO dispute that Mexico initiated in 2008.[42] In an interesting twist, the same NGO (Earth Island Institute) that brought the tuna-dolphin issue to the forefront of American consciousness is now partially responsible for administering the "dolphin safe" program private standard. One of Mexico's arguments is that, despite bringing its tuna-catching process into conformity with the standard that ensures the safety of dolphins, it still cannot regain access to the U.S. tuna market because the Earth Island Institute is holding its certification hostage.

The main point is that reliance on NGOs is not a panacea, because NGOs are driven by their own interests, which may not necessarily be the same as those of developing countries. The greater the influence of NGOs in the global trading system, the more likely it is that some NGOs will generate additional and unanticipated obstacles for developing countries in the WTO system as well.

NGOs, Trade Lawyers, and Litigation Support in Step 4 of the Extended Litigation Process

Finally, I consider a possible role for NGOs in the middle stage (step 4) of the ELP. In particular, I describe some of the implications of NGOs providing legal services to developing country policymakers and helping them prosecute a case. As issue-based organizations are taking on such a role in other legal contexts that I describe below, the same may occur in the WTO.

It is not far-fetched to imagine that some of the more technically sophisticated NGOs might offer legal services to developing countries in the context of WTO enforcement. Some NGOs have already submitted *amicus curiae* briefs relating to their organization's issue in formal disputes.[43] For example, the Centre for International Environmental Law (CIEL) has made *amicus curiae* submissions in disputes over trade and environment issues such as those litigated in

42. In October 2008, Mexico initiated the dispute *US–Measures Concerning the Importation, Marketing and Sale of Tuna and Tuna Products.* The impact of the Earth Island Institute lives on, as evidenced by Mexico's formal "request for consultations" in the dispute in which it claims explicitly that one of the U.S. measures that is inconsistent with the WTO is the ruling in *Earth Island Institute* v. *Hogarth,* 494 F. 3d 757 (9th Cir. 2007): "'The U.S. measures have the effect of prohibiting the labeling of Mexican tuna and tuna products as 'dolphin-safe,' even when the tuna has been harvested by means that comply with the multilaterally agreed 'dolphin-safe' standard established by the Inter-American Tropical Tuna Commission, while tuna products from most other countries, including the United States, are allowed to be labeled as 'dolphin-safe.'" See WTO (2008a).

43. In addition to those discussed in the text, other examples include a submission by the American Iron and Steel Institute in the *US–Carbon Steel* dispute, as well as a submission by the Interior Alliance group indigenous to Canada in the *US–Softwood Lumber* dispute (ICTSD 2002). For a discussion of WTO Panel and Appellate Body considerations of *amicus curiae* briefs in formal dispute hearings, see Mavroidis (2002); Appleton (2000); Durling and Hardin (2005).

the *US–Shrimp* and *Brazil–Retreaded Tyres* disputes. The former concerned the U.S. ban on imports of shrimp from countries that did not require shrimp boats to use turtle excluder devices (TEDs), while the latter concerned Brazil's ban on imports of retreaded tires that the Brazilian government justified on grounds of public health and environmental protection. Furthermore, the U.K. Consumers' Association submitted an *amicus curiae* brief on behalf of the Peruvian complainants in the *EC–Sardines* dispute, which challenged an EC consumer labeling scheme that refused to designate the imported Peruvian product as a sardine.[44] There is good reason to expect some issue-based NGOs to seek to expand their influence over WTO jurisprudence by offering to take on developing countries as clients and represent them, perhaps actually carrying out the full legal prosecution of a dispute, particularly if the dispute involves relatively novel legal areas that are likely to lead to the shaping of case law on topics of critical importance to the NGO's issue.

These suggestions are motivated by study of U.S. employment law, which Christine Jolls documents as having evolved such that issue-based organizations offer private clients the organization's attorneys and legal assistance for potential cases aligned with the organization's issue.[45] Not surprisingly, she finds that an organization's need to fundraise strongly influences its decisions on which cases to take on. For NGOs without a large endowment, which rely on fundraising to provide financial support of their issue, high profile and precedent-setting cases that lend themselves to media attention are of the greatest interest to pursue.

Given the existence of the Advisory Centre on WTO Law, which already provides to developing countries the legal services needed in step 4 of the ELP, donor funding in the case of WTO enforcement would be better placed elsewhere rather than expanding the capacity of development-focused NGOs to offer their own legal services. Unlike a legal assistance center such as the ACWL, issue-based organizations are most interested in covering the disputes relating to their core issue and not necessarily the broader self-enforcement needs of exporters in developing countries. The ACWL, on the other hand, does not have its own agenda other than to provide support to developing countries' foreign market access interests. Thus it takes on whatever cases come to it. This includes nonissue disputes over market access concerns that traditionally do not grab media headlines, such as antidumping actions, safeguards, customs measures, and other trade restrictions.

Nevertheless, there are additional roles for relatively sophisticated NGOs to play in providing technical support needed in step 4 of the ELP. While the

44. For the Centre for International Environmental Law submissions, see CIEL (1999, 2007). Shaffer and Mosoti (2002) describe the U.K. Consumers' Association's submission.

45. See Jolls (2005). Examples include employment discrimination allegations based on the issue of race (National Association for the Advancement of Colored People), sexuality (Lambda Legal Defense and Education Fund), age (National Senior Citizens Law Center), and gender (Legal Momentum).

submission of *amicus curiae* briefs is one role, perhaps more important is the provision of technical economic assistance, such as empirical evidence and economic modeling, in support of developing country cases.[46] What is particularly needed is economic modeling of markets that balances rigor with the transparency of how economic estimates and results have been generated. For example, given the experience of *US–Upland Cotton,* important evidence in future agricultural subsidy disputes may be estimates of the economic injury that foreign exporters suffer because of reduced market access caused by the price-suppressing effects of the subsidy. However, some of the economic models that generate the evidence introduced into the WTO dispute settlement process have made not only the lawyers but also the jurists (the Panel and the Appellate Body) uncomfortable, and in some cases unwilling to take a stand on the evidence.[47] While some of this discomfort reflects a lack of technical economic capacity, some responsibility also rests with economists who have not yet developed the right balance of rigor and technical sophistication relative to transparency and accessibility in models submitted to the WTO enforcement process. That being said, technical economic evidence continues to be an important element of the formal step 4 phase of WTO litigation.[48]

Although much modeling work and many refinements are needed to make economic evidence more comprehensible (while still maintaining its attractiveness due to its level of rigor), one NGO that is a research institute with the technical capacity to take on such a challenge is the International Food Policy Research Institute (IFPRI). In general, it will be interesting to see whether some of the other technically competent groups, such as the CGE modeling groups active in the Doha Round providing information that is used in the negotiations, are able to retool to provide economic analysis that would be useful as evidentiary support in future developing country WTO enforcement actions.[49]

46. The Advisory Centre on WTO Law does have access to a technical expertise fund to hire experts in disputes that are particularly intensive in scientific evidence, such as those relating to the Agreement on Sanitary and Phytosanitary Measures (SPS Agreement) or the Agreement on Technical Barriers to Trade (TBT Agreement). The ACWL can also use this fund to hire economic experts in support of its cases.

47. As an example, the Appellate Body Article 21.5 report in the *US–Upland Cotton* dispute takes issue with the Panel's unwillingness to consider such economic evidence by stating (paragraph 357), "Modelling exercises are likely to be an important analytical tool that a panel should scrutinize. The relative complexity of a model and its parameters is not a reason for a panel to remain agnostic about them. Like other categories of evidence, a panel should reach conclusions with respect to the probative value it accords to economic simulations or models presented to it."

48. For a discussion of the use of quantitative economic evidence in WTO dispute settlement cases, see WTO (2005); Keck (2004); Bown and Ruta (2010).

49. For more on the CGE modeling groups, see the section on development-focused NGOs. Note that Oxfam also published a commissioned empirical study of the impact of the cotton subsidy program on West African cotton farmers; see Alston, Sumner, and Brunke (2007).

*Other Roles for Development-Focused Researchers
in Assessing the WTO Enforcement Process*

There are other ways development-focused researchers can help developing countries in the area of WTO enforcement apart from assisting a developing country overcome one of the hurdles associated with steps 1 through 6 of a dispute in the ELP. In particular, scholars are needed to continually assess WTO legal rulings and to evaluate the process as well as the outcomes of these disputes.

A number of scholars have been contributing to this area; one example of intriguing collaborative and interdisciplinary research stems from the American Law Institute (ALI) project on the "Principles of Trade Law: The World Trade Organization."[50] One program of the ALI project teams legal scholars with academic economists to provide joint legal and economic assessments of WTO Appellate Body and (unappealed) Panel reports.[51] The resulting research has identified a number of areas of divergence between the WTO rulings and legal and economic scholarly perspectives, suggesting that there may be increasingly important need for dialogue between WTO insiders and WTO outsiders as the dispute settlement process and the case law continue to evolve.

From the perspective of economic scholarship, an important area of missing research is an impact assessment that analyzes how WTO rulings and acts of compliance affect trade flows and underlying economic activity, especially in developing countries. The needed research on how WTO dispute settlement affects markets should not be limited to the impact on complainants and the respondents, but also the impact on third party interests as well.

Conclusions

A number of development-focused NGOs have emerged to assist developing countries that seek to increase their engagement in the WTO system. While most of these NGOs have focused their efforts thus far on assisting developing countries during multilateral negotiations, a few have begun to also provide necessary assistance to the developing countries that use WTO disputes and the extended litigation process (ELP) to self-enforce the market-opening commitments of trading partners. Groups like the IDEAS Centre and ICTSD have helped firms and industries in developing countries overcome the costs of step 3

50. There are many important examples of non-ALI-sponsored research on WTO dispute settlement as well. In addition to the scholarship described in detail in chapter 4, work has been published in professional journals such as the *Journal of International Economic Law,* the *World Trade Review,* and the *Journal of World Trade.* The first two journals began publication after the establishment of the WTO in 1995.

51. Horn and Mavroidis (2004, 2005, 2006, 2008a, 2009a) contain the ALI assessments of seven years of WTO rulings (2001–07) from a legal and economic perspective.

of the ELP associated with organizing politically so as to engage their government policymakers to self-enforce foreign commitments in actual WTO disputes. In addition to making step 3 contributions, Oxfam has engaged media attention in noteworthy and creative attempts to help developing countries overcome the step 6 hurdle of generating respondent country compliance and policy reform at the very end of the ELP.

The remaining ELP hurdle that has not even begun to be addressed is the problem of insufficient information in step 1. This stage of the ELP requires developing countries to obtain the economic, legal, and political information on the cause of lost foreign market access. The technical information must derive from a synthesized analysis of economic data, legal knowledge of detailed WTO commitments, and a political analysis of the likelihood of foreign compliance and policy reform. Exporting firms in developing countries, and by extension their government representatives, too frequently lack information on the cause of lost foreign market access, as well as the expected benefits and costs to proceeding with self-enforcement. The current field of development-focused NGOs does not have the technical capacity to work on behalf of developing countries so as to generate or disseminate the critical information that is the starting point for triggering the ELP. The next chapter tackles this fundamental problem in step 1.

8

Monitoring and the Institute for Assessing WTO Commitments

D espite the efforts of a number of stakeholders—including policymakers, the Advisory Centre on WTO Law (ACWL), and even a number of development-focused nongovernmental organizations (NGOs)—to encourage the developing countries' self-enforcement efforts, a substantial hurdle continues to impede the access of exporting firms and their governments to the system. Developing country firms and their government representatives often lack information on the underlying cause of their industry's lost foreign market access. Since failure to recognize the cause leads to failure to recognize that the country's World Trade Organization (WTO) rights have been violated, the affected firm cannot even overcome the step 1 hurdle of the extended litigation process (ELP) described in chapter 5 (see figure 5-1).

This chapter focuses on the step 1 issue of information needed to trigger the WTO's extended litigation process. In order to focus on step 1, once again I consider this from the perspective of Michele Brown and her employer (see chapter 5), the kind of exporting firm whose trade is at the heart of WTO self-enforcement. Michele and her firm observe a reduction in its exports to a foreign market. What caused the reduced exports? Sometimes the cause of the export reduction is obvious to the firm and sometimes it is not. When the cause is something that is highly observable to the firm—imposition of foreign anti-dumping or countervailing measures, safeguards, or other new trade restrictions that occur at the border—the firm may not need assistance from outsiders to understand the cause of its plight.

However, an information problem arises when the exporting firm does not lose market access for these highly observable reasons but instead because the foreign demand shifts *away* from the exporter's product. In many instances the shift in demand away from the exporter's product results from changes in the "natural" economic environment that are not related to WTO-inconsistent measures.[1] Examples include foreign buyers substituting purchases of an exporting firm's products with a competitor's that are higher quality, better tailored for the consumer's end use, or simply offered at a lower price based on lower cost of production. Alternatively, foreign buyers may reduce their purchases of the firm's product for a reason that has nothing to do with a WTO violation, as when national income falls due to a recession. In these instances there is nothing that the exporting firm can or should do at the WTO—the lost foreign market access is due to changing natural economic conditions and not to a WTO-inconsistent policy that goes unchallenged.

The concern over the failure to self-enforce arises when the foreign demand shift is not caused by natural changes in economic conditions but by a WTO member's actions that violate WTO rules and membership obligations. Examples include foreign competitors attracting customers via lower prices resulting from government policies that are WTO illegal. One example of such a WTO-illegal policy is an explicit subsidy—a targeted foreign government transfer of funds to a competing producer. Another example is a policy that is not a direct subsidy but nevertheless creates similar economic incentives. Such policies include discriminatory use of the tax code to provide an advantage to domestic producers over foreigners. Alternatively, the foreign government may provide its firms with access to better terms for credit arrangements (for example, loan guarantees) not available to foreign firms. Likewise, the foreign government may have imposed export restrictions on products that were critical inputs to the product in question, thus implicitly subsidizing the foreign competitors' input costs and thereby allowing them to offer lower prices to buyers. Finally, a myriad of "behind the border" government regulations make it more costly for consumers to acquire imported products rather than their domestically produced equivalents. Examples include failure to enforce intellectual property rights or imposition of regulations that, although possibly motivated by considerations of consumer safety or environmental protection, are not well grounded in scientific risk assessment and are thus little more than disguised protection.

---

1. Even highly observable causes of a firm's lost market access that occur because of policy changes at the border are not necessarily WTO inconsistent.

A very real problem is that both the natural forces that are not WTO-inconsistent and WTO violations that illegally shift foreign demand may be operating at the same time. Exporters interested in self-enforcement are confronted with the technical problem of providing evidence that a major contributing cause of the adverse result is the WTO-inconsistent policy and that most of the injury suffered from lost market access is not due to something else. This is where formal economic analysis plays an important role, as it is not sufficient to know that there was a legal violation. If the WTO legal violation occurred at the same time as a major natural shock that was the chief underlying cause of the firm's lost foreign market access, a potential dispute may not be worth pursuing because correction of the legal violation will not restore the lost market access.

Putting aside this issue for the moment, are these sorts of changes in foreign market access—ones that are not economically natural but the result of WTO violations that illegally shift foreign demand—a quantitatively important source of disputes? As shown in chapter 4 (see figure 4-6), the evidence is that such causes of lost foreign market access are indeed an important source of disputes among WTO members. The data indicate dozens of trade disputes over these types of WTO-inconsistent policies imposed during the 1995–2008 period. Such policies are frequently imposed and are therefore present to be challenged. What is worrisome about the data in figure 4-6 is that most of the disputes challenging such measures have been initiated by industrialized country complainants.

Table 8-1 presents examples of actual WTO disputes stemming from these sorts of foreign market access violations. This list includes many disputes over products in which exports from firms in developing countries as well as developed countries have been adversely affected, and yet the complainants in these cases are typically developed economies. With the exception of Brazil, developing countries usually appear only as co-complainants, riding the coattails of disputes spearheaded by developed countries. One potential explanation that can be quickly ruled out is that the developed countries tend to dominate initiation of such disputes because the WTO-inconsistent policies disproportionately affect their own exporters. By their very nature, such policies are difficult for the imposing (respondent) country to construct in a way that would limit the adverse implications to only competitors in developed countries.[2] The main

2. It may, however, be a legitimate argument that disputes about WTO-illegal subsidies are more likely to involve developed country respondents, simply for the reason that developed countries have more efficient tax revenue generation systems and are better equipped to distribute subsidies. Developing countries, on the other hand, may be more likely to implement WTO-inconsistent policies that have the same market access effect as a subsidy but without the direct financial contribution from the government (for example, export restrictions on inputs or discrimination in the tax code).

Table 8-1. *Examples of WTO Disputes over Low-Observability Causes of Lost Foreign Market Access*

Type of cause	Disputes	Complainant(s)
Subsidy	*Australia–Automotive Leather II*	United States
	US–Offset Act (Byrd Amendment)	Australia, Brazil, Canada, Chile, EC, India, Indonesia, Japan, Korea, Mexico, Thailand
	US–Agriculture Subsidies	Brazil, Canada
Export subsidy	*Brazil–Aircraft*	Canada
	Canada–Aircraft Credits and Guarantees	Brazil
	Canada–Dairy	United States, New Zealand
	Canada–Wheat Exports and Grain Imports	United States
	EC–Measures Affecting the Exportation of Processed Cheese	United States
	EC–Export Subsidies on Sugar	Australia, Brazil, Thailand
	Hungary–Agricultural Products	Argentina, Australia, Canada, New Zealand, Thailand, United States
	US–Upland Cotton	Brazil
Export restriction conferring subsidy	*India–Measures Affecting Export of Certain Commodities*	EC
	Pakistan–Export Measures Affecting Hides and Skins	EC
Discriminatory domestic tax	*Chile–Alcoholic Beverages*	EC
	Japan–Alcoholic Beverages II	EC, Canada, United States
	Korea–Alcoholic Beverages	EC, United States
	US–Florida Excise Tax	Brazil
	US–Foreign Sales Corporation (FSC)	EC
Other regulation	*China–Intellectual Property Rights*	United States
	Japan–Agricultural Products II	United States

Source: Author's compilations from WTO (2009).

WTO-inconsistent aspect of these policies is not a violation of most-favored-nation (MFN) treatment (discrimination across different foreign sources) but a violation of national treatment (discrimination between domestic firms and all foreign sourced competitors).[3]

There are more compelling explanations for the failure of developing countries to initiate such disputes. The first is that is it more difficult for them to detect these low-observability causes, understand them, and disentangle them

---

3. See again the discussion of these GATT/WTO principles in chapter 1.

from other possible natural economic causes of lost foreign market access. For Michele Brown and her firm, this essentially underlies their inability to overcome the step 1 hurdle of the ELP. Without reliable and complete information on the source of the lost foreign market access, as well as political and economic information on the expected value of reclaiming this lost market access, Michele will be unable to trigger the forces within her firm (step 2), let alone trigger the mechanisms at the industry or policymaker level (step 3), to navigate the ELP of WTO self-enforcement.

A second problem arises when the cause of the lost foreign market access is an explicit or implicit subsidy or other regulatory barrier—a cause stemming from a more fundamental violation of the GATT/WTO principle of national treatment. Because policies that violate national treatment—that is, discrimination between domestically and foreign produced goods—typically affect firms from many exporting countries, there will be an additional free rider problem even beyond the ELP's step 3 political organization problem that was described in chapter 5. There, Michele Brown had to overcome the cost of organizing the other firms within her industry, but inside her country, to convince their government to pursue an action that is in their collective interest. The difficulty in organizing politically in order to collectively self-enforce at the WTO is compounded when the foreign WTO violation adversely affects exporters in multiple countries. Because the effect of the WTO-inconsistent trade policy is so far-reaching, the benefits of successful resolution would accrue to other countries as well. Even if exporting firms within one country politically organize and convincingly make the case that it is in their interest for the government to pursue a dispute, their government may find it worthwhile to pursue the case only if other countries join in to share in the costs. Table 8-1 includes some disputes in which this cross-country free rider problem has been overcome. Nevertheless, the difficulty of observing the cause of lost foreign market access to an exporting firm in any one country, understanding it, and disentangling the WTO-inconsistent policy from other factors is compounded when the next step is to communicate this information and politically organize exporters across countries.

This chapter therefore focuses on ways to increase information generation in support of exporting firms that themselves lack adequate knowledge of the economic, legal, and political causes of a WTO-inconsistent loss of foreign market access. Because firms find it costly to acquire such information on their own, they are often unable to initiate the ELP or to organize affected firms in their own country, let alone organize exporting firms in other countries over the same foreign market access issue. The result is the inability to self-enforce foreign market access.

To justify a role for the public sector, one must also ask why the market (private sector) has failed to provide sufficient information generation services.

What justifies the need for a new institution? First, the generation of such information has positive externalities; it is difficult to appropriate the information to make sure that potential private sector actors (for example, law firms) are able to recover their investment costs for providing it. Furthermore, because in many instances the foreign market access violation is a national treatment violation but is nevertheless applied on an MFN basis (and thus discriminates between foreign and domestic sources rather than across foreign sources), the positive externalities (benefits) from removing the violation extend across multiple countries. Thus the externality cannot be sufficiently internalized by creating domestic institutions within WTO member countries to confront the monitoring issues associated with foreign market access violations, despite the institutional efforts in a few developed economies to do so.[4]

Because of an unintended consequence of introducing the ACWL (described in chapter 6), the problem of insufficient information generation may be even more severe for exporting firms in developing countries. The existence of the ACWL reduces the incentives for private law firms to devote resources to generating information about violations for potential clients in developing countries. Once a law firm informs a potential client that it has identified a potential self-enforcement action that could be pursued at the WTO, developing country government officials could take that information and use the ACWL to provide litigation support services at (subsidized) lower cost than the law firm itself can provide. But because the ACWL's mandate is limited to step 4 of the ELP, the ACWL itself cannot fill the gap of generating step 1 information on potential disputes for developing countries to pursue. Therefore there is a need for increased public support of the step 1 information generation process, a need that some other entity must fill.

Calls for additional transparency, monitoring, and information generation are not new; the major contribution of this chapter is to provide context, details, and a coherent approach to how this could be done.[5] While many prominent analysts of the current system have called for more work in this area, no leadership has emerged to tackle the issue head on. The goal here is to do more. The global economic downturn begun in 2008 may create a political opportunity for efforts to increase transparency, information generation, and monitoring. Nevertheless, it is important to recognize that the self-enforcement problem confronting exporting firms in developing countries is systemic to the

---

4. See chapter 5, particularly the section "The Cost of Monitoring and Information Collection."

5. Indeed, especially with the spread of the global economic crisis in 2008-09 and the threat of a retreat toward protectionism, there were many calls for increased vigilance and surveillance. See, for example, the collection of proposals in Baldwin and Evenett (2009), and Hufbauer (2009). The Global Trade Alert (www.globaltradealert.org [July 2009]) is one new Internet-based initiative designed to improve monitoring. It was launched in June 2009 in the wake of the crisis.

current WTO framework. It is an issue that needs to be addressed regardless of the global macroeconomic climate.

To avoid redundant activity, it is also critical to understand what is already being done before making any explicit proposals on how to do more. The first section of this chapter therefore begins by describing the WTO's institutional role in improving the transparency of the international trading system and its "illumination" function. This section highlights areas in which the WTO makes important contributions to transparency; certain well-designed features of the institution allow exporters to quickly understand how policy decisions made at the national level in foreign countries lead to market access changes that directly affect them. The first section also identifies the limits to the WTO role and thus where there is need for additional initiatives by the outside community to address the previously described market failures that lead to insufficient monitoring undertaken by the private (commercial) sector itself. The discussion in chapter 5 on developed economy government initiatives to provide information on foreign market access violations to their exporters indicates that this informational market failure affects exporters in all countries. Thus it appears that the WTO's major contribution is establishment of a foundation and template that enables information generation, surveillance, and monitoring *by others*; the WTO itself does not and currently cannot fill this role effectively.

Are others using the WTO-established framework to fulfill this information generation role, particularly on behalf of exporters in poor countries? The second section in this chapter describes two efforts, the Global Subsidies Initiative and the Global Antidumping Database, that the external community has undertaken to generate and provide information that exporting firms in developing countries need so as to make an informed decision as to whether to trigger the self-enforcement process. While there is not yet formal evidence that the information provided by such initiatives has directly resulted in actual Dispute Settlement Understanding (DSU) cases, I describe what it would take for such information to be adapted to become useful for such a purpose. While some of these initiatives do generate useful information and data, much of that is admittedly not designed or yet packaged so as to be useful for facilitating the self-enforcement actions of developing countries. While the data created by these initiatives could be matched with other data to create the information that Michele Brown, her firm, and her country's policymakers ultimately need to make rational self-interested decisions, there is still much work to be done before this resource is ready for use in this way.

Therefore, in the third section, this analysis culminates with a proposal to establish a new institution—the Institute for Assessing WTO Commitments—with the mandate, resources, and capacity to provide the information generation services that developing countries require to self-enforce their foreign market access. This third section provides a detailed analysis of the scope of the proposed institution, including issue coverage and emphasis, funding, staffing, and governance structure.

Transparency and the Limits to What the WTO Offers

I have already emphasized that the WTO's third fundamental role—in addition to providing a forum for members to negotiate and litigate—is to illuminate. This section discusses how the WTO provides transparency for those involved in the trading system. Specifically, the WTO can help those with a stake in international trade understand the foreign changes to policies that are likely to affect trade flows.

While the main purpose of this chapter is to identify gaps in the process of information generation and dissemination—and thus where the WTO is not doing enough—it is important to begin by clarifying some areas in which the WTO makes fundamental contributions. The current WTO, which evolved from the General Agreement on Tariffs and Trade (GATT) foundation laid in the 1940s, provides a necessary institutional framework for reciprocal trade liberalization when viewed against the 1930s-era trading system during the Great Depression. The foundation for transparency that the WTO provides is likewise of tremendous value to the trading system when viewed through the lens of a hypothetical world in which it did not exist.

The following discussion examines two areas. The first subsection documents how the WTO foundation provides a set of rules, procedures, and reporting requirements that can substantially improve the process of information generation and dissemination to the commercial interests involved in trade and the government policymakers that represent their interests. The second subsection explores the WTO Trade Policy Review Mechanism and its contribution. The conclusion stemming from these sections is that, while the WTO itself does not provide enough information to allow exporters to self-enforce their trading interests, the WTO has created an infrastructure for others to use by developing and disseminating information needed to trigger members' self-enforcement of their access to foreign markets.

The WTO Basics and Ensuing Benefits

Dating back to the original Article X of the GATT 1947, the GATT/WTO has required its members to publish their national trade laws and regulations.[6] As

6. See Hoekman and Kostecki (2009, chapter 2). GATT 1947 covered only trade in goods. Similar requirements can be found in the new agreements added in 1995 covering services trade (Article III of the General Agreement on Trade in Services [GATS]) and intellectual property rights (Article 63 of the Agreement on Trade-Related Aspects of Intellectual Property Rights [TRIPS]).

discussed in chapter 2, when governments agree to membership, they bind their import tariffs and submit to the WTO the schedule of maximum tariff rates they can apply to each imported product. An implication of Article X is that WTO member governments must publish information on their basic tariff binding policies. With respect to agricultural products, many WTO members have also undertaken commitments beyond tariff bindings to also publish information on tariff rate quotas, limits on export subsidies, and certain other forms of domestic support payments.

While the WTO makes public the tariff binding information at the six-digit Harmonized System (HS) level, many countries actually apply their import tariffs on products defined at more disaggregated (eight- or ten-digit) levels.[7] However (as of 2008), the WTO does not provide full information to the public on the tariffs that its members actually apply. Exporters still cannot learn from the WTO even the basic, product-level MFN tariff bindings and thus the normal tariff that they should expect to pay when their goods arrive at the foreign border. As discussed in chapter 2, an average tariff at the six-digit HS level can mask substantial underlying variation (dispersion) in the tariffs actually imposed at a more disaggregated level, thus impeding access to the information exporters need to understand and plan for the foreign market conditions they confront. This issue is revisited later in the chapter.

A fundamental contribution that the WTO does make occurs through the reporting requirements with which WTO members must comply when they desire to change their policies in a way that affects the flow of international trade. While the WTO agreements contain a number of exceptions that permit members to impose higher trade barriers (above their official bound tariff rate) if certain conditions are satisfied, there are also reporting (and evidentiary) requirements. For example, the imposition of new import restrictions using antidumping and countervailing measures or safeguards requires that governments first undertake investigations and public notifications that the country is considering a change to its trade policy.[8] Under the WTO rules, set out in the Agreement on Antidumping, the Agreement on Subsidies and Countervailing Measures, and the Agreement on Safeguards, national governments must establish investigative procedures that require the provision of evidence on changing market conditions, such as injury to the domestic industry, as well as evidence of dumping,

7. See WTO, "Goods Schedules: Members' Commitments" (www.wto.org/english/tratop_e/schedules_e/goods_schedules_e.htm [February 8, 2009]).

8. A separate issue that I have already identified is that if the current applied tariff rate is significantly lower than the tariff binding, countries are free to raise the applied rate to a higher level that is still below the binding. A less frequently pursued option than antidumping and countervailing measures or safeguards is a procedure under Article XXVIII of the GATT that WTO members can follow to renegotiate tariff binding commitments as well. See again the discussion in chapter 1.

subsidies, or surges in imports that are alleged to be the cause of the injury. The agreements effectively mandate notification to either foreign exporting firms (antidumping or countervailing measures) or their governments (safeguards) that investigations are taking place and, ultimately, that new measures are being imposed.[9] Provided the investigating country follows the basic process required under WTO rules, the result generates substantial information for exporting interests about policy changes that may cause a change in their access to foreign markets.[10] This is a critical piece of information that exporters need to decide whether the new measure is worthy of a challenge through WTO dispute settlement—an action that is sometimes necessary in the self-enforcing system.

Such institutionalized procedures provide a monitoring framework through which other stakeholders can assist exporting firms and their governments. Making the information public allows such stakeholders (instead of firms or governments) to gather and disseminate the necessary economic, legal, and political information on the cause of the lost foreign market access and the expected value to having it restored. While the WTO does not itself provide extensive data or surveillance in this area, its establishment of rules and procedures that act as a template for how changes in trade policy may occur across member countries and who is to be notified constitutes a major contribution, as described in the subsection below on the Global Antidumping Database. This template provides those who need to know (exporters) with a source for where to look (foreign announcements of use of antidumping and countervailing measures or safeguards) to identify some important potential causes of reduced foreign market access.

On the other hand, this transparency function works only to the extent that these institutionalized exemptions are the mechanisms through which WTO

9. Since exporters also need information on the changing foreign market conditions they face relative to exporters from other countries, it is also relevant that they keep informed about the changes that may occur through preferential trade policies. For example, if two foreign countries sign a preferential trade agreement, the WTO must be notified as well.

10. Theorists have proposed a separate benefit from these sorts of WTO-permitted exceptions: they facilitate the actual process of trade liberalization by providing "insurance," as described in Hoekman and Kostecki (2009, chapter 9). See also the formal theories of Bagwell and Staiger (1990) and Fischer and Prusa (2003). Finger and Nogués (2005) provide a collection of case studies on Latin American country experiences that is suggestive of such a role. Formal empirical research, such that done by Moore and Zanardi (2009) and Crowley (2009), use cross-country regression approaches and find mixed evidence for such effects. However, such studies note that researchers confront a potentially daunting endogeneity issue that common political and economic factors may determine both the level of initial liberalization and the country's subsequent resort to exceptions for new protection. Bown and Tovar (2008) apply an alternative empirical approach to the special case of India and find that many of the tariff cuts associated with its exogenously mandated and unilateral liberalization in the early 1990s were subsequently offset by its resort to policies such as antidumping measures and safeguards.

members actually impose their new trade-restricting measures.[11] If countries instead turn to alternative instruments to restrict trade, then the beneficial aspect of transparency that these rules have provided is lost. Thus, while any outside monitoring and information gathering can start with examination of these exemptions for the underlying cause of lost foreign market access, in many instances policymakers will have chosen to use other nontariff barriers to trade, which WTO reporting procedures will not help to identify.

Trade Policy Review Mechanism

In addition to creating a master template for how WTO members are to report basic trade policy changes, the WTO's second major contribution to transparency and information generation is through the Trade Policy Review Mechanism (TPRM). The TPRM was introduced into the GATT system as a provisional feature during the Uruguay Round of negotiations, and it became a permanent part of the WTO under Article III of the 1994 Marrakesh Agreement.[12]

The TPRM has the mandate to review the trade policies of all WTO members. However, the frequency with which WTO members are reviewed differs. The four members with the largest shares of world trade (as of 2008, this was the European Community [EC], United States, Japan, and China) are reviewed every two years, the next sixteen largest traders are reviewed once every four years, and all other members are reviewed once every six years. Least developed country members may be reviewed even less frequently. The TPRM performed more than 200 trade policy reviews (TPRs) between 1995 and 2008. The United States (9), EC (8), and Japan (8) led the way with the most reviews. Major emerging market economies like Brazil and India were each reviewed four times, and Thailand led all developing countries with five reviews during 1995–2008. Reviews of other developing countries that have been discussed throughout the book include Colombia (1996 and 2006), Chad (2007), and Bangladesh (2000 and 2006). While China is now reviewed once every two

11. Analysts have argued that both changes to the rules made under the Uruguay Round (Bown 2002b) as well as how strictly dispute settlement Panels and the Appellate Body interpret member use of such exemptions are likely to affect the extent to which members rely on such instruments to implement new protection. For example, strict rulings on member misuse of safeguards (Sykes 2003; Irwin 2003) may have contributed to the relative decline in the reliance on safeguards in favor of antidumping measures. Continued strict rulings striking down use of antidumping actions may push countries to implement new protection in even less transparent ways, making the cause of the lost foreign market access less observable to affected exporting firms. See the discussions in Tarullo (2003), Durling (2003), and Cunningham and Cribb (2003).

12. For a discussion of the TPRM process and for the published TPRs for WTO member countries since 1995, see WTO, "Trade Policy Reviews" (www.wto.org/english/tratop_e/tpr_e/tpr_e.htm [February 8, 2009]).

years because it has grown to be one of the four largest traders in the system (recently displacing Canada), it has received only two TPRs (2006 and 2008) since it acceded to the WTO only in late 2001.[13]

A group of WTO member countries that form the Trade Policy Review Body (TPRB) undertake the TPRs in conjunction with permanent staff in the Trade Policies Review Division of the WTO Secretariat. Secretariat staff conduct the formal and technical analysis, and the TPR process then consists of a statement by the government being reviewed and the report of the WTO Secretariat, which are all presented at a meeting of the TPRB. Minutes of the meeting are reported subsequently, as are questions posed by other WTO members and the responses of the country being reviewed.

The TPR exercise can play a number of useful roles.[14] The reports are typically quite descriptive, and they provide newcomers with a coherent introduction to the various domestic institutions and policies that affect the country's overall trade regime. The reviews also provide useful summary data on the pattern of protection and openness across sectors within the country. If the timing of the review happens to be right—that is, if the scheduled review happens to occur during an episode of policy volatility that may affect international trade—the TPR also has the potential to provide useful information to foreign exporting interests about the changing trading environment. Separate from the issue of monitoring, the interactive process of engaging with the WTO in its conduct of a TPR can also provide a useful learning experience for developing countries with limited policymaking capacity, in principle helping the country to inventory its policies as well as to collect data.

The TPR of a foreign market is not designed to generate information that is sufficiently detailed and up to date to meet the needs of exporting firms engaged in the potential step 1 of the ELP of WTO self-enforcement. Because TPRs do not typically explain to an exporting firm (or someone seeking to assist that firm) why it has suffered a reduction in foreign market access that might be WTO inconsistent, they do not provide the smoking gun. At most, by revealing trends in some of the more aggregated data, the TPR might hint at potential areas of the member's trade policy regime that could be WTO inconsistent. An exporting firm or its information-gathering advocate would have to look deeper, examining more disaggregated and up-to-date data, to get a more accurate picture. Moreover, the TPRs are partially the result of a process that is influenced by political considerations, and thus they are written so as not to provoke

13. Hong Kong, China, was reviewed separately in 1998, 2002, and 2006; Macau, China, was reviewed separately in 2001 and 2007.

14. Some professional journals in international economics, including *The World Economy,* have commissioned academic economists to evaluate country TPRs. Prusa (2005), for example, provides a critical review of the 2004 TPR of the United States.

disputes or to provide evidence useful in litigation. Also, the reviews (especially of developing countries) are not frequent enough or detailed enough (in terms of disaggregated product coverage) to provide information needed for foreign firms and policymakers to make a rational economic, legal, and political assessment of whether any given WTO enforcement issue on behalf of an exporter has a high enough expected value (relative to self-enforcement costs) to be worth pursuing.

Before moving on, it is worth highlighting that since the TPRM does not play an effective step 1 role in generating information of use in the ELP, the TPRM system could be redesigned to expand upon the useful and positive role that it does play: capacity building in developing countries. In the case of TPRs of developing countries, the major positive effect of the process is on the country being reviewed. Many developing countries not only lack sufficient policymaking capacity to deal with WTO obligations, they also lack sufficient data and resources to perform self-assessments to help determine what is in their own economic interests. Only the United States, EC, Japan, and China are reviewed frequently enough to generate potentially useful time series data and information on changing market conditions that could be a starting point for foreign firms seeking information on those markets. Yet, for the United States and EC especially, the TPRs do not generate new information not already available from other public sources. To the extent that TPRs assist developing countries in taking inventory of their own policies and understanding their own WTO obligations and the economic implications of such obligations, the current system of conducting TPRs of developing countries at low frequency is the opposite of what is needed. Because the largest traders have an extensive network of private sector actors—think tanks, academics, NGOs, and the press—each with an incentive to collect, publish, and publicize data on these economies' trade policies and related activities, from a market failure perspective, these are the WTO members that are *least* in need of frequent (WTO) review. These economies also typically do not need assistance with capacity building that the TPR resources can provide to developing countries. If the primary benefit of the TPRM process is capacity building, basic data generation, and helping members create an inventory of their own policies, the WTO should reorient and focus the reviews on members with the least amount of outside information being generated.

Limits to the WTO's Illumination Role

While the WTO has done much to improve transparency and to create a better infrastructure for exporters and their advocates to use to identify and track some of the causes of lost market access, there is a limit to what the WTO offers. First, the WTO does not police, provide evidence, or highlight problematic actions that members have taken. Second, even though the WTO agreements do establish exemptions that allow members to raise trade barriers above tariff bindings temporarily—for example, through implementation of antidumping measures, countervailing duties, and safeguards—there are hundreds of instances in which members have restricted trade through other policies that may be WTO inconsistent. Thus, even if one were to rely on the WTO's lists of authorized exemptions, not all policy changes that affect international commercial trade and market access would be identified.

Therefore, while the WTO makes a fundamental contribution in the area of information generation and tracking WTO-inconsistent ways that members reduce foreign market access, the problem of inadequate surveillance remains. While perhaps the WTO itself could take on a heightened surveillance role, asking the WTO to do so might put into jeopardy some of the benefits it currently offers on other fronts. In particular, it might reduce the WTO's ability to provide a forum for trade liberalization negotiations and formal, neutral dispute resolution when conflicts arise and there is a need for members to self-enforce. Moreover, asking the WTO to take on a more aggressive surveillance role might upset the existing political balance between these three roles and introduce other unintended problems. This is much the same conclusion that arose from the analysis of the ACWL. While that institution performs a particular mandated task effectively, asking it to move beyond its mandate could reduce its ability to fulfill its current role.

Nevertheless, there is still much work on information generation and surveillance that needs to be done. Because the WTO is politically limited in what it can accomplish, there remains a role for the public sector in addressing the informational market failure. Indeed, as documented in chapter 5, a number of developed countries (for example, the United States, EC, Japan) have attempted to address this particular market failure confronting their exporters by generating national databases of foreign market access violations.[15] While the effectiveness of any particular national approach may be questionable, that policymakers have allocated resources for this purpose implies that even some of the most sophisticated users of the WTO system recognize the existence of an informational hurdle to using the self-enforcement system.

How might the public sector build on the WTO framework to provide more information to support self-enforcement efforts, especially on behalf of developing countries whose exporters and policymakers may not have the

15. In the United States, this database is the responsibility of the International Trade Administration under the Department of Commerce, in particular, the staff dedicated to Market Access and Compliance in the Trade and Compliance Center. In the EC this information is contained in the Market Access Database maintained by the Directorate General for Trade, and a similar database is maintained in Japan by the Ministry of Economy, Trade, and Industry.

resources necessary to do it themselves? The next section identifies examples of NGOs and the stakeholder community providing information for use in step 1 of the ELP. But such efforts by themselves are also insufficient to address the market failure. Thus, in the third section, I propose a major new institutional initiative to combat the problem.

Public Interest Monitoring—Building on the Work of Others

Some extra-WTO monitoring of and information generation about changing market access conditions around the world is already being done that might be of use to developing country firms seeking to self-enforce their foreign market access. This section describes two examples.

The intent is to take stock of what publicly available extra-WTO information exists. Doing so enables one to identify key gaps and hurdles that remain. This discussion also points out that while extra-WTO sources are currently providing some useful and additionally detailed information, the information is not yet being packaged in a way that is useful for exporting firms or their advocates in potential self-enforcement actions. Of course, this is because such initiatives were not intended to generate information for use by exporting firms in the ELP. Information already being generated could be adapted to make it useful for such purposes. However, any development-focused NGOs that hope to use such information to enable exporting interests in developing countries to engage in WTO self-enforcement will require personnel that have technical sophistication. They will need the capacity to turn economic, legal, and political information about actual WTO commitments into estimates—comprehensible to policymakers—on the likely economic benefits to firms and countries of pursuing such actions.

The Global Subsidies Initiative

One important example of a technically adept NGO taking an important step in the direction of information generation is the Global Subsidies Initiative (GSI).[16] The GSI attempts to bring increased transparency to WTO members' use of trade-distorting subsidies. As noted in earlier discussions, one country's subsidy to its own firms has an indirect impact on competing (nonsubsidized) firms that export to this or other markets. Nonsubsidized exporters lose foreign market access when consumers switch to buying the subsidized product for reasons that are difficult for the firms to observe. GSI provision of additional

---

16. See Global Subsidies Initiative (2007) and also www.globalsubsidies.org. Other NGOs that do related work on subsidies (described in chapter 7 and discussed below) include the Environmental Working Group and Farmsubsidy.org.

information concerning subsidy policies that may not be consistent with WTO member commitments is a well-targeted use of resources and generation of a public good.

While the WTO agreements do require members to self-report such subsidies (as part of the WTO's own transparency function), member compliance has often been both incomplete (insufficient notification of all subsidies) as well as delayed (not timely).[17] The GSI takes two steps to improve the situation. Its first contribution is to organize the subsidies that members self-report to the WTO into a more easily searchable Internet database and format accessible to the public. As a second step, the GSI has proposed a new format for WTO members to use in reporting their use of subsidies—including self-reporting of "no subsidies"—so that other WTO members are able to differentiate between when a trading partner claims to have imposed no subsidies versus when it simply fails to report the subsidies in a timely manner.

The GSI points out that a problem will persist even with the recommended change to the process by which countries self-report their subsidies to the WTO. A system of self-reporting creates an incentive for governments to underreport the number and amount of subsidies that they grant. To assess how large a problem underreporting is, the GSI commissioned a case study that compared Germany's subsidies as self-reported to the WTO with its actual use of subsidy programs in 2006 as reported in government publications of its national and state budgets.[18] Whereas Germany notified the WTO of 11 subsidies with a total value of €1.25 billion, the study identified 180 different programs of specific subsidies with a total value of €10.8 billion that should have been reported. As the GSI's study of Germany reveals, reliance on self-reporting is insufficient. More NGO resources are needed not only to replicate the GSI German study with regard to other counties but also to extend and deepen the level of detail. To provide full transparency, the studies would need to be performed comprehensively and routinely—year by year, country by country, and sector by sector—for all of the WTO's members.

From the perspective of the information needed by exporting firms to engage in self-enforcement, such efforts would be more useful if the GSI also extended the coverage of its database to include the underlying data on the specific subsidy programs that have gone unreported in addition to the subsidies that governments self-report to the WTO. Of course, unreported subsidies are more likely to be WTO illegal, and these offer the greatest (legal) scope for a self-enforcement action. While the ultimate decision of an exporter whether to

17. Article 25 of the WTO Agreement on Subsidies and Countervailing Measures requires WTO members to report use of such subsidies.

18. The GSI-commissioned case study of Germany is Thöne and Dobroschke (2008).

pursue a WTO dispute over a WTO-illegal subsidy requires additional information on the expected economic payoff from doing so, a necessary condition is that the firm has information on potential WTO violations affecting its foreign market access. For example, the GSI could create a companion database of unreported subsidies. A first step would be to fill in the unreported subsidy data unearthed in the German study and then extend the database to include data on specific subsidies generated from analogous studies of other WTO members. Furthermore, to the extent that much of the necessary data has already been generated for sectors like agriculture by NGOs such as the Environmental Working Group in its Farm Subsidies Database (U.S. agricultural subsidies) and Farmsubsidy.org (EC agricultural subsidies), efficiency could be improved if these NGOs work in concert and share data collection costs with the GSI.[19]

To reiterate, exporting firms from developing countries may need outside sources to provide them with information on the cause of their lost foreign market when such a cause is something difficult and costly for them to observe. A foreign subsidy is a critical example. The activities of the GSI are some of the most promising efforts that the extra-WTO community is undertaking to provide information that, if appropriately modified, adapted, and used, can help exporting firms in developing countries overcome the step 1 hurdle to applying the ELP to enforce their foreign market access.

But it is also important to recognize that the GSI is only a partial solution to the underlying problem. The GSI's greatest contribution may be providing accessible, accurate, detailed data and thus usable information on potentially WTO-inconsistent subsidies. As chapter 5 demonstrated, information on a possible legal violation is necessary but insufficient. Michele Brown and her firm still require complementary political and economic information to incorporate these data into a framework that allows them to make a rational choice about whether there is a sufficient expected payoff to justify using the WTO to self-enforce foreign market access. What is the size of the foreign market access (economic payoff) at stake? What is the (political) likelihood of foreign compliance in this instance? While the GSI may contribute technically necessary information, these data are only one input that technically sophisticated users of the WTO's self-enforcement process need to combine with other data to make a rational self-interested decision.

The Global Antidumping Database

The Global Antidumping Database is a second example of a transparency initiative that may also provide information useful to exporting firms in developing

---

19. See the subsection in chapter 7 on "Educating the Public on the Domestic Consequences of WTO-Inconsistent Policies."

countries seeking to self-enforce foreign market access rights. Like the GSI, it was not established with the intent of generating information for use in specific WTO enforcement actions.[20] However, the information that it provides could be readily transformed for use in this way.[21]

The WTO does play a transparency role in providing information on the membership's use of antidumping policies. As with subsidies, members are required to self-report to the WTO their own initiation of new antidumping investigations and new measures imposed. And as with subsidies, self-reporting of antidumping measures generates some problems. First, the reports arrive with a substantial time lag as members are asked to report their new antidumping activity to the WTO only once every six months. Second, the information provided to the WTO, which it subsequently makes public, is sparse. As of 2008 the WTO notifications typically list only the dates of investigations, the countries involved, and the names of the products being investigated, as well as the general outcome of the investigation in terms of the range of the size of new duties (or price undertakings) imposed.

The limited information on antidumping measures reported by the WTO is not useful for overcoming the step 1 hurdle of the ELP. Assume that an exporting firm in a developing country is hit with a new antidumping trade restriction, one that eliminates its access to a foreign market but is also WTO illegal. Then consider the role of a development-focused NGO or law practice that would like to assist this firm in fighting the imposition of this new antidumping trade restriction with a WTO self-enforcement action. One of the first things such a group would like to do is to identify (contact) the negatively affected

20. The Global Antidumping Database and the publication of version 1.0 in 2005 were intended to provide a publicly accessible, detailed database for trade policy researchers, who previously had little access to information on antidumping measures used by any WTO members other than the United States or EC. The original funding of research assistants to collect and publicize the data came from Brandeis University, the World Bank, and the Global Trade and Financial Architecture project initiative sponsored by the U.K. Department for International Development. Without access to detailed data, researchers were unable to assess the potential costs and benefits of WTO members' implementation of antidumping policies. The database has been updated and extended periodically, and underwent a major update to version 5.0 in 2009. But to make the database more useful in assisting the self-enforcement of trading partners' WTO commitments would entail continued and ongoing updates. This would require more resources than have historically been provided.

21. The Global Antidumping Database initiative is now broader than its name implies. It has evolved since 2005 to provide data on WTO members' use of countervailing measures and safeguard actions as well. Though the discussion below focuses on antidumping measures, the same basic arguments could be applied to the case of countervailing measures and safeguards. The only exception is that the antidumping and countervailing measure data in the Global Antidumping Database contain information at the firm level, since the measures imposed are firm specific. Since safeguard imposition is supposed to occur on an MFN basis, there is no firm-specific information related to safeguard measures in the database.

exporting firm. Interestingly enough, not only do the WTO-provided data contain no information on who the affected firms are, but there is virtually no way these groups could ever use the information provided to trace the identity of the negatively affected foreign firms.

However, such information is freely and publicly available in the Global Antidumping Database, which is generated from data provided by national government publications. Thus, unlike the GSI database, which currently reports only subsidy data that members self-report to the WTO, the Global Antidumping Database instead relies on original sources from national government publications. It is thus able to provide much more detailed data—details that members are not required to provide to the WTO (and thus that are not available for the WTO to report to the membership) but that such members nevertheless still make public voluntarily through other channels.

For example, most of the major countries that use antidumping measures do report to their public, via the Internet, relatively current information on how they are using them—information that foreign exporting firms (as well as private law firms or NGOs that might seek to assist them) need to use in a process of self-enforcement or restoration of lost market access. This information includes the names of the firms being investigated, the firm-specific measures that are imposed, and the HS product codes subject to the investigation and new measures.[22]

Consider how this information might be used from the perspective of an outside analyst at a development-focused NGO or pro bono private law firm. Such groups would like to assist Michele Brown at her small exporting firm in a developing country that has been subject to foreign antidumping actions. In this instance, while Michele can observe the cause of lost foreign market access because it is due to antidumping policies, she may benefit from outside assistance in information generation if she has no prior ELP experience. Her lack of prior ELP experience also indicates she is likely unaware of the existence of an outside analyst who may be equipped to help. Thus the outside analyst needs to contact Michele with the useful economic, legal, and political information on expected costs and benefits to using WTO dispute settlement that Michele

22. As a simple data collection matter, it currently appears relatively easier for the extra-WTO community to collect data at the country level on use of antidumping measures (via the Global Antidumping Database) than on use of subsidies (via the GSI). The major users of antidumping measures, for example, publicize their application of antidumping laws in national government documents, whereas tracking down subsidy data from national (and more local) government sources is relatively more difficult. This does raise an interesting question about why governments report use of these two policies to their domestic constituencies quite differently. While this question is not explored here, one likely contributing factor is that making subsidy information public could possibility elicit foreign countervailing measures (antisubsidy actions) against a country's own exporters that are receiving the subsidies.

requires to make a rational decision on behalf of her firm regarding whether to initiate the process and fight back.

To the outside analyst, the HS codes are particularly critical because much other information minimally required to understand the economic, legal, and political implications of the trade restriction can be derived from them—in particular, the actual trade flows associated with the HS product subject to the antidumping action.[23] Before attempting to contact Michele, the outside analyst's likely first step is to ascertain whether there is basic economic evidence that the antidumping action was warranted. Was there a potential WTO violation in the form of insufficient economic evidence of changing market conditions necessary to justify an antidumping measure? A first pass at the data collected from the period before the initiation of the antidumping investigation may reveal whether changes to the volume of trade and the prices of products subject to the investigation were in directions (trade volumes increasing, prices falling) typically consistent with evidence of injury caused by dumped imports.[24] Perhaps most important is what such access to the HS codes and the ability to assess the underlying market conditions from trade data imply for information generation. An analyst with access to these data can make an initial assessment of the economic market and context without first having to incur the costs of tracking down Michele. This helps outside analysts, even those at potential development-focused NGOs who themselves will still have to prioritize because of resource

23. As of 2008 the WTO reported only the name of the product subject to the antidumping investigation or measure and not the HS codes—for example, "carbon steel plate." This information is limited as there may be dozens of HS codes in a country's tariff schedule with products related to carbon steel plate, but some of these products involve only goods subject to the antidumping action, others only goods unaffected by the antidumping action, and some involve both types of goods. For an outside analyst to provide an accurate political and economic assessment of whether the policy is grounds for a potentially important self-enforcement action (as well as being able to identify the firms whose trade is at stake in the case), technical information on the HS codes is critical. As of the end of 2008, there was a new WTO initiative to also require members to self-report (to the WTO) the six-digit HS codes of the products under investigation (WTO 2008d). While this is certainly an improvement, even the six digit HS code is insufficiently disaggregated, however, since many countries impose measures at the eight- or ten-digit HS level.

24. The availability of sufficiently up-to-date and disaggregated import data (on volumes and unit values) at the HS product level differs substantially across countries, which presents another problem. For import markets like the United States, however, this is not a problem since the ten-digit import data are freely and publicly available, with only a short lag, from sources such as the U.S. International Trade Commission's DataWeb at http://dataweb.usitc.gov. However, domestic injury assessment in antidumping investigations also requires industry-level data (for example, sales, capacity utilization, and employment), which are not available at nearly the same level of disaggregation or frequency, even for an economy like that of the United States. The underlying problem of sufficiently available data, especially with respect to economic activity in developing countries, is not limited to the issue of WTO self-enforcement, of course. It is a problem that affects the ability to undertake program evaluation and impact assessments in almost any area of economic development policy.

constraints across multiple potential disputes, by reducing the likelihood that they would pursue dead ends.

Second, the trade flow information is also critical to help an analyst (and subsequently the exporting firm) put an expected value on the size of foreign market access that has been lost because of an antidumping measure. In addition to the necessary information on legal violations, Michele and her firm need accurate information on the expected payoff to pursuing a self-enforcement action if the firm is ultimately going to convince other firms and government policymakers to engage in the formal ELP on their behalf at the WTO.

However, it is necessary to qualify the importance of externally generated information on the use of antidumping policies, countervailing measures, and safeguards. Earlier chapters have described antidumping actions and counter-vailing duties as the most highly observable (from the exporting firms' perspective) causes of lost market access, and thus the least in need of public assistance and funding for overall improvements in transparency. The main argument here is not that major new resources should be allocated to improving the information collected on these policies; rather, this section is intended to illustrate the level of detail required and why this is necessary. One reason why exporting firms, especially in developing countries, are readily using the WTO to self-enforce their lost foreign market access due to antidumping measures is that the identity of the HS products and the names of the firms adversely affected are easy to ascertain. Creating similarly useful databases to address loss of foreign market access due to subsidies or other similar measures requires replicating this level of detail by providing HS product codes and names of adversely affected firms. Providing such information is more difficult in the case of subsidies than for antidumping measures, but this level of detail may be needed to create incentives for the self-enforcement process.

It is also worth highlighting that while lost foreign market access due to antidumping and countervailing measures is a major (and increasingly important) reason for formal WTO self-enforcement actions under the DSU (see figures 4-6 and 4-7), there are still many instances in which these policies go completely unchallenged. Consider the implications of table 8-2.[25] While close to 100 WTO disputes between 1995 and 2008 were related to these policies, these disputes covered only 134 of the antidumping and countervailing measures imposed during this time period. To put this into perspective, the data indicate that the 1995–2008 period witnessed almost 2,788 investigations and 1,752 measures imposed against exporters from WTO member countries. Only 134 of these antidumping and countervailing measure actions against WTO exporting countries resulted in formal DSU challenges. Developed economies

25. The more detailed data provided at the WTO member level are presented in table 4-3.

Table 8-2. *WTO Member Antidumping and Countervailing Measures: Initiations, Impositions, and DSU Challenges, by Category of Targeted WTO Exporter, 1995–2008*[a]

Targeted WTO member	New AD initiations	New AD measures	Exporter uses DSU to challenge new AD	New CVM initiations	New CVMs	Exporter uses DSU to challenge new CVM
Developed economy exporters	1,175	722	72	72	39	15
Developing economy exporters	1,416	909	38	125	82	9
Total	2,591	1,631	110	197	121	24

Source: Data for antidumping (AD) and countervailing measures (CVMs) were compiled by the author from Bown (2009a); WTO (2009). See also table 4-3 in this book.

a. Since some countries using AD and CV measures target exporters from the EC collectively while others target exporters from EC member states in separate initiations, to make the EC data consistent, I characterize a user as having at most one AD or CV measure initiated against the EC for any given product-level investigation.

used the DSU to challenge less than 12 percent of the measures imposed against their exporters, and developing economies challenged less than 5 percent of the measures imposed. Thus many more self-enforcement actions may arise as providers of assistance to developing country exporters gain access to the more detailed data provided in sources like the Global Antidumping Database.[26]

Toward a New Institution: The Institute for Assessing WTO Commitments

The market failure that continues to impede exporting interests in developing countries is the lack of sufficiently frequent and detail-oriented surveillance and monitoring to provide them with up-to-date information on the causes of their lost foreign market access. As explained in the first section of this chapter, the WTO system creates an institutional framework and environment in which active monitoring is possible, but the WTO also has limitations and currently does not (and perhaps politically may not be best suited to) provide active monitoring and surveillance. The two examples of piecemeal initiatives described in the second section, the Global Subsidies Initiative and the Global Antidumping

26. The likelihood of additional future DSU activity related to antidumping policies, in particular, is further supported by other underlying trends in the data: developing countries are increasingly using the ELP to self-enforce foreign market access provided by other developing countries, and they are increasingly turning to the use of antidumping measures to restrict foreign market access.

Database, use the WTO framework to generate data and materials that partially address the informational market failure. But despite such efforts, a substantial gap remains. In this section, I propose creation of a new institution designed to actively monitor compliance in support of the exporting interests of firms and industries in developing countries in order to help them self-enforce their ability to export. I refer to it as the Institute for Assessing WTO Commitments (IAWC).

This new institution would actively monitor WTO compliance and provide information to assist developing countries overcome the hurdles of step 1 and step 2 of the extended litigation process of WTO self-enforcement (see figure 5-1). The focus will be on institutionalizing much of the prelitigation provision of economic, legal, and political support about potential cases, thus ensuring access of developing country stakeholders to sufficiently detailed, accurate, and complete information. The ultimate goal is to help remedy the market failure by generating information on potential cases to pursue that the private sector does not provide.[27] This would allow developing countries to learn to assess for themselves where the largest expected political and economic "bang for the buck" (improvements in foreign market access) would be when deciding which of many different potential disputes to pursue and which WTO commitments to enforce. This proposal also describes the factors and trade-offs that should influence the IAWC as it sets priorities and selects areas to monitor.

The remainder of this section details the IAWC's key characteristics and elements of institutional design. It examines the potential role of the IAWC in the dispute resolution process, its mandate and functionality, and the need for it to be financed and staffed in a way that maintains its independence, long-term sustainability, and a commitment to quality output and service consistent with its mandate.

The IAWC's Basic Mandate: Economic, Legal, and Political Information on Likely Violations

The fundamental purpose of the IAWC is to provide a continually updated database of current WTO violations, with special focus on violations of potential interest to exporters in developing countries. In the context of the firm-level

---

27. Given the positive social cost of the IAWC in the form of resources that cannot be used for other productive activities, it is clear that even the IAWC will not be able to provide information on all causes of lost foreign market access that are not generated by the private sector. To maximize social welfare, in theory the IAWC would generate new information up to the point at which the marginal social benefit of information provided is offset by its marginal social cost. While the status quo equilibrium of "no IAWC" has arguably resulted in too little information generation, the socially optimal outcome is nevertheless likely to be reached before all potential information has been generated and therefore before all potential step 1 hurdles have been overcome. Thus, even from this perspective, some potential but unlitigated disputes will never be initiated.

example first introduced in chapter 5, the IAWC database would be a resource that Michele Brown and her firm (as well as outside analysts who might assist them) could use to help identify and assess the potential importance of foreign market access violations. To assist Michele, the IAWC would provide not only information about the legal merits of such potential cases but also an accessible combined political and economic assessment of the estimated value (expected improvements in economic well-being) of pursuing each potential case.

The information provided by the IAWC needs to be freely and publicly available so that exporting firms and developing country policymakers can access it and then use it to contact their own legal representation if they decide to pursue any given case. Unlike the ACWL, the IAWC would not be limited to contacts with government representatives. The immediate goal is to improve policy transparency by making technically rigorous but easily accessible information available to exporters, developing country policymakers, NGOs, and other groups with an interest in using international trade as part of a growth strategy to promote economic development.

While the IAWC would create a user-friendly database of relevant information, other groups would use the database for actual WTO enforcement in support of developing country firms' export interests. [28] Such groups would include private law firms, legal assistance centers such as the ACWL, and potentially also NGOs that eventually develop the legal capacity to assist developing countries prosecute actual disputes. Because these groups have different priorities, capacities, cost structures, and potential sources of external funding, each will have a different cost for providing legal assistance to a developing country in any given case. This implies that each group would likely provide litigation services—that is, the step 4 part of the extended litigation process—for different categories of actual disputes on behalf of developing country exporters.[29]

28. The creation of a new institution is distinctly different from, say, an approach that would attempt to overcome the information generation problem by subsidizing activities of existing private institutions (for example, law firms) or the ACWL to encourage them to create such information "in house." Because private law firms have to worry about profitability, they would not have the same incentive to pass along all information that they generate to the public—even if it is information they might not choose to act upon immediately themselves. They may have an incentive to privately hold such information into the future because of its option value. Private law firms are also less likely to generate information on potential violations that would be too small for them to pursue as the step 4 lawyers—for example, potential violations over small values of lost foreign market access. Furthermore, as discussed in chapter 6, the alternative of funding the ACWL to generate this kind of information is not possible given its current mandate, which confines its activity to step 4 of the ELP.

29. As I discussed in chapter 7, it is likely that issue-based NGOs (and even private law firms working pro bono) would be most interested in assisting developing countries in precedent-setting cases and those likely to generate media headlines, thus providing these groups with externality (fundraising) benefits to providing this assistance.

The purpose and mandate of the IAWC is to reduce the informational costs associated with getting exporting firms and policymakers in developing countries (and those interested in assisting them) over the hurdles to triggering potential use of the ELP. Ultimately, it is the government's decision to go forward with any one actual dispute. The IAWC can play an important role in assisting government policymakers who face such choices by providing detailed information (based on economic, legal, and political expertise) about the expected costs and benefits of each case that they could pursue. By providing policymakers with more complete information on their options, the IAWC would improve their capacity for informed decisionmaking about which potential cases should be given priority.

The next question concerns how the IAWC's work will be structured and whether it will be demand driven or supply driven. Will it be responsive to the interests and requests of developing country exporters and interested stakeholders, or will it rely on its own expertise and be able to know where to seek out potentially valuable WTO violations?

The IAWC will have to strike a balance. On one hand, as I have argued throughout, exporting firms themselves are frequently unaware of the WTO-inconsistent causes of their lost foreign market access, especially when the cause is something not readily observable, such as a foreign subsidy or discriminatory regulatory measure. If the firms are unaware, a demand-driven approach in which the IAWC is passively responsive to exporter requests may result in either too little service or researchers running off on wild goose chases.[30] This would suggest that the IAWC take a more supply-driven approach in which it relies on its own expertise, looking for violations exporting firms themselves may not have observed or completely understood. The IAWC must be able to track detailed data on trade flows and be kept up to date on public reports of policy changes at the national level—leads for it to investigate. The IAWC would also draw on already existing publicly available information and data (for example, the GSI's WTO Notifications Database and the Global Antidumping Database) and incorporate that information into its database on potential WTO enforcement cases for countries to pursue.

On the other hand, the IAWC should not waste good leads and other information that exporting firms and others "on the ground" might be able to provide. Thus it should not foreclose contact with these groups but instead create a mechanism by which such groups can log complaints into a database and suggest areas for the IAWC to examine. This complaint database should itself be

---

30. Furthermore, a model that requires the IAWC to be purely responsive to stakeholders' interests could lead to it being inundated with requests from one exporting country, industry, or NGO. In this case it would have to establish a rationing rule to set priorities.

publicly available so that if resource constraints at the IAWC prevent a complete economic, legal, and political assessment of all leads, other groups could pick up the slack.

Finally, the IAWC itself must be fully transparent. Since much of the information it provides will be based on economic and political analysis that relies on economic models, assumptions, and assigned probabilities of future events (for example, the likelihood that a respondent complies after an adverse legal ruling), the information that the IAWC provides will consist of estimates. It must anticipate that these estimates will frequently be subject to outside criticism. To clarify the underlying sources of conflicting estimates, and to ensure that the independence and competence of the institution itself are not called into question, the IAWC's data, methods, and assumptions must be fully available to scrutiny from outsiders.

Funding, Governance, and Staffing

The IAWC must retain political independence to remain credible, and it must not be responsive to political pressure from funders. This presents a challenge since the purpose of the institution is to generate the kind of information that governments would find politically sensitive and potentially damaging. So that the IAWC can steer clear of allegations that it is being influenced by (national) political considerations, the best case scenario is that it is not reliant on government financing. As was pointed out with respect to the ACWL in chapter 6, government financing of the ACWL is a factor that constrains its mandate to work effectively only within step 4 of the extended litigation process. For the IAWC financial sustainability suggests funding through contributions from private foundations, as well as perhaps from larger-budget NGOs. Also, the IAWC should be established with a multiyear endowment from the outset so that it is not under continuous pressure to fundraise for survival in ways that may affect its ability to retain political independence and focus on its core mission.

The IAWC must also have a governance structure that ensures transparency and accountability. This has strong implications for the quality and conduct of its staff, its oversight board, and the information that it generates as output.

The IAWC would be staffed by economists, lawyers, and experts in political science. As the discussion in chapter 5 concludes, only such comprehensive expertise can supply the range of technical knowledge required to engage the ELP of WTO self-enforcement. One potential model for the institution to pursue would be an "open source" framework. Drawing on insights in the open source software and "wiki" movements, the goal would be to allow technically qualified economists, lawyers, and political scientists to join the IAWC as experts and make voluntary contributions of their expertise and analysis to the evolving database. The outcome would be an online community of professionals contributing to the identification and assessment (valuation) of potential WTO violations.[31] The infrastructure could largely be virtual, increasing the likelihood of long-term sustainability by reducing operating costs and allowing for more contributors and access to additional expertise than a physically constrained institution would permit.

While one goal is to create an environment in which many capable researchers contribute to construction of the global database on WTO violations, it is also necessary to enforce technical standards and codes of conduct in order to ensure the quality of IAWC output. For example, no paid contributors—either permanent staff or outside contributors—would be able to consult on or litigate actual WTO enforcement cases. The possible involvement of IAWC personnel in an ongoing case creates a misalignment of incentives, as individuals may attempt to conceal information on potential violations from the IAWC community for their own personal (client-building) use.[32]

In addition, the IAWC staff must maintain actual, verifiable expertise in these technical disciplines, given the goal of generating accurate information for developing countries to rely upon when they make policy choices. The mandate of the IAWC is to be an information clearinghouse that creates and maintains its reputation based on the quality, accuracy, and accessibility of the information it provides to the public. Thus it must maintain mandatory, professionally verified quality standards for its output, which may therefore imply some required format for peer review.

In determining which countries are covered or assessed for potential WTO violations, the IAWC must not discriminate among countries and thus must provide information concerning WTO violations that may be politically damaging on any WTO member. Following WTO practice, the IAWC must implement a basic MFN policy of nondiscrimination—that is, no country's WTO violations are off limits for identification and dissemination. To retain credibility as an institution, the IAWC must also forgo any formal role for advocacy in actual disputes that are initiated.

The IAWC's Emphasis: Underanalyzed Areas of Market Access

While there are political sensitivity and political independence arguments in favor of having the IAWC keep an MFN-type balance so that no country's

---

31. Such an approach might attract useful expertise from experienced academics at a more advanced stage of their career who seek to shift from pure research to more applied (policy-relevant) endeavors.

32. While lawyers typically have formal training in ethical conduct and are subject to an oversight board (bar) to enforce basic ethical standards, this is a potential concern for professional economists and political scientists, for whom there is no equivalent institution—except, perhaps, professional reputation.

WTO violations go unexamined and unquestioned, inevitably resource constraints will require the IAWC to set priorities. Given the market failure argument for this institution, the major task of the IAWC must be to focus on areas
of lost foreign market access that are underanalyzed by the private sector and
existing institutions. Its mandate is to provide information of importance to
exporters in developing countries, with an emphasis on the causes of lost foreign
market access that are not currently being brought to light. Therefore the main
question is, which foreign markets and what causes of lost foreign market access
are being underanalyzed?

To identify which causes of lost foreign market access have been underanalyzed, recall the factors that contribute to the informational market failure.
First, if the cause of the lost foreign market access is difficult to observe and diffuse in its impact—such as a subsidy or regulatory measure—affected exporters
are unlikely to identify the source of the cause. If many exporting countries are
affected, this will also raise the cost of organizing politically to address it. Second, the private sector (for example, law firms) may not have brought attention
to the WTO violation due to a lack of economic incentives, either because the
affected exporters are themselves small or because the policy-imposing country's
import market is small. Third, countries involved in the WTO violation might
lack an oversight community—think tanks, research institutes, academics, and
critical independent media—that would generate information that private law
firms might not.

These possible reasons why some causes are underanalyzed suggest that if the
IAWC is going to focus on lost foreign market access violations in developed
countries, it should generate information on what is *not* already being covered
by the private sector. It should focus its information-generating efforts on the
adverse impact of explicit and implicit subsidies, since these causes of lost foreign market access are particularly difficult for exporting firms to observe,
understand, and then convince their government officials that these cases are
worth pursuing through the WTO. In terms of specific examples, the recent
efforts of Brazil in the *EC–Export Subsidies on Sugar* and *US–Upland Cotton* disputes indicate potential momentum for generating information on WTO violations of agricultural subsidy commitments that reduce foreign market access to
the United States and EC. [33] Furthermore, the massive government expenditures many countries included in their 2008–09 stimulus packages in response
to the global economic crisis have likely resulted in some government subsidy
programs that are at least questionable in terms of WTO rules and may have
adverse effects on foreign market access. Similar emphasis might be placed on

---

33. As noted above, the IAWC could use data from sources such as the Global Subsidies Initiative, the Environmental Working Group, and Farmsubsidy.org.

trade barriers resulting from WTO-inconsistent sanitary or phytosanitary measures—such as bans on food or consumer products that are not based on scientific risk assessments.[34]

However, the IAWC efforts to identify violations must not overemphasize
analysis of economies that are transparent. Indeed, a significant share of WTO
enforcement actions already focuses on the U.S. and EC. While some of this
emphasis can be explained by the large United States and EC import markets,
much can also be explained by their systems of government, decisionmaking
processes, and imposed policies, which are among the most transparent in the
world. More emphasis and dirty work on market access violations needs to
occur in places where there is *less* transparency. For example, while the EC and
United States are large providers of agricultural subsidies, a review of table 2-3
illustrates that the same can be said for the economies of Japan and Korea; even
developing countries such as Turkey, Mexico, and China have higher shares of
agricultural support in terms of GDP than does the United States.

Therefore a second major area of emphasis for the IAWC should be lost foreign market access within *developing* countries because of the WTO-inconsistent
policies that they themselves impose. Most of these countries are small, so there
is little private sector oversight, and they usually also lack a public oversight
community to monitor their policies. And yet, as previous chapters have documented with evidence from trade flows (see, for example, table 2-2) and realized
WTO trade disputes (see table 4-2), import markets in developing countries are
important to exporters in other developing countries. Since no one else is generating much information of use to developing country exporters on lost foreign
market access in other developing country markets, there is substantial need for
the IAWC to take on this task.

Furthermore, as the concluding chapter describes in more detail, information generation in developing country markets is likely to have substantial positive externality benefits beyond the additional WTO self-enforcement actions
that result.

Conclusions

Without additional assistance at the very beginning of the ELP of WTO self-
enforcement—the generation of necessary economic, legal, and political

---

34. Because the Global Antidumping Database is a useful resource, creating additional information on the lost foreign market access stemming from antidumping and countervailing measures
or safeguards should not be a high priority for the IAWC. For reasons already discussed at length,
exporting firms subject to these trade restrictions are relatively more aware of the cause of their lost
market access than firms experiencing loss of access due to subsidies or other domestic types of regulatory measures.

information for steps 1 and 2—the full benefits of participating in international trade will continue to elude the grasp of developing countries. There are increasing efforts by the outside community to help firms in developing countries organize politically (step 3), to provide subsidized access to high-quality litigation support through the ACWL (step 4), and even to create strategies to overcome the challenges to self-enforcement associated with limited capacity to retaliate over trade in goods by instead resorting to TRIPS retaliation (step 5) or to NGO political mobilization of potential allies of losers in the respondent country (step 6). However, the effectiveness of each individual effort may be limited. Addressing the very first hurdle to initiating the self-enforcement process—improving access to all the information necessary to recognize and evaluate potential WTO violations and enforcement actions that exporting firms and their policymakers might pursue—would allow developing countries to benefit even more from these other interventions at steps 2–6 of the ELP.

This chapter has highlighted the information market failure and proposed creation of a new institution to remedy the problem—the Institute for Assessing WTO Commitments. Exporters in developing countries need more information, especially relating to causes of lost market access that such firms are least able to observe and understand. This includes information on the foreign use of subsidies but also on all WTO violations that impede the access of developing country exporters to other developing country markets.

Of course, the biggest benefit from additional monitoring and transparency may be a long-run reduction in the need for actual enforcement actions. This is Jagdish Bhagwati's famous "Dracula Effect"—merely "exposing evil to sunlight helps destroy it."[35] Increased availability of information about WTO violations will improve the likelihood that the violations will stop before countries have to resort to the ELP. Over time, enhancing developing countries' access to the ELP will further enhance the reputation of their ability to self enforce. This may also result in a feedback effect, encouraging government policymakers among all WTO members to refrain at the start from imposing policies that violate WTO rules.

---

35. See Bhagwati (1988, p. 85).

9

Conclusions

The consensus among many analysts of and participants in the current international trading system appears to be that there are two distinct World Trade Organizations—one for rich economies and one for poor economies. I have attempted to make sense of this distinction and to argue how developing countries might enjoy further benefits from the system by enhancing their ability to self-enforce their trading interests.

For the developed economies, there is increasing evidence that the WTO is a well-designed institution. The history of the General Agreement on Tariffs and Trade and the WTO has resulted in a system that has allowed developed economies to achieve reciprocal access to import markets through multilateral trade negotiations and to sustain this market access in the face of changing political and economic conditions that over time threaten to result in new protectionist initiatives. The WTO system has some imperfections even from the perspective of rich countries, including the failure to liberalize trade fully in certain sectors, to discipline use of trade-distorting subsidies, and to halt the proliferation of preferential trade agreements that undermine the WTO's nondiscrimination principle of most-favored-nation (MFN) treatment. However, for the most part the WTO institution functions well. Today, after more than six decades and eight rounds of multilateral GATT/WTO trade negotiations, the WTO manages to sustain open markets by administering an effective system of dispute resolution. Although the developed economies have sometimes needed to use the WTO to fight minitrade battles, and some of these have been high profile, the system ultimately contained these battles and prevented them from escalating into trade wars. The WTO's dispute resolution system, on balance, has given developed economies the ability to self-enforce their foreign market access interests effectively.

For the developing country members of the WTO, the system does not yet work nearly as well. First and with regard to their own ability to import, the system has failed miserably. The GATT/WTO has been ineffective in getting poor countries to liberalize their own markets, lower their applied tariffs, and legally bind those tariffs at sufficiently low and meaningful levels to permit their consumers and consuming industries access to a well-diversified basket of goods and services at lower prices. Second and with respect to developing country exports, the story becomes slightly better. Under the WTO, developing country exporters do receive MFN treatment and thus face relatively low tariff bindings on average, especially in the import markets of the rich countries. However, the trade barriers that do remain disproportionately affect some major developing country exports. Above-average tariffs in sectors such as agriculture and textiles and apparel are pervasive in the import markets of the developed and developing country members of the WTO. Insufficient discipline over the trade-distorting agricultural subsidies of developed economies is another problem facing some developing country exporters. So while there is much WTO-enforceable foreign market access already available to developing country exporters, there is much useful trade liberalization of particular benefit to developing country exporters left to be successfully negotiated—some to be undertaken by developed economy importers, but much more to be undertaken by developing country importers themselves.

However, turning *potentially* valuable foreign market access to developing country exporters into *actually* valuable foreign market access requires these developing countries to self-enforce their WTO rights. As the rich countries have shown with their own history of using the WTO, access to foreign markets is not guaranteed by negotiations alone. Sometimes access needs to be self-enforced through formal dispute settlement activity.

One basic problem confronting developing country exporters is their inability to sufficiently self-enforce the commitments to potentially valuable foreign market access they have already received under the WTO. The lack of self-enforcement of existing commitments implies that firms and industries in developing countries do not export sufficiently. If they do not export, then the claim that a rules-based WTO trading system will complement their growth and development strategies is an empty promise.

The data and research on developing country involvement in self-enforcement through WTO dispute settlement indicate that at least three factors inhibit their access to the system, including cost; capacity to retaliate to induce respondent compliance with WTO legal decisions; and concern over extra-WTO counter-retaliation by respondents, through the elimination of bilateral aid or preferential access to developed economy markets under programs such as the Generalized System of Preferences (GSP). The second and third problems are systemic, and addressing them would require major institutional reform. In the near term, such reforms are not likely to be feasible politically.[1] Thus I have not said much about ways to address either of these two issues here.

My approach is to tackle the first problem, the costs to developing countries of using the WTO to self-enforce their foreign market access, since this can be addressed in the near term without embarking on systemic reform.

The long and complex nature of the extended litigation process (ELP) of WTO dispute settlement imposes many costs that impede developing countries from sufficiently exercising their right to self-enforce. I describe the ELP from the perspective of an exporting firm in a developing country that must navigate hurdles associated with a six-step process to achieve its self-enforcement objective, which is the restoration of lost foreign market access due to a trading partner's WTO violation. The length and complexity of the ELP is due in part to economics, to law, and to politics. I identify the costs that confront the exporting firm at each of the six steps: using economic and legal expertise to generate information and identify possible violations of WTO commitments by trading partners; using economic and political expertise to estimate the expected value of the restoration of lost market access; developing networks to organize politically with other firms in the industry to access government policymakers; hiring lawyers and expertise to prosecute the case at the WTO; using economic and political expertise to identify and implement credible and useful retaliatory threats; and using the results of these last two steps, along with other political strategies, to induce compliance by the respondent country with WTO legal rulings through appropriate policy changes.

While the ELP can be complex and has costs at each of these six steps, innovative groups have evolved to provide assistance to developing countries to help them overcome these costs and thus increases their use of the WTO system. For example, development-focused nongovernment organizations (NGOs) such as Oxfam, the IDEAS Centre, and the International Centre for Trade and

1. The possibility of developing countries using cross-retaliation under the Trade-Related Aspects of Intellectual Property Rights (TRIPS) Agreement may provide a partial solution to their current inability to engage in sufficiently credible goods (that is, tariff) retaliation. The continuing process of multilateral trade liberalization and the phenomenon of preference erosion may also slowly reduce the capacity of some respondents to use the GSP channel to engage in meaningful extra-WTO counterretaliation threats outside of the system.

Sustainable Development (ICTSD) have shown how outside groups can improve the ability of exporting firms to network with their national policy-makers and convince them to engage the WTO process on the exporters' behalf. Some developed countries worked with developing countries to establish and fund the Advisory Centre on WTO Law (ACWL), a legal assistance center for poor countries that has emerged as a potential major contributor to the system. It provides subsidized access to the WTO legal expertise that is critical in the litigation phase of the ELP, expertise that would be prohibitively costly for policy-makers in most developing countries to obtain from private law firms. Furthermore, groups like Oxfam, for example, have even begun to play a potential assistance role on behalf of developing countries in the final step of the ELP, which is the politically difficult stage of getting respondent countries to comply with WTO rulings by implementing appropriate policy reforms. Oxfam's effort to engage the media in support of agricultural policy reform during the *US–Upland Cotton* dispute was a particularly creative attempt to overcome the problem that developing countries lack credible retaliation capacity.

Despite the efforts and even some successes of the outside community to assist developing countries and improve their access to the ELP, one problem remains that this existing community cannot address. This is the lack of information available to exporting firms in developing countries, as well as their policymakers and their potential advocates in the ELP, on the underlying cause of their lost foreign market access. The exporting firms require this information at the very first step of the self-enforcement process under the WTO system—without it, there is no ELP, there is no self-enforcement, and there is no increase in exports. It is interesting that the problem of the lack of information facing all exporters at this stage is so pervasive that even some developed economy governments recognize it and are creating domestic information-generating institutions to confront it.

Nothing comparable is being done for uninformed exporters in developing countries, and the current assistance providers cannot offer much help in this area. The most useful institution assisting developing countries during the ELP—the ACWL—cannot provide such information services because its mandate disallows it. And the development-focused NGOs do not currently have the technical (economic, legal, political) expertise, the funding, or the mission to provide it.

Thus, I propose the creation of a new institution—the Institute for Assessing WTO Commitments (IAWC)—that will have the mandate, resources, and capacity to provide this information-generation service to developing country exporting firms, their policymakers, and their potential advocates in the WTO system. I have not, however, described one last externality benefit that the introduction of the IAWC would bring to the WTO system.

A Final Positive Spillover from More Disputes Initiated against Developing Countries

There is one additional benefit from providing increased support to developing countries during the ELP, including the generation by the IAWC of information on conditions of foreign market access in developing countries: a greater incentive for other developing countries to take on increased commitments to engage in the international trading system.[2]

As chapter 2 described, a fundamental problem of the international trading system is that most developing countries have not yet taken on serious enough commitments to participate in the WTO. In particular (see table 2-1), some middle-income developing countries and most of the least developed countries have not taken on sufficient commitments to bind (agree to set a maximum limit on) their import tariffs; moreover, many of those that have bound tariffs have not reduced those tariff bindings to sufficiently low rates. Even for developing countries with relatively low applied import tariff rates, the remaining "tariff overhang" (the difference between the applied rate and the bound rate) and thus the country's ability to raise the import tariff unilaterally without any WTO discipline or oversight creates substantial uncertainty for potential exporters in other countries about future market access. This uncertainty discourages foreign firms, including firms in other developing countries, from making the costly investments required to design and sell products in that export market.[3] This uncertainty, therefore, reduces the potential gains from trade.

Why have the political and economic forces of consuming industries within these developing economies (which would benefit from access to cheaper and better imported inputs, thus enhancing their own capacity to export) not mobilized to demand that their governments take on such commitments? The backbone of the WTO system is self-enforcement. The lack of external ex post enforcement of developing country commitments thus results in an ex ante failure to mobilize support for liberalization of import-restricting trade barriers in developing countries. Recall from table 4-1 that there have been virtually no WTO self-enforcement trade dispute actions filed against least developed country respondents. There are many economic, legal, and political explanations for this: for example, their markets are small, they have taken on fewer WTO legal commitments, no WTO member wants to be seen as picking on a poverty-stricken country. However, without a trading partner willing to file a formal

---

2. This section draws heavily on many of the arguments first made in Bown and Hoekman (2008).

3. See the discussion of the recent economic scholarship examining the fixed costs to exporting in chapter 5 (specifically the section titled "Firms Involved in International Trade and WTO Disputes and the Fixed Costs of Exporting").

trade dispute to self-enforce its own interests in the poor country's WTO commitment, there is no effective value to the poor country making a commitment in a self-enforcing system.[4] Because the commitment itself would be meaningless, there is no domestic incentive to spend political capital to push for the country to take on the commitment in the first place.

As I have detailed throughout, the historical and recent record of the GATT/WTO system offers many examples of how reciprocity can mobilize export interests. This occurs both in the initial opening of a country's own import market made as a reciprocal exchange during trade liberalization negotiations and in keeping that import market open by responding to a partner's retaliation threats of a reciprocal closure of market access if the country does not comply with its WTO commitments after DSU actions.

Consider a least developed economy such as Bangladesh or Chad, with the extremely high levels of tariff protection described in table 2-1. Assume that an industry in such an economy would have the potential to compete profitably in export markets if firms could access cheaper intermediate inputs by importing them. The industry thus needs to convince its government to take on WTO commitments to lower the tariffs on intermediate inputs. Under the normal reciprocity-based framework of the GATT/WTO system, the potential exporting industry in Bangladesh or Chad would lobby its government to lower the tariffs on those intermediate inputs and subsequently be able to expand its export capacity. However, the industry would need to spend political capital to counter the political pressure that the government faces from the domestic producers of intermediate inputs who would lose from increased import competition.

Why is the lobbying activity of export industries within these countries insufficient to achieve improved access to imported inputs? A partial explanation is

---

4. The more formal theoretical argument could be stated as follows. Consider a basic two stage, full-information game between a government and its domestic industry concerning lobbying over formation of trade policy. Suppose the government announces its future trade policy in the first stage (free trade or a tariff, for example), and then in the second stage, industries have the ability to lobby to influence the actual policy imposed. The problem is that the government implementing free trade in the second stage frequently does not result in a subgame perfect equilibrium. Even if the government announced a free trade policy in the first stage, it would face political pressure to renege on it in the second stage because of the lobbying of domestic industries that produce goods facing the new import competition. Without a counterweight to balance the concerns of adversely affected domestic industries, the subgame perfect outcome is for the government to give in to this pressure and raise the tariff. Thus, while the government can announce that it will impose lower tariffs, it can only commit credibly to such a policy if it faces a sufficiently high cost to reneging. The failure of foreign trading partners to self-enforce such commitments through formal dispute settlement reduces one potentially important cost to the government of reneging and thus increases the likelihood that the government will renege. As the process of the game is fully known to all of the players, no one emerges in the first stage to lobby the government for a trade liberalization announcement because everyone knows the government will not live up to it in the second stage. For related theoretical approaches, see Staiger and Tabellini (1987); Maggi and Rodríguez-Clare (1998, 2007).

the lack of external enforcement that is the subject of this book. Because the potential export industry knows ex ante that its own government will not be able to live up to its commitment to keep that import tariff low ex post, it does not invest in lobbying for a tariff reduction in the first place. For some of the poorest members of the WTO, such as Bangladesh and Chad, that potential foreign exporters are hesitant to use WTO dispute settlement to self-enforce their access to the markets of Chad and Bangladesh reduces Bangladesh's and Chad's own willingness to take on commitments, which is generated by the self-interest of domestic political and economic actors.

How do decisionmakers in the potential export industry within Bangladesh and Chad know that there will be no ex post external self-enforcement? They simply recognize the hurdles that limit the ability of foreign firms to self-enforce, which have been the focus of chapters 5 through 8 of this book. They understand the incentives built into the extended litigation process of self-enforcement in the WTO system, and they recognize that the costs of the six-step ELP are too high for foreign providers of these intermediate inputs to overcome so that consuming firms in Bangladesh and Chad have access to imports they need to be internationally competitive. Why are the costs too high? First, because there is no oversight or independently generated information about changes happening in the import market in a country such as Bangladesh or Chad, it is extremely costly for any foreign firm to understand the cause of a potential loss of market access (step 1 and step 2). Second, the intermediate input providers may be firms from other developing countries that themselves face cost constraints in using the ELP. The intermediate input providers may have difficulty overcoming the cost of organizing (step 3) to engage their own government officials. While they now may be aware that the ACWL can subsidize the cost of their actual WTO litigation (step 4), they may not have resources to spend on triggering compliance in Bangladesh or Chad (step 5 and step 6) even if they were to win the legal arguments.

Thus a final benefit of increased assistance to developing country self-enforcement efforts by the IAWC (chapter 8), the ACWL (chapter 6), and NGOs (chapter 7) should be an increased willingness of other developing countries to take on more market opening commitments of their own. If the IAWC, the ACWL, and the development-focused NGOs can ensure that the intermediate input providers from other developing countries will be self-enforcing their access to the liberalized Bangladesh or Chad market, a potential export industry in Bangladesh and Chad will find it worthwhile to lobby for those commitments to be taken on in the first place.

It is noteworthy that this demand for commitments within Bangladesh or Chad would be driven by internal political and economic forces and self-interest, rather than by the demands of an external institution. This motivation should not be confused with more politically problematic historical examples of external mandates to reform trade regimes as part of International Monetary Fund or World Bank conditionality. Here, trade reform would be triggered by domestic self-interest.

Finally, it is important to anticipate one likely result of the combined efforts of the IAWC, the ACWL, and development-focused NGO assistance on behalf of developing countries in the ELP: more WTO disputes initiated *against* developing countries.[5] Although disputes that self-enforce the foreign market access of developing countries would likely be initiated by other exporters from other poor countries, a relative increase in disputes initiated against developing countries may catch some WTO observers off guard. However, such an increase would simply contribute to an already observed trend in the data (table 4-2): during the 2001–08 period, 40 percent (67 out of 169) of all WTO disputes targeted a policy in a developing country respondent, which was slightly up from 37 percent (90 out of 246) during the 1995–2000 period. Because the WTO operates in such a sensitive political environment, it is nonetheless important to anticipate such an increase and prepare for the resulting reaction from those who look at trade disputes only through the lens of law (that is, winners and losers of legal arguments) rather than consider the combination of economic, legal, and political implications. The result of many WTO disputes is typically an economic win-win—the complainant values the improved market access to its foreign exporters, and the respondent discovers efficiency gains from compliance in the domestic economy, albeit discounted by some domestic political costs of having to engage in reform.

More disputes against developing countries would, in fact, be a strong positive signal.[6] It would indicate that exporters elsewhere found developing country market access valuable enough that they were willing to spend some (albeit subsidized) resources to ensure its continuance. What is worrisome in the historical data is that there have been no disputes over foreign market access violations in the poorest economies—in the immediate term, more rather than fewer disputes against developing countries may be what is needed.

---

5. Any increase in the overall number of disputes would also impose substantial costs on the WTO. Bown (2010) suggests that the Secretariat is not currently capable of mounting the resources to handle this increased workload, especially given the increasingly technical and economically complex evidence being provided by the parties involved. The WTO needs to expand capacity, improve quality, and restructure staff to introduce more technical economic competence.

6. This assumes that nothing else is changing, that is, that the reason for more disputes initiated against developing countries is more information and not an increase in the developing country imposition of WTO-inconsistent policies.

Appendix

Table A-1. *WTO Disputes Referenced in the Text*

Full case title	Dispute number (complainant)	Short title[a]
Argentina–Definitive Anti-Dumping Duties on Poultry from Brazil	DS241 (Brazil)	*Argentina–Poultry Anti-Dumping Duties*
Argentina –Definitive Anti-Dumping Measures on Carton-Board Imports from Germany and Definitive Anti-Dumping Measures on Imports of Ceramic Tiles from Italy	DS189 (EC)	*Argentina–Ceramic Tiles*
Argentina–Safeguard Measures on Imports of Footwear (DS121, DS123) *Argentina–Measures Affecting Imports of Footwear (DS164)*	DS121 (EC) DS123 (Indonesia) DS164 (United States)	*Argentina–Footwear*
Australia–Certain Measures Affecting the Importation of Fresh Fruit and Vegetables	DS270 (Philippines)	*Australia–Fresh Fruit and Vegetables*
Australia–Certain Measures Affecting the Importation of Fresh Pineapple	DS271 (Philippines)	
Australia–Subsidies Provided to Producers and Exporters of Automotive Leather	DS126 (United States)	*Australia–Automotive Leather II*
Brazil–Anti-Dumping Measures on Imports of Certain Resins from Argentina	DS355 (Argentina)	*Brazil–Anti-Dumping Measures on Resins*
Brazil–Export Financing Programme for Aircraft	DS46 (Canada)	*Brazil–Aircraft*
Brazil–Measures Affecting Imports of Retreaded Tyres	DS332 (EC)	*Brazil–Retreaded Tyres*
Canada–Certain Measures Affecting the Automotive Industry	DS139 (Japan)	*Canada–Autos*
Canada–Export Credits and Loan Guarantees for Regional Aircraft	DS222 (Brazil)	*Canada–Aircraft Credits and Guarantees*
Canada–Measures Affecting the Importation of Milk and the Exportation of Dairy Products *Canada–Measures Affecting Dairy Exports*	DS103 (United States) DS113 (New Zealand)	
Canada–Measures Relating to Exports of Wheat and Treatment of Imported Grain	DS276 (United States)	*Canada–Wheat Exports and Grain Imports*
Chile–Taxes on Alcoholic Beverages	DS87 (EC), DS110 (EC)	*Chile–Alcoholic Beverages*

247

Full case title	Dispute number (complainant)	Short title[a]
China–Measures Affecting Financial Information Services and Foreign Financial Information Suppliers	DS372 (EC) DS373 (United States) DS378 (Canada)	
China–Measures Affecting Imports of Automobile Parts	DS339 (EC) DS340 (United States) DS342 (Canada)	China–Auto Parts
China–Measures Affecting the Protection and Enforcement of Intellectual Property Rights	DS362 (United States)	China–Intellectual Property Rights
China–Measures Affecting Trading Rights and Distribution Services for Certain Publications and Audiovisual Entertainment Products	DS363 (United States)	China–Audiovisual Services
China–Value-Added Tax on Integrated Circuits	DS309 (United States)	
Colombia–Customs Measures on Importation of Certain Goods from Panama	DS348 (Panama)	
Colombia–Indicative Prices and Restrictions on Ports of Entry	DS366 (Panama)	Colombia–Ports of Entry
Dominican Republic–Measures Affecting the Importation and Internal Sale of Cigarettes	DS302 (Honduras)	Dominican Republic–Import and Sale of Cigarettes
EC–Anti-Dumping Duties on Certain Flat Rolled Iron or Non-Alloy Steel Products from India	DS313 (India)	
EC–Anti-Dumping Duties on Imports of Cotton-Type Bed Linen from India	DS141 (India)	EC–Bed Linen
EC–Anti-Dumping Duties on Malleable Cast Iron Tube or Pipe Fittings from Brazil	DS219 (Brazil)	EC–Tube or Pipe Fittings
EC–Anti-Dumping Measure on Farmed Salmon from Norway	DS337 (Norway)	EC–Salmon (Norway)
EC–Conditions for the Granting of Tariff Preferences to Developing Countries	DS246 (India)	EC–Tariff Preferences
EC–Countervailing Measures on Dynamic Random Access Memory Chips from Korea	DS299 (Korea)	EC–Countervailing Measures on DRAM Chips

Full case title	Dispute number (complainant)	Short title[a]
EC–Customs Classification of Certain Computer Equipment United Kingdom–Customs Classification of Certain Computer Equipment Ireland–Customs Classification of Certain Computer Equipment	DS62 (United States) DS67 (United States) DS68 (United States)	EC–Computer Equipment
EC–Customs Classification of Frozen Boneless Chicken Cuts	DS269 (Brazil) DS286 (Thailand)	EC–Chicken Cuts
EC–Duties on Imports of Rice	DS17 (Thailand)	
EC–Export Subsidies on Sugar	DS265 (Australia) DS266 (Brazil) DS283 (Thailand)	EC–Export Subsidies on Sugar
EC–Measures Affecting the Approval and Marketing of Biotech Products	DS291 (United States) DS292 (Canada) DS293 (Argentina)	EC–Approval and Marketing of Biotech Products
EC–Measures Affecting the Exportation of Processed Cheese	DS104 (United States)	
EC–Measures Affecting Trade in Large Civil Aircraft EC and Certain Member States–Measures Affecting Trade in Large Civil Aircraft (Second Complaint)	DS316 (United States) DS347 (United States)	EC and Certain Member States–Large Civil Aircraft EC and Certain Member States–Large Civil Aircraft (2nd Complaint)
EC–Measures Concerning Meat and Meat Products (Hormones)	DS26 (United States) DS48 (Canada)	EC–Hormones
EC–Protection of Trademarks and Geographical Indications for Agricultural Products and Foodstuffs, Complaint by the US	DS174 (United States)	EC–Trademarks and Geographical Indications (United States)
EC–Regime for the Importation of Bananas	DS361 (Colombia)	
EC–Regime for the Importation of Bananas	DS364 (Panama)	
EC–Regime for the Importation, Sale and Distribution of Bananas	DS27 (Ecuador, Guatemala, Honduras, Mexico, United States) DS105 (Panama)	EC–Bananas III

Full case title	Dispute number (complainant)	Short title*
EC–Selected Customs Matters	DS315 (United States)	EC–Selected Customs Matters
EC–Trade Description of Sardines	DS231 (Peru)	EC–Sardines
Ecuador–Definitive Anti-Dumping Measure on Cement from Mexico	DS191 (Mexico)	
Egypt–Anti-Dumping Duties on Matches from Pakistan	DS327 (Pakistan)	Egypt–Matches
Egypt–Definitive Anti-Dumping Measures on Steel Rebar from Turkey	DS211 (Turkey)	Egypt–Steel Rebar
Guatemala–Anti-Dumping Investigation Regarding Portland Cement from Mexico	DS60 (Mexico)	Guatemala–Cement I
Guatemala–Definitive Anti-Dumping Measures on Grey Portland Cement from Mexico	DS156 (Mexico)	Guatemala–Cement II
Hungary–Export Subsidies in respect of Agricultural Products	DS35 (Argentina, Australia, Canada, New Zealand, Thailand, United States)	Hungary–Agricultural Products
India–Anti-Dumping Measure on Batteries from Bangladesh	DS306 (Bangladesh)	
India–Anti-Dumping Measures on Certain Products from the Separate Customs Territory of Taiwan, Penghu, Kinmen and Matsu	DS318 (Chinese Taipei)	
India–Measures Affecting Export of Certain Commodities	DS120 (EC)	
India–Measures Affecting the Automotive Sector India–Measures Affecting Trade and Investment in the Motor Vehicle Sector	DS146 (EC) DS175 (United States)	India–Autos
India–Patent Protection for Pharmaceutical and Agricultural Chemical Products	DS79 (EC)	India–Patents (EC)
India–Patent Protection for Pharmaceutical and Agricultural Chemical Products	DS50 (United States)	India–Patents (US)

Full case title	Dispute number (complainant)	Short title[a]
Indonesia–Certain Measures Affecting the Automobile Industry	DS54 (EC) DS55 (Japan) DS59 (United States)	*Indonesia–Autos*
Japan–Countervailing Duties on Dynamic Random Access Memories from Korea	DS336 (Korea)	*Japan–DRAMs (Korea)*
Japan–Measures Affecting Agricultural Products	DS76 (United States)	*Japan–Agricultural Products II*
Japan–Measures Affecting Consumer Photographic Film and Paper	DS44 (United States)	*Japan–Film*
Japan–Taxes on Alcoholic Beverages	DS8 (EC) DS10 (Canada) DS11 (United States)	*Japan–Alcoholic Beverages II*
Korea–Anti-Dumping Duties on Imports of Certain Paper from Indonesia	DS312 (Indonesia)	*Korea –Certain Paper*
Korea–Definitive Safeguard Measure on Imports of Certain Dairy Products	DS98 (EC)	*Korea–Dairy*
Korea–Measures Affecting Imports of Fresh, Chilled and Frozen Beef	DS161 (United States) DS169 (Australia)	*Korea–Various Measures on Beef*
Korea–Taxes on Alcoholic Beverages	DS75 (EC) DS84 (United States)	*Korea–Alcoholic Beverages*
Mexico–Anti-Dumping Duties on Steel Pipes and Tubes from Guatemala	DS331 (Guatemala)	*Mexico–Steel Pipes and Tubes*
Mexico–Anti-Dumping Investigation of High Fructose Corn Syrup (HFCS) from the US	DS132 (United States)	*Mexico–Corn Syrup*
Mexico–Certain Measures Preventing the Importation of Black Beans from Nicaragua	DS284 (Nicaragua)	
Mexico–Definitive Anti-Dumping Measures on Beef and Rice, Complaint with Respect to Rice	DS295 (United States)	*Mexico–Anti-Dumping Measures on Rice*
Mexico–Measures Affecting Telecommunications Services	DS204 (United States)	*Mexico–Telecoms*
Mexico–Provisional Anti-Dumping Measure on Electric Transformers	DS216 (Mexico)	

Full case title	Dispute number (complainant)	Short title[a]
Mexico–Tax Measures on Soft Drinks and Other Beverages	DS308 (United States)	Mexico–Taxes on Soft Drinks
Pakistan–Export Measures Affecting Hides and Skins	DS107 (EC)	
Peru–Provisional Anti-Dumping Duties on Vegetable Oils from Argentina	DS272 (Argentina)	
South Africa–Anti-Dumping Duties on Certain Pharmaceutical Products from India	DS168 (India)	
South Africa–Anti-Dumping Measures on Uncoated Woodfree Paper	DS374 (Indonesia)	
South Africa–Definitive Anti-Dumping Measures on Blanketing from Turkey	DS288 (Turkey)	
Thailand–Anti-Dumping Duties on Angles, Shapes and Sections of Iron or Non-Alloy Steel and H-Beams from Poland	DS122 (Poland)	Thailand–H-Beams
Trinidad and Tobago–Anti-Dumping Measures on Pasta from Costa Rica	DS185 (Costa Rica)	
Turkey–Certain Import Procedures for Fresh Fruit	DS237 (Ecuador)	Turkey–Fresh Fruit Import Procedures
Turkey–Restrictions on Imports of Textile and Clothing Products	DS34 (India)	Turkey–Textiles
Turkey–Restrictions on Imports of Textile and Clothing Products	DS47 (Thailand)	
US–Anti-Dumping Act of 1916	DS136 (EC)	US–1916 Act
US–Anti-Dumping and Countervailing Measures on Steel Plate from India	DS206 (India)	US–Steel Plate
US–Anti-Dumping Duty on Dynamic Random Access Memory Semiconductors (DRAMS) of One Megabit or Above from Korea	DS99 (Korea)	US–DRAMS
US–Anti-Dumping Measures on Cement from Mexico	DS281 (Mexico)	US–Anti-Dumping Measures on Cement
US–Anti-Dumping Measures on Polyethylene Retail Carrier Bags from Thailand	DS383 (Thailand)	

Full case title	Dispute number (complainant)	Short title[a]
US–Continued Dumping and Subsidy Offset Act of 2000	DS217 (Australia, Brazil, Chile, EC, India, Indonesia, Japan, Korea, Thailand) DS234 (Canada, Mexico)	US–Offset Act (Byrd Amendment)
US–Countervailing Duties on Certain Carbon Steel Products from Brazil	DS218 (Brazil)	
US–Countervailing Duty Investigation on Dynamic Random Access Memory Semiconductors (DRAMS) from Korea	DS296 (Korea)	US–Countervailing Duty Investigation on DRAMS
US–Definitive Anti-Dumping and Countervailing Duties on Certain Products from China	DS379 (China)	
US–Definitive Safeguard Measures on Imports of Certain Steel Products	DS248 (EC) DS249 (Japan) DS251 (Korea) DS252 (China) DS253 (Switzerland) DS254 (Norway) DS258 (New Zealand) DS259 (Brazil)	US–Steel Safeguards
US–Equalizing Excise Tax Imposed by Florida on Processed Orange and Grapefruit Products	DS250 (Brazil)	US–Florida Excise Tax
US–Final Countervailing Duty Determination with Respect to Certain Softwood Lumber from Canada	DS257 (Canada)	US–Softwood Lumber IV
US–Final Dumping Determination on Softwood Lumber from Canada	DS264 (Canada)	US–Softwood Lumber V
US–Import Prohibition of Certain Shrimp and Shrimp Products	DS58 (India, Malaysia, Pakistan, Thailand) DS61 (Philippines)	US–Shrimp
US–Laws, Regulations and Methodology for Calculating Dumping Margins ("Zeroing")	DS294 (EC)	US–Zeroing (EC)
US–Measures Affecting the Cross-Border Supply of Gambling and Betting Services	DS285 (Antigua and Barbuda)	US–Gambling

Full case title	Dispute number (complainant)	Short title[a]
US–Measures Affecting Trade in Large Civil Aircraft	DS317 (EC)	US–Large Civil Aircraft
US–Measures Affecting Trade in Large Civil Aircraft–Second Complaint	DS353 (EC)	US–Large Civil Aircraft (2nd Complaint)
US–Measures Relating to Shrimp from Thailand	DS343 (Thailand)	US–Shrimp (Thailand)
US–Measures Relating to Zeroing and Sunset Reviews	DS322 (Japan)	US–Zeroing (Japan)
US–Provisional Anti-Dumping Measures on Shrimp from Thailand	DS324 (Thailand)	
US–Rules of Origin for Textiles and Apparel Products	DS243 (India)	US–Textiles Rules of Origin
US–Subsidies and Other Domestic Support for Corn and Other Agricultural Products (DS357) US–Domestic Support and Export Credit Guarantees for Agricultural Products (DS365)	DS357 (Canada) DS365 (Brazil)	US–Agriculture Subsidies
US–Subsidies on Upland Cotton	DS267 (Brazil)	US–Upland Cotton
US–Sunset Reviews of Anti-Dumping Measures on Oil Country Tubular Goods from Argentina	DS268 (Argentina)	US–Oil Country Tubular Goods Sunset Reviews
US–Tax Treatment for "Foreign Sales Corporations"	DS108 (EC)	US–FSC
US–Transitional Safeguard Measure on Combed Cotton Yarn from Pakistan	DS192 (Pakistan)	US–Cotton Yarn

Source: Author's compilations from WTO (2009).

a. Disputes only receive a "short title" once they have resulted in a Panel being established, so any dispute that settles or terminates at an earlier stage of the DSU process does not have a short title associated with it.

Table A-2. *NGOs Submitting Position Papers to the WTO, 1999–2007*

ActionAid
Africa-Europe Faith and Justice Network (AEFJN)
All India Association of Industries (AIAI)
Alliance for Global Business (AGB)
American Chamber of Commerce to the European Union
American Electronics Association (AEA)
American Farm Bureau Federation
American Institute for International Steel, Inc.
American Lands Alliance
APRODEV
Asia-Pacific Research Network
Asociación Interamericana de la Propiedad Industrial (ASIPI)
Asociación Internacional Para la Protección de la Propiedad Industriale Intelectual (AIPPA)
Association Internationale pour la Protection de la Propriété Intellectuelle (AIPPI)
Association of European Consumers (AEC)
Australian APEC Study Centre
Bahá'í International Community
Bäuerliches Zentrum Schweiz
Brazilian Business Coalition (CEB)
Brazilian National Confederation of Industry (CNI)
British Chamber of Commerce in Belglum
Bundeskammer fur Arbeiter und Angestellte
Bundesverband der Deutschen Industrie e.V. (BDI)
Business and Industry Advisory Committee to the OECD (BIAC)
Canadian Agri-Food Trade Alliance
Canadian Egg, Dairy and Poultry Farmers
Canadian Federation of Agriculture
Caribbean Policy Development Centre
Caritas Internationalis
Carnegie Endowment for International Peace
Catholic Agency for Overseas Development (CAFOD)
Center for International Environmental Law (CIEL)
Center for Science in the Public Interest
Centre for Agriculture & Environment (CLM)
Centre for International Economics (CIE)
Centre for Science and Environment (CSE)
Centre of Concern
Chambre de Commerce et d'Industrie de Paris
Chinese National Federation of Industries
Christian Aid
Coalition of Service Industries (CSI)
Comité Européen de Liaison des Commerces Agro-Alimentaires (CELCAA)
Committee of Agricultural Organisations in the European Union (COPA)
Commonwealth Business Council
Communauté de Travail (Suisse)
Confédération des Industries Agro-alimentaires de l'UE (CIAA)
Confederation of Asia and Pacific Chambers of Commerce and Industries (CACCI)

Confederation of Asia-Pacific Chambers of Commerce and Industry
Confederation of British Industry
Confederation of Norwegian Business and Industry (NHO)
Confédération Pan-Africaine des Employeurs
Conference of European Churches
Consumer Project on Technology
Consumers' Association
Consumer's Choice Council
Consumers International
Consumers Union
Consumers Unity & Trust Society (CUTS)
Coopération Internationale pour le Développement et la Solidarité (CIDSE)
Coordination SUD
Cordell Hull Institute
Council of Canadians
Dairy Farmers of Canada
Danish 92 Group
Danish North/South Coalition
Dutch Interchurch Aid
EcoLomics International, Switzerland
Essential Action
Ethical Sugar
EU Oil and Proteinmeal Industry (FEDIOL)
Eurochambres
Eurocommerce
European Aluminium Association
European Apparel and Textile Organisation (EURATEX)
European Centre for Nature Conservation (ECNC)
European Chemical Industry Council (CEFIC)
European e-business Tax Group
European Environmental Advisory Councils
European Information, Communications and Consumer Electronics Technology Industry
    Association (EICTA)
European Services Forum (ESF)
European Services Network (ESN)
European Small Business Alliance (ESBA)
European Spirits Organization (CEPS)
European Trade Union Confederation
European Union of Alcohol Producers (UEPA)
Evian Group
Fair Trade Alliance
Fairtrade
Federación Interamericana de Empresas de Seguros
Federal Trust
Fédération des Exportateurs de Vins et Spiritueux de France (FEVS)
Fédération International des Conseils en Propriété Industrielle (FOCPI)
Fédération Internationale des Vins et Spiritueux (FIVS)
Federation of German Industries (BDI)

Food and Drink Federation (FDF)
Foreign Trade Alliance
Foreign Trade Association (FTA)
French International Solidarity and Environmental Protection Organizations
Friends of the Animals International
Gaddafi Foundation for Development (Libya)
General Committee for Agricultural Cooperation in the European Union (COGECA)
Global Information Infrastructure Commission (GIIC)
Global Traders Conference (GTC)
Grain and Feed Trade Association (GAFTA)
Greenpeace International
Group of Fifteen, Federation of Chambers of Commerce, Industry and Services
Health Action International
Health Gap Coalition
Hong Kong Coalition of Service Industries
Hong Kong People's Council for Sustainable Development
Icelandic Farmers Union
Institute for Agriculture and Trade Policy (IATP)
Institute for Globalization and Sustainable Development (GLOBUS)
Institute of Science in Society
International Agricultural and Food Sectors
International Centre for Human Rights and Democratic Development
International Centre for Trade and Sustainable Development (ICTSD)
International Chamber of Commerce (ICC)
International Coalition for Development Action (ICDA)
International Confederation of Free Trade Unions (ICFTU)
International Council of Chemical Associations (ICCA)
International Council of Securities Associations
International Federation for Alternative Trade (IFAT)
International Federation of Agricultural Producers (IFAP)
International Federation of Intellectual Property Attorneys (FICPI)
International Federation of Library Associations and Institutions (IFLA)
International Federation of Pharmaceutical Manufacturers Associations (IFPMA)
International Financial Services
International Food and Agricultural Trade Policy Council
International Gender and Trade Network (IGTN)
International Institute for Sustainable Development (IISD)
International Kolping Society (IKS)
International Management and Development Institute
International Organization of Employers (IOE)
International Policy Council on Agriculture, Food and Trade
International Protection
International Road Transport Union (IRU)
International Trademark Association (INTA)
International Union for Health Promotion and Education (IUHPE)
International Union of Pure and Applied Chemistry (IUPAC)
ITDG
Ja Zenchu

Japan Electronics and Information Technology Industries Association (JEITA)
Japan Services Network (JSN)
Keidanren (Japan Federation of Economic Organizations)
Korea Fisheries Association
Korea International Trade Association
Korean Advanced Farmers Federation
Liberalizing Agricultural Trade and Developing Countries
Lutheran World Federation
Marine & Fire Insurance Association of Japan
MARQUES (Association of European Trade Mark Owners)
Médecins Sans Frontières (MSF)
Mouvement des Entreprises de France (MEDEF)
National Agricultural Cooperatives
National Agriculture Cooperative Federation (NACF)
National Federation of Fisheries Cooperative Associations (JF Zengyoren)
National Foreign Trade Council (NFTC)
National Research Council of the National Academies
Non-Aligned Movement Business Council
Norges Bondelag
Northwest Ecosystem Alliance
Norwegian Farmers Union
Norwegian Small Farmers Association
OriGIn
Overseas Development Council (ODC)
Oxfam International
Pacific Basin Economic Council (PBEC)
Pacific Economic Cooperation Council (PECC)
Performing Arts Employers Associations League Europe (PEARLE)
Quaker United Nations Office
Research and the Information System for the Non-Aligned and Other Developing
     Countries (RIS)
Réseau des Organisations Paysannes et de Producteurs Agricoles
Réseau Foi et Justice Afrique-Europe (RFJAE)
Réseau pour l'Environnement et le Développement Durable en Afrique (REDDA)
Royal Institute of International Affairs
Save the Children Fund
Seattle Round Agricultural Committee (SRAC)
Solidarité
South Centre
Southeast Asian Council for Food Security and Fair Trade
Stichting Oecumenische Hulp (SOH)
Stichting Onderzoek Multinationale Ondernemingen (SOMO)
Svenskt Näringsliv (Confederation of Swedish Enterprise)
Swedish Federation of Trade
Swiss Farmers Union
Syndicat National des Fabricants de Sucre de France
Tambuyog Development Center
Third World Network

Traidcraft
Trans Atlantic Consumer Dialogue
Transatlantic Environmental Dialogue (TAED)
Transnational Institute (TNI)
UBUNTU—World Forum of Civil Society Networks
UK NGO Trade Network
Union maraîchère Suisse
Union of Industrial and Employers' Confederation of Europe (UNICE)
UNISFÉRA
Uniterre
War on Want
Wemos Foundation
WIDE (Network Women in Development Europe)
William Davidson Institute
Women's Caucus
Women's EDGE
Women's International League for Peace and Freedom
World Alliance of Reformed Churches
World Business Council for Sustainable Development (WBCSD)
World Confederation of Labour
World Council of Churches
World Development Movement (WDM)
World Economic Forum (WEF)
World Federation of the Animal Health Industry
World Federation of Trade Unions (WFTU)
World Information Technology Services Alliance (WITSA)
World Spirits Alliance
World Vision (WVI)
WWF International
Zentralverband Elektrotechnik–und Elektronikindustrie e.V. (ZVEI)

Source: Data compiled by the author from WTO's website "NGO Position Papers Received by the WTO Secretariat" (www.wto.org/english/forums_e/ngo_e/pospap_e.htm [January 2009]).

References

Abbott, Frederick M. 2010 (forthcoming). "Cross-Retaliation in TRIPS." In *The Law, Economics, and Politics of Retaliation in WTO Dispute Settlement,* edited by Chad P. Bown and Joost Pauwelyn, chapter 22. Cambridge University Press.

Advisory Centre on WTO Law (ACWL). 2007. "How to Use the Services of the ACWL: A Guide for Developing Countries and LDCs." Geneva (December) (www.acwl.ch/pdf/how_to.pdf).

———. 2008. "Assistance in WTO Dispute Settlement Proceedings since July 2001." Geneva (www.acwl.ch/e/dispute/wto_e.aspx [December 5, 2008]).

Alston, Julian M., Daniel A. Sumner, and Henrich Brunke. 2007. "Impacts of Reductions in US Cotton Subsidies on West African Cotton Producers." Washington: Oxfam America.

Appleton, Arthur. 2000. "*Amicus Curiae* Submissions in the *Carbon Steel* Case: Another Rabbit from the Appellate Body's Hat?" *Journal of International Economic Law* 3 (4): 691–99.

Aw, Bee Yan, Xiaomin Chen, and Mark J. Roberts. 2001. "Firm-Level Evidence on Productivity Differentials and Turnover in Taiwanese Manufacturing." *Journal of Development Economics* 66 (1): 51–86.

Baden, Sally. 2004. "White Gold Turns to Dust: Which Way Forward for Cotton in West Africa?" Briefing Paper 58. Washington: Oxfam International (March).

Bagwell, Kyle, and Robert W. Staiger. 1990. "A Theory of Managed Trade." *American Economic Review* 80 (4): 779–95.

———. 1999. "An Economic Theory of GATT." *American Economic Review* 89 (1): 215–48.

———. 2002. *The Economics of the World Trading System.* MIT Press.

———. 2006. "What Do Trade Negotiators Negotiate About? Empirical Evidence from the World Trade Organization." Working Paper 12727. Cambridge, Mass.: National Bureau of Economic Research (December).

Bagwell, Kyle, Petros C. Mavroidis, and Robert W. Staiger. 2006. "The Case for Tradable Remedies in WTO Dispute Settlement." In *Economic Development and Multilateral Trade Cooperation,* edited by Simon J. Evenett and Bernard M. Hoekman. Washington: Palgrave Macmillan and the World Bank.

———. 2007. "Auctioning Countermeasures in the WTO." *Journal of International Economics* 73 (2): 309–32.

Baldwin, Richard, and Simon J. Evenett, eds. 2009. *The Collapse of Global Trade, Murky Protectionism, and the Crisis: Recommendations for the G20.* London: VoxEU.org.

Barton, John H., Judith L. Goldstein, Timothy E. Josling, and Richard Steinberg. 2006. *The Evolution of the Trade Regime: Politics, Law, and Economics of the GATT and the WTO.* Princeton University Press.

Bayard, Thomas O., and Kimberly Ann Elliott. 1994. *Reciprocity and Retaliation in US Trade Policy.* Washington: Institute for International Economics.

Bernard, Andrew B., and J. Bradford Jensen. 1995. "Exporters, Jobs, and Wages in U.S. Manufacturing: 1976–87." *Brookings Papers on Economic Activity: Microeconomics*: 67–112.

———. 1999. "Exceptional Exporter Performance: Cause, Effect, or Both?" *Journal of International Economics* 47 (1): 1–25.

Bernard, Andrew, J. Bradford Jensen, Stephen Redding, and Peter Schott. 2007. "Firms in International Trade." *Journal of Economic Perspectives* 21 (3): 105–30.

Bernard, Andrew B., and Joachim Wagner. 2001. "Export Entry and Exit by German Firms." *Weltwirtschaftliches Archiv* 137 (1): 105–23.

Bhagwati, Jagdish. 1988. *Protectionism.* MIT Press.

———. 2004. *In Defense of Globalization.* Oxford University Press, a Council on Foreign Relations book.

Bhagwati, Jagdish, and Hugh T. Patrick, eds. 1990. *Aggressive Unilateralism: America's 301 Trade Policy and the World Trading System.* University of Michigan Press.

Bhagwati, Jagdish, and V. K. Ramaswami. 1963. "Domestic Distortions, Tariffs, and the Theory of Optimum Subsidy." *Journal of Political Economy* 71 (1): 44–50.

Blonigen, Bruce A., and Chad P. Bown. 2003. "Antidumping and Retaliation Threats." *Journal of International Economics* 60 (2): 249–73.

Borrell, Brent. 1994. "EU Bananarama III." Policy Research Working Paper 1386. Washington: World Bank (December).

Bouët, Antoine, and Valdete Berisha Krasniqi. 2006. "The 'Black Box' of Trade Modeling." Washington: International Food Policy Research Institute (June).

Bown, Chad P. 2002a. "The Economics of Trade Disputes, the GATT's Article XXIII and the WTO's Dispute Settlement Understanding." *Economics and Politics* 14 (3): 283–323.

———. 2002b. "Why Are Safeguards under the WTO So Unpopular?" *World Trade Review* 1 (1): 47–62.

———. 2004a. "Trade Disputes and the Implementation of Protection under the GATT: An Empirical Assessment." *Journal of International Economics* 62 (2): 263–94.

———. 2004b. "Trade Policy under the GATT/WTO: Empirical Evidence of the Equal Treatment Rule." *Canadian Journal of Economics* 37 (3): 678–720.

———. 2004c. "On the Economic Success of GATT/WTO Dispute Settlement." *Review of Economics and Statistics* 86 (3): 811–23.

———. 2004d. "Developing Countries as Plaintiffs and Defendants in GATT/WTO Trade Disputes." *World Economy* 27 (1): 59–80.

———. 2005a. "Trade Remedies and World Trade Organization Dispute Settlement: Why Are So Few Challenged?" *Journal of Legal Studies* 34 (2): 515–55.

———. 2005b. "Participation in WTO Dispute Settlement: Complainants, Interested Parties and Free Riders." *World Bank Economic Review* 19 (2): 287–310.

———. 2009a. "Global Antidumping Database." Brandeis University. Version 5.0, July (http://people.brandeis.edu/~cbown/global_ad/).

———. 2009b. "MFN and the Third-Party Economic Interests of Developing Countries in GATT/WTO Dispute Settlement." In *Developing Countries in the WTO Legal System*, edited by Chantal Thomas and Joel P. Trachtman. Oxford University Press.

———. 2010 (forthcoming). "The WTO Secretariat and the Role of Economics in Panels and Arbitrations." In *The Law, Economics and Politics of Retaliation in WTO Dispute Settlement*, edited by Chad P. Bown and Joost Pauwelyn, chapter 19. Cambridge University Press.

———. Forthcoming. "China's WTO Entry: Antidumping, Safeguards, and Dispute Settlement." In *China's Growing Role in World Trade*, edited by Robert Feenstra and Shang-Jin Wei. University of Chicago Press.

Bown, Chad P., and Meredith A. Crowley. 2009. "Self-Enforcing Trade Agreements: Evidence from Antidumping Policy and WTO Dispute Settlement." Brandeis University (January).

Bown, Chad P., and Bernard M. Hockman. 2005. "WTO Dispute Settlement and the Missing Developing Country Cases: Engaging the Private Sector." *Journal of International Economic Law* 8 (4): 861–90.

———. 2008. "Developing Countries and Enforcement of Trade Agreements: Why Dispute Settlement Is Not Enough." *Journal of World Trade* 42 (1): 177–203.

Bown, Chad P., and Rachel McCulloch. 2007a. "U.S. Trade Policy toward China: Discrimination and Its Implications." In *Challenges to the Global Trading System: Adjustment to Globalization in the Asia Pacific Region*, edited by Sumner La Croix and Peter A. Petri. Oxford, U.K.: Routledge.

———. 2007b. "Trade Adjustment in the WTO System: Are More Safeguards the Answer?" *Oxford Review of Economic Policy* 23 (3): 415–39.

Bown, Chad P., and Joost Pauwelyn, eds. 2010 (forthcoming). *The Law, Economics, and Politics of Retaliation in WTO Dispute Settlement*. Cambridge University Press.

Bown, Chad P., and Michele Ruta. 2010 (forthcoming). "The Economics of Permissible WTO Retaliation." In *The Law, Economics, and Politics of Retaliation in WTO Dispute Settlement*, edited by Chad P. Bown and Joost Pauwelyn, chapter 6. Cambridge University Press.

Bown, Chad P., and Patricia Tovar. 2008. "Trade Liberalization, Antidumping, and Safeguards: Evidence from India's Tariff Reform." Brandeis University (March).

Brander, James A., and Barbara J. Spencer. 1985. "Export Subsidies and International Market Share Rivalry." *Journal of International Economics* 18 (1–2): 83–100.

Broda, Christian, Nuno Limão, and David E. Weinstein. 2008. "Optimal Tariffs and Market Power: The Evidence." *American Economic Review* 98 (5): 2032–65.

Busch, Marc L. 2000. "Democracy, Consultation, and the Paneling of Disputes under GATT." *Journal of Conflict Resolution* 44 (4): 425–46.

Busch, Marc L., Rafal Raciborski, and Eric Reinhardt. 2008. "Does the Rule of Law Matter? The WTO and US Antidumping Investigations." Emory University (May).

Busch, Marc L., and Eric Reinhardt. 2001. "Bargaining in the Shadow of the Law: Early Settlement in GATT/WTO Disputes." *Fordham International Law Journal* 24 (1): 158–72.

———. 2002. "Testing International Trade Law: Empirical Studies of GATT/WTO Dispute Settlement." In *The Political Economy of International Trade Law: Essays in Honor of*

Robert E. Hudec, edited by Daniel L. M. Kennedy and James D. Southwick. Cambridge University Press.

———. 2003. "Developing Countries and GATT/WTO Dispute Settlement." *Journal of World Trade* 37 (4): 719–35.

———. 2006a. "Fixing What Ain't Broke? Third Party Rights, Consultations, and the DSU." In *WTO Dispute Settlement Reform,* edited by Kim Van der Borght and Dencho Georgiev. London: Cameron.

———. 2006b. "Three's a Crowd: Third Parties and WTO Dispute Settlement." *World Politics* 58 (3): 446–77.

———. 2009. "With a Little Help from Our Friends? Developing Country Complaints and Third Party Participation." In *Developing Countries in the WTO Legal System,* edited by Chantal Thomas and Joel P. Trachtman. Oxford University Press.

Busch, Marc L., Eric Reinhardt, and Gregory Shaffer. 2008. "Does Legal Capacity Matter? Explaining Patterns of Protectionism in the Shadow of WTO Litigation." University of Minnesota (August).

Bütler, Monika, and Heinz Hauser. 2000. "The WTO Dispute Settlement System: A First Assessment from an Economic Perspective." *Journal of Law, Economics, and Organization* 16 (2): 503–33.

Cadot, Olivier, and Douglas Webber. 2002. "Banana Splits: Policy Process, Particularistic Interests, Political Capture, and Money in Transatlantic Trade Politics." *Business and Politics* 4 (1): 5–39.

Centre for International Environmental Law (CIEL). 1999. "*Amicus* Brief to the Appellate Body on *United States–Import Prohibition of Certain Shrimp and Shrimp Products.*" Geneva.

———.2007. "*Amicus Curiae* Brief to the Appellate Body in *Brazil–Measures Affecting Imports of Retreaded Tyres.*" Geneva.

Cerra, Valerie, and Sweta C. Saxena. 2002. "What Caused the 1991 Currency Crisis in India?" *IMF Staff Papers* 49 (3): 395–425.

Charnovitz, Steve. 2000. "Opening the WTO to Non-Governmental Interests." *Fordham International Law Journal* 18 (2): 173–216.

Clerides, Sofronis, Saul Lach, and James Tybout. 1998. "Is Learning by Exporting Important? Micro Dynamic Evidence from Colombia, Mexico and Morocco." *Quarterly Journal of Economics* 113 (3): 903–47.

Collier, Paul. 2007. *The Bottom Billion: Why the Poorest Countries Are Failing and What Can Be Done about It.* Oxford University Press.

Conybeare, John A. C. 1985. "Trade Wars: A Comparative Study of Anglo-Hanse, Franco-Italian, and Hawley-Smoot Conflicts." *World Politics* 38 (1): 147–72.

———. 1987. *Trade Wars: The Theory and Practice of International Commercial Rivalry.* Columbia University Press.

Copeland, Brian R., and M. Scott Taylor. 2003. *Trade and the Environment: Theory and Evidence.* Princeton University Press.

Crowley, Meredith A. 2009. "Why Are Safeguards Needed in a Trade Agreement?" In *Law and Economics of Contingent Protection in International Trade,* edited by George A. Bermann, Petros C. Mavroidis, and Kyle W. Bagwell. Cambridge University Press.

Cunningham, Richard O., and Troy H. Cribb. 2003. "Dispute Settlement through the Lens of 'Free Flow of Trade': A Review of WTO Dispute Settlement of US Anti-Dumping and Countervailing Duty Measures." *Journal of International Economic Law* 6 (1): 155–70.

Dam, Kenneth W. 1970. *The GATT: Law and International Organization.* University of Chicago Press.

Davis, Christina L. 2003. *Food Fights over Free Trade: How International Institutions Promote Agricultural Trade Liberalization.* Princeton University Press.

———. 2009. "Why Adjudicate? Enforcing Trade Rules." Manuscript. Princeton University (February).

Davis, Christina L., and Sarah Blodgett Bermeo. Forthcoming. "Who Files? Developing Country Participation in WTO Adjudication." *Journal of Politics.*

Davis, Christina L., and Yuki Shirato. 2007. "Firms, Governments, and WTO Adjudication: Japan's Selection of WTO Disputes." *World Politics* 59 (2): 274–313.

De Loecker, Jan. 2007. "Do Exports Generate Higher Productivity? Evidence from Slovenia." *Journal of International Economics* 73 (1): 69–98.

Devereaux, Charan, Robert Z. Lawrence, and Michael D. Watkins. 2006a. "Banana Wars: Challenges to the European Union's Banana Regime." In *Case Studies in US Trade Negotiation: Resolving Disputes,* vol. 2, chapter 2. Washington: Institute for International Economics.

———. 2006b. "Brazil's WTO Cotton Case: Negotiation through Litigation." In *Case Studies in US Trade Negotiation: Resolving Disputes,* vol. 2, chapter 5. Washington: Institute for International Economics.

———. 2006c. "Standing Up for Steel." In *Case Studies in US Trade Negotiation: Resolving Disputes,* vol. 2, chapter 4. Washington: Institute for International Economics.

Dunoff, Jeffrey L. 1998. "The Misguided Debate over NGO Participation at the WTO." *Journal of International Economic Law* 1 (3): 433–56.

Durling, James P. 2003. "Deference, but Only When Due: WTO Review of Anti-Dumping Measures." *Journal of International Economic Law* 6 (1): 125–53.

Durling, James P., and David Hardin. 2005. "*Amicus Curiae* Participation in WTO Dispute Settlement: Reflections on the Past Decade." In *Key Issues in WTO Dispute Settlement: The First Ten Years,* edited by Rufus Yerxa and Bruce Wilson. Cambridge University Press.

Eaton, Jonathan, Samuel Kortum, and Francis Kramarz. 2006. "An Anatomy of International Trade: Evidence from French Firms." Working Paper. New York University, Department of Economics.

Elliott, Kimberly Ann, and Richard B. Freeman. 2003. *Can Labor Standards Improve under Globalization?* Washington: Institute for International Economics.

———. 2005. "White Hats or Don Quixotes? Human Rights Vigilantes in the Global Economy." In *Emerging Labor Market Institutions for the Twenty-First Century,* edited by Richard B. Freeman, Joni Hersch, and Lawrence Mishel. University of Chicago Press.

Environmental Working Group. 2007. "Farm Subsidy Database" (http://farm.ewg.org/ sites/farm/ [November 23]).

Estevadeordal, Antoni, Caroline Freund, and Emanuel Ornelas. 2008. "Does Regionalism Affect Trade Liberalization toward Non-Members?" *Quarterly Journal of Economics* 123 (4): 1531–575.

Esty, Daniel C. 1998. "Non-Governmental Organizations at the World Trade Organization: Cooperation, Competition, or Exclusion." *Journal of International Economic Law* 1 (1): 123–48.

Evenett, Simon. 2010 (forthcoming). "Sticking To the Rules: Quantifying the Market Access Protected by WTO Retaliation." In *The Law, Economics and Politics of Retaliation in WTO Dispute Settlement,* edited by Chad P. Bown and Joost Pauwelyn, chapter 7. Cambridge University Press.

Farmsubsidy.org. 2007. "Who Gets What from Common Agricultural Policy" (http://farm subsidy.org/ [November 23]).

Fatoumata, Jawara, and Aileen Kwa. 2004. *Behind the Scenes at the WTO: The Real World of International Trade Negotiations*. London: Zed Books.

Feinberg, Robert M., and Kara M. Reynolds. 2006. "The Spread of Antidumping Regimes and the Role of Retaliation in Filings." *Southern Economic Journal* 72 (4): 877–90.

Findlay, Ronald, and Kevin H. O'Rourke. 2007. *Power and Plenty: Trade, War, and the World Economy in the Second Millennium*. Princeton University Press.

Finger, J. Michael. 2002. "The Uruguay Round North-South Bargain: Will the WTO Get Over It? Comment." In *The Political Economy of International Trade Law: Essays in Honor of Robert E. Hudec*, edited by Daniel L. M. Kennedy and James D. Southwick. Cambridge University Press.

Finger, J. Michael, and Julio J. Nogués, eds. 2005. *Safeguards and Antidumping in Latin American Trade Liberalization: Fighting Fire with Fire*. Washington: World Bank.

Finger, J. Michael, and Alexander Yeats. 1976. "Effective Protection by Transportation Costs and Tariffs: A Comparison of Magnitudes." *Quarterly Journal of Economics* 90 (1): 169–76.

Fischer, Ronald D., and Thomas J. Prusa. 2003. "WTO Exceptions as Insurance." *Review of International Economics* 11 (5): 745–57.

Francois, Joseph, Henrik Horn, and Niklas Kaunitz. 2008. "Trading Profiles and Developing Country Participation in the WTO Dispute Settlement System." Working Paper 730. Stockholm: Research Institute of Industrial Economics (IFN).

Friedman, Thomas L. 2005. *The World Is Flat: A Brief History of the Twenty-First Century*. New York: Farrar, Strauss and Giroux.

Galanter, Marc, and Thomas Palay. 1995. "Public Service Implications of Evolving Law Firm Size and Structure." In *The Law Firm and the Public Good*, edited by Robert A. Katzman. Brookings.

General Agreement on Tariffs and Trade (GATT). 1993. "EEC–Member States' Import Regimes for Bananas: Report of the Panel." DS32/R. Geneva (June 3).

———. 1994. "EEC–Import Regime for Bananas: Report of the Panel." DS38/R. Geneva (February 11).

German Marshall Fund of the United States (GMFUS). 2005. *Perspectives on Trade and Poverty Reduction: A Survey of Public Opinion—Key Findings Report 2005*. Washington.

Global Subsidies Initiative. 2007. "WTO Notifications Database." (www.globalsubsidies.org/private/modules/knowledgebox/external/index.php?kb=wto [November 23]).

Goldstein, Judith L., Douglas Rivers, and Michael Tomz. 2007. "Institutions in International Relations: Understanding the Effects of the GATT and the WTO on World Trade." *International Organization* 61 (1): 37–67.

Guzman, Andrew, and Beth A. Simmons. 2002. "To Settle or Empanel? An Empirical Analysis of Litigation and Settlement at the World Trade Organization." *Journal of Legal Studies* XXXI: S205–S235.

Harrison, Ann, and Jason Scorse. 2006. "Improving the Conditions of Workers? Minimum Wage Legislation and Anti-Sweatshop Activism." *California Management Review* 48 (2): 144–60.

———. Forthcoming. "Multinationals and Anti-Sweatshop Activism." *American Economic Review*.

Heinisch, Elinor Lynn. 2006. "West Africa versus the United States on Cotton Subsidies: How, Why and What Next?" *Journal of Modern African Studies* 44 (2): 251–74.

Hoekman, Bernard M. 2005. "Operationalizing the Concept of Policy Space in the WTO: Beyond Special and Differential Treatment." *Journal of International Economic Law* 8 (2): 405–24.

———. 2007. "Doha, Development and Discrimination." *Pacific Economic Review* 12 (3): 267–92.

Hoekman, Bernard M., Henrik Horn, and Petros C. Mavroidis. 2009. "Winners and Losers in the Panel Stage of the WTO Dispute Settlement System." In *Developing Countries in the WTO Legal System,* edited by Chantal Thomas and Joel P. Trachtman. Oxford University Press.

Hoekman, Bernard M., and Robert Howse. 2008. "*EC–Sugar.*" *World Trade Review* 7 (1): 149–78.

Hoekman, Bernard M., and Michael M. Kostecki. 2009. *The Political Economy of the World Trading System: The WTO and Beyond.* 3rd ed. Oxford University Press.

Hoekman, Bernard M., and Petros C. Mavroidis. 2000. "WTO Dispute Settlement, Transparency and Surveillance." *World Economy* 23 (4): 527–42.

Hoekman, Bernard M., Francis Ng, and Marcelo Olarreaga. 2002. "Eliminating Excessive Tariffs on Exports of Least Developed Countries." *World Bank Economic Review* 16 (1): 1–21.

Holmes, Peter S., Jim Rollo, and Alasdair R. Young. 2003. "Emerging Trends in WTO Dispute Settlement: Back to the GATT?" Policy Research Working Paper 3133. Washington: World Bank (September).

Horn, Henrik. 2006. "National Treatment in the GATT." *American Economic Review* 96 (1): 394–404.

Horn, Henrik, Giovanni Maggi, and Robert W. Staiger. Forthcoming. "Trade Agreements as Endogenously Incomplete Contracts." *American Economic Review.*

Horn, Henrik, and Petros C. Mavroidis. 2001. "Economic and Legal Aspects of the Most-Favored-Nation Clause." *European Journal of Political Economy* 17 (2): 233–79.

———, eds. 2004. *The WTO Case Law of 2001.* Cambridge University Press.

———, eds. 2005. *The WTO Case Law of 2002.* Cambridge University Press.

———, eds. 2006. *The WTO Case Law of 2003.* Cambridge University Press.

———, eds. 2008a. *The WTO Case Law of 2004–5.* Cambridge University Press.

———. 2008b. "WTO Dispute Settlement Database." (http://go.worldbank.org/X5EZPHXJY0 [December 29]).

———, eds 2009a. *The WTO Case Law of 2006–7.* Cambridge University Press.

———. 2009b. "The WTO Dispute Settlement System 1995–2006: Some Descriptive Statistics." In *Trade Disputes and the Dispute Settlement Understanding of the WTO: An Interdisciplinary Assessment,* edited by James C. Hartigan. Bingley, U.K.: Emerald Group Publishing.

Horn, Henrik, Petros C. Mavroidis, and Håkan Nordström. 2005. "Is the Use of the WTO Dispute Settlement System Biased?" In *The WTO and International Trade Law/Dispute Settlement,* edited by Petros C. Mavroidis and Alan Sykes. Cheltenham, U.K.: Edward Elgar.

Hudec, Robert E. 1970. "The GATT Legal System: A Diplomat's Jurisprudence." *Journal of World Trade Law* 4: 615–65.

———. 1975. The *GATT Legal System and World Trade Diplomacy.* New York: Praeger.

———. 1987. *Developing Countries in the GATT Legal System.* Aldershot, U.K. and Brookfield, Vt.: Gower. Published for the Trade Policy Research Centre, London.

————. 1993. *Enforcing International Trade Law: The Evolution of the Modern GATT Legal System.* Salem, N.H.: Butterworth Legal Publishers.

————. 1998. "GATT/WTO Constraints on National Regulation: Requiem for an 'Aim and Effects' Test." *International Lawyer* 32: 619–49.

————. 1999. "The New WTO Dispute Settlement Procedure: An Overview of the First Three Years." *Minnesota Journal of Global Trade* 8 (1): 1–53.

Hufbauer, Gary Clyde. 2009. "Slowing the Protectionist Juggernaut." RealTime Economic Issues Watch. Washington: Peterson Institute for International Economics (www.peterson institute.org/realtime/?p=478 [February 13]).

Hufbauer, Gary Clyde, and Kimberly Ann Elliott. 1994. *Measuring the Costs of Protection in the United States.* Washington: Institute for International Economics.

Hummels, David. 2007. "Transportation Costs and International Trade in the Second Era of Globalization." *Journal of Economic Perspectives* 21 (3): 131–54.

International Centre for Trade and Sustainable Development (ICTSD). 2002. "WTO Members Comment on Indigenous *Amicus* Brief in Lumber Dispute." *Bridges* 2 (9). Geneva (May).

Irwin, Douglas A. 1991. "Mercantilism as Strategic Trade Policy: The Anglo-Dutch Rivalry for the East India Trade." *Journal of Political Economy* 99 (6): 1296–314.

————. 2002. *Free Trade under Fire.* Princeton University Press.

————. 2003. "Causing Problems? The WTO Review of Causation and Injury Attribution in U.S. Section 201 Cases." *World Trade Review* 2 (3): 297–325.

Irwin, Douglas A., Petros C. Mavroidis, and Alan O. Sykes. 2008. *The Genesis of the GATT.* Cambridge University Press.

Jackson, John H. 1969. *World Trade and the Law of GATT.* New York: Bobbs-Merrill.

————. 1997. *The World Trading System: Law and Policy of International Economic Relations.* 2nd ed. MIT Press.

————. 2002. "Perceptions about the WTO Trade Institutions." *World Trade Review* 1 (1): 101–14.

Johnson, Harry G. 1953–54. "Optimum Tariffs and Retaliation." *Review of Economic Studies* 21 (2): 142–53.

Jolls, Christine M. 2005. "The Role and Functioning of Public-Interest Legal Organizations in the Enforcement of the Employment Laws." In *Emerging Labor Market Institutions for the Twenty-First Century,* edited by Richard B. Freeman, Joni Hersch, and Lawrence Mishel. University of Chicago Press.

Jones, Kent. 2003. *Who's Afraid of the WTO?* Oxford University Press.

Karacaovali, Baybars, and Nuno Limão. 2008. "The Clash of Liberalizations: Preferential vs. Multilateral Trade Liberalization in the European Union." *Journal of International Economics* 74 (2): 299–327.

Keck, Alexander. 2004. "WTO Dispute Settlement: What Role for Economic Analysis?" *Journal of Industry, Competition and Trade* 4 (4): 365–71.

Kovenock, Dan, and Marie Thursby. 1992. "GATT, Dispute Settlement, and Cooperation." *Economics and Politics* 4 (2): 151–70.

Krugman, Paul R. 1990. *The Age of Diminished Expectations.* MIT Press.

Lawrence, Robert Z. 2003. *Crimes and Punishments? Retaliation under the WTO.* Washington: Institute for International Economics.

Lileeva, Alla, and Daniel Trefler. 2007. "Improved Access to Foreign Markets Raises Plant-Level Productivity . . . for Some Plants." Working Paper 13297. Cambridge, Mass.: National Bureau of Economic Research (August).

Limão, Nuno. 2006. "Preferential Trade Agreements as Stumbling Blocks for Multilateral Trade Liberalization: Evidence for the U.S." *American Economic Review* 96 (3): 896–914.

Limão, Nuno, and Kamal Saggi. 2008. "Tariff Retaliation versus Financial Compensation in the Enforcement of International Trade Agreements." *Journal of International Economics* 76 (1): 48–60.

Ludema, Rodney D., and Anna Maria Mayda. 2009. "Do Countries Free Ride on MFN?" *Journal of International Economics* 77 (2): 137–50.

Maggi, Giovanni. 1999. "The Role of Multilateral Institutions in International Trade Cooperation." *American Economic Review* 89 (1): 190–214.

Maggi, Giovanni, and Andrés Rodríguez-Clare. 1998. "The Value of Trade Agreements in the Presence of Political Pressures." *Journal of Political Economy* 106 (3): 574–601.

———. 2007. "A Political-Economy Theory of Trade Agreements." *American Economic Review* 97 (4): 1374–406.

Maggi, Giovanni, and Robert W. Staiger. 2008. "On the Role and Design of Dispute Settlement Procedures in International Trade Agreements." Working Paper 14067. Cambridge, Mass.: National Bureau of Economic Research (June).

Mavroidis, Petros C. 2002. "*Amicus Curiae* Briefs before the WTO: Much Ado about Nothing." In *European Integration and International Co-ordination: Studies in Transnational Economic Law in Honour of Claus-Dieter Ehlermann,* edited by Armin von Bogdandy, Petros C. Mavroidis, and Yves Meny. Alphen aan den Rijn, Netherlands and London: Kluwer Law International.

———. 2007. *Trade in Goods.* Oxford University Press.

Melitz, Marc J. 2003. "The Impact of Trade on Intra-Industry Reallocations and Aggregate Industry Productivity." *Econometrica* 71 (6): 1695–725.

Moore, Michael O., and Maurizio Zanardi. 2009. "Does Antidumping Use Contribute to Trade Liberalization in Developing Countries?" *Canadian Journal of Economics* 42 (2): 469–95.

Nordström, Håkan. 2010 (forthcoming). "The Politics of Selecting Trade Sanctions in the European Community: A View from the Floor." In *The Law, Economics, and Politics of Retaliation in WTO Dispute Settlement,* edited by Chad P. Bown and Joost Pauwelyn, chapter 10. Cambridge University Press.

Nordström, Håkan, and Gregory Shaffer. 2008. "Access to Justice in the World Trade Organization: A Case for a Small Claims Procedure?" *World Trade Review* 7 (4): 587–640.

Olson, Mancur. 1965. *The Logic of Collective Action.* Harvard University Press.

Organization for Economic Cooperation and Development (OECD). 2008. *OECD in Figures 2008* (www.oecd.org/dataoecd/44/17/41733586.pdf).

Ostry, Sylvia. 2002. "The Uruguay Round North-South Grand Bargain: Implications for Future Negotiations." In *The Political Economy of International Trade Law: Essays in Honor of Robert E. Hudec,* edited by Daniel L. M. Kennedy and James D. Southwick. Cambridge University Press.

Prusa, Thomas J. 2005. "Review of World Trade Organization Trade Policy Review—The United States 2004." *World Economy* 28 (9): 1263–275.

Prusa, Thomas J., and Susan Skeath. 2002. "The Economic and Strategic Motives for Antidumping Filings." *Weltwirtschaftliches Archiv* 138 (3): 389–413.

Reinhardt, Eric. 2001. "Adjudication without Enforcement in GATT Disputes." *Journal of Conflict Resolution* 45 (2): 174–95.

Reynolds, Kara M. 2009. "Why Are So Many WTO Disputes Abandoned?" In *Trade Disputes and the Dispute Settlement Understanding of the WTO: An Interdisciplinary Assessment,* edited by James C. Hartigan. Bingley, U.K.: Emerald Group Publishing.

Roberts, Mark, and James Tybout. 1997. "The Decision to Export in Colombia: An Empirical Model of Entry with Sunk Costs." *American Economic Review* 87 (4): 545–65.

Rodrik, Dani. 2007. *One Economics, Many Recipes: Globalization, Institutions, and Economic Growth.* Princeton University Press.

Rose, Andrew. 2004. "Do We Really Know That the WTO Increases Trade?" *American Economic Review* 94 (1): 98–114.

Sapir, Andre, and Joel P. Trachtman. 2008. "Subsidization, Price Suppression, and Expertise: Causation and Precision in Upland Cotton." *World Trade Review* 7 (1): 183–209.

Scholte, Jan Aart, Robert O'Brien, and Marc Williams. 1999. "The World Trade Organization and Civil Society." *Journal of World Trade* 33 (1): 107–24.

Shaffer, Gregory. 2003. *Defending Interests: Public-Private Partnerships in WTO Litigation.* Brookings.

———. 2006. "The Challenges of WTO Law: Strategies for Developing Country Adaptation." *World Trade Review* 5 (2): 177–98.

———. 2009. "Developing Country Use of the WTO Dispute Settlement System: Why It Matters, the Barriers Posed, and Its Impact on Bargaining." In *Trade Disputes and the Dispute Settlement Understanding of the WTO: An Interdisciplinary Assessment,* edited by James C. Hartigan. Bingley, U.K.: Emerald Group Publishing.

Shaffer, Gregory, and Victor Mosoti. 2002. "The *EC-Sardines* Case: How North-South NGO-Government Links Benefited Peru." *Bridges* 6 (7). Geneva: International Centre for Trade and Sustainable Development (ICTSD).

Shaffer, Gregory, Michelle Ratton Sanchez, and Barbara Rosenberg. 2008) "The Trials of Winning at the WTO: What Lies behind Brazil's Success." *Cornell International Law Journal* 41: 383–501.

Spar, Debora L. 2002. "Hitting the Wall: Nike and International Labor Practices." Case 9-700-047, rev.. Harvard Business School (September 6).

Srinivasan, T. N. 2000. *Developing Countries and the Multilateral Trading System: From the GATT to the Uruguay Round and the Future.* Boulder, Colo.: Westview Press.

———. 2001. "India's Reform of External Sector Policies and Future Multilateral Trade Negotiations." Discussion Paper 830. Yale University, Economic Growth Center.

Staiger, Robert W. 2006. "What Can Developing Countries Achieve in the WTO?" Book review of Jawara Fatoumata and Aileen Kwa, *Behind the Scenes at the WTO: The Real World of International Trade Negotiations. Journal of Economic Literature* 44 (2): 428–42.

Staiger, Robert W., and Guido Tabellini. 1987. "Discretionary Trade Policy and Excessive Protection." *American Economic Review* 77 (5): 823–37.

Steinberg, Richard H., and Timothy E. Josling. 2003. "When the Peace Ends: The Vulnerability of EC and US Agricultural Subsidies to WTO Legal Challenge." *Journal of International Economic Law* 6 (2): 369–417.

Subramanian, Arvind, and Shang-Jin Wei. 2007. "The WTO Promotes Trade, Strongly but Unevenly." *Journal of International Economics* 72 (1): 151–75.

Sykes, Alan O. 2003. "The Safeguards Mess: A Critique of WTO Jurisprudence." *World Trade Review* 2 (3): 261–95.

Tarullo, Daniel K. 2003. "Paved with Good Intentions: The Dynamic Effects of WTO Review of Anti-Dumping Action." *World Trade Review* 2 (3): 373–93.

Thöne, Michael, and Stephan Dobroschke. 2008. "WTO Subsidy Notifications: Assessing German Subsidies under the GSI Notification Template Proposed for the WTO." University of Cologne, FiFo Institute of Public Economics (April).

Tomz, Michael, Judith L. Goldstein, and Douglas Rivers. 2007. "Do We Really Know That the WTO Increases Trade? Comment." *American Economic Review* 97 (5): 205–18.

Topalova, Petia. 2004. "Trade Liberalization and Firm Productivity: The Case of India." Working Paper 04/28. Washington: International Monetary Fund.

Trebilcock, Michael J., and Robert Howse. 1999. *The Regulation of International Trade.* 2nd ed. London and New York: Routledge.

Trefler, Daniel. 2004. "The Long and Short of the Canada-U.S. Free Trade Agreement." *American Economic Review* 94 (4): 870–95.

Tumlir, Jan. 1985. *Protectionism: Trade Policy in Democratic Societies.* Washington: American Enterprise Institute.

Tybout, James R. 2000. "Manufacturing Firms in Developing Countries: How Well Do They Do and Why?" *Journal of Economic Literature* 38 (1): 11–44.

U.S. Trade Representative (USTR). 1999. "Implementation of WTO Recommendations Concerning EC–Measures Concerning Meat and Meat Products (Hormones)." *Federal Register* 64 (143) (July 27): 40638–0641.

———. 2009. "USTR Announces Revised Trade Action in Beef Hormones Dispute." Press release. Washington (January 15).

Van Biesebroeck, Johannes. 2005. "Exporting Raises Productivity in Sub-Saharan African Manufacturing Firms," *Journal of International Economics* 67 (2): 373–91.

Van den Bossche, Peter. 2008. "NGO Involvement in the WTO: A Comparative Perspective." *Journal of International Economic Law* 11 (4): 717–49.

Van der Borght, Kim. 1999. "The Advisory Centre on the WTO Law: Advancing Fairness and Equality." *Journal of International Economic Law* 2 (4): 723–28.

Vietor, Richard H. K., and Forest Reinhardt. 1995. "Starkist (A)." Case 9-794-128. Harvard Business School (January 20).

Waters, W. G. 1970. "Transport Costs, Tariffs, and the Patterns of Industrial Protection." *American Economic Review* 60 (5): 1013–020.

Watkins, Kevin. 2002. "Cultivating Poverty: The Impact of US Cotton Subsidies on Africa." Briefing Paper 30. Washington: Oxfam International.

Williams, Marc. 2005. "Globalization and Civil Society." In *Global Political Economy*, edited by John Ravenhill. Oxford University Press.

Wilson, Bruce. 2007. "Compliance by WTO Members with Adverse WTO Dispute Settlement Rulings: The Record to Date." *Journal of International Economic Law* 10 (2): 397–403.

Winston, Morton. 2002. "NGO Strategies for Promoting Global Corporate Social Responsibility." *Ethics & International Affairs* 16 (1): 71–87.

WTO. 1995. *Analytical Index: Guide to GATT Law and Practice*, vols. 1 and 2. Geneva.

———. 1997. *Panel Reports under the MFN Agreements and Arrangements (Tokyo Round Codes) of 1979.* Geneva.

———. 2005. "Quantitative Economics in WTO Dispute Settlement." In *World Trade Report 2005*, pp. 171–212. Geneva.

———. 2008a. "United States—Measures Concerning the Importation, Marketing and Sale of Tuna and Tuna Products: Request for Consultations by Mexico." WT/DS381/1. Geneva (October 28).

————. 2008b. "WTO Dispute Settlement: One Page Case Summaries (1995–December 2007)." Geneva. (www.wto.org/english/res_e/booksp_e/dispu_summary08_e.pdf).

————. 2008c. *World Tariff Profiles 2008.* Geneva: WTO and International Trade Centre UNCTAD/WTO.

————. 2008d. "Committee on Anti-Dumping Practices: Format for Semi-Annual Reports of Anti-Dumping Actions Pursuant to Article 16.4 of the Anti-Dumping Agreement." G/ADP/1/Rev.1. Geneva (November 3).

————. 2009. "Dispute Settlement: The Disputes—Chronological List of Disputes Cases" (www.wto.org/english/tratop_e/dispu_e/dispu_status_e.htm [January 5, 2009]).

Zunckel, Hilton. 2005. "The African Awakening in *United States–Upland Cotton." Journal of World Trade* 39 (6): 1071–093.

Index

ACP. *See* African, Caribbean, and Pacific
  countries
ActionAid, 184
ACWL. *See* Advisory Centre on WTO Law
Adidas, 201
Advisory Centre on WTO Law (ACWL):
  benefits, 140–42, 174; case types, 165;
  client firms, 139; compared to nongovernmental organizations, 204; complainant countries represented, 149–52;
  cost-shifting effect, 161; demand for
  services, 145–47; effects on DSU caseload, 148–49, 153–64; empowerment
  channels, 158–61; establishment, 140;
  external legal counsel, 147, 151, 167–69;
  fees, 145–46; funding, 142–44, 165;
  governments using, 146–47, 155–61,
  171; information collection and monitoring, 231; input mix, 144–45; legal
  opinions issued, 165–67; limitations,
  139, 157–58, 170, 174, 213; mandate,
  139, 140, 213; membership, 140, 144;
  nonmembers, 142, 146, 162; organizational structure, 140; participation in
  WTO disputes, 138, 147–53, 169–70,

241; performance, 145, 169–70; policy
  issues, 170–74; postlitigation phase role,
  171–72; repeat clients, 152; scale effect,
  148–49, 161–64; spillover effects,
  167–69; staff, 145; third parties assisted,
  151, 157, 172; use of services, 147–53
Africa, cotton producers, 189, 194–95, 199.
  See also individual countries
African, Caribbean, and Pacific (ACP)
  countries, 49–50, 60, 61
Agreement on Agriculture, 38, 39, 75–76
Agreement on Antidumping, 119, 216–17
Agreement on Safeguards, 119–20, 216–17
Agreement on Subsidies and Countervailing
  Measures, 216–17
Agreement on Textiles and Clothing (ATC),
  38, 75
Agreement on Trade-Related Aspects of
  Intellectual Property Rights. *See* Trade-
  Related Aspects of Intellectual Property
  Rights, Agreement on
Agricultural subsidies: corporate recipients,
  199, 201; in developed economies,
  30–31; disputes related to, 4, 205; effects
  on developing country exporters, 29–31,

273